After the Black Death

THE MIDDLE AGES SERIES

Ruth Mazo Karras, Series Editor
Edward Peters, Founding Editor

A complete list of books in the series is available from the publisher.

After the Black Death

Plague and Commemoration Among Iberian Jews

Susan L. Einbinder

UNIVERSITY OF PENNSYLVANIA PRESS

PHILADELPHIA

Published by
University of Pennsylvania Press
Philadelphia, Pennsylvania 19104-4112
www.upenn.edu/pennpress

Printed in the United States of America on acid-free paper
10 9 8 7 6 5 4 3 2 1

Library of Congress Cataloging-in-Publication Data
Names: Einbinder, Susan L., 1954– author.
Title: After the Black Death : plague and commemoration among
    Iberian Jews / Susan L. Einbinder.
Other titles: Middle Ages series.
Description: 1st edition. | Philadelphia : University of Pennsylvania
    Press, [2018] | Series: The Middle Ages series | Includes
    bibliographical references and index.
Identifiers: LCCN 2017051661 | ISBN 9780812250312 (hardcover :
    alk. paper)
Subjects: LCSH: Black Death—Iberian Peninsula—Religious
    aspects—Jews. | Black Death—Iberian Peninsula—Religious
    aspects—Judaism. | Jews—Iberian Peninsula—History. |
    Antisemitism—Iberian Peninsula—History—To 1500. | Jewish
    literature—Iberian Peninsula—History—To 1500.
Classification: LCC RC178.S7 E46 2018 | DDC
    616.9/2320899240366—dc23
LC record available at https://lccn.loc.gov/2017051661

Contents

Introduction   1

Chapter 1. Before the Plague: Anti-Jewish
Violence and the Pastoureaux   14

Chapter 2. Emanuel ben Joseph:
Trauma and the Commemorative Lament   32

Chapter 3. Abraham Caslari: A Jewish Physician on the Plague   57

Chapter 4. Stones of Memory: The Toledo Epitaphs   88

Chapter 5. Bones and Poems: Perpetrators and Victims   117

Appendix. The Toledo Plague Epitaphs: Translations   148

Notes   163

Bibliography   211

Index   225

Acknowledgments   231

Introduction

He died of the plague in the month of Tamuz in 5109.
Just days before his death
He had married.
Then the voice of the bride and groom
Became a voice of weeping,
And a father is pained and pining.
God of the heavens, grant him consolation.
Restorer of souls, [grant him] progeny.
    —From the epitaph of Asher ben Turiel, in Toledo

Wise and learned men asked of me that I inform them of my opinion
for treating these fevers, and that I write a tractate about this. I have
fulfilled their request. Let any learned man benefit from it concerning
these illnesses, whether the benefit is for the present [fevers] or as a
model for those to come.
    —Abraham Caslari, *Tractate on Pestilential and Other Types
    of Fevers*, in Besalú

THE FOURTEENTH CENTURY is known for its catastrophes, but among them,
the Black Death still stands out for its magnitude. As a result, it has merited out-
size attention in modern times. Even so, as a cursory scan of the literature reveals,
studies of the second pandemic, as it is more soberly known, have been experienc-
ing a renaissance.[1] One of the most exciting aspects of the newer research is its collaborative, interdisciplinary nature. Geneticists and medievalists have combined
their talents to establish firmly the identity of the medieval plague bacillus, now
confirmed as *Yersinia pestis* (bubonic plague), and the route it took from Asia into
the Middle East, North Africa, and Europe.[2] Among medievalists, the collaboration of historians of religion, science, technology, and institutions has produced a

more accurate picture of how medieval societies responded to the devastating fevers that swept across Europe from the time Genoan sailors returning from Caffa set anchor in Sicily, and then in Marseilles. Within months, the pestilential fevers that they brought with them had spread across continental Europe, reaching Provence by the late spring of 1348 and continuing westward over the Pyrenees down to Barcelona and across the Iberian Peninsula. At the same time, we now know, a second plague vector crossed the Iberian Peninsula from the south, reaching from Mallorca to Valencia and heading north and westward. By July 1348, pestilence was devastating Aragon and Catalonia. Slowed by the aridity of higher altitudes, the onset of winter, and patterns of human and animal traffic, it reached Castile the next spring, tapering over the next year or two.[3]

Mortality figures for the plague's impact in Europe generally hover between 30 percent and 66 percent. However, one yield of recent scholarship is the realization that the effects of the pandemic were not uniform, a view confirmed by medieval records and early local studies. The plague struck urban and rural settings differently, mountains and lowlands, sometimes rich and poor. During winter months, the disease also mutated into pneumonic, septicemic, and gastrointestinal versions that were highly contagious, speedily transmitted, and almost always fatal. Some regions were further crippled by years of drought or rain, high or low temperatures, cattle disease and crop failure—the erratic climate conditions of what Bruce Campbell has called the "Medieval Climate Anomaly."[4] Some regions, like Aragon, were also in the grip of political turmoil that made institutional responses to disease haphazard and ineffectual. These variable political, social, and environmental conditions all played a role in determining the character of the pandemic in a particular locale. Forensic archaeologists, demographers, and historians, with the help of new methods for extracting aDNA, have also tapped the evidence of plague burial pits and cemeteries, in order to understand the variable demographics of plague mortality; these studies suggest that bubonic plague had greater "success" among individuals already weakened by famine and malnourishment.[5] So, too, the familiar triad of flea-rat-human has been modified considerably with evidence that many insects and mammals can transmit plague from animals to humans. Greater attention is now focused on the plague as an endemic disease, hosted more or less permanently in the ecosystem and periodically transmitted to humans. Marmots, rabbits, black as well as brown rats, and other mammals can harbor it, and lice as well as different varieties of fleas can deliver it to human hosts.[6] At the same time, scholars are beginning to look closely at the ways later (human) plague outbreaks, which would occur at intervals of five to ten years for the next five centuries, reshaped and distorted the ways the initial outbreak was perceived by those who were unfortunate enough to encounter it in 1348.[7] To these investigations, scholars of literature, liturgy, religion, and art have begun to make their own contributions.[8] All these stories find sharper focus almost daily, and with them an ever richer picture of how individuals and communities responded to crisis continues to unfold.

In all this, Jewish studies has lagged behind. As a topic in Jewish social, cultural, or literary history, the Black Death has hardly been treated as an epidemiological event, scholars having focused almost exclusively on the violence against Jews that often accompanied its journey across European lands. Jews were active in mercantile and medical arenas, both of which were profoundly affected by the pandemic. Yet I know of no studies addressing the activities of Jewish merchants, middlemen, or lenders during the plague. Jewish physicians have garnered more interest, especially in the last decade and with regard to a substantial corpus of Hebrew plague tracts; but most of the primary texts are still unpublished, and much work remains to be done. With respect to anti-Jewish violence, the publications have been few but sobering. The early essay in the 1906 *Jewish Encyclopedia* is still the one that naive Googling may turn up most quickly. The authors recount the plague's arrival in Europe from the Crimea to ports in Sicily and Marseille. But the plague itself does not interest them so much as the accusations of Jewish responsibility for maliciously spreading it. The essay concludes with a grim list of Jewish communities that succumbed to violence in the wake of these accusations, a memorial litany that consists entirely of central and eastern European towns, mostly German, with representation from the Lowlands, Cracow, and Trent.[9] A very few early studies focused on individual attacks, such as Adolphe Crémieux's study of plague-inspired violence against the Jewish communities of Toulon and Hyères, and local studies continue to appear that detail the eruption of violence in settings characterized by different degrees of earlier tension or harmony.[10] More recent decades have also seen a trend to synthetic overviews, again mostly focused on Germany and central Europe. Joseph Shatzmiller's 1974 survey of violence against Jewish communities in Provence, František Graus's or Alfred Haverkamp's surveys of anti-Jewish attacks in Germany, David Nirenberg's measured attempt to contextualize episodes of violence in Aragon as expressions of antiroyalist resentment—all these works, to some extent, grapple with a need to establish and understand the scope of the violence while resisting essentializing explanations. Samuel Cohn's 2007 essay, auspiciously titled "The Black Death and the Burning of the Jews," returned to the familiar geography of Germany and eastern

Europe. Rejecting the case for class or economic-based motives for the outbreaks, Cohn simultaneously rejected "transhistorical explanations" while invoking recurring motives of "religious hatred." The fury and sheer punch of this now-classic essay have undoubtedly given it traction despite the unease that its conclusions may engender.[11] I have surely omitted other studies, and most surveys of medieval Jewish history include some reference to the plague as one more harbinger of persecution, expulsion, and slaughter. Anti-Jewish violence, in sum, has been the overwhelming focus of modern scholarship on Jewish experience during the Black Death.

Surprisingly, especially given the recent surge in interest and publications on the second pandemic, a study of individual and collective responses of Iberian Jews to the Black Death has yet to appear. While this book is by no means a comprehensive account, I hope that it will begin to fill a gap in the scholarly literature. As the most visible minority of the European Christian kingdoms, the Jewish men and women who lived and died in the shadow of the plague years have something to offer to more general studies of this period, as well as to studies of Jewish literature, thought, institutions, and relations with the Christian majority.

*   *   *

In theory, at least, the commemorative corpus in Hebrew should be rich—and not merely because of the rapacious pandemic. Anti-Jewish libels and the attacks that they precipitated were the stuff of traditional commemorative chronicles and laments and what twentieth-century anthologies excelled in finding. Nonetheless, with the exception of a handful of laments from central and eastern Europe, Jewish history books and anthologies cite almost no commemorative and contemporary writing that responds to the plague, especially from Provence and the Iberian Peninsula, the focus of this study.

Among other claims, I argue in this book that this is not because traditional forms of commemoration ceased to be meaningful in a shattering moment of crisis. Some of those traditional forms were grappling with challenges of relevance, along with competition from vernacular and extra-liturgical genres that are not the subject of this study but that surely existed alongside the Hebrew texts that I examine here. Yet the evidence of the few liturgical laments that are extant suggests that this most conventional of genres remained a viable form of expression after the pandemic, even if today it is not so easy to identify which hymns served that end. Significantly, the very ordinariness of this corpus, which continued to rely on familiar tropes, techniques, and sentiments, suggests that the Black Death, as it was experienced from its European outbreak in 1347 until its dissipation in the early 1350s, was not perceived as a truly cataclysmic event until later times. Equally important, violence was not omnipresent in Iberian settings; in Castile, it was unheard of, and in Aragon, when it did occur, sometimes it was resisted or suppressed. Familiar genres and concepts could still be enlisted to explain it; sacred and scientific narratives strained but express no sense of rupture. No enduring crisis of faith, meaning, or language characterized this moment.

This conclusion, which the following chapters reach from several angles, may seem counterintuitive, but it is sustained not only by the evidence of the texts but by the corroborating studies of social historians and historians of science. The extant commemorative literature suggests that the Black Death did not shatter the faith or worldview of the men and women who survived it, even when it did come with terrible violence. Among the Jewish texts treated here, neither liturgical laments, medical treatises, chronicles, nor epitaphs demonstrate meaningful rupture with received conventions for representing catastrophe. Amazingly, the old ways of explaining—and expressing—destruction and loss remained intact. This observation is of a piece with recent findings, whether in the form of focused studies of the 1348–50 pandemic or in comparisons of the effects between the initial and subsequent outbreaks.[12] As the newer scholarship concurs, despite its extraordinary mortality and devastation, the Black Death did not upend a traditional way of viewing life or the cruel blows that it might deliver. While in some cases, the great mortality of the pandemic motivated technological innovations or strengthened (or weakened) labor markets and wage earners, agricultural practices, or guilds, the Black Death caused no revolutionary change in institutions of government or religion.[13] As David Mengel has put it, the "presumed connection between high plague mortality and profound historical effects" does not hold.[14] This book reinforces this observation and extends it to individuals, families, and communities. Arguably, the continuing *return* of the plague proved more unsettling to old ways of feeling and making meaning. That is a subject for future study.

Implicit in the framing of this project is a secondary question about the viability of current theoretical paradigms, particularly the ever-expanding realm occupied by theories of trauma and its literary representations, for describing medieval catastrophe. Chapter 1 addresses this question directly; but in its own way, each of the subsequent chapters returns to the question of whether the modern concept of psychological trauma, or the wealth of works on "trauma theory" or a "trauma aesthetic" have relevance for mid-fourteenth-century Jews and Christians. To the degree that the answer is no, I ask what remains useful conceptually or descriptively in the recent literature but also what the medieval context may offer those who are interested in the present-day phenomenon and theory.

This project began as a quest for Hebrew liturgical laments (*qinot*) that responded to the Black Death. The dearth of such texts is striking but not unique: absence also characterizes the liturgical commemoration composed in the wake of Pastoureaux violence, when a combination of local inhabitants and migratory bands of "shepherds" attacked Jewish communities in Provence and Aragon in the summer of 1320. Many of those same communities were attacked again in 1348, with the arrival of the Black Death. In a prefatory mode, Chapter 1 treats the Pastoureaux attacks, their commemorative traces, and their possible lingering effects in later decades, with a specific scrutiny of the assumptions governing current trauma theory and their applicability to medieval contexts. Two Hebrew laments and one survivor's marginal notation in a biblical codex serve as the focus for analysis. To what extent did the events that they describe endure in the memories of survivors? How did medieval Jewish institutions and authorities enlist familiar genres and themes, or harness individual anger and grief, to unify shattered survivors and communities? How did the literary records of Christian institutions likewise emphasize corporate unity over individual experiences of remorse or shame? I conclude that neither the medieval Hebrew laments nor the autobiographical inscriptions behave in ways consistent with assumptions of modern Western models. Instead, they emphasize a shock to communal over personal honor; affirm resistance and resilience over victimhood; and ratify collective tropes of suffering (and redemption) over an intra-psychic experience of pain, shock, or bereavement. Significantly, many of the same techniques, motifs, and theological perspectives recur in the two plague laments discussed in later chapters. This continuity of form and faith is one indication that the task of writing about the Black Death—hence the task of explaining and giving it meaning—did not pose insurmountable challenges to these authors. Contrary to recent emphases on an essential linkage between traumatic experience and a breakdown in language, these men were satisfied with the vocabulary and sensibility conveyed by existing idioms and forms.

Chapters 2 through 5 are dedicated to the Black Death. Although scholars can point to a handful of Hebrew laments included in the standard lachrymose anthologies of the mid-twentieth century, all but one of these examples come from central or eastern European communities. The exception, a Sephardic lament copied in fifteenth-century Calabria, refers to plague-related violence. Its author, Emanuel ben Joseph, is not otherwise known; his hymn is preserved in a collection of Sephardic *qinot* whose fifteenth-century copyist penned them in Sephardic script. Emanuel's lament emphasizes communal resilience, drawing on familiar techniques and themes. "Let me lament in bitterness and fasting" ("Aqonen bemarah vetzom") refers to a combined assault of sickness and violence, an absentee ruler, and the flight or expulsion of survivors, all factors that characterize Jewish experience in Aragon/Catalonia. The lament also alludes to cattle plague or slaughter, perhaps a nod to the great cattle panzootic (possibly rinderpest) associated with the middle years of the Great Famine (1315–21). Significantly, some of the other texts considered in this book also allude to forms of environmental catastrophe such as drought, famine, and bad weather. While it would be unwise to make too much of these echoes, they suggest that the disastrous climate conditions of the mid-fourteenth century and their impact on agriculture, economy, and animal and human life were not far from the minds of medieval writers when they thought about plague.

Liturgical poetry, of course, was not the only vehicle for preserving one's views on the pandemic. The elusiveness of traditional sources, particularly in the form of liturgical laments, led me to a variety of Jewish texts that shed light both on plague demographics and on the social, institutional, psychological, and spiritual impact of the pandemic on those who lived through it. One genre that emerged with the Black Death and showed continuing vitality over the years was the plague tractate, a medical composition. The physician-authors of these tractates included Christians, Muslims, and Jews, who wrote in Latin, Arabic, Hebrew, and, occasionally, Romance vernaculars. In Christian Spain and Provence, the Christian authors had been educated in the most prestigious medical schools of their day, and their Jewish counterparts were men who had mastered their curriculum from beyond the university walls and endorsed their methods and theories. In recent years, tagging the rise in interest in the plague and in the history of medieval medical knowledge and practice, the activities of Jewish physicians during the plague years have merited some attention. Like their Christian and Muslim colleagues in Provence, Aragon, and Castile, Jewish physicians treated plague patients—sometimes dying as a result—and wrote their own plague tractates, while others translated into Hebrew some of the Christian treatises that circulated in their milieu.[15] One prominent Jewish practitioner, Abraham Caslari, was an exile from Narbonne who had set up a flourishing practice in Besalú. Abraham had already written a work on epidemic fevers before the plague reached Catalonia in the late spring of 1348. Chapter 3 treats a new Hebrew tract, *On Pestilential Fevers*, that specifically responded to the extraordinary fevers of that year.

The beginning of Abraham's tractate testifies to the author's awareness of the regional extent of the pandemic, which he describes sweeping from Provence to "Catalonia, Valencia, the region of Aragon and some of Navarre and Castile."[16] Recall that the plague crossed Spain in two converging paths, one originating in the north and coming via Perpignan over the Pyrenees, and then moving south and westward; the other via Mallorca into Valencia and moving north and west. Castile, where the plague is very poorly documented, was near the end of this double trajectory. The plague struck Castile in the summer of 1349 and lingered another year or two; if Caslari knew that the terrible pestilence had reached this kingdom, he was writing no earlier than late 1349. Yet his is one of the earliest known plague tractates. In Catalonia, it was preceded by a vernacular work by a physician in Lleida affiliated with the small medical faculty at the university there. Before succumbing to the plague himself, Jacme d'Agramont wrote a preventive regimen in the vernacular, directing his composition to the municipal officials charged with preparing the town for the epidemic.

Today, Jacme's tractate is often singled out for two reasons. First was the author's unusual division of pestilence into two equally pernicious categories of physical and moral disease. Second, Jacme thought that the plague could be artificially manufactured by people of ill will, arguing that someone might intentionally seed the waters or air with a poisonous substance that could cause an epidemic. The other well-known proponent of this view was Jacme's contemporary at the more famous University of Montpellier, Alfonso de Córdoba. Neither of these authors explicitly pointed a finger at the Jews. Nonetheless, attacks on Jewish communities accused of spreading the plague emerged precisely in their orbits. Chapter 3 looks at Abraham Caslari's tractate is to see whether he might be responding to a theoretical argument associated with anti-Jewish violence, or to the post-hoc knowledge of the brutal attacks on Jewish communities to the south and west of him.[17]

Previously untapped sources also form the basis of Chapters 4 and 5. Chapter 4 turns to the medieval Jewish cemetery in Toledo, the capital of Old Castile. Now mostly lost, the Jewish tombstones of Toledo were still visible in the early sixteenth century, when a Jewish tourist transcribed nearly eighty epitaphs from the stones. In 1841, Samuel D. Luzzatto published a copy of these transcriptions made by Joseph Almanzi.[18] Of the seventy-six epitaphs in the collection, twenty-eight describe deaths from plague between 1349–52, twenty-five of those during 1349–50. Toledo was not a site of anti-Jewish violence, and these elegant epitaphs permit a rudimentary assessment of the impact of the plague in Toledo, particularly among its better-off residents. The mere fact that these men and women were individually buried and commemorated in verse suggests that the pandemic's effects were mitigated in this locale. Epitaphs, certainly, are not intended to be genre-breaking, either in literary or theological terms, and these are no exception, wedding a recurring series of tropes and encomia to more or less succinct details of biography.[19] Chapter 4 argues that the continuity in style and convention between the pre- and post-plague epitaphs is further evidence that the Black Death did not cause a profound rupture in Jewish institutions or communal fabric. A secondary conclusion is that the plague epitaphs also preserve evidence of the tension that characterized the interactions of Toledo's acculturated Jewish aristocracy and its imported, Ashkenazi-born, religious elite.

In 2007, archaeologists discovered six communal graves in an exploratory survey in Tàrrega, west of Barcelona and several miles east of Lleida. Their race to analyze and identify the remains was galvanized by the interference of religious groups that ultimately succeeded in halting the excavation and reburying the human remains. Despite the obstacles, the remains were identified as the Jewish victims of a 1348 massacre described in a contemporary Hebrew chronicle; new archival and archaeological sources have permitted reconstruction of the most brutal episode of anti-Jewish violence associated with the outbreak of the Black Death. The forensic analyses of the remains are unique not only as a medium but because we may ask something about their Christian authors from the way they left their marks. Ironically, it is in the silent traces of fury and pain that the bones of Tàrrega's Jews tell two sides of a story. In this context, I am interested in engaging the insights of recent sociological and anthropological studies of intercommunal and interethnic violence to complicate the stereotypical representation of Christian perpetrators as an undifferentiated mass. This disaggregation reveals a number of distinct actors and agendas in the assault on the *aljama* (Jewish community).

Complexity also characterizes Tàrrega's Jewish victims, some of whom survived with the help of Christian neighbors. One survivor, Moses Nathan, was one of the wealthiest Jews in Catalonia prior to the plague; spirited to Bellpuig, he would spend the next decade or so trying to recuperate the loans, property, and capital lost in one bloody day in July. In addition to his financial interests, Moses authored a variety of writings. His Catalan and Hebrew proverbs, composed a few years before the plague, have merited some attention; and in 1354, he was among the coauthors of a pact signed by representatives of the Catalonian *aljamas*. In Chapter 5, I argue that Moses' lament for the great fast day of the Ninth of Av commemorates the attack on the Targarin *aljama*. A close reading of the text permits this study to come full circle by returning to the traditional, liturgical lament in closing. Again, the problem of generic topoi of catastrophe and the challenges that they pose for historians must be raised. On the one hand, Moses' lament demonstrates that, whatever tragedy he commemorated, he had no problem defaulting to the literary and religious tropes embraced in earlier writing: preexisting idioms "worked" to supply the meaning that he sought for himself and his readers. On the other hand, texts like Moses' also "worked" because their imagery and intertextual allusions had local resonance and relevance. Now lost to us, elements of melody and performance once enriched their ability to heighten passions of grief or anger, and then proffer consolation. Laments like this one also survived in fast-day liturgies whose familiar and solemn verses, processions, and shofar blasts nested present catastrophes in the collective memories and rhythms of a liturgically constructed past. These settings, too, might heighten local details without detaching them from familiar foundations. In the echoes of repeatable history, a lament composed for one kind of liturgical use might even be retroactively associated powerfully with a later, local event. That process of commemorative imagination is also part of this story, and meaningful whether or not the original author had this eventual misreading in mind.

The range of genres, ideas, and affect invoked in these chapters is also a reminder that the writing of the Middle Ages largely bequeaths us voices modulated by institutions and their authorities. Sometimes the institutions are religious, sometimes political or legal, sometimes medical; sometimes, they are the voices of convention and belief that constitute the invisible glue of a human community even when no law or doctrine officially prescribes them. The survival of dissident voices from the medieval past is rare, and this may be truer of Hebrew than of Latin and the European vernaculars. To write in Hebrew was already to situate oneself among sacred texts and authorities. Fragments and tantalizing references assure us that the medieval Hebrew corpus coexisted with a rich vernacular analogue. Unfortunately, vernacular authors, performers, and audiences rarely thought to write down their texts, or no one thought to save them. Recent research on a vernacular (*aljamiado*) fifteenth-century text that belongs to the famous *danza de la muerte* (*danse macabre*) tradition confirms that by the fifteenth century, at least, Iberian Jews had a robust investment in Romance genres circulating around them. But, as Michele Hamilton has shown, the *danse* itself reaches back to the experience of the plague, and its early prototypes may have been embraced by Jewish users.[20] Hamilton has thoroughly discussed this unusual text, which I do not include here, but whose existence reminds us that vernacular expressions of mourning and commemoration supplement the

Hebrew genres that interest me in this book. So, too, as stray manuscripts and the material artifacts of the Tàrrega dig confirm, fourteenth-century Jews, like their Christian neighbors, had recourse to amulets, spells, and forms of prophylaxis and healing elided by canonic religious texts. These, too, regrettably fall outside the scope of this study.

Even when it was not partnered with acts of horrific violence, the plague was certainly the kind of external event emphasized in twentieth-century definitions of trauma. Nonetheless, it turns out that the shape of that event was not even or consistent. If these studies suggest that the severity of the pandemic varied from region to region, so, too, did the way people experienced it. Like those of all grand catastrophes, its full contours may always escape us, projecting the kinds of gaps and discontinuities that trauma theorists love to find. In this case, the gaps and discontinuities may be more significant as they are reified over time. The turbulent shocks of the fifteenth century and the blows that they dealt to Jewish communities; the end of Jewish life on the Iberian Peninsula following the expulsion of 1492; the dominance of Castilian Jewish identity among post-expulsion Iberian exiles; and the lachrymose historiography favored by the early Spanish exiles themselves and reinforced by German Jewish scholars in the decades following the Holocaust: all shaped the Jewish past, highlighting details and texts that confirmed an anticipated narrative while suppressing others. Literary texts are chief among the casualties of belated simplification; they are, by definition, mediated, allusive, and often figurative representations and yet fall victim to the flat literalism that conforms them to the expectations of modern narratives of the past. This is starkly evident in the naive assumption that medieval Jewish chronicle, liturgical, or martyrological genres accurately represent the complexity of Jewish or Christian responses; the same may be said for Christian sources. This study tries to honor both the meaning of these institutionalized ways of seeing and to peek behind, around, and underneath them for glimpses of an unrulier reality.

Unlike much of my previous work on anti-Jewish violence, which has treated incidents of judicial violence, these chapters also confront experiences of collective catastrophe—plague and violence—that were largely indiscriminate in their impact. In keeping with my interest in the applicability of recent trauma models and concepts for medieval contexts, this double focus permits scrutiny of what I think is one of the weaker points of contemporary theory: the theorization of collective trauma. By collective or cultural trauma, I refer to a shocking historical event that constitutes a threat to a group's physical survival and sense of identity. Although these catastrophic events have an impact on groups as well as individuals, the theoretical literature on trauma is poorly equipped to describe collective process or distress. Beginning with Freud himself, a number of authors have tried to justify a case for collective trauma that mimics the individual phenomenon. Some of their claims are as problematic as they are sweeping, beginning with the biological analogy itself.[21] A group of human beings does not behave like a larger version of a single individual, and a singular event will affect members of a group in different ways, both in the short and long term. The ready conflation of individual and collective trauma, moreover, reinforces "event-based" models that are already problematic and according to which trauma results inevitably upon exposure to a certain kind of terrible event.[22] In contrast, some sociologists usefully emphasize the role of "culture carriers" or "memory makers" who shape public memory and forgetting; from this perspective, "collective trauma" (like collective memory) is largely a social construct.[23]

The prominence of event-based trauma models is especially associated with American psychological trends and with the political, legal, and social legacy of the Vietnam War and the large numbers of veterans treated for posttraumatic stress disorders, on the one hand, and the rising feminist movement, with its interest in childhood sexual abuse, on the other. The theorization of collective trauma also owes much to early interviews and encounters with Holocaust victims, where the desire to weight external conditions over intrapsychic factors was both obvious and understandable.[24] For similar reasons, studies of children exposed to violence, or wartime atrocities against civilian populations (including sexual violence targeting women) also emphasize exposure because they understandably do not wish to blame the victims of horrific abuse.[25]

At the same time, psychoanalytical models are, by definition, models of individual mental perception and processing; the very concept of psychological trauma emerged from a psychoanalytic focus on individual experience and remains conceptually tethered to that language.[26] Thus, to an exceptional degree, Western models of trauma "tend to locate the cause and onus of responsibility within the individual."[27] Exported to other settings, the focus both on event and individual may actually have the effect of alienating victims from traditional networks of support and "impair their struggle to reconstitute a shared sense of reality, morality and dignity."[28] These critiques are apt for medieval contexts as well, where the distinctions between self, community, and world are not identical with our own. Indeed, even the meaning of "world" in a medieval setting may conflate past, present, and future as well as sacred and profane in ways alien to educated and largely secular Western scholars. Medieval victims are, of course, safe from whatever damage our obtuseness may inflict on them. But if we want to understand their experience and their world, the casual application of modern psychoanalytic categories may not be ideal.

This is not to say that the phenomenon of mass trauma does not exist. The plague is an excellent example of an outside event that had a devastating impact on entire communities. It is harder to map its psychological effects than its sociological or economic ones, but surely they were real—and varied. I am, however, suggesting that the impact of a mass event of this sort is inadequately described by trauma theory and that the concept of collective or cultural trauma has specific historical and cultural limitations that may not reasonably apply to different contexts or times. For that purpose, other disciplines or discourses may serve us better—for instance, sociology and anthropology, which are equipped to describe institutional or otherwise authoritative voices that shape public memory—unsurprisingly, often in ways that uphold the institutions and authority that they represent. For the interplay of group identities and agendas that produce interethnic or interreligious violence, social and political theory are again more useful than psychoanalysis or psychology. I have, accordingly, relied on a variety of studies, from a variety of academic disciplines. None of them can ultimately explain why human beings do the terrible things to one another that we do, or why, despite the calamitous horrors that human beings endure, the capacity for resilience and renewal is never entirely extinguished. Perhaps these questions have no answer. But each of these disciplines can nevertheless probe a tiny piece of the puzzle and offer up its lesson. I have learned something from them all. Above all, I have learned from the voices of my texts, moving and eloquent in their very fragility, objects wrought of parchment and stone, text and bone, preserved these many years—in the words of Dayas Quinoni, a brand plucked from the fire. To spend time with the written testimony is to appreciate with humility and awe the ability of their authors to render layers of meaning and complexity in language shaped by a dialogue with the past even as it grasps for present meaning. To contemplate the language of ravaged bones is to humbly acknowledge the hand of fortune and the measure of faith that levels or preserves us all. Sadly, we have again reached a historical moment where that lesson is worth pondering.

Chapter 1

Before the Plague: Anti-Jewish Violence and the Pastoureaux

THIS BOOK TREATS the Black Death, but it starts almost three decades earlier, during the summer of 1320, when Jewish communities in Provence and Aragon faced attacks by a mix of roving and local forces identified as "Shepherds," or Pastoureaux. Launched under the banner of a popular crusading movement, these attacks were characterized by excessive violence and heavy Jewish casualties. Christian chronicles, letters, and archives document the movement of crusading bands from Normandy toward Paris, south toward papal Avignon and over the Pyrenees into Aragon. These accounts are generally terse, but they emphasize the lawlessness of the attackers and fears of popular revolt that they inspired among the chroniclers and the men whose views they shared and sought to represent. Occasionally, a chronicler resorts to hyperbole, as in Jean de Saint-Victor's description of embattled Jews who exhaust their stock of projectiles and hurl their children over the walls.[1] By contrast, Jewish sources are scarce, even among the traditional forms of liturgical commemoration that often preserve some memory of anti-Jewish violence. However, while dozens of verse laments (*qinot*) mark the roughly contemporary anti-Jewish attacks known as the Rindfleisch massacres in Germany, for Pastoureaux violence, there are two—perhaps.

Over the years, scholars have disagreed over the reliability of Jewish liturgical poetry as a historical source. Yet, whether they have related to the *qinah* genre as documentary testimony, as an affective (literary) supplement to the historical record, or something in between, they have largely agreed that the liturgical lament records and reflects the direct shock of historical trauma. This chapter challenges this notion, beginning with some historical background and then turning to two Hebrew laments associated with Pastoureaux violence. How do these laments commemorate traumatic violence? I argue that liturgical representations of violence and trauma are not "memory" in the conventional sense, traumatic or otherwise. Rather, the liturgical lament attempts to unify and regulate communal responses to catastrophic events, reclaiming individual loss for a public domain. The second half of this chapter expands the question of traumatic response to other sources. Stray bits of testimony suggest the presence of disruptive grief and institutional efforts to address it among victims and perpetrators. These efforts I consider, along with the question of perpetrator trauma, a subject rarely, if ever, raised in discussions of medieval anti-Jewish violence.[2] Together, these questions and considerations create a baseline for the chapters to follow, which treat Jewish commemorative responses to the Black Death in the same general region that saw the depredations of the Pastoureaux. One of the claims of this book is that the Black Death did not lead to a dramatic rupture with existing conventions for commemorating collective trauma or catastrophe. This first chapter therefore performs an important task by asking what traditional commemorative genres looked like just before the Black Death, and as they would have been activated in the wake of mass violence and loss.

"Trauma" is a word that has acquired popular as well as technical currency, and even its technical (medical, legal, and psychological) meaning has shifted over time. For the purposes of this book, it may be defined generally as a delayed reaction to abnormal or violent events, a reaction that the theoretical literature characterizes by amnesia, intrusive behaviors, flashbacks, dissociative disorders, and somatized symptoms of distress. How much what is commonly swept under the rubric of trauma refers to a universal response to catastrophic events, and how much to a more culturally, geographically, and temporally limited phenomenon is a question implied throughout this and later chapters.[3] In modern times, the term has proved highly expansive, especially as it has been linked to themes of subjectivity ensnared in Foucauldian grids of power and state, technology and industrialization, slow and sudden violence.[4] Although one psychologist describes trauma as a "conception of the self, a certain life narrative," it is not at all obvious that this perspective makes sense beyond Western contexts and modern times.[5] What we know about Pastoureaux-related attacks against Jewish communities, as well as how those communities responded to them, permits us to probe the limits of contemporary trauma models for understanding medieval episodes of intercommunal violence and collective catastrophe. How did medieval Jews and Christians experience and make sense of anti-Jewish violence in the decades preceding the Black Death? In certain respects, I will argue, the medieval example challenges core assumptions of contemporary "trauma theory." I concentrate where the theory is weak, first in the assumption of continuity between individual and collective trauma, and then in the leveling of distinction between victim and perpetrator.

When Philip V of France announced plans for a new crusade in 1319, it was not at all evident that he intended to go. Lifting their banners, the men and women who began to assemble in small groups headed initially for Avignon and Paris, meant to hold him to his word. The chroniclers refer to them as "shepherds" (*pastoureaux, pastorelli*), a term perhaps intended to convey contempt more than sociological fact. Nonetheless, legend soon attributed their inspiration to a young shepherd's vision, and shepherding imagery signaled the crusading ambitions of the early bands.[6] The Shepherds' corollary objective was to purify the kingdom of corruption, a goal that did not initially target Jews but wealthy Christian officials and clerics. Indeed, as William Jordan has noted, Jews had only recently been readmitted to France after their expulsion by Philip's father in 1306. For the small numbers who returned, their timing could not have been worse. Years of famine and pestilence added to the economic hardships bred of war and relentless taxation; restricted to lending for survival, Jews were an easy target for desperate Christian locals. Jordan attributes the brutality of Pastoureaux attacks, with more than a hundred casualties in Toulouse, to popular resentment over a renewed Jewish presence.[7] David Nirenberg's extensive analysis, which concentrates on Aragon, emphasizes antiroyalist motives: the Jews, under direct protection of the Crown, were a visible extension of royal policies and repression.[8]

More recently, Georges Passerat has retraced the French itinerary of the Pastoureaux, seeking to identify the participants as well as the victims in anti-Jewish attacks.[9] For Aragon, Jaume Riera i Sans has also tried to disaggregate the ranks of Pastoureaux bands and identify perpetrators, local supporters, and victims; his analysis balances the savage attack on the Jews of Montclus with the relatively pacific movement of the Pastoureaux through other towns.[10] Riera traces the Shepherds' origins to Gascony, noteworthy not only because of a Gascon predisposition to anti-Frenchness (which would support a reading of antiroyalist motives in French lands) but because Gascony had expelled its Jews permanently in 1287. Thus, by 1320, whatever Gascons felt about Jews was not based on current experience or neighbors. At the same time, the expulsion was not in the distant past: in fact, recent scholarship has treated the Gascon expulsion as a laboratory for the large-scale English expulsion that followed three years later.[11] In turn, these early expulsions provided a precedent for King Philip IV of France, who ordered the mass expulsion of French Jews in 1306.

Although they wrought considerable havoc in France and Provence, the Pastoureaux had relatively little success attacking Jewish communities in Aragon.

Only Montclus, with several hundred casualties, suffered a serious assault.[12] Historians have detailed the flight of the attackers and their pursuit by royal agents, several dozen exemplary executions, and ongoing legal exertions to retrieve looted property. They have noted the flood of remissions granted most of the municipalities and authorities accused of negligence or active participation in the violence and looting. The royal obsession with cash—Jaume II's and Philip the Tall's—made financial penalties appealing; the remissions demonstrate that royal motives were more about preserving royal possessions and authority than any sympathy for Jews. Nonetheless, whatever royal motives were in Aragon, Jewish pleas for tax relief in the aftermath of the Pastoureaux attacks were granted swiftly, especially in the fall and winter of 1320, while the communities were encouraged to rebuild.

All of the old and new studies have exhaustively combed the chronicles, royal registers, and papal correspondence. The moving story of Baruch, a survivor of the Toulouse massacre who converted under duress, is another important testimony; Baruch was deposed by the inquisitor Jacques Fournier (later Pope Benedict XII).[13] Riera has added new archival material to argue that the crusader peasants were largely nonviolent and received as such in most localities. Certainly, the chroniclers' distaste for populist uprisings colors their accounts and echoed the haste with which Pope Jean XXII disowned the would-be crusaders. Still, Riera's attempt to recuperate the Shepherds, which joins a number of important studies on peasant revolts and popular crusades, has been unique for its sympathetic perspective.[14] The problem is not that we lack solidarity with peasants but that these peasants murdered Jews.

Complicating matters further, as already suggested, they were not entirely peasants. Modern historians treat the label "Pastoureaux" as metaphor, a theological identification for participants and a dismissive stereotype for the chroniclers.[15] Although conveniently deemed outsiders later, when it was time for someone to blame, the attackers were a mix of crusaders and local folk who must have known their victims. In Montclus, they include "des alcaids, un justicier, dos lloctinents de justícia, el guarda de la sal, tres battles locals, 4 notariis."[16] In Lézat, the local butcher and a handful of townsmen and nobles joined the fray.[17] Royal officials who failed to protect Jewish lives and property were punished,[18] but many of the actual rioters fled quickly, some across borders. Those who were prosecuted were men who could not activate local networks of support.[19] Where they did find support, it appears not merely in several accounts of local mobs freeing jailed attackers but also, for instance, in the refusal of local residents to bid on the impounded goods of men arrested for participation in violence and looting.[20]

The dearth of Jewish sources on the Pastoureaux is striking. Three chronicle accounts, by Solomon ibn Verga, Samuel Usque, and Joseph haCohen, are the work of Spanish exiles. They were written in the 1550s, far removed in time and place from the events that they describe; their sources are unknown. Scholars rightly relate to them with caution. The authors jumble chronologies and places, invoking biblical topoi and inflating enemy forces and Jewish casualties. All three of the early modern chroniclers view earlier events through the prism of their own post-expulsion experience, much as later twentieth-century historians would read their chronicles through a Holocaust warp. Strangely, more conventional forms of Jewish testimony do not survive. There are almost no commemorative liturgical texts, no references to fast days or sumptuary restrictions, and no legal disputes or inquiries that offer glimpses of the shattered rhythms and relationships of daily and ritual life. Two colophons to legal manuscripts identify the son of a victim and another contemporary figure to the violence; these documents are treated below.

The brief span of time between the attacks in Toulouse (June 15) and the attack in Montclus (July 7) marked the Jewish fast days of the Seventeenth of Tamuz and the Ninth of Av—marked on the tenth of Av in 1320 because the ninth fell on a Saturday.[21] The penitential liturgies for these fast days have historically attracted laments connected to local and general Jewish tragedies, and we might logically expect manuscript liturgies from Aragon and Provence to preserve responses to the violence of 1320. It would be a monumental task to find them. No database catalogs *piyyutim* by such categories, and the generic tropes of tragedy resist classification by event. My early efforts in this direction were not very profitable. Of two laments by an otherwise unknown poet, Solomon b. Joseph of Avalon (in Burgundy), one has been linked to the Pastoureaux attacks.[22] A second lament, by the poet Emanuel, I have identified from a Provençal liturgy. These are the Jewish commemorative records closest to the experience of Pastoureaux-related violence; thus it would be reasonable to assume that their representation of events tells us something about Jewish responses, official or otherwise, to the attacks on their communities. Let us look, then, at how these laments represent individual and collective trauma, and ask what that representation seeks to achieve.

Solomon's lament, "Abi'a miqreh" (Let me tell the story), explicitly alludes to Shepherds and indiscriminate violence on a Sabbath evening in the month of Tamuz. The poet comments bitterly:

ועדו רועים מפיצים בחורי ובתולותי

זממו להפר מצותי, חקותי ותורותי

אמונים במאנם דרכו קשת משחיתי
יסבו עלי רביו יפלח כליותי.

The Shepherds gathered and scattered my young men and women.
They plotted to break my commandments, my laws, and my Torah.
The destroyers drew bows against my faithful ones who refused [to convert].
His archers surround me, they slash open my kidneys.
 (Job 16:13) (vv. 21–24)

Some verses later, "the band of shepherds" calls to their supporters to lock the
market gates and annihilate the Jews (vv. 73–76) (השחיתו בעם וסגרו בשוק דלתיים).
Some of the attackers are mounted (v. 64) and carry swords (v. 105), and they inflict
head injuries on their victims (v. 57). This is consistent with testimony preserved
in royal inquests. In Lézat, for instance, local nobles joined the attackers and proceeded to the Jewish quarter with "swords, long knives, lances, javelins, shields,
helmets, and other types of weapons."[23] The description also matches with what
we know about anti-Jewish violence during later plague-related attacks, when
again an impromptu mob relied on a blend of make-do and formal weaponry
against local Jews.[24]

 Martyrological vignettes constitute the main part of Solomon's lament.
Many describe the suicide-martyrdoms of family units; one stanza describes
forty-eight Jews who tried to hide in a cave and were drowned. The forty-eight
victims were all women, who feature prominently elsewhere in the poem. Their
fate is described in a kaleidoscope of cultic, domestic, and nightmarish images:

צוחתם עלתה, קראה פרח לרעותיה
כולנו האשה וילדיה תהיה לאדוניה
בפירורי חבית התשירה מנחת חביתיה
חגרה בעוז מתניה ותאמץ זרועותיה.

Their shrieking went up. Every blossom called to her companion "Each
 one of us—women and children!—will be the Lord's!"
With cake crumbs, she made her meal offering.
She girded her loins in strength and braced her arms.
 (Prov. 31:17) (vv. 69–72)

The motif of the cultic meal offering recurs a bit later, simultaneously evoking
women's baking and labors as well as the Temple cult (perhaps intentionally

linking an image of women's place in the domestic sphere to the most plebian of ritual offerings):

רצחו היפה בנשים, ידו אליה
דמים בדמים נגעו יתרון לבעליה
אשה עולצת שמטו ביושר מעלליה
פתות אותה פתים ויצקת עליה.

> They murdered the most beautiful of women, they shot at her!
> Blood mingled with blood, a credit to its owners.
> The woman rejoices that her deeds have earned her release
> *To crumble [the meal] into pieces and pour oil on it.* (Lev 2:6) (vv. 77–80)

The biblical verb *y-d-h* ("hurl" or "shoot") refers generally to the use of projectiles, but Solomon cites directly from Jer. 50:14, with its call to archers; he follows this prooftext with a verse fragment from Nah. 3:1 describing women exiled while their children are killed. Hosea 4:2 provides the image of the commingled blood of the dead. Rashi and Qimhi read the verse from Hosea to refer to accumulated debts (חובין על חובין מוסיפין); as he certainly knew these glosses, Solomon may be alluding to credit activity among the victims. In its surface meaning, the image strikingly valorizes the submerging of individual in communal identity: the blood (or credit) of the individual victims is mingled with that of her sisters. The "release" of the following verse, tapping Deut. 15:2, was also glossed by the medieval rabbis as release from debt.

In other stanzas, Solomon's lament returns to the image of archers, describing an assault on the market and the scattering of fleeing Jews, instances of forced baptism, and vain attempts to hide. Biblical allusions add subtexts of credit and debt imagery, deceitful Shepherds, and violence that has driven Jews out of one kingdom (France, 1306?) into another, where they remain threatened. Several allusions to cattle plague are curious and could invoke the panzootic that marked the end of the Great Famine. For instance, Solomon says, "The foe made a daily offering of Your herd" (v. 85), meaning that the Christians slaughtered the Jews as if it were a regular practice, or that the mundane fact of slaughter was something that went on day after day. The biblical prooftext, however, is from Exod. 9:3, where it refers to the plague on Egyptian "cattle . . . horses, asses, camels, herds, and flocks." Suggestively, Nachmanides, a thirteenth-century commentator from northern Spain, explained that since the Egyptians treated shepherds as abominations(!), their flocks might have been kept outside the city.

If Solomon knew this tradition (and Nachmanides' glosses were well read in Solomon's day), he may have been seeking to create a compound set of allusions—the surface image of unrelenting slaughter, bringing with it reminders of royal hostility to the Shepherds and attempts to bar them entry to Aragonese towns, along with a memory of great animal death. I have claimed elsewhere that this widespread mortality of livestock also charged competing images of shepherding and sanctity, and here it may suggest that the panzootic was a sign of divine displeasure with the Pastoureaux.[25]

Solomon's attention to antifemale violence reflects historical reality—such violence did occur—but it is also a poetic device.[26] The trope of female violation in a traditional, specifically a liturgical, setting, charges the greater theme of the blow to Jewish honor and sanctity. But it would be anachronistic to read these tableaux as a sensitive homage to female valor. On the contrary, these scenes are designed to elicit the mutual horror of men, while diverting the desire for revenge to higher theological terrain. God's vengeance, perhaps, was lagging, but it would be spectacular in its time. The poet's decision to focus on female figures points to an accepted mechanism for the regulation of individual (male) grief and outrage within liturgical time and space. The need to cultivate this kind of affective response in a liturgical setting is, at the same time, a need to manage it, to subordinate personal rage and anguish to group solidarity. Indeed, the failure to contain individual grief could be costly. The royal registers of Aragon drily record a case of infuriated Jews from a half-dozen localities who had come to rebury the victims of Montclus and went on to vent their fury on a number of trees, pigs, and bridges. The communities that sent the delegation were heavily fined and were probably lucky that that was all.[27]

The institutional conscription of the personal that we see in this lament is one method of coping with the traumatic aftereffects of shocking violence. The long series of vignettes highlighting the sacrifice of families, of cherished wives and children, consciously claims scenes of individual and intimate loss on behalf of a communal narrative. In real life, individuals react to traumatic episodes in different ways, and one challenge of recent theoretical work has been to account for the varying degrees of resilience or disability among men and women exposed to the same traumatic event.[28] It is no surprise that communal accounts of such events override or enlist difference to emphasize common destiny and values.[29] Survivors tempted to dwell on personal grief, perhaps even to express that grief dangerously, are counseled to see their singular agony as part of a larger whole. In the case of the Hebrew lament, this reliance on individualized vignettes has been insistently misread as a transparent report of historical events. This misreading misses the point: first, these are *literary* representations, not documentary reports; and second, these representations of individual martyrdom exist only to be absorbed into a collective narrative. The liturgical lament is, above all, a public genre; it is designed not for the subjective expression of personal grief but for the articulation of social ideals and behavior. To paraphrase Arthur Kleinman, the *qinah* becomes a vehicle for a "transformation of social life."[30] In the solemn sanctity of martyrdom, the living remnants of a community recover the social and religious values that lie shattered in the real world outside.[31] Can we say that the relative dearth of other laments commemorating these episodes signals a failure of this idiom? If that dearth reflects an actual failure to enlist this genre in a time of stress, I suppose that it is possible. But even these few examples tell us that the failure was not total and that, for some Jews and their descendants, it continued to have meaning.

Significantly, the figure of the martyr is consistently keyed to themes of resistance and community and not to the emphasis on victimhood and individuation that dominates modern treatments of trauma. This is illustrated by the description of the commingled blood of the women, which is valued more than the blood of an individual offering.[32] It is evident in the scriptural prooftexts concluding the quatrains, many of which draw on cultic or legal passages that have meaning only as part of a system of communal regulation that is preoccupied with communal purity. It is also evident in the stylized presentation of the vignettes, a frozen diorama of collective sanctity suspended in a timeless present, each tableau encapsulating the theme of commitment unto death. The image of the victim that is central to the modern trauma narrative is both absent from and inconceivable in the Hebrew lament. Rather, the "victim"—the word has no analogue in medieval Hebrew—is a voluntary offering whose identifying gestures signal resistance, faith, and transfiguration.

One other extant hymn, also a lament, is attributed to Solomon b. Jacob. "She'erit Sheleimei" ("The remnant of the peaceable ones") also describes "foreign" attackers who assault a tower and hunt, capture, and kill the Jews, some of whom are dragged through the streets.[33] The attackers are instruments of divine wrath delivering punishment to His people for misdeeds of the ancient past, and Solomon alternates allusions to the assault of the unworthy upon God's chosen ones with cries for revenge. This lament includes no personalized vignettes and only one, negative, allusion to women: Solomon compares the disgrace and pariah's status of the Jews who have been "conquered and consumed" to a menstruating (ritually impure) woman, "a mockery, a *niddah*, for vileness and rebuke" (v. 16). This poem was preserved as a penitential hymn and may or may not relate to Pastoureaux violence. I leave it aside to turn to a lament that is a much stronger candidate for that category.

"Ez'aq bemar" ("I shall cry out bitterly"), by the poet Emanuel, survives in a fourteenth-century Provençal liturgy for the Ninth of Av, where it appears among a group of laments by Provençal poets.[34] We know nothing about this poet, and the lament has not been previously associated with the Pastoureaux. It is still unpublished but is among the otherwise unknown liturgical poems collected by Benjamin Bar-Tikva of Bar-Ilan University, who provided a transcription for my use. Emanuel describes an attack in Av that kills the leaders and "nobles" of the community, destroys the synagogue, and wrecks walls and towers. Young people are killed and survivors flee. The attackers are idolaters who prostrate themselves to alien gods and afflict themselves harshly. Again, the fleeing Jews are trapped between two kingdoms, and Emanuel calls on God to put the attackers "in shackles and prison" (v. 25). Halfway through the poem, he describes the havoc wrought by the onslaught, polemically transferring the "shepherds" label to God's true shepherds, the Jews:

עלי היכל / אשר אוכל / הילילו הרועים
ושק חגרו / כי שברו / האנשים התועים
חומותי / וטירותי / ויטבחו השועים
ולחגה / ודאגה / שמו שכני רעים
מכון שבתי / ואדמתי / היתה גולה וסורה.

O shepherds, wail and wear sackcloth for the Temple
That was consumed! For the erring ones broke down
My walls and towers and slaughtered the nobles.
Evil ones made a mockery and concern of my neighbors.
I was removed and exiled from my dwelling place and homeland.
   (vv. 15–19)

As in Solomon's lament, Emanuel's flattened description of the attackers reflects disinterest in historical representation. He does offer the unusual detail of their ascetic displays (flagellation?). He indicates also that their brutality is indiscriminate, targeting fortified towers where Jews take refuge as well as their quarter and synagogue. In this lament, there are no references to women or heroic portraits of ordinary Jews; the poet focuses on communal leaders and the youth. His call for vengeance includes a wish for his enemies' arrest, a wish that reflects actual occasions when royal officials were able to arrest Pastoureaux and

cart them off to prison, often to be liberated by local mobs. These historical details are generic enough to survive in anthologized collections recited by the
Comtadin Jews who preserved this liturgy without necessarily remembering
their local meaning, but not generic enough that they lasted beyond that rite.
That liturgical hymns like Emanuel's were used repeatedly (until they were not)
is only half the story; they were composed with the *anticipation* of repeated use
in settings where their often vague allusions did not require much decoding. In
the shadow of their familiar topoi, men were permitted to mourn and yearn for
justice and revenge. Consciously, the liturgy contains and constrains their private suffering for communal ends.

Understandably, later readers have tended to treat commemorative texts as
preserving a collective memory of episodes of communal violence. Nonetheless,
the liturgical lament does not record an act of recollection—individual or collective. It is not memory per se and does not "remember" episodes of violence; it
constructs the communal meaning of events after the fact, much as Mitchell
Merback has described the emergence of libel narratives *after* outbreaks of violence belatedly explained by them.[35] From a communal perspective, the very
multiplicity of individual memories is unruly; almost in compensation, the collective narrative explains disaster as divine while sanitizing the chaos and un-
predictability of human responses by representing them in the mythic language
of courage, commitment, and faith. The commemorative lament does not exist
to supply memory where there was amnesia. Rather, it works to unify multiplicity, turning to familiar themes, melodies, and liturgical contexts to restitch
what is experienced as rupture to a fabric of conventionally accepted meaning.[36]
Obviously, the scenes of individual pathos were not representations destined for
the victims, who were dead, but for the survivors. In terms of who could literally
understand the language and allusions of the texts, the target audience was
male. But if we consider the solemnity of the penitential liturgy and synagogue
setting, it is clear that less literate members of the community could respond to
other, nonverbal elements of a lament's recitation. Solomon's lament was sung to
a preexisting melody associated with earlier hymns that had their own rich associations, and the strophic format of the laments enlisted congregational participation, alternating a solo rendition of each stanza with a choral refrain.
Moreover, Emanuel's lament appears as one in a sequence of laments from which
it drew and to which it contributed meaning, and the penitential liturgy to
which they belonged interspersed biblical and liturgical passages that could be
recited by rote and added charge to the whole. Through this richly evocative
performance, a particular historical trauma assumed its place in a series of

catastrophes stretching back to biblical origins; at once metaphor and metonym, echo and extension, one community's experience was subsumed in a familiar sacred narrative. In subsequent chapters, I will ask if that narrative span embraced the plague and its aftermath. In the aftermath of Pastoureaux-inspired violence, these laments suggest that traditional forms of mourning and commemoration, as well as the meaning that they conveyed, still worked.

However effective this transformation of present misery into sacred meaning might have been, there were surely limits to the consolation that it offered. This was not simply because the intensity that characterized liturgical drama ended with the return to quotidian reality. The conflation of liturgical and everyday time, like the conflation of biblical Israel's collective history with that of individual, postbiblical Jews, blurred the boundary between sacred and mundane worlds. But it is also true that communal tragedy did not strike all members of medieval communities equally. Someone's children were slaughtered while someone else's survived. Others were baptized or raped, physically maimed or psychologically shattered in their own varying degrees. Someone salvaged or hid some valuables, while someone else lost everything he owned. Someone's house was auctioned off to Christians, but someone else had properties out of town. Someone sought justice in court and received compensation, while someone else waited years in vain. Even if this historical inequity were not inevitable, exposure to the same terrible event does not affect everyone equally, from a psychological perspective; some individuals and communities prove more resilient than others.[37]

When the time for prayers was over, and daily life resumed, Jewish survivors of Pastoureaux attacks may have drawn comfort from sacred narratives, but just as possibly the narratives might wear thin. In the singularity of suffering, the survivor not only stood out among others, but stood out to him or herself. This was the problem that the liturgy tried to solve but could never have solved perfectly. One copyist of a fourteenth-century legal commentary signed off with a cascade of recent woes:

פירשתי מסכתא זו בשעת הדחק אני טודרוס בן יצחק פ' תוספות הצרפתים בשנת פ"ג ויציאת פ"א היא שנת צר ומצוק גזרת המצורעים הבאה אחר יללת הרועים ... ולפני האפי- פיור . . . עלו מרשיעים להנחיר תורת אמת.

In 1323, in a time of oppression, I, Todros ben Isaac, commented on this tractate on the glosses of the French Tosafists. The year 1321 was one of distress and misery, the persecution of the lepers that followed the wailing of the shepherds. . . . Then accusers went to . . . the Pope to denounce the True Law.[38]

Todros aligns himself with recent historical touchstones that conclude with a threat to the Talmudic texts whose glossators his work of copying and commentary has preserved. Oddly, his memory was confused: Pope John XXII's call to confiscate the Talmud was issued in early September 1320, following the Shepherds' attacks but preceding the Lepers' Plot: apparently, firsthand experience is not a guarantee of proper recall, as trauma scholars know.[39] Todros's interest in French Tosafists suggests that he or his parents had northern connections, but we have no information on his particular circumstances. Nor does he suggest that any of these events touched him personally. Nonetheless, his decision to preserve a work of Talmudic commentary so soon after such works were destroyed suggests a gesture of defiance and even risk. It was a commitment to rebuild in parchment as well as stone.

Another extant colophon testifies more personally to loss. This copyist was in Candia (Crete). His hand is Byzantine, so he was a native. For some reason, his father journeyed to France or Aragon in 1320, where he was killed by the Pastoureaux. In the son's words:

נשלם מכתב יד ימיני זכריה בן הקדוש ה"ר משה החזני קילו"ר בעי"ן בראשי תיבות סימנו ופירושו לכל יושבי תחכמוני כי בגזירת הרועים הלך באור יי' לקדושתו קדוש יאמר לו ואל רחום בגן עדן ישים נפש מתו א"ס נכתב ונחתם בלקניאה באי קנדיאה בשנים עשר יום לירח מרחשוון שנת חמשת אלפים ופ"ה לבריאת העולם.

Completed by my hand, Zechariah the son of the Martyr, Rav Moses Hazani, QILUR Be'AYiN in acrostic, meaning to all who are clever that during the persecution of the Shepherds he walked by God's light to his sanctification. *He shall be called a holy martyr, and the merciful Lord will place the soul of the dead in paradise,* Amen Selah. Written and sealed in Canea on the island of Candia, on the twelfth day of Marheshvan 5285 = 1325 C.E.[40]

Zechariah's connection to the Shepherds was personal. His father committed suicide, a saintly martyr who preferred dying in faith to baptism. The acrostic QiLUR Be'AYiN derives from the verse fragment קדוש יאמר לו ואל רחום בגן עדן ישים נפש מתו ("he is called a martyr/saint and the merciful God will place his soul in paradise"), cited immediately after the abbreviation; the first letter of each word in the verse produces the acrostic. Of itself, the word *qilur* refers to collyrium, and *be'ayin* means "in the eye." Indeed, collyrium was known as an eye salve. Was the father a physician, or does the unusual expression intend only to refer to his healing presence? I do not know. What is certain is that for Zechariah, the legacy of his father's martyrdom is now a way of defining himself. A sacred category and social identity are grafted to the space of personal loss.[41] What we would call trauma and treat as a personal encounter with violence and death, Zechariah agreed to reconfigure as part of a larger social and sacred narrative. This was not because Zechariah did not suffer real and private pain. Rather, the available forms of commemoration responded to that pain in the language of collective meaning. For Zechariah, that language was sufficient, and his suffering was reabsorbed into the language of communal grief and resilience as he himself embodied living witness: Zechariah ben haQadosh, son of the holy martyr.[42]

The privileged status of martyrological kinship is attested abundantly in Jewish sources from medieval Europe.[43] It is rarely noted, however, that the designation extends the reach of the rabbis beyond the prayer house into private life, offering collateral consolation to martyrdom's innocent bystanders. The extension into daily life served a measure of healing even as it repaired the frayed lines of institutional authority: the bereaved received the salve of communal acknowledgment while in exchange, like a living billboard, he exemplified the supreme values of sacrifice and faith.[44] Recent trauma studies sometimes underscore the victim as a signifier of universal humanity or, by extension, the condition of trauma as a mark of that same humanity. The medieval model does not serve this function. The sanctity of medieval victim and proxy affirms a Jewish particularist identity, not a universal human one. The designations of proximate martyrdom likewise single out select survivors or relatives of survivors as unique figures in the community, tokens rather than types of the collectivity. Correspondingly, even as their representations of the victims emphasize Jewish chosenness, the Hebrew liturgical laments deliberately flatten the humanity of their attackers.

Beyond the liturgical landscape, commemorative idioms—honorifics, sumptuary restrictions, cemetery pilgrimages, and the rhythms of sacred learning—sought to alleviate the grief of the bereaved while shoring up the institutional status quo. In so doing, they, too, might allocate a privileged status to those related by blood or discipleship to the sacred dead.[45] Although not all these derivative victims were witnesses to the terrible fate of the man or woman whose aura they reflected—Zechariah was presumably in Crete when his father was killed in Provence—some surely were. Perhaps their corollary status served its own therapeutic function, offsetting survivors' guilt.[46] What of the actual perpetrators and bystanders, who were firsthand witnesses to these traumatic episodes, too? According to recent studies, perpetrators of violence can be trauma victims, too.[47] But the legitimacy of perpetrator trauma remains very much a political affair: as Richard Rechtman has pointed out, no one worries about whether Pol Pot's minions suffer from perpetrator trauma, or the Taliban. Yet if the category is real, we should ask whether it applies to those everyday medieval men and women who rose up against their Jewish neighbors.

Daniel Baraz has argued that medieval Christians associated Jews with violence, an association that encouraged anxiety and fear and that justified repression.[48] Similarly, Anthony Bale describes a world in which, despite the reality of medieval Christian power, Christians imagined themselves threatened by a variety of forces but especially by Jews.[49] In such a medieval context, it may be unnecessary to look for lingering distress among those who committed acts of anti-Jewish violence. Certainly, the question of post-slaughter remorse does not interest Jewish or Christian sources. The Hebrew laments emphasize Jewish solidarity and resilience, and Christian writers express their own version of this ideal. Here is the famous "equilibrium" of Nirenberg's model, which is really about balance only from the fulcrum's upside view. But within these meta-narratives, occasionally a detail rubs the wrong way. From the Jewish side, allusions to converts, pleas for tax relief, fines for disturbing the peace (the poor trees and pigs of Monzón), and even the frantic scramble for new privileges by the Jewish elite describe the experience of "equilibrium" from a less secure perch. There are signs of nonconformity to narrative expectations on the Christian side, too. That narrative is better policed but not perfectly.

Dragged to the baptismal font by an angry mob in Toulouse, Baruch the Jew pleaded for his "great friend" the friar Jean Alamand (Johannen Alamanum), ostensibly to sponsor Baruch's conversion but actually to buy time that might save him from baptism and death.[50] When the mob refused to wait for Jean to be found, Baruch sought protection from the *sous-viguier*, Pierre de Saverdun, hoping that Pierre might offer rescue.[51] Pierre did shelter him temporarily, and then counseled him to flee, which Baruch failed to do, leading to his tragic baptism and injury.[52] Let us fast-forward to 1324, when the Crown was auctioning Jewish property in Toulouse. In general, the alacrity with which notaries and small-scale burghers moved into the spaces of erstwhile Jewish clients and creditors suggests eagerness to appropriate Jewish property and the absence of compunction in doing so. One exception was a small plot of vacant land in front of the old synagogue. Intriguingly, that plot was bought by Baruch's old friend Pierre de Saverdun, and his brother, a purchase that Passerat proposes was motivated by the desire to honor the memory of the man he could not save.[53] Pierre de Saverdun did not kill any Jews. Still, if Passerat is right, his gesture defies the dominant narrative of Christian complicity or tacit approval. It describes equilibrium but also describes reproach. Within safe limits, Pierre de Saverdun's was an act of resistance.

Pierre was not alone. In 1332 and 1335, two French clerics sought and received papal dispensations for their part in the events of 1320. One pleaded that he had only been a youth of fifteen at the time of the uprising in Arbois, where he had "carried wood to burn the Jews." The other recalled tossing "two sticks" onto a pyre where Jews were burned in Nuits-Saint-Georges.[54] Unlike the abundant references to remissions granted to other participants in Pastoureaux violence and looting, these pardons stand out not merely because they are so late but because they enrich neither those who bestow them nor those who received them. On the contrary, the detailed yet fragmentary memory of the man who cast "two sticks" on the fire suggests the disabling persistence of a nightmare. The generic phrase "burning the Jews" veils any personal connection that the clerics may have had with real men and women on the pyre.[55] Still, what was to be gained from these pardons but peace of mind? It would be generous to call these traces "scanty." But they reinforce my suggestion that the private and individual lives of men and women who lived outside the institutional narratives sometimes responded to trauma in ways the official transcript preferred to suppress.

Many questions and challenges raised in this chapter also apply to the records of attacks on Jewish communities of the same region during the Black Death. There, too, we have a surprising paucity of commemorative texts, especially when compared with the detailed laments that have survived from Ashkenaz. The same Hebrew chronicles that confusedly describe Pastoureaux violence are our chief sources for plague-related violence in Provence and Aragon—one difference being that one of Yosef haCohen's sources has now been identified as the lost chronicle of a near-contemporary witness, Hayim Galipapa of Monzón.[56] While individuals in specific localities had economic and political resentments against Jews and their royal patrons, it is not really possible to invoke this all-purpose rationale to explain the virulence of plague-related violence against Jews. Nor does the older reflexive argument of irrational anti-Jewish hatred serve. In Chapter 5, I treat the story of plague-related violence against the Jewish community of Tàrrega, which was virtually annihilated in July 1348.[57] The victims' bodies were deposited in an empty cistern, and, as in 1320 Montclus, a delegation returned later to transfer them to the Jewish cemetery. Yet by 1362, with the next plague outbreak, we find a Jewish physician in Tàrrega drawing a municipal salary. Over the next century, moreover, municipal contracts confirm that a majority of the medical men who treated the citizens of Tàrrega, and to whom they entrusted their lives, were Jews—despite secular and ecclesiastical leg-islation prohibiting their hiring.[58] Irrational hatred of Jews cannot explain this.

Nor, as modern studies of intercommunal and interethnic violence increas-ingly show, is it possible to indict one class of perpetrators only. As Riera i Sans and Passerat have both meticulously demonstrated, the mobs that assaulted Jewish communities in Provence and Aragon were not limited to uneducated peasants and shepherds. Nor were peasants and a disgruntled underclass blindly directed by nefarious "leaders" from the urban guilds or local aristocracy. True, those elements played a role in inciting violence, but violence would not have been so effective if lower-class artisans and angry peasants had not calculated some gain in it for themselves. As for whatever equilibrium ensued, it was an equilibrium that was brutally imposed from above, at royal command, and bru-tally enforced by royal authority. Another, more horizontal, form of equilib-rium likely emerged from the choreography of local violence. Again, studies of twentieth-century intercommunal or interethnic violence sometimes note that the proportion of perpetrators to victims is exceedingly high and that the victims—frequently old or young or weak—were often no match for their op-ponents. Killings also unfolded in public spaces where they were widely seen. These factors created a sense of collective complicity that would have benefited the unrepentant while silencing uneasy participants or bystanders who felt lin-gering qualms of conscience.[59] There is no evidence that all Christians secretly hated their Jewish neighbors. Some of them probably did, and some hostility was surely mutual. More likely, a good many Christians did not hate Jews at all but at a certain moment, both hatred and violence became strategic means to an end. Was that end achieved? Hardly, and it rarely is. But some participants suf-fered more than others, some paid a higher price for their roles in the mayhem than others, and some knew that it was wrong.

*   *   *

Before proceeding to the following chapters, it becomes important to ask a methodological question: Is the concept of psychological trauma a useful cate-gory for medievalists? I think that "trauma" has the potential to make us think carefully about the experience of extreme violence, deprivation, or catastrophe in medieval settings; the category of trauma, even where it is anachronistic, also reminds us to scrutinize carefully the ways we read our sources when we look for psychological or social affect that are generally associated with other, more modern, contexts. Does medieval anti-Jewish violence modify current theory? I

think yes, especially for the American assertion that the experience (and therefore treatment) of trauma is universal. The affective residue of anti-Jewish violence suggested in this chapter is distinct in important ways from what we now
call trauma. The distinction lies first in the medieval emphasis on communal
narrative and experience, so that institutional forms of commemoration (which
are often our primary sources) seek to regulate personal suffering and memory
and subordinate them to the collective. Second, in Jewish contexts, at least,
trauma also produces a derivative figure, not a direct victim of violence but related by blood or discipleship. In what I have called "collateral consolation," the
son, brother, father, or student of the martyr acquires a secondary aura of sanctity. This sacred transfer parallels the deference to dynastic authority in other
medieval Jewish contexts—familial, political, and religious; in a martyrological
context, it extends power precisely along those social lines where rupture would
be dangerous.

Perhaps one of the most significant divides between medieval and modern
trauma lies in their respective attitudes toward suffering. For the medieval Jew
or Christian, suffering evoked a range of social, judicial, and sacred images that
could make it a virtue or a punishment, but always within a system of greater
meaning.[60] Individual trauma, in our sense, is rarely invoked. By comparison,
trauma may now be ubiquitous, but no one really wants to suffer; suffering is
generally seen as an undesirable impediment to life and not an integral part of it.
Medieval men and women were not inured to suffering or violence, but they had
a vocabulary and way to give them meaning. In that arena, we lag far behind
them. The following chapters treat a variety of genres and responses to the next
great catastrophe of the century, the Black Death (1347–50). In addition to
shedding greater light on Jewish experience of and responses to the plague, each
chapter continues to probe the relevance of modern assumptions about trauma
and the challenges of representation that it poses. The preliminary work of this
chapter also permits us to ask whether continuity or rupture characterizes the
literary records of the Black Death.

Chapter 2

Emanuel ben Joseph: Trauma and the Commemorative Lament

[H]ere, overt communication transfers an undercode, an afterimage, a shared emotional substance, that renders a testimony collective speech—speech ethically and emotionally accountable to a wounded and defaced collective.

—Allen Feldman, "Memory Theaters, Virtual Witnessing, and the Trauma-Aesthetic"

THE HEBREW LITURGICAL laments known as *qinot* (singular, *qinah*) may be the most traditional genre of Jewish commemorative literature to come down to us, with biblical prototypes in the book of Lamentations or David's lament for King Saul. These prototypes inspired and sanctioned the composition of later laments that constituted a thriving genre of liturgical and para-liturgical hymns (singular, *piyyut*; plural, *piyyutim*) in Hebrew or sometimes Aramaic. During the classical period of *piyyut* composition in Palestine and the Byzantine East, the *qinah* flourished in liturgies that commemorated national or collective memories of catastrophe, such as the Destruction of the Temple and the Roman siege of Jerusalem. Medieval European Jews, especially in Ashkenaz and northern France, continued to recite many of these older laments, some of which they interpreted in ways similar to sacred text.[1] But medieval Europe also produced its own *paytanim*, or liturgical poets, and in a novel twist, some of their *qinot* took a historical turn. These so-called persecution laments thus have added significance as the official memory of recent events, a rich but understudied poetic corpus that preserves, in a distinctive poetic idiom, the encounters of Jewish communities with different forms of violence—crusader, judicial, and mob violence and attacks on people, property, or books.[2]

This chapter treats one particular and long-neglected liturgical lament that survives in a single copy in a fifteenth-century Sephardic liturgy. The author, Emanuel ben Joseph, is not known from other sources, nor is his lament especially striking for its literary quality. Nonetheless, it is one of two traditional Hebrew laments from a Sephardic context that may be linked to the Black Death and to plague-related attacks on a Jewish community. The second lament, which was discovered in the course of writing this book, is treated in Chapter 5 with the other sources that respond to the combined effects of plague and violence in the Catalonian town of Tàrrega. I begin my investigation of Jewish responses to the Black Death with Emanuel's text precisely because it is a traditional text, of a type we would have expected to find in greater abundance but do not; it therefore offers a way to begin thinking about the role of traditional commemorative activity in the wake of the plague. This chapter asks what kind of response Emanuel's lament offered to the traumatic experience that it commemorates, and whether it succeeded. As with the Pastoureaux laments discussed in Chapter 1, the stylistic techniques enlisted by the poet, as well as the message that he sought to convey, are noteworthy for their distance from the agendas and approaches highlighted in recent theoretical writings on trauma and what is now called the "trauma aesthetic."[3] At the same time, Emanuel's lament is noteworthy for its continuity with the earlier examples. Poignantly, Emanuel's lament points simultaneously to the genre's durability and fragility, a faith in familiar ways of understanding catastrophe undercut by some unease.

More than any other genre of medieval Jewish literature, the Jewish prayer book is a diary of the past. Although the basic format of the Jewish liturgy had been fixed since the early ninth century, each region modified the scaffolding of fixed prayers with local variations, stamping regional liturgies with their own distinctive character. This was especially true in the case of the *piyyutim* that adorned the festival and fast-day liturgies, when there was no haste to disband a community in worship for other sorts of activity: on a long fast day, when it was not even necessary to break for meals, additional distraction must have been welcomed. In the East, some communities salvaged hymns that they had long recited and were unwilling to jettison. In the West, European Jewish communities added local favorites to the received repertoire, nurturing regional hymn collections, generally for use in penitential liturgies. Some of these hymns were transmitted from the east and greatly revered; others were the work of local poets who lived among their communities and shared their moments of celebration and sorrow. These local voices spoke on behalf of real as well as imagined communities, and frequently in compositions that were linked to specific episodes and memories. Their writings are therefore a great resource for scholars seeking clues to communal identity and to communal responses to particular events.

The great virtue of Hebrew liturgical hymns is, alas, also their great weakness, for several reasons. The Jewish communities of the European Middle Ages, especially the later span of that broad period, did not have stable histories. From the thirteenth through the end of the fifteenth centuries, many of these communities were subject to political, economic, and social pressures that disrupted daily life and fractured cultural continuity. The degree and constancy of these pressures varied over time and place; occasionally, the weakening or expulsion of Jewish settlements in one region sent Jews into more hospitable territory for longer or shorter sojourns. Unless the refugees were represented in considerable numbers or had considerable cultural dominance—as happened with the Castilian communities expelled to Italy, Palestine, the Balkans, and North Africa in 1492—their local poets and history were soon submerged into that of their hosts. A hymn that embraced generic tropes of sin and redemption, exile and return, affliction and salvation, undoubtedly had a better chance of surviving than a hymn that commemorated a particular moment in the life of a vanished community. For European Jewish communities, the fourteenth and fifteenth centuries were a period of considerable dislocation, one that concluded with few identifying Jews on European soil. The kinds of local memory that once bound small communities together could not always withstand the pressure of successive and greater blows. These are all reasons that the traditional voices of collective memory for earlier and more local events may be difficult to find now.

By the sixteenth century, with the rise of the printing press, Jewish liturgical particularity would suffer another challenge. The introduction of print liturgies also jettisoned local in favor of more generic hymns, in part because they consolidated the traditions of smaller communities and in part because print liturgies needed to appeal to a broader group of consumers. Even these print liturgies often had limited lives, as illustrated by the fate of the volumes that appeared in the Comtat Venaissin in the 1760s and 1770s representing the liturgical rites of Jews in Avignon, Carpentras, L'isle-sur-Sorgue, and Cavaillon. The emancipation that came with the French Revolution shortly thereafter was extended to Comtadin Jews, who rapidly dispersed into greater France. Elsewhere, I have treated a number of hymns from these liturgies as rare examples of commemorative responses to the Great Expulsion of French Jews in 1306. The Comtadin liturgies also contain hymns by many stalwart favorites of Provençal Jews, as well as some by poets who have been remembered minimally, if at all. On the other hand, many manuscript liturgies survive from this region, largely because handwritten prayer books were the rule even after the rise of printing, which small communities could not afford. These manuscript liturgies preserve many more instances of local compositions, testifying to local practices and memories that have been lost with dispersion and neglect.

Among the events that shaped these old communities, the Black Death must have played a part, and it may be that any number of penitential laments among the liturgical codices that served Provençal and Hispanic Jews refer to this catastrophe. But there is no catalog or index that sorts them for this theme, and if their language is sufficiently generic, it would not be obvious today that this is the crisis that they were written to address. Conversely, it is also true that laments that may have been composed as generic hymns of catastrophe and mourning came to be associated with the Black Death later; this is possibly the case of the lament by Moses Nathan discussed in Chapter 5. Moreover, of the handful of penitential laments that may even tentatively be associated with the Black Death, only two—Emanuel ben Joseph's is one of them—derive from a Sephardic liturgy. The remainder come from central or eastern European communities. Like the extant plague laments from Ashkenaz, moreover, the Sephardic lament survived because it recorded a compound experience of disease and anti-Jewish violence.[4] As will be evident, Emanuel's images of plague are subordinated to his representation of a brutal assault on a Jewish community, although both are presented as forms of divine punishment.

The liturgical hymns found in old prayer books pose other obstacles for scholars interested in responses to particular catastrophes of the past. For modern, predominantly Western, historians of history and literature, this quest has often been construed as a search for traces of individual, private affect. Nonetheless, *piyyut*—liturgical poetry—preserves the voice of a community, and any vignettes of individual affect that it included were mediated through well-established formulas and conventions. The liturgical poet was himself a product of authoritative institutions and learning, a man who frequently served in an institutional capacity as a rabbi or cantor, scholar or teacher, or judge. His voice was not trained to sound radical harmonies: the fact that his texts were preserved testifies to their ratification by communal authorities and their embrace by a worship community. This must have been true even of those hymns that we read today as expressions of great distress or anger, such as Ephraim of Bonn's great lament for the victims of an auto-da-fé in Blois in 1171, or Isaac bar Shalom's astonishing challenge to God in a lament for victims of Second Crusade violence in Germany.[5] The liturgical poet was, above all, charged with the formation of collective memory. In the case of collective catastrophe, his hymns could focus

that memory on particular details while providing cues for interpreting and responding to them, thus playing an important role in defining the meaning of
disturbing events.[6]

To this end, the individual details as well as the themes of the historical lament are carefully selected. Modern readers of historical *qinot*, including myself,
have been greatly drawn to the insertion of family tableaux, or vignettes of individual or collective martyrdom, in these texts. Certainly, these vignettes represent
a commitment to narrative realism that is new to the medieval *qinah* and owes
much to narrative developments in the surrounding vernaculars. Nonetheless, it
would be a mistake to confuse these poetic vignettes with documentary snapshots
committed to a realist aesthetic alien to this genre. The individuals who appear in
the Hebrew laments commemorating historical catastrophes have been shaped to
represent a communal ideal, an ideal that promoted stubborn resistance and voluntary suffering on behalf of their faith. As the example of Emanuel ben Joseph's
plague lament demonstrates, both individuals and the actions for which they are
recalled are consciously typed. The historical individuals they represent are real;
but as literary figures, they serve to ratify communal values of purity and devotion.
As literary signifiers, the historical individual and his or her feelings and behavior
are not so much lost as inessential; they must be subordinated to the larger and
corporate objectives of the genre.

Moreover, this literature aimed at a range of users, from the cantor who recited the stanzas to the men of variable literacy who chimed in on the refrain, to
the women and children who heard the plaintive melody, often contrafacted
from another well-known hymn. It taught its listeners the proper response to a
horrifying episode that directly or indirectly threatened an entire Jewish community. To some extent, its success lay in organizing the disorganized emotions,
passions, and thoughts of the individuals who constituted a collectivity. This is
the official voice of what is now called collective trauma, and why that concept
has been so linked to that of collective memory.[7] Nonetheless, both in the short
and long term, the tropes invoked to cohere a community would also be used by
individuals seeking a vocabulary and grammar for expressing what had
happened to them personally. To see how fluid the exchange between public and
private grammars of grief might be, the closing section of this chapter offsets
Emanuel's lament with a text that initially appears to be at the opposite end of
the literary and traumatic spectrum: a personal inscription scrawled in a Pentateuch by a survivor of plague and Christian assault. The moving words of Dayas
Quinoni, who owed his survival to a business trip, speak from outside the collective legacy while simultaneously reflecting it back to itself: collective trauma's

vocabulary and grammar could be adapted to articulate individual meaning, but they continued dialectically to coexist, each drawing meaning and life from the other.

*   *   *

Emanuel ben Joseph's lament, "Let me lament in bitterness and fasting" ("Aqonen bemarah vetzom"), survives in a lush two-volume codex now in the Biblioteca Palatina in Parma. The codex is a work comprising several parts and copied in a Sephardic script; several colophons date its completion to 1481. The first volume announces its contents as "prayers of the Sephardim," a designation confirmed by rite and authorship of its many *piyyutim*. The second volume includes prayers and hymns for fast days—first the prescribed fasts of the Jewish calendar year, and then an occasional liturgy for catastrophes of nature or history that called for public fasting and prayer rituals whose origins go back to the Mishnah.[8] It is not uncommon, especially in manuscript liturgies, for fast-day rites to preserve the shards of otherwise forgotten events—for instance, a pogrom or custom enhanced by ritual anti-Jewish violence.[9] Alternatively, local hymns can preserve evidence of Jewish solidarity with Gentile neighbors, such as the "Yom Tzarfat" or "Yom Sefarad" hymns that mark the defeat of French or Spanish troops on Italian soil.[10] In the case of the Calabrian codex, MS Parma 1929/1935, the modern catalogers describe its public fast liturgy as an alternation of benedictions and penitential hymns with the blowing of the shofar. As they observe, the Parma codex's fast-day liturgy is characterized by an "emphasis on plague," a recurring motif in its prayers and hymns.[11] The concluding prayers also enlist a Mishnaic appeal designated for times of plague.[12]

Emanuel's lament was preserved in the liturgy for the Ninth of Av, where it was to be recited over the Torah on the Sabbath of that week. Not only is this the calendar date associated with cumulative Jewish catastrophes, but it was the time of the year that saw plague-related attacks on the Jewish communities of Cervera, Tàrrega, and nearby towns.[13] The hymn consists of nineteen verses, although its concluding lines differ slightly in the sources. An acrostic running through the initial letters of each verse spells out the poet's name; the acrostic is marred in its final four verses, which yield an unidentifiable place of origin for the poet. In full, the acrostic, as we have it, reads: "I am Emanuel ben Yosef S-Sh-N-A." The lament may have been willfully or unintentionally emended over time, a fate that was not uncommon and could reflect a desire to adapt a text to later conditions.[14]

Over the centuries, the Parma codex had a number of owners, many of whose names adorn its flyleaves, along with censor's marks dated to the late sixteenth century. In the 1830s, the hefty codex came to the attention of the learned rabbi and bibliophile Samuel D. Luzzatto ("Shadal"), who copied sections of it, including our lament; his transcription was included among his published letters in 1882.[15] Subsequently, the text of the lament was republished by Lazar Landshuth in his *'Amudei ha'avodah* and included in a classic "lachrymose" anthology, Simon Bernfeld's *Sefer haDema'ot*.[16] Otherwise, the poem has been ignored. No one can definitively say that it is or is not a poetic response to the great plague of 1348. Emanuel wrote in response to some episode combining illness and violence, although it could have been a later outbreak of plague or some other disease. Nonetheless, I believe that the historical details that the poem embeds, as well as its plaintive depiction of illness accompanied by a level of violence not associated with later outbreaks, make possible and even plausible its identification with the 1348 pandemic. If I am wrong, the hymn still illustrates what such a text might look like, what conventions it would utilize, and what message it would seek to convey. If its genesis lay in a slightly later event, the poet relied on earlier models for inspiration and guidance, in which case the great pandemic still lurks behind his text.

Emanuel's lament is formally simple. It is heralded in the Parma manuscript with a bold incipit reading מרתיה קודם תגלה—which should probably be translated as "I lamented [to the melody of] 'Before You reveal.'"[17] The lament is built on a monorhyme, so that each verse ends with the syllable *-im*, carefully obeying the grammatical requirement for Hebrew rhyme of a vowel and two consonants. Each verse contains two hemistichs, and each hemistich has eight syllables. The lament opens conventionally, with the speaker assuming the role of spokesman for the community in the wake of tragedy; a series of nonnarrative and fragmentary descriptions of the disaster follow, with a concluding appeal to God to hear his people's prayer and redeem them. My translation follows the Hebrew text.

Parma Biblioteca Palatina Heb. 1929, 1935;
IMHM Microfilms F 13085, F 13090 fol. 71b
Emanuel b. Joseph S"ShNA

מרתיה קודם תגלה
אֲקוֹנֵן בְּמָרָה וְצוֹם וַעֲצָרָה עַל הַתּוֹרָה וְעַל הַנְּבִיאִים
נִבְרִים קְדוֹשִׁים זְקֵנִים יְשִׁישִׁים אֲדוֹנִים קָשִׁים [1] בְּמַסְגֵּר מְבִיאִים

יָרַד הֲדָרָם וְחָשַׁךְ מְאוֹרָם וְאַרְצוֹת מְגוּרָם אוֹתָם מְקִיאִים
עֲזוּבִים לְחוֹרֶב מְנוּיִם [2] לְחֶרֶב בֹּקֶר וָעֶרֶב בְּפִיּוֹת לְבָאִים
מְרוּדִים [3] בִּידֵי נוֹגֵשׂ וְרוֹדֶה וְרָחַק פּוֹדֶה וְגָבְרוּ מַשְׂנְּאִים
נְתוּשַׁי [4] חוֹמָה טְרוּדִים בְּחֵמָה לְקַצְוֵי אֲדָמָה וְאֶל גּוֹי שְׁבָאִים [5]
וְשֻׂדְּדוּ נֶהֱרַג לְעֵינֵיהֶם [6] וְכָל קִנְיָנֵיהֶם בָּתִּים מְלֵאִים
אֲחָזוּם בְּמַקְשָׁם [7] מְבַקְשֵׁי נַפְשָׁם וַיִּשְׁחָטוּם שָׁם כְּעֶדְרֵי טְלָאִים
לָחוּצִים בְּדַלּוֹת אֲמֵלִים בְּשִׁפְלוּת כֻּלָּם בְּגֵלוּת יָהֹגּוּ אַךְ נְכָאִים [8]
בָּנִים אֲהוּבִים בְּחָצוֹת סְחוּבִים וְאָבוֹת כּוֹאֲבִים בְּמוֹתָם רוֹאִים
נְעִימִים כַּשַּׁחַר עוֹרָם שָׁחַר וּמֵתוּ אַחַר מִמּוֹתֵי חֲלָאִים
יְמוֹתָם סָפוּ יְדֵיהֶם רָפוּ יוֹם נִגְּפוּ לִפְנֵי טְמֵאִים [9]
וְכָשְׁלוּ רַגְלֵי שָׁבוּי וְגוֹלָה בְּמִדְבָּר מָלֵא פִּגְרֵי רְפָאִים
סָר צֵל הוֹדָם וְשָׁפֵל כְּבוֹדָם וְהָלְכוּ בְּאֵידָם רְעֵבִים צְמֵאִים
פְּנֵיהֶם קָדְרוּ וַיִּתְנַכְּרוּ בְּחַיִּים נִקְבְּרוּ יָרְדוּ פְּלָאִים
סְמוֹךְ נְפִילָתָם צוּר כְּפוֹרַתָם הָאֵר אֲפֵלָתָם יוֹצֵר בְּרוּאִים
טַהֵר לְבָבָם וְיַשֵּׁר נְתִיבָם וּמְחוֹת לְחוֹבָם וְהַעֲבֵר חַטָּאִים [10]
שְׁעֵה שַׁוְעָתָם מְקוֹם מִנְחָתָם וְדַם חַטָּאתָם וְחֵלֶב [11] מְרִיאִים
נְחֵה עַמְּךָ יָהּ כִּנְאוּמֶךָ לְמִקְדָּשׁ שָׁמֶיךָ [12] יְשׁוּבוּן פְּדוּאִים
[אַשְׁרֵי אֱמוּנִים בְּיָהּ מַאֲמִינִים וְאַשְׁרֵי בָנִים עִם אֵל קְרוּאִים] [13]

הערות:
[1] לאנדסהאוט וברנשטיין, אנשים ונשים.
[2] לאנדסהאוט וברנשטיין, מטים לחרב.
[3] לאנדסהאוט וברנשטיין. מסורים.
[4] לאנדסהאוט וברנשטיין. נתוצי.
[5] בדפוס, "גיא שבאים" ועיין יואל ד:ח, גם "גיא שמנים" ביש' כח:א,ד.
[6] למול עיניהם – חסרה הברה אחת.
[7] לאנדסהאוט וברנשטיין, אחוזים ביוקשם.
[8] הברה מיותרת.
[9] חסרה הברה אחת.
[10] שורה זו חסרה בלאנדסהוט ובברנפלד.
[11] לאנדסהאוט וברנשטיין, כחלב.
[12] לאנדסהואט וברנשטיין. הדומיך. ויש פה הברה מיותרת.
[13] השורה הסרה בכתב היד אבל מופיעה בברנפלד ובלנדסהאוט.

I lamented [to the melody of] "Before You reveal":

1. I shall lament in bitterness, fasting, and prayer, on behalf of the Torah
    and prophets.

2. Saintly men, pure of heart, and venerable elders were imprisoned by harsh lords.

3. Their glory dwindled, their radiance dimmed; the land where they dwelled spit them out.

4. They were left desolate, appointed for the sword; morning and evening in the mouths of lions.

5. [They were] brought down by attackers and oppressors. Their redeemer is distant while those who hate them grew strong.

6. Their wall destroyed, they were driven by anger to the ends of the earth, to a nation of captors.

7. Before their eyes, they plundered their homes, houses filled with belongings.

8. Those who sought their lives trapped them and slaughtered them like flocks of lambs.

9. They were pressed in poverty, wretched in baseness; all were sent into exile uttering wails and grief.

10. Beloved sons were dragged in the streets, and aching fathers saw their deaths.

11. They had been radiant as the dawn, [but now] their skin turned black. They died of deadly diseases.

12. Their days ended, their grasp weakened, the day they were struck down before the impure ones.

13. The feet of captive and exile stumbled in a wilderness full of ghostly corpses.

14. The Glory that had shaded them departed, their honor fell. In their misfortune, they went in hunger and thirst.

15. Their faces grew dark and unrecognizable. They were buried alive; they had a terrible descent.

16. Catch their fall, O Rock, just as You scattered them! Illumine their darkness, Creator of all!

17. *Purify their hearts and straighten their path; wipe out their debt and take away [their] sins.*

18. Hear their cry in place of their sacrifice, the blood of the sin-offering, the fat of calves.

19. Lead Your people, O God, as You have spoken, to Your heavenly Temple; let them return redeemed.

20. Happy are those who have total faith in the Lord, and happy are the children who are called the people of God!

Notes. 1. *Prayer* (עצרה)—a communal assembly; cf. Joel 1:14, 2:15, with Rashi and Abraham Ibn Ezra. **3.** Cf. Lev. 18:25, 28; 20:22. **5.** *Were brought down*—Landshut and Bernfeld have "were handed over." **6.** *Driven by anger*—reading טרד as it is used in rabbinic Hebrew, as banish/expel; see, e.g., Lam. R to I, 21; Targum Y Gen III, 24. *To a nation of captors*—the Parma manuscript reads לגוי שבאים, while Bernfeld has לגיא שבאים, "the valley of the people of Sheba." I read the Parma version as Emanuel's pun on the Aramaic word for "captors," which is a homonym for the people of Sheba, known in Hebrew Scriptures as traders of ancient Arabia (e.g., 1 Kings 10; 2 Chronicles 9; or Ezek. 27:22–23, 38:13; and elsewhere). Thus, the expression may also mean "a people of traders." In Bernfeld's version, Emanuel alludes to Joel 4:8, where God says that He has sold Judah's sons and daughters to other men of Judah who have sold them to Sheba. See the discussion following. The verse may also ironically echo Isa. 28:1, 4, where the prophet refers to גיא שמנים, the "fertile valley" (NIV). **8.** *Trapped them*—or, as per Landshut and Bernfeld, "they were trapped [by] those who sought their lives." **9.** *All were sent into exile*—cf. 2 Sam. 20:13, with its back story of antiroyal revolt, royalist suppression, violence and murder, and a corpse in the road. The expression could also be translated "will lament in exile." *Uttering wails and grief*—Isa. 16:7. **10.** *Aching fathers—* אבות כואבים. Compare the phrase אב נכאב ונדאב, a recurring trope of the Toledo epitaphs discussed in Chapter 4. **11.** *Skin turned black*—Ezek. 30:30, and see verse 15 below. *Died from deadly diseases*—Jer. 16:4. The context from Jer. 16:4 is evocative: "they will die and lie unburied in the streets; they will also die of hunger and by sword, and birds will eat their corpses." Qimhi glosses the catastrophe as famine; the Tosafist commentary, *Metzudat David*, says that the dead will not be eulogized; they are too many to bury and they will be cast on the ground like garbage. The Jeremiah passage also refers to an unsparing mortality and inability to bury the dead. **12.** *Struck down*—נגפו, with its echoes of plague, hence perhaps "the day they were smitten (by plague and violence)." See Lev. 26:17, which follows the promise of disease (consumption and fever) in 26:16. **13.** *Ghostly corpses*—פגרי רפאים. The phrase is unusual. **14.** *The Glory . . . departed*—see Num. 14:9. *Hunger and thirst*—Ps. 107:5. **15.** *Grew dark*—perhaps, "unrecognizable." This is also a plague symptom. I am not sure how to read ויתנכרו. *A terrible descent*—Lam. 1:9. **16.** The text appears to read נפזרתם, which I have emended to כפזרתם following the suggestion of Professor Naoya Katsumata. As he notes, there is also an extra syllable in the second hemistich, and perhaps אפלתם should read אפלם; the meaning is unchanged. **17.** This whole verse is only in MS Parma, not in the print versions. The reference to debt is perhaps an association of later users (including the copyist). **20.** This verse appears only in the print editions, not in MS Parma.

The contents of Emanuel's poem unfold rapidly in a nonlinear narrative. Nonetheless, the temptation to read nonlinearity as an attempt to mimic traumatic recall would be out of place. While linear narrative in the Hebrew lament characterizes several compositions from the late twelfth century on, chiefly from northern French contexts, it is a technique imported from contemporary prose and exegetical trends and never really conquers the *piyyut* genres.[18] The vast majority of Hebrew laments, in contrast, begin in media res, summoning earlier tragedies from the sacred past as the backdrop to a recent historical event. From his opening words, which engage a well-worn topos, Emanuel is relating a story that is contained and conveyed by a traditional view of the bitterness of Jewish life in exile, a fate that the Jews have merited by their many sins. By plying these recurring motifs, the medieval poets assured their works a degree of durability that more historically specific narratives often failed to have. It was not particularly necessary for later chanters or listeners to identify Emanuel's text with a specific historical location or event: the cyclical repetition of history was what validated each particular instantiation of its rules. In the case of European Jewish memory, those rules would cohere around a narrative of chosenness and divine protection that they had willfully betrayed, a foolish repudiation that led inexorably and repeatedly to dispossession, suffering, and exile. The notion of "a new kind of historical event . . . that requires a shift in understanding, as well as unprecedented modes of action and response" is not even on the horizon for Emanuel and his contemporary listeners, or for the later generations who recited his lament in Calabria.[19] If it had been, they would not have recited the lament at all. The loss of this and other laments, or their reduction to academic artifacts, is as much a function of modernity as it is a consequence of the turbulence of late medieval Jewish experience.

In fact, no traditional Jewish genre of commemoration, from fast-day liturgies to tombstone epitaphs to the rare instance of this lament, treats the plague as a catastrophe of previously unknown dimensions. The concept of a singular and unprecedented irruption in cyclical time was not necessary, as it was, for instance, to explain the Jewish suicide-martyrdoms commemorated in twelfth-century Ashkenaz. There, in contrast, we do find Hebrew chronicles and laments voicing stupefaction before a reality that had never been encountered before. In the case of the Black Death, an impression of its novelty was either irrelevant or absent. At least within a liturgical framework, this catastrophe sounded familiar and could be described in familiar ways; it could still be assimilated to preexisting theological rubrics of punishment and penitence. The notion of trauma's singularity and resistance to conventional narrative description, a theme frequently invoked in contemporary trauma theory, was not a problem for Emanuel, at least as he expressed himself in his lament. In rare cases, we do find liturgical poets who violate the formal symmetry of a composition to suggest the incapacity of form and language to represent traumatic grief— Ephraim of Bonn's brilliant lament for the thirty-two men and women burned at Blois in 1171 is an excellent example—but more often, the resilience of the tropes is striking. Emanuel described a terrible and searing event, but he could do so without breaking with the conventions of the lament genre.

And yet, along with its dependence on familiar conventions, Emanuel's lament incorporates local details into the generic and cyclic version of history that they uphold. On the level of content, the text refers to imprisonment, dispossession, slaughter, the plundering of homes and property, children dragged through the streets before the eyes of helpless parents, entrapment and starvation on the road, and corpses unburied while others are buried alive. Scattered through these images are more evocative images of sickness and disability that allude to fatal illness, fever, weakness, disfigurement, and impaired mobility. Both kinds of disaster—social and biological—are characterized in the language of shame and dishonor. The human enemy is explicitly invoked only in the first half of the poem: the victims confront "harsh lords" (3), "lions' mouths" (4), the "attacker and oppressor" and men of hate (5), a Gentile nation (6), and men "who seek their lives" (8) and are "impure" (12). With the exception of the "harsh lords" of verse 3, and perhaps the "lions" of verse 4, these are generic terms for Christian attackers, emphasizing the contrast between Christian and Jew in theological binaries of aggressor versus (sacrificial) victim, Gentile versus chosen, impure versus pure.

The flattened representation of attackers and victims conveyed more to Emanuel's contemporaries than they do to us now. Who were the "harsh lords" who arrested the Jews? Were they municipal officers, judges, or bailiffs, who held the Jews in anticipation of attacks (and who may have yielded to the attackers and turned them over)? Emanuel writes that the Jews were "destined (appointed) for the sword"; does this refer literally to sword-bearing, hence upper-class or professional fighters, or is it just a metaphor for armed violence? A wall is destroyed—near the Jewish quarter, or perhaps even their place of imprisonment. In verse 5, a ruler who might have intervened was instead far off, which emboldened the attackers. This was the case in Catalonia, where Pere III (of Catalonia, also referred to as Pere or Pedro IV of Aragon) was trapped in Valencia for part of this period; royal correspondence attests to a lag in his information about the attacks as well as to an inability to quash them.[20] According to Emanuel, the flight of survivors was also characterized by terror, famine, and hardship; roadsides were littered with dead (from violence or plague?), including the sick.[21]

Emanuel's record of compound catastrophe is also shaped by its omissions. Notably, it describes a world populated exclusively by males. Men constitute the evildoers, and men are their victims. Harsh lords, prisoners, polluted attackers, like the sick and the dead, the lions and lambs—all male. Sons are killed and fathers watch them, and even the grammatically feminine "lands" that expel them are transformed into masculine entities to conform with the rhyme: the verb "spit them out" is in the masculine third-person plural when, grammatically, we would expect the feminine. Recent research has challenged the view that the plague was universal in its impact, and mortality studies have demonstrated that the demographics of plague mortality varied in different locales. The following two chapters, treating a medical treatise from outside Girona and epitaphs from Toledo, confirm this picture of the varied impact of the plague even across the Iberian Peninsula. Overall, a higher percentage of young adult victims characterized the 1348 pandemic, and there was a lesser impact on toddlers and the elderly. (The year 1362, the next plague wave, is, by contrast, sometimes referred to as the plague of children.) Anecdotal suggestions that women fared better than men in the first wave of plague (i.e., in 1348) have not been substantiated. King Pere lost his queen to the pandemic when he left her and his daughters in Valencia. Nor were Jewish women exempt from the violence of the attacks on Jewish *calls* (quarters) in 1348; as the grim evidence from Tàrrega confirms, they were killed as brutally and in the same ways as men.

Emanuel's decision to craft an exclusively male tableau, while not unusual, upholds particular genre conventions. At least one of the Hebrew laments commemorating Pastoureaux-inspired violence, treated in Chapter 1, chose to highlight vignettes of female purity and death. That decision was not motivated by an interest in women so much as it reflected a focus on communal male honor and a rallying point for recovery. Here, on the contrary, Emanuel does not articulate a strong call for spiritual or material restitution, and he may have been too close to the events that he described to offer such language honestly. So, in a sense, his lament may also testify to some uneasiness about the nature of the catastrophe around him. His concluding petition beseeches God to honor His ancient promises—"lead Your people to Your sanctuary, *as You have said*" (19); and, in the print version of the text, a wobbly reassurance that death in faith is rewarded in heaven. Perhaps this verse was added later, after all, and if so, its addition acknowledges the anemic quality of consolation that precedes it.

As verse 6 has come down to us, it has two possible readings. Emanuel announces that the victims have been banished to the "ends of the earth," an assertion that he follows in the Parma manuscript with the words אל גוי שבאים, which I have translated "to a nation of captors." This reading of שבאים as the Aramaic "captor" suggests a pun with the proper noun for which it is a homonym, the *Sheva'im*, or people of Sheba. Inexplicably, Bernfeld has emended the phrase to read אל גיא שבאים, to the *valley* of [the people of] Sheba. In his version, then, the Jews who have fled their attackers in Spain have ended up (in captivity) in an Arab land. Bernfeld's version also puns by inverting the image of the fecund valley evoked in Isa. 28:1 and 28:4 to describe a place of captivity. Indeed, in Joel 4:8, God announces that He will sell the people of Judah to other Judae-ans who will sell them "to the people of Sheba, to a distant nation." Either way, Emanuel tells us that the Jews have fled far away; he may also imply that, stripped of all resources, the survivors were vulnerable to indenture or debt. Bernfeld's reading would imply that their inhospitable landing was in an Islamic territory, but we have no evidence of Jews fleeing Aragon in 1348 for Islamic refuge. If Bernfeld's emendation was correct, the verse—and hence the lament—would have to refer to a later catastrophe. The obvious suggestion would be 1391, when Jews did flee Aragon for the Maghreb, but not during a wave of plague. Later Sephardic laments by the great Rashbatz, Rabbi Simon b. Tzemah, also refer to penury and servitude in Islamic lands, along with pestilence and famine. But the Rashbatz survived the terrible pogroms of 1391 by fleeing to Algeria, and his laments belong to a late fourteenth-century Maghrebi context. Did Emanuel understand "Sheba" as "really far away," or as a specific location?[22] Did a later user or copyist tamper with Emanuel's language to extend its meaning to later experience? Did Bernfeld, the German twentieth-century editor, retroject a similar conflation of experience into Emanuel's lament?

If we take the first option, this line suggests that the poem was not composed in the immediate wake of the event that it describes, because the narrator has knowledge of the survivors' destination. If we take the second option, the narrator has this information, too, perhaps because he has experienced later episodes of plague, violence, and expulsion that drove Jews to Arab lands. In this case, we must read this lament as a kind of polytext that fuses multiple voices and histories spanning a century or more. However, we would then also have to explain how this lament and its fellows traveled from an Islamic context back to Italy and the Parma copyist in Calabria. If we take the third option, we have a twentieth-century, historiographical problem, but one that tells us nothing about Emanuel or his world. In all three readings, we see the delayed construction of collective mem-ory and trauma as they are shaped by agents of institutional authority in and out of the synagogue. This is not an illustration of the classic latency, or delayed emer-gence, of traumatic symptoms or memories in an individual—say, Emanuel. Rather, it is an illustration of the institutional shaping of collective memory as a way of making sense out of catastrophe and of the shakiness of that memory over time.[23] For now, that may be our safest conclusion.

The Christians in Emanuel's lament are frequently realized through the use of third-person plural forms that portray them as a monolithic bloc that acts with anger and brutality: "they imprisoned" (v. 4), "they plundered their houses"

(v. 13), "they slaughtered them" (v. 16). The Jews find themselves delivered into the hands of a generic foe, "the oppressor and tyrant" (v. 9) who implacably hates them (v. 10). In contrast, the victims are passive recipients of violence, the objects of Christian terror. They are handed over (v. 9), their walls are broken, and they are harassed (v. 11), they are seized and trapped (v. 15), "pressed in poverty" (v. 17), and their sons are dragged through the streets (v. 19). This binary technique constructs two undifferentiated collectivities: the Christians are uniformly characterized by murderous intent and the Jews uniformly as powerless victims. Strikingly, in the second half of the poem, the Christians are mentioned only once, as the "impure ones" of verse 12. Appearing just past the halfway mark of the poem, verses 11–12 illustrate how Emanuel can reinforce specific themes by means of biblical prooftext:

> Beautiful as the dawn, their skin was radiant. They died from deadly disease.
> Their days ended, their grasp weakened, the day they were struck down
> before the impure ones.

נעימים כשחר עור[ם] שחר / ומתו אחר ממותי חלאים
ימותם ספו ידיהם רפו / יום נגפו לפני טמאים.

The first of the two verses is unclear and perhaps corrupt. The print versions read עוד[ם] ("they still") where I have read עור[ם] ("their skin"). I do not understand what sense the other reading offers. The verb שחר is also slippery. It appears in noun form in the first unit of the hemistich, where it means "dawn." The verb form can either refer to radiance or shining (like the dawn), or to darkness (the adjectival form שחור means "black"). A nimble poet would have avoided the same root with the same meaning twice in one verse; the technique of *tajnis*, the iteration of homophonic words with different meanings, is beloved by Sephardic poets. As a result, I am pushed to read "their skin is/turned black." The second half of the verse draws directly on Jer. 16:4, Jeremiah's terrifying assertion that God has removed His mercy from the people and they will die of sickness, young and old, with no one to bury or lament for them. In Emanuel's verse 12, this dire prophecy is seconded by an allusion to Lev. 26:17, which warns the people of Israel that they shall be "smitten" before their enemies. Lev. 26:16 is explicit that "smitten" refers to disease, consumption, and fever. While Emanuel seems, therefore, to be depicting the helplessness of Jewish men and women stricken first by disease and then by enemies whose beliefs are abhorrent ("impure"), the subtexts of Jeremiah and Leviticus point an ominous finger at the victims, who, in straying from God's way, have brought this terrible punishment on themselves. Blackened skin, for that matter, and sudden weakness were symptoms of the plague fevers noted by contemporary physicians, and the verses may deliberately summon their descriptive relevance.

Emanuel emphasizes that the degradation suffered by the Jews is all the greater for taking place in full view. Before all, "their splendor diminished, their light darkened" (v. 3). The Jews are forced helplessly to witness their downfall: "they plundered their homes and all their property before their eyes" (v. 7), they were "slaughtered . . . like flocks of lambs" (v. 8), and survivors spilled into exile. Fathers must watch their sons as they are dragged through the streets (v. 10). Recurring images of vertical descent are linked to those of public dishonor. The Jews' splendor "has gone down" (v. 3), they are "brought down/oppressed" by the enemy (v. 5), they are wretched and abased (v. 9), their honor "goes down" (v. 14), and they are even buried alive (v. 15). As the echo of Leviticus 26 in verse 12 implies, this spectacular fall is viewed triumphantly by their enemies. Accordingly, God is beseeched in verse 16 to halt the downward moral and physical trajectory of His people: "support their fall, O Rock who dispersed them."

More than personal shame, the poet describes a blow to communal honor, a threat to corporate identity and survival. This, too, distinguishes medieval Jewish conventions for representing catastrophe or trauma from the modern emphasis on personal shame and affect.[24] It is not, therefore, "universally" true that the doubled traumatic impact of plague and violence will find mimetic representation in disrupted narration, fragmentary imagery, temporal discontinuity, and aporia.[25] In its liturgical formulation and for its fourteenth-century audience, the language of communal threat still summoned familiar sorts of meaning. No sense of rupture with past catastrophes was necessary, or of a moment unprecedented in collective history. The events described by the poet are surely terrible, but the biblical prooftexts tether them to scriptural contexts and theological meanings that span from the sacred past to the messianic future. The jagged narrative, constructed of incomplete vignettes of horror, is not enlisted to convey shattering trauma or the shock of the unspeakable so much as it is to insert images of meaningless violence into a meaningful, ultimately scriptural, frame. So, too, the language of honor weaves unity out of the disparate experiences of sickness, violence, shock, and dispossession that constitute the surface matter of the poem. Significantly, these nonlinear features of Emanuel's text are fairly standard to the genre, and what appears to be incoherent and inexplicable is, by design, braced by intertextual supports to frame an institutionally sanctioned (if shaky) message of consolation. At the same time, the actual experience of Emanuel's ravaged community, and what was recalled by survivors in individualized landscapes of terror, disease, destruction, and exile, are reabsorbed as a part of a cyclic narrative of collective trauma in the familiar rites of the liturgy and its laments.

Ironically, both versions of the poem's conclusion support my reading. In each, the poem concludes with a plea to God to uplift the fallen, to hear their cry, and to restore them to their home. According to the Parma manuscript, the poet also asks God to "purify their hearts, straighten their path; wipe out their debt and remove [their] sins" (v. 17). The list of requests links purity to straightness (rectitude) and "debt" to sin. Emanuel uses the Hebrew word חטא for sin, which etymologically casts "sin" as "missing the mark" or "straying"; the verse pleads for God to lead His people from a crooked path (sin) to a straight one. The reference to debt could be metaphorical, in the sense of debts accrued to God, but it could equally imply monetary debts such as those suggested by verse 6's allusions to servitude or indenture. Royal correspondence and archives from Aragon for the 1350s refer to the economic devastation of *aljamas* attacked in 1348 and to their struggle to recover from the combined blows of violence (which included burned ledger books), plague, famine, and civil war. In the desperation that might characterize life under these conditions, "debt" might indeed incline one toward "sin," perhaps conversion, and perhaps lesser forms of familial or communal betrayal.

But if so, this may have been a message deemed less pleasant or relevant as the years went by. This verse is missing in the print editions, where we find instead a final verse that is absent in the Parma copy and which reads: "Happy are the faithful who believe in God, and happy are the sons who are called the children of God!" (v. 20). Where the Parma version concluded in the language of sin, the print version chose to turn away from this theological denouement to insist on the rewards of unswerving faith. Despite their differences and the different register of the two conclusions, they both remind their listeners that catastrophe comes from heaven and that those whom it befalls must cling to their faith.

The conclusion—in either version—is striking for another reason. A quick examination of the four long plague laments from Ashkenaz (central Europe) that accompany Emanuel's text in Bernfeld's 1924 anthology confirms that all of them incorporate grim calls for revenge against their Christian foes. The first, by a R. Meir, concludes each stanza with a refrain inherited from earlier Crusade-era laments, asking: "For these [martyrs], will You hold back, O Lord?" "Bring them down beneath the waves/ like a stone in water," cries Baruch bar Yehiel toward the end of an exhausting description of torments and plunder suffered by the Jewish victims. Another long lament, by Israel bar Joel Zusselin of

Erfurt, details attacks on a series of communities, and then swings toward an extended peroration with a bitter vision of retribution against a personified Christian nation: "The Rock will judge you and bring you down / [to Sheol] with your uncircumcised ones," he predicts, and "Zion, then you will see / vengeance and rejoice." The same lament concludes with assurances that God will (someday) behead their enemies, "tear off head and skull," and crush and annihilate those who have attacked them. A third very long text also depicts attacks on a series of Jewish communities. Its author, Akiva ben Eleazar, concludes with relative restraint: "Our Father, our King, avenge us / sevenfold among our neighbors."[26] In contrast, Emanuel has chosen to conclude without so much as a murmur for vengeance against the perpetrators whose brutality he records in his lament. The omission is not initially surprising: Israel Yuval has argued that the Sephardic lament, unlike its Ashkenazi counterpart, avoided calls for retribution of the Ashkenazi variety. However, Yuval also claimed that, in place of retribution, the Sephardi laments imagined the *conversion* of their enemies as their own brand of messianic justice.[27] Emanuel's lament is devoid of any such utterance, emphasizing instead faith, penitence, and redemption from suffering—for the Jews. The cruel foes who have attacked and dispossessed the Jews have been relegated to the background; they are instruments of divine wrath but insignificant in themselves.

In its day, Yuval's essay was attacked for highlighting the raw aggression of the Ashkenazi revenge motif, which he treated as evidence of symmetry between Christian and Jewish expressions of hate. Certainly, any argument for symmetry would be misleading in important ways. The Jewish desire for revenge remained precisely that: wishful thinking safely expressed in Hebrew and securely confined to a liturgical setting. Its speakers had neither the means nor the opportunity to act on vengeful thoughts, which, in any case, were deferred for divine implementation. Christian violence against Jews, however, was real; it exceeded the bounds of liturgical and aesthetic expression (which often served to justify it) and was translated into action. From a psychological perspective, it is possible to read expressions of vengeance in Jewish penitential hymns and laments as one means of coping with the aftermath of violence, especially in a context where physical retribution was denied.[28] The Hebrew laments situate scenes of communal and personal violation in a familiar emplotment of sin, punishment, and atonement. The affective recitation of these laments, the heightened pathos that they would have acquired with the addition of music and a penitential setting, would contribute to the therapeutic repetition and catharsis that defined the genre.

Thus, the real question is not why Emanuel elides any call for revenge in his lament, but why he elides a closing vision of restored justice in any form at all. What does it mean that Emanuel's poem concludes without the dramatic release otherwise conventional to these poems? One possible answer is that his lament is not a very good piece of poetry; it is true that this lament falls below other exemplars in conception, imagery, and power of expression. But another, equally valid, answer is the possibility that Emanuel had no riveting consolation to offer. Emanuel's "I shall bitterly lament" may or may not have been composed in the immediate aftermath of the episode that it describes, but the instability of the text became one of its features, including the evidence that lines and phrases have been altered deliberately or accidentally over the years. What remained was a text that struggled to imagine the wheels of divine justice coming full turn. This surely may be read as traumatic affect. It is a failure of speech on poetic, theological, and therapeutic levels: what it offers is a transcription of numbness, an inability to convert lived experience into the tropes of meaning otherwise at hand. This is not, as Caruth and others have argued, because the poet does not have access to memory of the traumatic event that he tries to narrate. On the contrary, the bits and pieces of what transpired are embedded throughout the composition: the event is neither inaccessible nor its recall belated.[29] The loss of chronological or narrative coherence may reflect disordered recall, but it is not atypical for the lament genre. Rather, as I have argued above, while Emanuel's informative bits and pieces lack the forward momentum that we associate with narrative, they are snugly tethered to a vertical history that locates them meaningfully between a biblical past and an anticipated future. What nonetheless suggests tremendous shock is that Emanuel is unable to articulate that future with any conviction or in the language of explicit reassurance.

What, finally, are we to make of this poem's incipit? The Sephardic *qinah* tradition evolved over time to embody special liturgical texts and traditions. Laments for the four official fast days of the Jewish liturgical year (the fasts of Esther, Gedaliah, Tamuz, and Tisha b'Av) were gathered into a *Seder qinot le-'arba' ta'aniyyot* (Order of laments for the four fast days). Emanuel's lament survived in one such collection. Some of these laments were intended for solo recitation, and others for solo recitation with choral or congregational refrains; almost all were performed to preexisting melodies that are occasionally indicated in the manuscript by means of the first few words of the original melody.[30] Although rarely acknowledged by scholars of text, that melody also added a layer of affect to the words that it supported and may have equally guided their interpretation.[31]

Emanuel's lament is prefaced by three words: *Martiha qodem teggaleh*—"I lamented" (or "performed this lament"), according to "Before You reveal," presumably the opening words of another, preexisting lament. We recall that whoever arranged this liturgy inserted Emanuel's text in the morning service for the Ninth of Av, where it was to be recited prior to the reading from the Torah. Another lament followed the scriptural reading, and that lament, too, begins with a similar incipit: *Martiha Elohim al nidrash ladin 'oni verash*: "I lamented [to the melody of] 'O God, the poor and afflicted should not be sentenced to judgment.'" These are the only places in this manuscript where the term *martiha* appears. The copyist/arranger may have been familiar with the cognate Arabic verb, which means "to lament," or he may have inherited the term as a technical one (like the use of the Arabic *lahan* for "melody"), indicating a style of recitation.

In Hebrew, the root *m-r-r* commonly referred to bitterness, with lamentation a secondary association. Perhaps coincidentally, perhaps not, the Hebrew verb appears in Isa. 24:9, amid a description of a land and people laid waste by God. All shall share the same fate—laypeople and priests, slaves and servants, with their lords and mistresses, buyers and sellers, lenders and borrowers. The earth is polluted and cursed because of human sin. Joy has vanished, musical instruments have fallen silent, and verse 9 adds that men no longer drink and sing songs, but drink is bitter (*yeimar*, from *marar*) to them. The chapter continues with images of chaos in the city and with God's anticipated punishment of the celestial forces and earthly rulers whose transgressions have roused His wrath. As biblical predictions go, this one might easily have evoked plague-struck cities to readers after the mid-fourteenth century. Does it also confirm a special type of lamentation that was recited in times of plague? Perhaps it does, and we should look for more examples of its use.

Both the "titles" of the contrafacted hymns referred to in the manuscript liturgy are unknown to us today. No poems beginning with these words appear in Davidson's thesaurus or surface in the Institute for Microfilmed Hebrew Manuscripts database. Both melodies and lyrics are impossible to retrieve. Nonetheless, they were familiar to a group of worshipers who associated them with a common past that was itself associated with plague. Following the fixed fast-day liturgies, Parma 1935 appended a liturgy for public fasts designed for catastrophes of the moment and alternating benedictions and shofar blasts. Customarily, the sorts of catastrophes that might be covered by such a liturgy ranged from droughts and famines to epidemics and wars. The catalogers note that in the case of Parma 1935, the disaster that preoccupied the copyist of the manuscript is clear: each liturgical segment concludes with the words "Our eyes remain fixed on You until You have favor upon us and remove the plague and pestilence and destroyer from among us today, O Holy One."[32] In other words, by the time the copyist of the Parma double-codex finished his work, Emanuel's lament was not only associated in the collective memory of his community with a late summer convergence of plague, violence, and expulsion, but it was a touch-stone of that memory that provided its own sort of vertical ballast for later communities exhausted by recurring epidemics and dislocation.

The liturgical arc of the Parma codex illuminates the process according to which, over decades and even centuries of use, the memory of a particular episode might be transplanted to new settings and users, becoming constitutive of a shared "memory" of the past. As the sociologist Jeffrey Alexander has noted, collective trauma, like collective memory, is invariably such a construct. It is distinguished from direct and personal experience precisely by its delayed formation and appearance, and it must be shaped by what Alexander calls "culture carriers" who are invested in a certain view of the past.[33] That perspective makes sense for this context as well. It may have been more than a repeatedly battered and dispersed community could manage to invoke a common memory of a long-ago pandemic. Too many local experiences were shaken together in the stories of survivors and refugees, too many subsequent disasters had intervened to make the Black Death seem so singular. What mattered, ironically, was not what exactly had happened but that it kept on happening, and that very repetition became a kind of meaning, as well as testimony of faithfulness, of its own. Once again, trauma is not the unprecedented or inconceivable event. Rather, it is a familiar cycle of similar catastrophes, whose cumulative repetition forges the common history and identity of those who perceive themselves to be its subjects. Nor does this perception leave them bereft of agency: their abandonment of God's Law and betrayal of God's Covenant led to terrible chastisement, and repentance and return would restore them—one day—to God's favor.

The caprice that attends this poem's survival, like the instability of its transmission, characterizes the textual record of much of the medieval Jewish past. A century and a half after these events, there would be no Jews on the Iberian Peninsula, and within another decade or so, they would have been expelled from most of Provence into the Comtat Venaissin. Hebrew liturgies from northern Africa that preserve the legacy of Iberian exiles most often do so from a late fifteenth- to sixteenth-century vantage point. From that perch, anthologists and copyists, like the communities they lived among, looked back on the expulsion from "Sepharad." Beyond the high peak of 1492, the dimmer outlines of the previous century and a half were dimly visible, a long period characterized by fortune and prosperity as well as by harassment and loss. It is not so surprising if 1348 is more of a landmark on our backward vista than it was on theirs. In either of its versions, Emanuel's weak gesture toward consolation may have guaranteed his lament's survival; a more robust assertion of renewal would have seemed like folly, and a more documentary kind of poetry would have gone the way of an old newspaper clipping. Who knows but that the exhausted poverty of his vision may have been precisely what lent it credibility to a further battered age? Even the survival of Emanuel's lament in a later plague liturgy testifies to its incorporation into a communal memory marked by recurring plague outbreaks and expulsion. What mattered to its sixteenth-century users was not its uniqueness but its sheer repeatability, the way sickness, like expulsion, had become an "idiom of distress" encompassing unending cycles of Jewish suffering and divine displeasure.

Caprice and instability destroy but also salvage, and it is due to a measure of both that we find a unique record of an individual survivor of plague and violence in 1348 from nearby Provence. This record is at the opposite end of the textual spectrum from Emanuel's. It was not composed for communal recitation, or according to liturgical theological or prosodic norms. It was not composed by a poet, for that matter, and not intended to voice the experience of a collective. At this register, rather, we see a rare glimpse of personal testimony and, yes, trauma. As detailed in Joseph Shatzmiller's early study, the Jews of La Baume, near Sisteron on the Durance River, fell in a wave of massacres that swept the region with the arrival of the Black Death. The attack at La Baume, which occurred in mid-May, annihilated the community.[34] The sole survivor owed his life to his wealth and importance. After the plague had subsided, other sources name him as one of the delegates from Jewish communities who convened to coordinate a response to royal demands for funds; at that convocation, Dayas (Yedaiah) Quinoni negotiated a huge tax deduction for himself. A one-percenter for sure, Dayas was not in La Baume when his fellow Jews were attacked, but in Avignon, where Queen Jeanne had summoned him. After the destruction of that spring and summer, he settled in Aix, where he scribbled a note in the margin of a Pentateuch that had, like Dayas himself, survived. Shatzmiller has analyzed the inscription carefully; and I supply his transcription here with my own translation:

הלא זה מוצל מאש ביום האף והחמה ששפך השם באש חמתו על קהל הקדוש
מלבמא דשטרון כי כלם קדשו השם ית' טף ונשים ביום אחד בעונותינו הרבים בשנת
קח' לפרט ו' פרשה והעבירו תער על כל בשרם והובא אלי זה החומש בעיר איגש
בשנת ק"ט לפרט ז, פרשה שוב אשוב אליך ונשארתי רק אני לבדי כי הוזמנתי ונקרוא

נקראתי י' ימים קודם הגזרות לבא לפני אדנתינו המלכה העירה אבינון ושמה ישבתי
ובכתי במר נפשי השם ברחמיו יזכנו לראות בנחמות .יהודה וישר' ובנין אריא' ויזכני
להגות בו אני וזרעי עד עולם

This is a brand saved from the fire, the day of wrath that God poured out on
the holy community of La Baume de Sisteron in the fire of His wrath. For all
of them sanctified God's Name, may He be blessed, infants and women on
the same day, on account of our many sins, in the year 5108, the Friday of the
weekly portion, "And they shall shave themselves entirely" (Num. 8:7). This
Pentateuch was brought to me in Aix in 5109, during the weekly portion "I
shall surely return to you" (Gen. 18:10). Only I remained, for I had been
summoned ten days prior to the pogroms to our Lady the Queen in the city
of Avignon, and there I stayed and wept in bitterness of soul. May God in
His mercies merit us to see the consolation of Judah and Israel, and the
rebuilding of Ariel. And may He merit me to go there, I and my descendants,
forever.

Dayas's moving notation permits several observations. The first is that he
identifies with a book of sacred Scripture as having been saved like himself; he is
part of what Brian Stock has termed a "textual community" that dialogically and
powerfully defines itself in relationship to its books. The Pentateuch brought to
him—by whom? Jews returning to La Baume who ransomed or salvaged it? sympathetic Christians who may have done the same?—is a metaphor for himself. The
codex is "a brand rescued from the fire," in the words of the biblical prophet Zechariah. In Zechariah's vision, the Temple priest Joshua stands before the angel of
God, who is flanked by "the challenger" (the "satan"). The Lord rebukes the prosecuting angel and expresses His intention to protect Jerusalem, the brand saved
from the fire (Zech. 3:2). In the biblical text, there is already a conflation of man
(priest) and city/community (Jerusalem), and Dayas intuitively adopted its resonance. Time, in his account, is also tethered to Scripture and is marked by the cycle
of weekly scriptural readings: the attack on La Baume took place during the week
of "They shall pass a razor over all their flesh" (Num. 8:7), from Parashat
Beha'alotkha, which would have been read in late June or early July. The salvaged
Pentateuch is "brought" to him during the week of "I shall surely return to you"
(Gen. 18:10), from Parashat Vayera, read later, in September, and beginning with
the account of angelic visitors to Abraham and Sarah to announce the future birth
of their child. Dayas has chosen to focus on a verse in which Abraham's mysterious
visitor announces that the elderly couple will give birth and that he "will surely
return" at that time. The subtext of promised progeny is made explicit in Dayas's

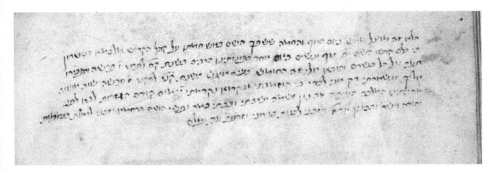

FIGURE 1. The inscription by Dayas Quinoni, a survivor of plague-inspired violence against the Jews of La Baume, in a biblical codex, Vienna Austria Cod. Heb. 28, fol. 362b, at the Austrian National Library. Reproduced by permission of the National Library of Israel, which holds the digital copy.

concluding lines; perhaps, privileged though he was, he lost a son or a wife in the violence at La Baume.

Unlike Emanuel, Dayas has no problem highlighting the deaths of women and children in the attacks at La Baume. The fact that the attackers did not spare "infants and women" is an added condemnation. Yet Dayas moves swiftly from this notation to attribute their collective fate to "our many sins." This motif may have been so pervasive in medieval thinking that it unconsciously found expression; yet it is noteworthy how finely it is woven into the language of a nonliterary man. The violence at La Baume reflects the outpouring of God's wrath, and it befell the community on account of their sins (what sins of ordinary people, more skeptical writers would ask, could demand such repayment?).[35] The passage from Zechariah 3, with its vivid image of a single brand plucked from the flames, also embeds a lesson on sin and repentance: the priest Joshua must shed his filthy robe for a new garment, which the angel of the Lord explains pointedly: "See, I have removed your sin from you and you shall be dressed in priestly robes" (Zech. 3:4). The angel adds a "pure turban" and instructs Joshua to follow in God's paths if he wishes to officiate in God's "house" (Zech. 3:5–6). Terrible things had happened at La Baume, and Dayas was left to contemplate their meaning. But meaning still resided in the familiar forms of human failing and repentance, in the hope for divine mercy.

Even so, the desire to see Dayas merely as an individual expressing individual trauma demands a willful distortion of the ways that he locates himself as part of a collective, from the invocation of scriptural markers of time to the assumption of his role as witness. Dayas somberly describes his shock and agony upon learning of his community's destruction while he was safe in Avignon,

writing that "there I stayed and wept in bitterness of soul." His phrasing, שם
ישבתי ובכיתי, "there I stayed [or sat] and wept," adapts Ps. 137:1 by converting its
collective to his singular usage. The individual is a microcosm of the collective
in this schematic more than the macrocosm—the community—is personified
as an individual. Dayas's inscription concludes by yearning for mythical restoration of people and land, a future time when he and his descendants may
"meditate" upon the Holy Land. In sum, Dayas's sense of divine reliability and
forgiveness holds strong. It is a faith in the resonant verticality of history, the
lingering echo of its chords of punishment and redemption, exile and return. It
is also a faith that does not erase the fact that he is equally a stunned and lonely
survivor, a man whose community has been extinguished, its final embers reduced to a man and a book.

Clinicians and scholars who discuss contemporary trauma, in the words of
Derek Summerfield, remain committed to a "tradition both in Western biomedi-
cine and psychology to regard the singular human being as the basic unit of
study."[36] In other words, even when making claims for collective trauma, trauma
theory tends to revert to individual experience as its basic unit of study and treatment. This bias toward an "individual-centric" model of trauma has been critiqued
by a number of postmodern scholars, more often in literary and cultural studies
than in clinical psychology. The tension between individual and collective, as it
has emerged in this chapter, does not really mesh with current theory. Emanuel
wrote as a spokesman for a community, in a long-recognized genre. His lament
describes the human experience of shock in the face of extraordinary mortality
and violence, which are inexplicable except in the language of sin, repentance, and
anticipated redemption. The shattered social and psychological reality that he depicts in his verses, however, is tethered to a vertical brace of meanings, a backdrop
of sacred prooftexts and situations that cohere the shards of images and memories.
Dayas, for his part, writes as an individual—for some kind of posterity, certainly,
but not for collective performance or in a collective voice. His personal experience
governs his narrative, but it, too, is tethered securely to the same tropes of meaning
and affirmation that undergird the hymn. The language that gives meaning to the
collective is what is available to him for expressing meaning as an individual, too.
Are the tropes that Emanuel and Dayas invoke under strain? Yes, I think that in
both cases, that sense of strain comes through. But these tropes are still holding,
and neither of these men is ready to relinquish them. Institutional or intimate,
poet or banker, the old answers were the only ones still. For other Jews, that was
not the case, as Chapter 3 suggests.

Abraham Caslari: A Jewish Physician on the Plague

THIS CHAPTER TREATS the *Tractate on Pestilential and Other Types of Fevers*, by Abraham Caslari, a Jewish physician in Besalú, not far from Girona and at the eastern tip of Catalonia. Composed sometime in 1349, Abraham's work is one of a number of extant tractates written during or immediately after the period of the Black Death, which reached Besalú in May 1348.[1] As an early record of a physician's perspective on the pandemic, Abraham's tractate is important as a medical witness. The first half of this chapter, accordingly, considers the tractate as a medical composition, comparing it with the slightly earlier plague tract of Jacme d'Agramont. The second half of this chapter examines aspects of Abraham's tractate that are not directly related to his medical argument, in order to see what light they shed on the social, religious, and human crisis precipitated by the Black Death.

For several reasons, Jacme d'Agramont's *Regiment de Preservacio* is a useful foil to Abraham's tractate. Jacme held the chair in medicine at the university in Lleida, a city located 200 kilometers west of Besalú. It was where Abraham and his family had spent several years following their expulsion from Languedoc in 1306.[2] The *Regiment de Preservacio* was written in April 1348, making it the first known medical treatise to respond to the Black Death and the first original medical treatise produced at the University of Lleida).[3] Jacme's work was unique among the early tractates as the only example of a plague regimen written in the vernacular (in this case, Catalan) and intended for ordinary people; his preface addresses the good councillors of Lleida, who wished to know how to defend their city against pestilence and to advise their citizens how to protect themselves. (If Jacme's readers sought theory or pharmaceutical recipes, he recommended that they consult a learned physician, for that was not the goal of his work.) In contrast, Abraham Caslari's tractate was intended for a reader learned in medicine and in Hebrew—not just the limpid biblical Hebrew of the Iberian Hebrew poets but the stilted, highly technical Hebrew that characterized medieval Hebrew philosophical and scientific prose. Despite this rarefied circulation, Hebrew, too, shared some of the attributes of a vernacular for a textual community of rationalist, scientifically inclined Jews, crossing dialects and national boundaries and contributing to the common intellectual formation of Abraham and his peers, Christian as well as Jewish.

Whether the men were personally acquainted, or whether Abraham actually encountered Jacme's text, we do not know. By the summer of 1348, like many of his fellow Lleidans and despite whatever preventive measures they implemented, Jacme would be dead of plague, and the Lleida *aljama* would be the target of a pogrom fueled by rumors blaming Jews for the pestilence. In contrast, and at the other end of the peninsula, Abraham treated many patients who, like him, survived the pandemic; his tractate was written after the fevers had ebbed and the violence to his west and south had quieted. These similarities and differences make it useful to compare what these two men had to say about the greatest professional crisis of their careers. As the first half of this chapter demonstrates, both men drew on similar textual traditions, particularly the work on epidemic fevers by the revered tenth- and eleventh-century Persian physician known to the west as Avicenna (Ibn Sinā). Nonetheless, they plied this common learning to reach very different conclusions about the causes and nature of the plague. Abraham insisted that the devastating fevers that he had survived and treated were not true pestilential fevers and that if properly and quickly diagnosed, many victims of such fevers could be saved. In contrast, Jacme thought that the plague represented a universal pestilence, a type of pestilence originating in an astronomical (celestial) event such as an eclipse or planetary conjunction; for Jacme, this kind of pestilence was ordained by God in punishment for human sin.[4] Interestingly, from a medical perspective, their divergent views are reflected in plague demographics: in Besalú, mortality was not as high as in cities farther south or west, giving Abraham reason to think that it was treatable. In Lleida, mortality from the plague was much higher, as it was in cities like Barcelona, whose fate was known to Jacme. It may not be so surprising that Abraham's sense of confidence was not echoed by his peers, or that his tractate preserves a perspective on the pandemic that was distinctly in the minority. The second half of this chapter asks if plague demographics entirely explain the expressions of isolation and frustration that occasionally surface in Abraham's work.

Today, Jacme's treatise is often invoked by historians for its claim that plague could be "manufactured" by evil men, a notion that has been linked to violence against local Jews. Indeed, Abraham's treatise was written not just in the wake of a devastating outbreak of plague but in the wake of a series of violent attacks on local Jewish communities to the east, south, and west of Besalú. The nearest of those attacks, in April 1348, was in Perpignan, approximately 40 kilometers away.[5] On May 17, when the plague had reached Besalú and Girona, the Jewish *call* (quarter) in Barcelona—approximately 130 kilometers to the south—was decimated and some twenty Jews killed; a domino series of attacks accompanied the plague west and south of Barcelona, causing varying degrees of destruction. (A second plague route through Iberia began in Majorca and touched the mainland in Almería, and then proceeded north and west.) Informed of the Barcelona attacks, King Pere IV of Aragon (also known as Pere III of Barcelona) sent letters to the cities of Cervera, Lleida, and Huesca ordering local authorities to protect their Jews.[6] While the efficacy of these letters has been debated by scholars, there is evidence that municipal officials in these towns attempted to comply with their demands. In Tàrrega, in contrast, the mayor and possibly the city councillors participated actively in the looting and murder of several hundred Jews; I treat their story in Chapter 5. There are no known records of anti-Jewish violence in Besalú or in Girona, the nearest city for which the impact of the plague has been studied.[7] Still, it was likely that, by the summer of 1349, Abraham knew of the assaults on Jewish life and property elsewhere. In April 1348, a traveler from Provence to Girona had brought news of the arrest and torture of Jews accused of poisoning the water to cause plague in Narbonne, Carcassonne, and LaGrasse.[8] By the following summer, when Abraham composed his tractate, refugees from Monzón, Tàrrega, and Solsona had sought shelter in Barcelona and surrounding towns, seeking refuge and redress; many refused to return to their ravaged homes despite enticements to do so. Some news of these men and women must have reached the ears of Jews farther east, and Abraham's connections to the royal court and royal patients surely brought links to other informants as well.

Abraham's tractate makes one reference to these events, alluding in his introduction to a contemporary Jewish chronicler's description of the attacks on the *aljamas*. The second half of this chapter moves away from scientific questions to examine aspects of Abraham's composition and prose style that shed light on concerns that the author consciously or unconsciously chose not to address outright. I focus on three specific features of the text: (1) the use of authorial interjections and assertions of personal experience or authority; (2) the use (or avoidance) of biblical illustration or citation; and (3) the elision of psychological or emotional factors in Abraham's discussion of diagnosis and treatment.

These "accidents of the soul" fall under the rubric of the sixth "nonnatural"—factors that influence health or illness and that are subject to manipulation. On the one hand, Abraham's tractate reflects the lack of anti-Jewish violence experienced in his immediate environment. His apparent reticence may signal the temporary collapse of the institutions and networks that voiced and sustained traditional responses to violence. In contrast, as the plague tracts demonstrate, the lines of communication among physicians, despite their relatively high mortality levels, remained intact. On the other hand, Abraham's decision to invoke, by means of intertextual citation, a contemporary account of plague-related violence points to the need to look beyond traditional commemorative genres to understand how different sorts of Jews responded to religious and political catastrophe of 1348.

But I want to begin Abraham's story earlier, in the late summer of 1306. When Abraham Caslari, his wife, and his father, David, left their home in Narbonne and crossed the Pyrenees in the late summer or fall of 1306, they were one family amid the great Jewish exodus from France.[9] The Jews of Languedoc, which included Narbonne, were subject to the decree of expulsion that King Philip IV had issued in August; many proceeded south and west toward Catalonia or eastward into the Savoie and Dauphiné. For the former, Perpignan was their first destination. Today part of France, in the early fourteenth century it was territory belonging to the kingdom of Aragon; as such, it constituted an important haven for French and Languedocian Jews. The Jewish refugees quickly overwhelmed the local community and its resources, and many, like the Caslaris, pushed on farther, over the mountains toward Girona, Barcelona, and Lleida. After some years in Lleida, the Caslari family relocated back toward the border, receiving royal permission to open a medical practice in Besalú. In 1320, Abraham requested royal permission again—this time, to take a second wife in addition to the wife who had accompanied him from Languedoc. His new wife, Bonadona sa Sala, also came from a medical family that had originated in Perpignan and reestablished itself in Besalú; perhaps Abraham was trying to boost his local connections.[10] Bigamy was not a common practice among Iberian Jews, but it was not outlawed, and Abraham must have been willing to risk some domestic strain for the sake of his career.

One of his marriages ended in divorce, but the professional gamble paid off, as Abraham dots the royal archives with increasing visibility over the coming years.[11] Throughout the 1320s and 1330s, he amassed franchises and lawsuits, contracts, loans, and debts. In the late 1320s, he was granted a thirty-year exemption from new tax assessments by the king; by then, a son, Yahacel, had died, and the king guaranteed that Abraham's privileges would be extended to his daughter Bonadona. By 1339, Abraham was under contract to provide medical care to the Infante Joan.[12] During these years, he authored several Hebrew tracts on medical topics, including an early essay on vital spirits, followed by the "Alei ra'anan" (Fragrant leaves), a work on fevers composed in 1326.[13] When the plague reached Catalonia and Aragon in the summer of 1348, Abraham was still actively practicing medicine.[14] He treated victims of the plague and, shortly afterward, wrote the treatise that is our concern here.[15]

While some of the prominent Jewish physicians of his time were known also as men of letters, dedicating themselves to traditional religious texts and contemporary belles lettres as well as to science, Abraham's name is not linked to any belletristic achievement. In this respect, he differed from his father, David, who, in addition to his medical interests and writings, was a lover of poetry. A renowned physician in Narbonne, David translated a work by Galen from Latin into Hebrew. David also boasted a personal friendship with the local rhetorician and poet Abraham Bedersi, who dedicated a poem to him and nominated him to judge a poetry competition.[16] David died in Catalonia in 1315 or 1316; we know of nothing that he wrote from the day he left France.[17] In contrast, Abraham did invest time in writing, but as two of his three extant treatises attest, his abiding interest was not in poetry but fevers. In penning one of these medical works, moreover, Abraham Caslari bequeathed us a record of his views on a crucial topic of his day: the unprecedented fevers that swept through Provence and across the Iberian Peninsula in 1348 and 1349.

Abraham was one of a handful of physicians whose firsthand experience in 1348 led him to compose a formal tractate that discussed the diagnosis, prevention, and treatment of the plague. A new literary genre that emerged in 1348, the plague tractate remained popular for several centuries. Hundreds of tractates appeared over this period, most of them responding to later plague outbreaks and authored by Christian physicians, clerics, and astrologers. Many of these texts have now been gathered and studied by modern scholars. Much work remains, however, for the study of Jewish and Muslim tractates, only a few of which have appeared in critical editions.[18] A dated but important essay by Ron Barkai sought to survey the extant Jewish plague tractates, both those that were original compositions and those that were translations of Christian or Muslim works.[19] As Barkai noted, and as other studies confirm, Abraham's treatise is one of the earliest plague tractates in any language; other works composed by university-based physicians during or immediately after the appearance of the plague in 1348 were by Jacme d'Agramont in Lleida; the commissioned and jointly authored tractate by the medical faculty at the University of Paris; the anonymous Montpellier author responding to the Paris tractate; Alfonso de Córdoba, also in Montpellier; and Gentile da Foligno in Perugia. Both Jacme and Gentile were dead from the plague by June 1348, Gentile while revising two earlier tractates that he had written before the devastating force of the pandemic was evident.[20]

A central argument of the *Ma'amar beqaddahot divriyyot uminei qaddahot* (Tractate on pestilential and other types of fevers) was that plague patients often suffered because physicians misdiagnosed the kind of fever that they were treating, confusing pestilential and non-pestilential fevers. As Melissa Chase has observed, this concern was shared by other plague authors, for whom fever was not (as now) a symptom but "a category of disease characterized by excess heat within the body."[21] Fevers, as a rule, might be divided into three categories based on the parts of the body that they primarily affected: hectic fevers originating in the solid members, ephemeral fevers in the spirits, and putrid (corrupting) fevers in the humors. Pestilential fevers differed because they began *outside* the body, with a corruption of the air; when inhaled, the bad air went to the heart, where it generated excess heat and moved to other organs.[22] The buboes that appeared on plague victims represented the body's attempt to expel excess heat to the "emunctory" closest to the affected organ (the groin, armpit, or neck)—what we now identify with the lymphatic network.

Like a few of his contemporaries, Abraham was not convinced that the fevers of the past year were truly pestilential, despite their heavy mortality.[23] While this view is not extraordinary, it holds interest because of Abraham's description of a patient's reasonable chances for survival if properly diagnosed. Some sick men and women recovered, he noted. But when physicians misdiagnosed the fevers that they were treating, patients often died unnecessarily. Significantly, studies of the impact of the Black Death in Girona, the nearest city for which I have found data, do conclude that the mortality rate there was markedly lower than in Barcelona or towns farther west. Guilleré estimated an overall mortality rate of 14.5 percent for Girona, which may be contrasted with the estimates of 40 percent to 60 percent or higher for Barcelona.[24] Ironically, Abraham may be accurately describing the plague demographics suggested by modern historians, although he attributes the better survival rate among "his" patients to his greater medical expertise. The same pattern of thinking led later physicians to assume that they were more successful in treating subsequent plague outbreaks, which in general were not as deadly as the Black Death.[25]

Even so, and no matter how they tried to prepare for it, the plague dealt the inhabitants of western Catalonia a harsher blow than anything that Abraham could have previously seen. The sense of extraordinary catastrophe is correspondingly heightened in Jacme's hometown of Lleida, where mortality was high. On the one hand, the *Regiment de Preservacio* testifies to the rising prestige of university medicine in general society. As the modern editors of Jacme's text observe, the fact that *el catedrático* Jacme d'Agramante wrote at the behest of *los paers* is evidence of the burghers' confidence in the new university medicine.[26] Jacme's turn to a lay audience also underlines his conviction that "average" people stood to benefit from medical knowledge and that this was knowledge that they supposedly desired to have. On the other hand, despite its concessions to a lay audience, Jacme's text remained an official and authoritative pronouncement on the advancing pandemic.

Because Jacme was primarily interested in what laypeople might do to protect themselves from the plague, he avoided theoretical discussions. He felt that it was important, nonetheless, to provide his readers with a basic explanation for the causes of the plague and hence why certain kinds of prophylactic actions were preferable to others.[27] The tractate begins with an explanation of the crucial role played by air in times of epidemic. Air may become corrupted after undergoing two types of change—in its quality or in its substance—and these may have local or widespread ("universal") effects. A qualitative change can be natural (as in seasonal change) or contra-natural (as in abnormally warm winters or frigid summers). A substantive change is manifested as putrefaction and can also take two forms: one that generates living things (reptiles and insects) or one that does not. Six chapters follow. Chapter 1 defines pestilence as a contra-natural change in the air that may be qualitative or substantive but that leads to corruptions and sudden death among living creatures. Chapter 2 discusses the possible causes of pestilence. A "universal pestilence" of the sort unfolding to the east had three possible causes, all stemming from corruption of the air. The first, as his biblical examples illustrate, was sin, which God might punish by means of plagues. The second possibility was that wicked men might actually concoct a toxin to corrupt food and water sources. The third possibility was corruption of air due to celestial factors, such as an eclipse or planetary conjunction.

Not all pestilence was universal, of course, either in the sense of originating in celestial activity or in the sense of ranging far and wide. Local conditions might generate local pestilence. Jacme considers these conditions in his second chapter, discussing factors of diet and excessively indulgent bathing or sex, poor ventilation, or people with infectious ailments like leprosy or other types of fevers or skin diseases. Other possibilities included freakish weather or bad winds, poor sanitation, or smelly locations where "bad air" (bogs, butchers' or tanners' streets, sewers, unburied corpses) might contaminate the local environment. As for celestial changes that translated into pestilence on earth, these had warning signs in the natural world—for instance, the strange behavior of animals and birds, or blighted crops.

Chapter 3 enumerates these signs of pestilence in the heavens and in the natural world; here Jacme draws directly from Avicenna's discussion of pestilential fevers while adding the possibility that God might be chastising "faithful Christians" with pestilence. Chapter 4 explains how corrupt air affects the human body, generating excess heat and corrupting humors that seek to evacuate the surplus by removing it to the "sewers" of the body (the emunctories). Chapter 5 offers a preventive regimen for hot and cold seasons, emphasizing the need to correct the imbalance in the air with fumigations and fragrant bonfires. Medications may be useful but should be obtained from a physician. In constructing this regimen, Jacme relied on the familiar categories of the "six nonnaturals" inherited from Galen: climate (air); diet; evacuation (purging, bleeding, and bodily evacuations); sleep; exercise; and moods. He urges his readers to avoid strenuous exercise and certain foods, to sleep lightly and to undergo purging and bleeding at a physician's hands, and he offers practical tips for verifying that someone is dead. Chapter 6 is dedicated to "moral pestilence." It, too, is caused by a contra-natural change but in people's minds, leading to war and civil disorder, social chaos, and suffering.[28] As Arrizabalaga observes, for Jacme the term "moral pestilence" was not a metaphor; it expressed a link between natural and "moral" life, between individual disease and collective disorder.[29]

The serious attention that Jacme dedicated to moral pestilence is one aspect of his tractate that scholars often note. The other is his conviction that it was possible for malicious people to manufacture plague. The physician does not explicitly refer to Jews, yet some historians have grimly noted that attacks on Jews took place in the very localities where this tractate might have circulated. Certainly, elsewhere, burghers and city officials—Jacme's target audience—have been linked specifically to attacks on local Jews.[30] Attacks on Jews also occurred in Provence, where Alfonso de Córdoba made a more pointed assertion that the plague had been maliciously seeded by human beings, and a similar hypothesis in the plague tractate of the anonymous Montpellier author appeared in a context of accusations and anti-Jewish violence. But were these physicians legitimizing what was already a widespread belief, or were they suggesting something new? Arrizabalaga tends to the former reading, contending that d'Agramont was "just echoing the information that he had received from . . . trans-Pyrenean regions." Even so, he argues, the inclusion of this possibility in a learned document could have encouraged its malicious dissemination and violence.[31] I am less convinced by this possibility. Plague-related attacks on Jews took place far beyond Aragon and Provence, reaching deep into central and eastern Europe, where medical literature has never been blamed for inciting them. In fact, Jacme clearly indicates that he is writing a preventive regimen for a *universal* pestilence (celestial in origin). *Manufactured* pestilence, in his own words, is not universal, but rather is engineered via the poisoning of foods, not air. Jacme dismissed the possibility that this was the cause of the current epidemic:

> Per altra rahó pot venir mortaldat e pestilència en les gents, ço és a saber, per malvats hòmens fiylls del diable qui ab metzines e verins diverses corrompen les viandes ab molt fals engiynn e malvada maestria, *ja sie ço que pròpriament parlan, aytal mortalitat de gents no és pestilència de la qual ací parlam*, mas he.n volguda fer menció per ço car ara tenim temps en lo qual s'a[n] seguides moltes morts en alcunes regions prop d'ací axí com en Cobliure, en Carcassès, en Narbonès e en la baronia de Montpesler e a Avinyó e en tota Proença.

> Another cause of mortality and pestilence is men, as is known, by wicked men, sons of the devil, who with venoms and diverse poisons corrupt foods with great cunning and evil skill. *But properly speaking, this mortality is not the pestilence of which we speak here*, although it must be mentioned because in this time in neighboring lands there have been many deaths, as in Cobliure, Carcassonne, Narbonne, and in the barony of Montpellier, in Avignon and all Provence.[32]

Jacme's *Regimen* survives today in only one copy, which was found in the ecclesiastical archives of Santa Maria de Verdú, in the diocese of Solsona, about halfway between Lleida and Besalú.[33] Although written specifically for the town of Lleida, it may have had a briefly wider life. Nonetheless, it is not cited by other writers and seems not to have been widely known.[34] If it did circulate beyond Lleida, Abraham could easily have been among an audience of medical practitioners or local officials who were read or given a copy. When he composed his own tractate the next year, however, Jacme's "popular" model was not what interested him, but rather the academic and analytical style of tractates more conventionally associated with the genre. Duran-Reynals and Winslow, who published a translation of Jacme's tractate in the late 1940s, stated emphatically that Jacme's and Abraham's tractates could not be more dissimilar, for the right and wrong reasons. As they correctly noted, Abraham Caslari had actually treated victims of plague, and he includes treatment considerations in his regimen; Jacme's regimen was purely preventive and written before the plague had reached him. Unfortunately, neither Duran-Reynals nor Winslow had actually read Abraham's work, which they encountered in Pinkhof's (faulty) 1891 edition and Dutch translation. As a result, they concluded that Abraham's work was "not a scholarly one and must stem from a medical tradition" unlike that tapped by Christian physicians in his milieu, especially as it bore "no trace of the influence of Galen and Avicenna upon the author's philosophy of disease."[35] It is true that Abraham's tractate makes no explicit reference to the categories of naturals, nonnaturals, and counter-naturals associated with the Galenic texts admired by his Christian peers. However, it is unlikely that he was not exposed to Galen's writings, either in Arabic or in Hebrew translation, because they were both popular and circulating in his time and milieu, as well as foundational for Avicenna. Abraham was definitely at home with Avicenna's writings, and his tractate reflects the shared learning and intellectual attitudes of Jewish and Christian physicians in this region and time. How much that was so is evident from a comparison of Jacme's and Abraham's works, which, despite their distinctive agendas and positions, share a dependence on Avicenna's Canon.

As Abraham explains in his introduction, he organized his treatise to discuss definitions, and then causes, signs, and treatment, concluding with his thoughts on the fevers of the past year and how they should be treated.[36] The tractate consists of eight chapters, beginning with a definition of pestilential fever. "True pestilential fever" requires a "poison-like corruption of the air" that enters the spirit of the heart. He lists its possible terrestrial or celestial causes, adding that celestial causes are beyond the competence of most physicians because they have not studied astronomy. Chapter 2 discusses the signs of pestilential fevers, and Chapter 3 the "early signs" that also interested Jacme: these are early indications of celestial change that are visible on earth. Although humoral-pestilential fevers will closely resemble pestilential fevers, they are not the same; neither is the spread of disease an indication that it has necessarily become pestilential. In Chapter 4, Abraham presents a regimen for true pestilential fevers that stresses correction of the corrupted air, light sleep, and recommendations for diet and bleeding. Chapter 5 elaborates a treatment regimen for people with pestilential fever, recommending that people leave an infected area, if possible. If this is not possible, the fevers should be treated like humoral-pestilential fevers or fainting fevers, the regimen for which follows in chapter 6 and is tailored to the humoral complexion of the patient. Above all, it is important to strengthen the heart. Chapter 7 considers the fevers of the past year, which behaved more like humoral fevers than pestilential ones—and mixed-humoral fevers, at that. Many of the afflicted were cured with or without medical intervention. Abraham speculates that the fevers had a material cause, possibly bad regimen due to famine and scarcity; a particularly malevolent astrological conjunction (i.e., celestial cause) is another possibility. Chapter 8 concludes the tractate with a regimen for "this year's fevers," if similar fevers recur. The regimen is not strictly intended for Jewish patients, as it refers to pork.[37] Although it does not use the terminology of nonnaturals, the tractate covers the topics of air, sleep, exercise, diet, sexual activity, bathing, bleeding, and purging that are standard touchstones for five of the six nonnaturals invoked in the writings of contemporary physicians. The only nonnatural that Abraham ignores is the sixth, which deals with mood or emotional well-being, an elision that I return to below.

Throughout the *Tractate on Pestilential and Other Types of Fevers*, Caslari refers to the opinions of both learned and not-so-learned physicians (respectively, those with whom he agrees and those with whom he does not), indirectly letting us know that he has been closely following the debates over the season's fevers. It would have helped modern scholars had he named his sources and rivals; not atypically, he chose not to do so.[38] His familiarity with the core medical reading of his time, especially Avicenna's Canon, is nonetheless evident; some of the passages that Abraham cites from Avicenna's work are also cited by Jacme. Despite Duran-Reynals and Winslow's claim that Abraham displayed ignorance of this learning, this is not surprising. Abraham, we recall, came from Narbonne, where Jewish medical learning and practice benefited from the prestige of medicine throughout Provence and Languedoc. The contemporary center for medical learning that would have influenced him was Montpellier, where the university faculty in medicine was renowned throughout Europe. Not far away, in Avignon, the papal court also attracted important physicians, some with faculty positions in Montpellier. Aragon imported physicians from Montpellier, while encouraging locally an "open" system of medical education that permitted non-Christian access to the profession in this region. Jews were not permitted to enroll at the universities but maintained a parallel system of instruction, largely through apprenticeships of young students to established physicians, and a licensing exam.[39] Abraham Caslari was presumably trained by his father in this way. The so-called open system of licensing and practice in Aragon made it possible for Jewish physicians to follow the university curricula by means of a parallel corpus of translations that permitted them to master essential texts.[40] When they were ready, the students were examined, often by a pair of examiners—one Christian, one Jewish—in the texts that constituted the formal university curriculum.

Among those works, Avicenna reigned supreme. For Jacme, that meant the Canon in Latin. Gerard of Cremona's translation had been circulating since the twelfth century and was incorporated into the university medical curriculum in the thirteenth.[41] Gerard was responding to a growing hunger for Arabic medical works in Latin at a time when most Jewish physicians were still able to read the Canon in the original Arabic. A century later, this was less and less the case, and the need for a Hebrew translation became pressing, especially in those regions of Christian Europe where Avicenna was now central to medical instruction and where Jews no longer knew Arabic, or enough Arabic, to read the original.[42] For Jews, the Canon in Latin was also largely inaccessible. Toward the end of the thirteenth century, two Hebrew translations appeared almost simultaneously in Rome: one by Nathan haMe'ati (1279) and one by Zerahiah ben Shealtiel Hen (Gracian) (1280). Sometime before 1402, Joshua haLorqi—soon to become a famed apostate—retranslated parts of Me'ati's books 1 and 2.[43] According to Benjamin Richler, a number of anonymous translators also took up the challenge of rendering the Canon in Hebrew, and their efforts survive in fragmentary form.[44] In Richler's words, the eleventh-century Avicenna's writings constituted "the most important component of Jewish intellectual activity in the fourteenth century."[45] And, as he has noted, if the number of manuscript copies is any indication of its popularity, the hundred-plus copies of Hebrew versions of the Canon testify that it "was by far the most popular medical book among the Jews in the Middle Ages."[46] Near the close of the fifteenth century, the Hebrew Canon would be the first Hebrew book ever printed, rolling off the press in Naples in 1491; this edition bears the additional distinction of being the first printing of the Canon in any language. Gerard of Cremona's twelfth-century Latin translation would not appear in print until 1522, and the original Arabic text was not printed until 1593.

The Canon was a huge work, and completing an entire translation would have been a remarkable achievement. Divided into five books, the Canon's introductory theoretical expositions attracted the most attention from translators.[47] At the other extreme, the pharmacological compendium of book 5 held practical appeal. Book 4, on illnesses that involve more than one body part, contains Avicenna's discussion on general and epidemic fevers.[48] In addition, the Canon generated its own commentary tradition among Christians and Jews. The Hebrew commentaries flourished, especially in Provence and Languedoc, which Hagar Kahana-Smilansky has argued reflects the Canon's practical value. Two late thirteenth-century commentaries come from Abraham's native region: one was authored by Yedaiah Bedersi, yet another Narbonnais intellectual

resettled in Perpignan, whose father, we may recall, counted Abraham's father
as a friend. The other was by Moses b. Joshua Narboni (i.e., "of Narbonne"), also
in Perpignan, the stopping point for all Languedocian Jews fleeing toward Aragon in 1306.[49] It is thus highly likely that Abraham Caslari had seen and thoroughly digested the contents of this important work.

The terminology that Abraham uses to distinguish among various kinds
of fevers supports the claim that he was familiar with the Canon. Avicenna
begins book 4 of the Canon by defining fever as an "alien" heat that ignites
and expands via the spirit and blood through the vessels of the body: חום נכרי
מתלקח בלב ויצמח ממנו באמצעות הרוח והדם אשר בשריינים והעורקים בכל הגוף.[50]
Abraham defines a pestilential fever as an "alien" corruption of heat and humidity in the air: עפוש האויר בחום ולחות נכרי;[51] he repeats the term when describing fevers that cause putrefaction of the spirit, מקרה לחום נכרי משנה
הרוח.[52] The same echoes of Avicenna that sound in Jacme's work also sound in
Abraham's, underlining the systematic approach to their medical problem
that sent both physicians back to this primary text. Jacme notes that in times
of pestilence, "we see how serpents and other reptiles flee from their holes and
issue hurriedly from them, the birds leave their nests and flee. . . . [W]heat and
other fruits growing from the earth are affected . . . and carry such great infection that they are like poisons to all who eat them."[53] Abraham writes that a
pestilence caused by celestial change will be signaled on earth by changes in
nature:

שהבורא ית' הטביע בבעלי חיים הרגשת האוירים הטובים וברח מהאוירים הרעים הנפסדים
וביחוד קצת מיני העופות כעורב ומינו ותור וסיס ועגור . . .

> For the Creator, blessed be He, gave animals [the ability to] sense when the
> air is good and to flee when it is bad and putrid, especially certain types of
> birds like crows, doves, and swallows.[54]

In fact, one reason he cites in defense of his argument that the mortality of the
past months was not due to a universal pestilence (cosmological in origin) was
that these signs were not in evidence:

והנה לא נראו האותות באויר באביב ולא בסתו ולא מערפליות ושאר ובריחת העופות מקניהן
והרמשים מחוריהן ולא נראה בפירות עפוש יותר מן העפוש הרגיל הטבע להם . . .

> But these signs were not evident in the air, neither in the spring nor the fall,
> not in fogs or such, or in the fleeing of birds from their nests or reptiles from
> their holes. The fruit showed no more rot than usual for their nature.[55]

Both men's claims rely on Avicenna's Canon, book 4, which contains the author's treatment of fevers. Avicenna also divides his discussion of pestilential fevers into causes, signs, and treatment. He notes that pestilential fevers have celestial and terrestrial causes and that celestial changes may be observed in the peculiar behavior of birds and reptiles on earth. In Me'ati's medieval translation:

ואמנם האותות על דרך הדמיון לסבה כמו שתראה הצפרדעים הנה הרבו במים ותראה הר־
משים הנולדים מן העפוש וממה שיורה על זה שתראה העכבר וב"ח השוכבים בתוך הארץ
יברחו על פני הארץ ותראה בעלי החיים נקי הטבע כמו אל לקלאק הם אגסים וכיוצא בהם
יברחו מקניהם וירחקו ממנו ואולי יעזבו ביציהם.

> Moreover, the signs as they appear for this cause may be that you see frogs multiplying in the water, and that you'll see reptiles [or insects] generated by the corruption and what indicates [corruption]; you will see mice and animals that live in the earth flee, and you will see "bad-natured" animals like the stork, i.e., the *agasim*, and the like fleeing from their nests and departing, perhaps even abandoning their eggs.[56]

Jacme observes that pestilence can be local or general; it can begin in a single house or street or city and spread, or it can originate in a greater region.[57] His analysis emphasizes the impact that local climate and, for that matter, lifestyle, could have on public health. The types of winds and air circulation that characterize a given locale, the ways people store food, the types of trees, "especially high ones such as poplars, which hinder the ventilation of the air, or walnut trees, which have a special tendency to corrupt the air, and also fig trees" will influence regional susceptibility to epidemics.[58] So, too, local sanitation, or an area where animals are slaughtered or tanners work, can produce infection—particularly for someone predisposed by temperament to disease, which is also a "lifestyle" hazard encouraged by those who bathe or have sex too frequently, or who overeat and drink.[59]

Abraham similarly believes that corruption of the air can have an initial toxic effect on one or many people. Like Jacme, he notes that pestilence can begin in a house—even a part of a house—a city, or region and spread, and that bad diet or an unbalanced regimen can aggravate its effects.[60] Again, both men echo the Canon, book 4, article 4, where Avicenna states that once corrupted air has entered the heart and spread to other organs, the result is pestilential fever—for those bodies who are susceptible to it. This includes people whose complexion is characterized by heat and humidity, but also people who have "bad humors" as a consequence of excessive behaviors, like people who indulge too much in sex.[61] Jacme and Abraham also concur that local climate or individual susceptibility play a role in epidemic fevers.[62] For Jacme, however, the diagnosis of "universal" pestilence made individual susceptibility less relevant, as the primary cause was divine. For Abraham, the fevers of 1348 were not a universal pestilence, and individual temperament mattered.

Complexion (temperament) was relevant for Abraham even in terms of planetary influences, which primarily affect those persons and places predisposed to their influence:

ולא יעשה רושם בבלתי מוכנים לקבל זה, והם שמזגם חולק והפכי לזה השפע. ולולא זה כבר
כל האנשים אשר עומדים באויר הדבריי יחלו חליים דבריים בעת הדבר ימותו מהם או יבראו
ואיננו כן שיש שיחלו ויש שלא יחלו וסבת זה ההכנה לקבול השפע והבלתי הכנה.

> They will have no effect on those who are not predisposed to receive it, or on
> those whose complexion is contrary or divergent from this influence. Were
> this not the case, all the people found in pestilential air would get pestilential
> illnesses; [all] would die from them or [all] get well. But this is not the case,
> since some get sick and some do not, and the reason is the predisposition or
> lack of predisposition to this influence.[63]

Even his own treatise, he cautions his readers, should be read with the understanding that it describes the action of an individual disease in specific individuals. Every experience of illness is unique: שאין אחד וחליו שוה לאחד וחליו. Although he seeks to offer guidance in case this kind of fever should recur, the savvy reader will "add or subtract as his intellect recommends."

This is not a point unique to Abraham but is one that he repeatedly emphasizes. He saw many people die, but not all of them, and for him, this variability demonstrates that the plague was not a universal pestilence. Likewise, he insists on modifications in his treatment plan based on the humoral complexion of the patient—which would be irrelevant in the case of universal pestilence. He begins his treatise with a sharp critique of the fatalities that he attributes to physicians' misdiagnosis of the season's fevers, whose "mixed" signs made them difficult to classify. Again, his observations may simply reflect his personal reality in the context of relatively low plague mortality rates in the Girona region. From Abraham's perspective, however, the problem was not regional epidemiology but the physician's failure to apprehend the true significance of his patients' symptoms.

Both Abraham and Jacme also followed Avicenna in describing the kinds of corruption that could propagate disease locally. Among the terrestrial factors, all three men emphasized local climate and environment. Abraham's examples include mildewed crops; putrid waters; or plants and trees of a corrupting nature, "as empirics and researchers have agreed."[64] The unhealthy qualities of fig and nut trees were likewise noted by Jacme.[65] Jacme, we recall, also singled out people associated with odiferous settings and poor ventilation, as well as those who indulged in bad regimens: these were men and women whose potential to transmit infection was based on their occupational or habitual conditions. Finally, human beings afflicted with certain disease conditions were capable of transmitting infection that could corrupt their surroundings (or other people). Jacme listed these conditions as *lebrositat ho meseleria e roynna e tiseguea e lagaynna, febre pestilencial, pigota e sarampió e tiynna.*[66] In a parallel passage, Abraham ignored occupational hazards but listed disease conditions that generate corruption, including leprous or fevered people who might transfer their own corrupted humors to the air and hence to other people.

For pestilential fevers, and for the "humoral-pestilential" fevers he diagnosed in his patients, Abraham offers a standard repertoire of remedies. To treat humoral-pestilential fevers, it is critical to strengthen the heart, and therefore foods that might be shunned in the case of pure pestilential fevers are cautiously allowed. Abraham admits that the fevers of the past year did not fit cleanly into any of these categories. Relying again on Avicenna, he notes that the pulse and urine of the patient might be deceptively normal, and then suddenly he would die:

ולכן היה דפקי אלה ושתניהם קרובים לטבעיים עם היותם קרובים למות הגיעם ללב וקרבתם
להמוח עד שלא יוכל הרופא להקדים הידיעה במותם.

> Thus their pulses and urine will be close to normal even as they are close to
> death. They [the corrupted humors] have reached the heart and brain so that
> the physician is unable to anticipate death.[67]

Thus, while they behaved in many respects like humoral-pestilential fevers, in other respects the recent fevers behaved as if the source of corruption were external and "poison-like." For pestilential fevers, fumigations, and wood fires might counteract the corrupted substance of the air; Abraham adds familiar warnings to avoid exposure to "bad" air currents or breezes, to cover windows that let in air. Beneficial foods are those that emphasize astringent (cold, dry) qualities; they include citrus and poultry, land birds, and fish roasted in vinegar or pomegranate juice. Sweet fruits and dairy products, which increase humidity (phlegm) should be avoided, as should emetics and bleeding, which deplete the patient's strength.

But since fevers such as those experienced recently are not pure pestilential fevers, Abraham concludes his tractate with specific recommendations for fevers like those of the past year. Patients should be given silk compresses on their hands, face, and heart; arms and legs should be washed twice daily with herbal blends.[68] Purging and bleeding are prescribed according to the number of days from the fever's onset and the time of day. A mild emetic should target all the humors, "which are mixed in these sicknesses"; this is preferable to purgative drugs of bad or toxic qualities.[69] Abraham prescribes ointments to combat headaches and recommends scenting the air lightly with myrtle, cinnamon, and citrus. Soups made with melon seeds, lentils, or chickpeas are good; almond milk, however, aggravates head pain. Meat and wine should be avoided, but since it is so important to bolster the patient's strength, the rules may be bent: it is better for the patient to eat familiar foods than medically prescribed ones that are alien to his or her regimen.[70] Unlike Jacme, Abraham offers no cost-cutting options for his recipes, which may say something about the social circles of his clientele; he does, however, indicate several times that dosages or remedies should be modified for children.[71]

To conclude the first segment of this chapter, therefore, Abraham and Jacme not only drew upon some of the same written authorities and texts for their work, particularly Avicenna, but they shared a way of thinking about health and sickness. Abraham's failure to enlist the categories of the six non-naturals seems noteworthy. Yet even without explicitly invoking this terminology, Abraham covers five of its six categories; the missing rubric, to which I turn below, is that of moods or emotional well-being. Overall, Abraham's approach to the medical challenge posed by the recent pandemic is logical, systematic, and clearly in dialogue with opinions and texts circulating around him. All the plague writers considered definitions, causes, and signs, followed by options for treatment and/or prevention. Their conclusions may have differed, but the process for reaching them was the same, whether the writer was Christian or Jewish, university-trained in Latin or privately tutored in Hebrew. Abraham understood the rules of the genre. Abraham's tract is also distinctive because it is based on his personal experience during the plague epidemic and in a region that experienced that epidemic in milder form than did other regions, some fairly nearby. His analysis and treatment recommendations reflect his conviction that he had not witnessed a universal epidemic of pestilential fever.

The relative optimism of Abraham's insistence on the ability of many patients to recover correctly reflects his experience treating them, but is unusual for the first-generation tractates. As Ann Carmichael has noted, physicians rapidly rebounded from their initial sense of helplessness in encounters with the plague. Whether because subsequent outbreaks were less virulent, so that medical practitioners were convinced that their treatment regimens were successful, or whether repeated outbreaks dulled the shock of 1348, later tractates convey a tone of optimism and confidence notably lacking in the tractates of the first generation.[72] Again, Abraham's view of the fevers that he treated suggests a milder epidemiological context from that encountered elsewhere. That his experience was anomalous is also reflected in his exasperated disparagement of other physicians, some of whom presumably were located in cities and towns where the plague wrought greater devastation. Abraham's sense of estrangement from the elite circles of medical opinion, which he voices periodically in his tractate, may thus be explained as an epidemiological fluke. At the same time, less explicitly "medical" aspects of the *Tractate on Pestilential and Other Types of Fevers* suggest that other factors may also have contributed to this feeling.

*   *   *

Is there any evidence that Abraham's distress, like his fevers, was motivated by nonacademic factors? Here a closer look at some of the stylistic features of his tractate is instructive, as they suggest something of the social and psychological context in which he wrote. The second segment of this chapter examines three literary aspects of Abraham's plague tractate: (1) its use of personal interjections; (2) its near paucity of biblical allusions; and (3) its elision of the sixth nonnatural, those psychological or emotional factors that influence the forms and experience of illness.

On the surface, Abraham's passion seems reserved for what look like questions of medical theory and policy. The season's fevers had "mixed" signs, and physicians had never seen anything like them before; moreover, people fell ill so suddenly that they often did not seek out physicians until it was too late.[73] Abraham repeatedly condemns the physicians whose *mis*diagnosis of the fevers has contributed to fatalities: physicians who erroneously believed that they were treating pestilential fevers would prescribe meat, chicken, and wine at the onset and augmenting phase of the fevers, and defer purging. "And I saw them [the patients] follow this regimen and die."[74]

Medicine is a social art, not just for the relationships that it fosters between doctor and patient but among physicians themselves. Abraham does not refer directly to social, religious, or political events, and he does not differentiate among his patients in terms of religion or nation. Likewise, as a learned physician, he was part of a medical community that included practitioners of different sorts: men and women; Christians, Jews, and Muslims; empirics and university men.[75] Despite the diversity of medical practitioners around him, the world of learned medical men is what he notices; this is the group with which he identifies and is, significantly, medicine's most prominent social class. At one point, his tractate refers to a כת מהרופאים—a sect, or group, of physicians, perhaps alluding to an organized professional guild or group with political or university connections.[76] In this context, Abraham's repeated invocation of personal experience, like his use of personal asides and interjections, unintentionally testifies to the medical networks and relationships that connected university physicians and their more prominent Jewish peers. He begins his treatise announcing that he has been inspired to write by the unprecedented fevers of the summer and late spring. He describes the geographical range of the epidemic and then its symptoms: continuous fever with much fainting, pain, and weakness. The onset of the fever is accompanied by great sweating, mental confusion, weakness, hemorrhage, vomiting, diarrhea, and worms. The afflicted often "experienced diarrhea or vomiting or strong hemorrhaging from the nostrils, but many were healed and their strength held; some would die from a loss of strength and sudden and excessive evacuation." Despite their bewildering symptoms, however, "no *learned man* would doubt that these are not true pestilential fevers . . . and when I examined many people for them, [I found them to be] mixed, not simple" [emphasis mine].[77] Abraham's introduction informs us that he has written at the request of "wise and learned men":

ושאלו ממני אנשים חכמים ונבונים שאודיעם סברתי בהנהגות הקדחות האלה ושאכתוב
בזה מאמר והשלמתי רצונם ויקבל תועלת כל חכם לכיוצא בחלאים האלה אם יקרו ויהיה
התועלת להההווים ויהיה המשל ודוגמא לבאים . . .

Wise and learned men asked of me that I inform them of my opinion for treating these fevers, and that I write a tractate about this. I have fulfilled their request. Let any learned man benefit from it concerning these illnesses, whether the benefit is for the present [fevers] or as a model for those to come.[78]

At the same time, Abraham suggests that he has another goal as well—namely, to record for posterity a view that has been marginalized by some of these learned experts:

וראיתי כי אם לא אודיע בברור הקדחות האלה מאי זה מין הם לא יפרסם אמתת סברתי
בדרכי הנהגתם.

And I saw that if I did not make explicit what kind of fevers these were, the truth of my opinion about treating them would not be disseminated.[79]

In Abraham's judgment, the fevers that he treated were humoral-pestilential, not a universal pestilence. This implied, among other things, that the immediate causes were local (terrestrial) and not cosmological. One possible culprit was bad diet; it was a year of famine and poor-quality foodstuffs and people were eating grains and seeds that they did not customarily consume, "pips and chestnuts and acorns."[80] True, the primary causes of climate change were celestial, but celestial changes did not of themselves necessitate pestilence; this was ultimately up to God.[81] Abraham notes again, with some asperity, that by relying on astrological signs, "a number of would-be sages" had boastfully proclaimed the year's sicknesses pestilential. But the behavior of the planets is not sufficient for such a diagnosis: astronomical conditions might dictate an epidemic on earth, but only God determines whether it will be pestilential.[82]

Like Jacme, Abraham declares that he is writing for "the common good" (תועלת כללי[ת]). He insists that his readers are free to disagree with him. Should these fever types recur in the future, he adds, his readers are free to modify his recommendations as seems sensible to them. The tone of this passage oscillates between two not quite concordant claims. On the one hand, Abraham tells us that he is not writing for any personal stake or renown, that other men have implored him to write, and that he does so to serve a greater good. On the other hand, he lets slip several times that he has a perspective on the pandemic that other authorities have dismissed and that he writes to ensure that he gets a hearing. He has been among other physicians or with the patients they have treated, and he has decided that the physicians were wrong: it is hard to imagine that this would have been a harmonious scene. Now, Abraham feels that he must disseminate his view or have its traces lost forever. In other words, Abraham's asides and interjections preserve the traces of an impassioned debate over the causes, nature, and treatments of the plague.

Abraham's opinion was one of a variety of written judgments on the year's fevers, undoubtedly supplemented by oral discussions that are lost to posterity. If he had encountered Jacme's regimen, he knew Jacme's relatively heterodox consideration of possible causes, as well as his conviction that universal pestilence came to chastise Christendom for its sin. If he was unaware of Jacme's text, by the summer of 1349 he may have had some idea of the analyses circulating in the tractate of the anonymous writer from Montpellier or that of Alfonso de Córdoba. Alphonse, even more than Jacme, emphasized the possibility of human causes for the plague, whose final phase he attributed to concocted poisons that corrupted the air.[83] For both Alfonso and the Montpellier author, this kind of pestilence was untreatable by human means. This, too, was a view that Abraham would have adamantly opposed. Among the early tractates described by Arrizabalaga, only Giovanni della Penna diagnoses a form of humoral pestilence similar to Abraham's reading, but Abraham was unlikely to have seen this work. Thus, among his peers, men educated in the orbit of Montpellier to the east and Lleida to the west, Abraham's opinion would have been in the minority.[84] And, apparently, it was rejected.

Abraham's discord with his colleagues surfaces throughout his tractate. In cases of true pestilential fever, he comments, their celestial cause can translate into sudden mortality without any of the early warning signs typically observed on earth. Physicians are not trained to read astronomical signs, and they are therefore confused about how to treat their patients.[85] Discussing pestilential fever, he refers to a position taken by the כת מהרופאים, a guild or group of physicians that he identifies with certain medical opinions.[86] As he goes on to argue for his own diagnosis of humoral-pestilential fever, where corruption of a humor in the body—not the air outside, or a celestial event—causes fever, Abraham interjects four times the phrase "as I have said" and once the phrase "as I mentioned earlier." The force of the repetition intensifies his argument and underlines his interest in this fever category. At one point, Abraham brusquely cuts short his treatment regimen to send his readers to other books, as "I have left off mentioning this regimen in this tractate." Indeed, he concludes:

המאמר הזה חברתיו ביחוד לבאר בהנהגת הקדחות שקרו בשנה הזאת ומקריהן ואותותיהן המשיגים והמפורסמים גם להמון וכ״ש לחכם רופא ולפי האותות לא יספק אחד מן החכמים כשאינן דבריות אמתיות. . . .

> I have written this tractate especially to clarify the regimen for the fevers
> that occurred this year, their symptoms and their accidental signs, which are
> obvious even to common people and all the more to a learned physician. And
> according to the signs, no learned man would doubt that they were not true
> pestilential [fevers].[87]

Doubt only arises, he continues, when trying to distinguish between humoral-pestilential fevers and humoral-fainting fevers, which present very similarly; in this case, the early signs are critical, such as the quality of the air. In any event, the fevers that he saw were "mixed," not simple, perhaps due to material causes such as poor diet in time of famine, or perhaps due to celestial causes like a planetary conjunction. It is up to God whether celestial events translate into pestilence, but he mentions celestial causes because "would-be sages" have declared that a planetary conjunction was definitely responsible.

Taken together, these personal interjections buoy a drily clinical argument with passion and permit us to detect a medical community struggling to react to a new kind of crisis. From our perspective, an argument over a diagnosis of "true pestilential" or "humoral-pestilential" fever may seem like useless hairsplitting. We know that, either way, the prognosis of a plague patient was unlikely to be affected. But we would be wrong to shrug off the intensity and urgency of the debate from the perspective of men who were putting their own lives at risk to treat the sick.[88] Was Abraham ostracized or sidelined among the prestigious physicians he encountered at the court and bedsides of his well-to-do patients? He expresses just such a fear. Perhaps his views were marginalized because they did not reflect the epidemiological reality of the plague's devastation to the east, south, and west of him. Or perhaps being sidelined in a medical debate had other kinds of associations as well as consequences in the summer and fall of 1348. If so, Abraham's occasional testiness may have other causes, a conjecture strengthened by other features of his prose.

Abraham's *Tractate on Pestilential and Other Types of Fevers* is characterized by a near-total avoidance of biblical allusion. This is especially observable when contrasting his language to Jacme's, but also in contrast to the mosaic of biblical phrases and puns that were second nature to Hebrew belletristic writers of his day.[89] With rare exceptions, of course, Hebrew writers distinguished sharply between belletristic and scientific language: the former modeled on Arabic genres and emphasizing a biblical purity of language; and the latter modeled on secular, scientific, or philosophical Arabic and Latin works characterized by cumbersome syntax, foreign terminology, and neologisms. Biblical illustration has no place in this literature, either as exemplar or stylistic guide.[90] In contrast, Jacme's second article defines universal pestilence, first citing the example of Exodus 10, where God punished Pharaoh with, "among other plagues and curses, scorching wind and locusts."[91] Contra-natural change in the air causing pestilence may, he continues, be "sent by God because of our sins," for which claim he cites Deuteronomy 28.[92] Immediately following, he invokes 2 Kings 24, Exodus 7–11, and Numbers 14 as other illustrations of divinely wrought plague. In the same article, part 2, chapter 2, Jacme states that pestilential diseases will spread unless God mercifully restrains them, and article 3 invokes Sodom and Gomorrah (Genesis 19), advising the "faithful Christians" who are his readers that they must accept divine chastisement for their sins.[93] Article 5 introduces Jacob's spotted sheep (Genesis 30). Finally,

Jacme's final chapter, on moral pestilence, draws on New Testament passages, beginning with a cascade of references to Matthew and Luke and concluding with the solemn assertion that a truly "universal" pestilence would be a sign of the antiChrist, as proved by Mark 13.[94] For Jacme, as for his colleagues at the University of Paris, the medical crisis posed by the pandemic was never entirely separable from the theological apparatus and language that shaped their view of history and human suffering. Medical science affirmed theology and remained securely subservient to it.[95]

Not all Christian physicians held this view. Arrizabalaga's survey of six tractates written by university physicians in 1348–49 describes two that barely mention God, two that consider divine factors of secondary importance, and two that consider "divine intervention" a plausible cause of universal pestilence.[96] Abraham's tractate concords with the views of the second group, reminding his readers that God ultimately controlled the celestial factors that cause plague on earth and that God decided whether astronomical events would translate into epidemics on earth.[97] Otherwise, heavenly motives play a minor role in Abraham's analysis and recommendations, although he is careful to refer to "God's will" in reviewing the case for astrological causes for pestilence.[98] His tractate emphasizes the importance of correct diagnosis and that the summer's epidemic was not a universal pestilence. He even ponders an explanation that some historians would reconsider more than six centuries later: years of erratic climate and bad harvests had led to widespread famine, and people were not eating well. Deviation in diet and regimen had led to humoral imbalances and corruption, with disastrous results.[99]

Abraham's disinterest in theology is reflected in his scientific commitments, which were rooted in his belief in scientific knowledge as rational and nonpartisan. That attitude was shared by many of his Jewish peers. In this context, Abraham's prose avoids biblical echoes so efficiently that it must be by design.[100] The two exceptions that I could identify in Abraham's *Tractate on Pestilential and Other Types of Fevers* are revealing. The first comes in the opening description of the devastation wrought by the plague as it moved from east to west through "Provence, Catalonia, Valencia, the district of Aragon, Navarre, and Castile." Abraham writes: לא היתה קריה ועיר ששגב[ה] מקדחות—"there was no town or city mightier than the fevers."[101] The line, with its sweeping geographical arc, draws on a verse from Deuteronomy that, ironically, describes the biblical Israelites' conquest of the lands and peoples of Canaan. In Deut. 2:36, we read לא היתה קריה ששגבה ממנו, "there was no town mightier than they" (lit., "he," referring eponymously to the people). Abraham added "city" to the biblical "town" and inverted a scene of Israelite conquest to one of epidemiological defeat. In the biblical context, the anticipated conquest is the realization of divine promise. It is brutally imagined: no *Gentile* woman or child shall survive the onslaught, and entire populations will be slaughtered, their property plundered and only their cattle spared. Abraham "borrows" this language to depict the raging devastation of a pandemic frequently accompanied by violence against Jews. Now a reversal of biblical promise, the phrase describes a moment when outside forces emerged to slaughter and plunder local populations. This time, however, the victims were not Canaanites, Moabites, or Amalekites. They were Jews.[102]

No similar allusion appears anywhere else in the treatise, which implies that it was not a theme that Abraham sought consciously to reinforce. Nonetheless, it also holds pride of place at the head of his tractate and exploits a biblical reference that his medieval audience would have recognized without difficulty. The description deftly links the geography of destruction wrought by the plague to that subtended by attacks against Jews. It is artful enough that it could easily have prefaced a very different kind of account. In fact, it does: in his account of plague-related attacks on Jewish communities, Joseph haCohen, the sixteenth-century Hebrew chronicler, cites a (now-lost) chronicle by Hayim Galipapa, an eyewitness to anti-Jewish violence following the plague's appearance in Monzón.[103] As Hillel Barzilay has recently shown, haCohen embeds excerpts from Galipapa's contemporary account in two of his own histories, which include the following citation in almost identical form:

והיה בשנת חמשת אלפים ומאה ושמנה . . . דבר כבד מאד ממזרח שמש ועד מבואו ולא
היתה קריה אשר שגבה ממנו ככתוב ב[ספר] עמק רפאים לר' חיים גאלייפפה.

In the year 5108 [=1348] . . . a weighty thing occurred, from east to west, and there was no town that was mightier than it, as written in the [book] *The Valley of Ghosts* by R. Hayim Galipapa.[104]

Was Abraham deliberately quoting Galipapa's chronicle, amplifying the chronicler's "east to west" with names of specific regions and their cities and towns? If so, he was very much aware of the link between the plague and anti-Jewish violence. Conceivably, Abraham's insistence on the fatal consequences of misdiagnosis was also an acknowledgment that not all plague fatalities were a consequence of disease; some were the result of violence. Alternatively, perhaps Abraham unconsciously recalled Galipapa's description and its biblical overtones in composing his own work. This reading, too, has its strengths. Nowhere else do we see Abraham repeat this kind of allusion, or express explicitly or implicitly any concern with religious violence. Yet even as an unconscious echo, Abraham's language marks a convergence of professional and political powerlessness. The passage's significance is not so different, either way.

Abraham strikes a biblical chord with one other phrase in his tractate. It appears in a passage that I have mentioned before, where he discusses local sources of pestilential fevers:

והארציות יהיה משכונת העפושים מפסידים האויר כשכונת בעלי הגדמות והצרעות והנשד־
פים והחרחורים. המתעבר הפסדם לאויר והפעולות

> The terrestrial [causes] are proximities of corruption that cause a change of substance in the air as from the proximity of *gedemot* and lepers, *nishdafim* and *kharkhurim* whose substance is transmitted to the air.[105]

Abraham's list of corrupting conditions draws on Deuteronomy 28, the chapter detailing the curses that will befall the Israelites if they fail to heed God's word. Deut. 28:22 includes a list of diseases that will strike land and people: בשחפת ובק־ דחת ובדלקת ובחרחור ובחרב ובשדפון ובירקון, translated in the Revised Standard Version as "with consumption and with fever, inflammation and fiery heat, and with drought and with blasting and with mildew."[106] Medieval commentators recognized that the list mixed human and environmental categories, and they tried to distinguish between them.[107] Today, we cannot know exactly what conditions the Hebrew words describe, and the RSV translators have opted wisely for capacious terms. Some of these words also went on to develop modern meanings that do not accurately convey their biblical and medieval referents. *Giddem*, in modern Hebrew, refers to an amputee, but this is only part of the picture summoned by the medieval condition, which is treated by Avicenna in the same book 4 on fevers that served Abraham as a reference. In Me'ati's translation of book 4, fen 3, article 3, Avicenna discusses במין הצרעת ונקרא בלשוננו גד'מות ובלשון ערבי גדאם ובלטין ליפרה—"a type of leprosy that is called in our [Hebrew] language *gidhmut*, in Arabic *gudham* and in Latin *lepra*." As the Arabic and Latin terms clarify, *giddem* in Me'ati's translation describes a leprous condition in which facial features and limbs disintegrate and eventually fall off. *Kharkhur* ("gangrene," in modern Hebrew) is read by the biblical glossators as a kind of fever—according to Rashi, an internal fever that causes great thirst. Abraham has thus taken two words directly from the Deuteronomic verse (*kharkhur* and *shidafun*) and changed a third (*shidafun*, "blight") to *nif'al* form, where it seems to describe a human, not an agricultural, condition: *nishdafim*. The biblical passage makes no reference to lepers: Abraham has added them to his list.

As we have seen, Jacme's plague tractate included a similar claim. His list of disease conditions that might be a catalyst to pestilence mentioned leprosy and a variety of conditions characterized by fever and skin irruptions.[108] Jacme also referred to tanning, meat markets, and bridgeheads, as well as winds and corpses, as sources of local corruption.[109] In both cases, people afflicted by illnesses caused by putrefaction might be expected to transfer that putrefaction to the air that surrounded them.[110] Among these conditions, leprosy held a special taint because of its association—going back to the Bible—with sin and moral delinquency. The leper's physical deformity was an outward manifestation of spiritual disease—a familiar concern of Jacme's but nowhere evidenced in Abraham's writings. Indeed, when Abraham discusses the treatment of pestilential fevers, he includes "toxic" patients among those being treated, implying that he does not see their condition as morally predicated at all.[111] Considering Abraham's overall disinterest in questions of moral corruption, his list carries with it a subtext of moral taint or sin that is an unexpected sting. Again, whether the sting was intentional or unconscious, the consequences do not much differ. In this case, Abraham's choice of language betrays a cultural prejudice shared across confessional lines, reminding us of how easy it was to move associations from a moral field to a medical one. To be a Jew did not bestow greater sensitivity toward the plight of other marginal groups.[112]

As a social datum, Abraham's catalog also reflects the trend toward segregation of lepers, prostitutes, and Jews in Aragonese towns—ironically, often near one another.[113] It may also reflect his distance from sites of relatively recent violence. In 1321, Abraham was already in Besalú when rumors linking lepers and Jews to a conspiracy to poison Christian wells fueled pogroms across Languedoc, the papal Comtat-Venaissin, and Aragon. Lepers were arrested, tortured, and burned, and then it was the turn of the Jews, who suffered particularly vicious attacks in Toulouse and Barcelona, Cervera, Huesca, Barbastro, Tarazona, and elsewhere. Significantly, the "Lepers' Plot" led to anti-Jewish violence along much the same trajectory that it would follow in 1348. In contrast, Girona and surrounding towns, like Besalú, are not mentioned in the accounts of attacks against lepers or Jews in 1321. More than two decades later, Abraham surely knew about these episodes. But when he wrote his tractate, lepers, like those who suffered from the other afflictions on his list, were not political victims. On the contrary, they posed a potential threat to public health—the "common good" that he and Jacme both invoke, and whose emergence as a discursive category owes much to the Black Death.[114] As a matter of public health, their moral status was irrelevant, but it roused no particular compassion or regard in the Jewish physician.

Another feature of Abraham's plague tractate bears consideration. This feature is one of omission—specifically, his disinterest in emotional or psychological factors that are otherwise standard considerations of a medieval treatment regimen. As Naama Cohen-Hanegbi has recently demonstrated, the source and management of emotions was a topic vigorously debated by medieval physicians, who struggled to reconcile Galen and Avicenna on this and other questions.[115] Cohen-Hanegbi notes that the popular genre of the preventive regimen did not invariably include the sixth nonnatural, otherwise known as "accidents of the soul"; physicians were not unanimously convinced that it belonged in their domain.[116] Elsewhere, she asserts that omission of this topic became increasingly rare; however succinctly, plague regimens routinely referred to the familiar set of emotional states treated in the standard regimen.[117]

The omission of emotional factors in Abraham's work distinguishes him from his Christian peers: all six of the Christian tractates written in the wake of the 1348 plague defer to the Galenic categories of the six nonnaturals, emotions (or "mood") constituting the sixth of these factors that were subject to the physician's manipulation. Three of those tractates, by Jacme, the Paris faculty, and Gentile da Foligno, thoughtfully consider the sixth nonnatural's "accidents of the soul," especially the importance of neutralizing fear.[118] Jacme invokes this last of the nonnaturals by citing Genesis 30, the story of Jacob's notched rod, which miraculously increased the birth of spotted lambs among his uncle's flocks. For Jacme, this story is proof of the suggestive power of the "spotted" bough to the ewes, who saw its stippled pattern and gave birth to spotted offspring. This testimony to the power of suggestion tells us how great the power of fear is in times of pestilence and how important it is not to lose hope. Jacme recommends suspending the practice of chiming bells for deaths in times of pestilence, as it encourages morbid imaginings.[119]

The three Hebrew tractates besides Abraham Caslari's that have been published to date are later fourteenth-century works responding to later plague outbreaks, but they are all from the same region and explicitly enlist the six nonnaturals, including consideration of "accidents of the soul." The first, by Abraham ben Solomon Hen, recommends that the sick try to maintain good spirits to boost vital spirit.[120] The second, an anonymous Sephardic tractate recently published by Bos and Mensching, elaborates on psychological factors to a surprising degree. In times of pestilence, the author states, it is important to make an effort to avoid sadness, worry, and melancholy, and likewise anger, "bad thoughts," and isolation. All these things arouse bad humors and burn up the good ones. Thus it is critical to tilt to the other extreme and distance oneself from anger and bad things, "while rejoicing in one's lot and giving praise to God for one's life, enjoying companionship, good music, and tranquillity."[121] In the third example, written in the aftermath of the 1362 plague in Avignon, Isaac b. Todros also warns his readers to avoid anger and melancholy or thinking about things that arouse fear and worry. He advises the sick (or potentially sick) to avoid studying difficult subjects but to study what is easy to grasp and gives one pleasure.[122]

In contrast, the question of psychological or emotional affect seems almost irrelevant to Abraham. In his defense, Avicenna's Canon, book 4, does not emphasize these factors in its discussion of epidemic or pestilential fevers, either. The Canon, however, includes an impressive list of quotidian (ephemeral) fevers linked to affective causes that ranged from excessive joy to excessive fear, melancholy, fainting, or pain, and whose treatment calls upon remedies similar to those just mentioned.[123] So, too, the treatise on fevers by Ibn al-Jazzar, which preceded Avicenna's but, like his work, found a secure niche in the thirteenth- and fourteenth-century curricula of European Christian universities, understands one cause of short-cycle fevers to be excessive emotion. The author's list includes "anger, grief, and fury," for which he recommends treatment with "words and deeds that appease and please the soul," as well as comforting diversions, friends, and aromatic plants.[124] Abraham Caslari notes these categories when he considers the potential origins for putrefaction of spirit, some of which are humoral, and some in the heart or blood or spirit itself: "actions of the soul like anger and melancholy and others change the spirit's [humoral] complexion."[125]

Abraham may have assumed that physicians seeking a detailed treatment of this condition could consult other tractates; in several places, he mentions that he is eliding a topic because it is amply treated elsewhere. But even given this possibility, the total absence of psychological factors in Abraham's tractate leaves a strange gap in the expected coverage of his subject matter. Only in the beginning of his tractate do we find a reference to "accidents of the soul": when listing the signs of a true pestilential fever, Abraham refers to the power of fear, which, however, he medicalizes as a consequence of illness. Due to a suppression of vital spirit in the brain, the patient can experience lethargy, weakness, loss of appetite, and confusion. This physiological condition, in turn, creates "fear and a dread of death."[126] He offers no specific treatment to soothe or comfort the frightened patient.

For Abraham, the physician's primary goal when treating fevers like those that have ravaged Aragon is to maintain the strength of the patient's heart. This may require cautious deviation from the regimens, especially if a patient yearns for a food that is not recommended.[127] Here Abraham acknowledges a sort of psychological factor, by granting weight to a patient's particular tastes or cravings.

But the dietary cravings of a sick man are a meager concession to his mental anguish and fears. At the least, Abraham's failure to address this category suggests that in a time of medical emergency, he did not think a patient's emotional state was the physician's priority. And perhaps, by extension, the low premium that Abraham set on "accidents of the soul" tells us something about his own temperament. A man who survives expulsion from his home, community, landscape, and language, and then rebuilds his life in a new setting, adding a new wife and language and powerful patronage in the construction of a flourishing career, is not a man who gives in to fearful imaginings.

Alternatively, the lacunae tell us nothing of the sort, and Abraham simply chose to emphasize points of diagnosis and treatment that he felt were critical and on which he differed from prevailing medical opinion. A comparison with Abraham's 1326 fever treatise, the "Alei ra'anan," might bolster one view or the other. Alas, it is still unpublished, and for now, we can only say that for Abraham, his patients' state of mind was not his most pressing medical concern, even that of patients he had lived among and perhaps treated for almost three decades. Neither, as noted above, does he distinguish among the sick in terms of class, profession, or gender, only deferring occasionally to modify recommendations for the very young. He does refer to patients of different humoral temperament (particularly sanguine and phlegmatic) and to men who overindulge in food or sex or bathing. But these are categories taken from Avicenna and do not necessarily describe Abraham's particular milieu.

What can be learned from these three literary aspects of Abraham's tractate? First, Abraham's interjections and asides betray a glimpse of himself and his colleagues as they treated the sick. They furthermore testify to the heated debates taking place among medical professionals during the course of the plague and in its immediate aftermath. That debate began with questions of diagnosis that taxed received categories of disease (specifically, fevers) in new ways, pushing to the fore questions of transmission and contagion, as well as causality, and pressuring physicians to reconcile the gap between their experience and their books. Abraham's insistence that the fevers should not be classified as universal pestilence is accompanied by his observation that many patients recovered. This anomalous assessment seems to reflect lower plague mortality in the vicinity of Girona and may partially explain the rejection of his view by other physicians (as well as his rejection of their plague realities).

Second, albeit indirectly, the tractate also reflects the author's distance from episodes of plague-inspired violence against Jewish communities—and equally from the sites of violence against lepers twenty-seven years earlier. There is only one place in Abraham's text where he may allude to anti-Jewish violence, and that is in his opening description of the trajectory of the pandemic. This description not only cites a biblical passage evocative of violent slaughter and dispossession but is also the identical passage invoked by a contemporary eyewitness of the violence in Monzón who survived to write about the attacks on the *aljamas*. The fact that it remains an isolated example makes it impossible to ascertain how consciously Abraham recycled Hayim Galipapa's account. In either case, I have argued, the remarkable intertext reinforces a subtext of frustration in Abraham's tractate that may speak to more than a professional dispute. Moreover, if his source was Galipapa's chronicle, then this, too, indirectly suggests that more conventional genres of commemoration controlled by rabbinic authorities (fast days, penitential liturgies, and laments) were not the dominant genre shaping his views—because they were not relevant to him or because they were in trouble. Although these conventional genres did offer consolation to plague survivors, as I argue in Chapters 2 and 5, they may have competed with other forms of expression. For a man of science like Abraham, they may have lacked the kind of truth that he found in scholastic medicine.

    *   *   *

Abraham Caslari was a man who had survived his own dose of trauma and loss. His medical writings testify less to great gifts of intellect or synthesis than to his astounding resilience in a life that he had rebuilt from scratch and as a refugee in a foreign land with a father, wife, and children to support. His steady trajectory toward professional recognition, financial comfort, and political privilege document his canny mastery of the social and professional challenges that he faced along the way. In this sense, his personal quirks may be on display precisely where he believes he has escaped them: in ordered, technical prose. Conversely, Abraham's prose betrays signs of stress. He worries that his views go unheard, he refers both to clinical and bookish disputes with other physicians, and he is tellingly contradictory in explaining his motives for writing. The fact, nonetheless, that he seeks to overcome these challenges in the form of a medical tractate reminds us that he saw his rivals as well as his followers as members of an intellectual and professional community whose language and commitments he continued to share in a time of crisis. This is a gesture of faith comparable to that of the liturgical poet who continued to ply the conventions of that genre when its assumptions were equally under stress. But the genre difference counts. The two types of writers envision different audiences: a community of learned physicians versus a community of pious Jews. A poet like Emanuel, whose lament was treated in Chapter 2, speaks on behalf of a collective by tapping the shared tropes and language of sacred texts. Abraham Caslari also taps a shared canon of authoritative writing, but it is not sacred, and the voice that he proclaims emerges from his individual experience.

Strikingly, Abraham Caslari was also a survivor of earlier catastrophes, dating back to the great expulsion of French Jews in 1306. Over the four decades since his forced departure from Languedoc, he had built himself an enviable fortune and reputation, a prestigious career as a physician with access to the royal court and patients, not to mention a long list of royal privileges that he could transfer to his daughter and her family. Trauma may be a part of Abraham Caslari's story. But if so, it is trauma that has become inextricably interwoven with his sense of overcoming the blows of the past, confident that his success is a vindication of personal merit. Whether or how much he identifies with the reports of devastation in other regions—devastation wrought by high plague mortality as well as specifically Jewish losses to disease and violence—is a difficult question to answer. I have focused on elements of Abraham's tractate that, in some sense, destabilize the orderly logic of his prose, some of which may be rooted in his awareness of anti-Jewish violence. Even so, I am hesitant to claim that these factors are evidence of a deeply unsettled soul. With the exception of his opening line, his tractate never reverberates with any sense of a communal blow, a sense poignantly voiced in contemporary Christian plague tractates. Was Abraham content to leave this work to rabbis and poets, or did he repel grief and fear in the language of medical reason? I do not know.

What became of Abraham Caslari after the grim season that initiated the second great pandemic? He disappears from the records after 1349. That was just about when the plague made its first real appearance at the other end of the peninsula, in Castile. And that is where we turn our attention next.

Chapter 4

Stones of Memory: The Toledo Epitaphs

And seven days prior to his death
He sent away his dove
To find him a resting place
She found a place to rest her feet
Then her husband followed after her.
　　　—From the epitaph of Meir haLevi Abulafia (who died in
　　　Toledo of the plague, Marheshvan 1350)

THE PLAGUE CAME late to the lands of Castile, having traversed the eastern
end of Iberia and ravaged Catalonia, Aragon, Valencia, Navarre, and Granada.
It also lingered, appearing late in 1348 or early in 1349 and slowly tapering into
1351–52. As the case of Castile illustrates, the pandemic was experienced differently in different regions, both in its epidemiological impact and in the responses of communities and institutions. Mortality was high but not as high as
in Catalonia and Aragon. Even within the kingdom, the effects of the plague
were variable, and apparently more destructive in the lowlands than in the
mountains. (This was also the case in Aragon, where the dry, cooler mountain
climate provided a less hospitable setting for fleas and possibly their carriers.)[1]
So, too, it spread more quickly—and efficiently—in the towns along commercial and pilgrimage routes and, according to one older study, struck rural areas
more severely than urban ones. Its general impact was harsher on the poor than
the elite, although the predictable categories of professional men were eroded,
and the loss of bailiffs, notaries, jurists, and priests disrupted the institutions
and rhythms of daily life.[2] Castile's best-known victim was her king, Alfonso
XI, who died in 1350 in Gibraltar, where the plague took no side in wars of religion and expansion.[3]

The few studies of the plague's impact in Castile point to familiar signs of stress and depopulation: higher labor costs, a spike in ecclesiastical benefices, neglected farmland, and pleas for relief in debts owed to Jews. One old study invokes anti-Jewish hostility as part of a larger array of "violent psychological reactions" in severely afflicted areas.[4] Nonetheless, there is little evidence that anti-Jewish violence typified the reaction to this first outbreak of the plague; the second wave, in 1361–62, was a death blow to a number of struggling settlements and towns and may have tapped a greater sense of desperation and rage. In 1349, however, the records of such violence are not there. The distinct history of Castilian Jews leading up to this period may be part of the explanation: their role in royal administration and resettlement of the frontier, as well as their historical visibility as courtiers, scholars, translators, astronomers, and physicians, both in the orbit of Toledo, the capital of Old Castile, and in the penumbra of a perpetually migrating royal court.[5] Among physicians, Castile's lack of a university and university culture also permitted Jewish physicians to flourish in high circles; many of these men still derived their knowledge of medicine directly from Arabic sources and composed in that language.[6] This does not mean that Christian Castile, like other European kingdoms, was free of hostility or prejudice toward its Jews, although (and partly because) royal protection of Castilian Jews remained strong. Even though the years preceding the Black Death show signs of interfaith tensions, especially between local urban elites and their Jewish counterparts, this region had long been characterized by what historian Maya Soifer Irish has described as an "evolution of accommodations for the Jewish minority."[7] In the late thirteenth and early fourteenth centuries, a distinctive social, political, economic, and cultural structure in Castile kept tensions in check, and this difference made itself felt during the years of the Black Death.

This chapter examines an unconventional source of documentation for Jewish responses to the Black Death in Castile, a set of more than two dozen epitaphs written for Jewish victims of the plague in Toledo in 1349 and 1350. Significantly, none of these epitaphs refers to anti-Jewish violence as a compounding cause of death—a sharp contrast to the situation in Provence, Catalonia, Aragon, Valencia, and central Europe, where Jewish communities were routinely attacked on suspicion of causing the plague. Many of the epitaph texts, moreover, are polished literary compositions. In addition to details of biography and lineage, they trace a chronology of the epidemic in the most important Jewish center in Castile and among its major dynastic families. The formal conventions that gild the lives of the deceased with expressions of piety, honor, and righteousness shed light on the construction of public memory as it crystallized around the lives of powerful Toledan Jews in a time of crisis. That construct was intended for later generations as much as for the immediate survivors.

But that is not all that they can tell us. Even when the sentiments that they express are heavily dependent on conventional formulations, the authors of these texts often succeed in balancing cliché and idiosyncratic description, permitting us to glean details of private life behind the measured lines of public eulogy. As Rachel Greenblatt has noted of the sixteenth- and seventeenth-century epitaphs in the Jewish cemetery in Prague, this is a special kind of literature: in material form as well as in language, it marks a meeting place of public and private, living and dead. In their elegant platitudes and careful portraiture, in their stonework and their verses, the epitaphs of Toledo are exceptional in their artistry; but like lesser exemplars, they pay homage to the ways this community wished to remember the dead and hence themselves. At the same time, they testify to a reciprocal and ongoing traffic between the here and hereafter in which the dead also played an active part as intercessors for the living. They, too, were asked to remember.[8]

The preeminence of the Toledo Jewish community makes this investigation important in other ways. The post-expulsion dominance of Castilian identity among Iberian exilic communities may have contributed to the silence of Jewish sources on the Black Death in Iberia, if only by overshadowing other experience and records. Alternatively, the instability and crisis of later Castilian-Jewish history may have dulled memory of a disaster that gave way to graver, more irrevocable kinds of crisis. Either way, Castilian memory of the Black Death may have accorded it less significance than subsequent catastrophes.[9] Then, too, as this book argues, even communities that were more severely affected, such as those in Catalonia, found it possible to rely on familiar tropes and forms of commemoration in the wake of the Black Death. Rupture did not characterize their commemorative efforts except in cases where extreme violence made such commemoration impossible. Nonetheless, the Castilian experience, which did not include anti-Jewish violence, also seems to have been shaped by the milder impact of disease, at least in 1349–50. In each regional case, different factors influenced the forms of commemorative activity and the subsequent fate of written texts.

The artistry of the Toledo tombstones is unique to Toledo; no other community in Iberia or outside it seems to have adopted their physical form, and none can match the sophistication of their texts. There has been a recent flurry of interest in Jewish gravestones and an attempt to theorize burial practices and analyze epitaph texts.[10] Each new excavation has also brought new controversies over the fate of human remains.[11] Over the last few decades, too, there has been a smattering of articles or collections treating Jewish epitaph poetry in Amsterdam, Italy, and the New World, all postmedieval exemplars. Among them, the literary flourishes of Amsterdam Jewry's seventeenth-century gravestones, the poetic texts published by David Malkiel from northern Italy, and even the mix of Hebrew, Spanish, or Portuguese poetry that adorned the headstones of wealthy and prominent Jews in Bermuda or Jamaica, clearly sustain a literary tradition with origins in Castile.[12] The Toledo epitaphs thus hold interest far beyond their chance inclusion of almost thirty records of death by plague, and I will try to suggest their wider meaning in these pages.

This chapter examines the Toledo plague epitaphs as literary texts, material remains, and cultural artifacts: What do they tell us as expressions of literary commemoration in a time of catastrophe? And in what ways do they point to beliefs, rituals, and cultural practices that go beyond the chiseled words on stone or paper? I begin with the story of how these inscriptions have come down to us.

*   *   *

Sometime in the early sixteenth century, a Jewish "tourist" to Toledo wandered the extraordinary cemetery of that medieval Jewish community. Who he was, we do not know, nor do we know what motivated him to transcribe almost eighty inscriptions from the tombstones that he encountered there.[13] Some of the stones may already have been uprooted and recycled by Christians, or preemptively dismantled by Toledan Jews on the eve of the 1492 expulsion.[14] A few, according to the anonymous copyist, were in a local home, whose owner had collected and saved them.[15] From that moment on, the story of this *ignoto curioso*, as Cantera called him, is a mystery, until his transcriptions resurface three centuries later in Turin in the royal library founded in 1723 by the king of Sardinia, Victor Amadeus II of the House of Savoy.[16] Cantera and Millás thought that they were donated to the Turin library in 1809 by the Italian Orientalist Tommaso Valperga-Calusio, and copied shortly thereafter by the Paduan Jewish poet and bibliophile Joseph Almanzi. In their account, Almanzi's interest was serendipitous, as the library caught fire soon afterward and many manuscripts were destroyed.[17]

As other records show, this account is not quite accurate. Although Valperga may indeed have owned the manuscript copy in 1809, the collection of which it formed a part did not reach the royal library in Turin until 1818.[18] Sometime later, it was read by Almanzi, who made his own copy and sent it on to his friend the rabbi and scholar Samuel David Luzzatto, otherwise known by the acronym

"Shadal."[19] Shadal published the inscriptions in 1841, with a brief introduction and Almanzi's notes. Both the original copy and Shadal's publication are mentioned in the 1880 catalog of Hebrew manuscripts in the Turin library produced by B. Peyron.[20] Peyron's entry for the miscellany includes the names of two previous owners inscribed in the flyleaf, one a Jew from Palestra and one from Casale. Both towns are within 100 kilometers of Turin-Mantua. From 1500 until the late seventeenth century, Palestra was governed by Spain, which means that a Jewish presence during those years is unlikely. In the seventeenth century, the region passed to the House of Savoy; the Jewish owners may date to this period, or, alternatively, they may have been earlier owners who lost possession of their books under Spanish rule. The infamous fire mentioned by Cantera occurred In January 1904, and it almost entirely destroyed the collection of Hebrew manuscripts.[21] A number of recent publications based on surviving fragments, painstakingly restored since the 1970s, offer moving descriptions of the state of the tattered remnants.[22] According to Richler, the anonymous transcription, which miraculously survived three centuries of migration and unknown hazards, was not so lucky in 1904; it appears to have been destroyed.[23]

The survival of the actual gravestones also proved precarious. The anonymous sixteenth-century traveler recorded seventy-six inscriptions, but the stones that originally bore them have mostly disappeared. Four transcriptions correspond to stones that are currently in the archaeological museum in Toledo.[24] One, Shadal's inscription no. 70 (= Cantera no. 82), is for Jacob son of Isaac al-Sarqastan, who died of plague in 1349.[25] The large trapezoidal slab was discovered in the wall of a private home in 1915, where it had been serving as a laundry or wash basin; it was moved to the museum in 1926.[26] A second, Shadal's inscription no. 1 (= Cantera no. 71), was discovered in a convent in 1930, where it, too, had spent centuries as a washing trough. Reassembled, this five-piece tombstone commemorates a woman called Sitbona. Like Jacob the son of Isaac, she died of plague in 1349. Sitbona was linked by birth and marriage to the Sahwan and haLevi dynasties, two prominent Castilian Jewish families. The survival of her complete tomb illustrates clearly a striking feature of their curious design: the text not only covers five sides of the trapezoidal stone but is inscribed in wraparound form, so that the reader must circle the grave in order to read the inscription. While there is evidence for a medieval Ashkenazi custom of circling a graveyard, the notion of circumambulating a particular grave is not described in the literature.[27] I shall return to this custom below.

A third piece of stone, composed of two fragments, preserves three lines of an epitaph corresponding to Shadal's inscription no. 43 (= Cantera no. 85). The

deceased is Dona, daughter of Solomon ben al-Bagal and wife of Abraham son of
Reb Moses ben Sasson; she, too, died of plague in 1349. These fragments were discovered in 1771 in building debris. Moved to the church of San Nicolas, they were
then acquired by an antiquities collector, Domingo Rivera, in 1779. They then
passed to Cardinal Lorenzana, who installed them in the public library that he
had established in the Palacio Arzobispal. From there, the stones were transferred
to the archaeological museum.[28] Finally, two slender fragments of stone, bearing
one incomplete line of text, were uncovered in the rubble of a demolished barrio in
San Andrés in 1835, the site of a new Seminario Conciliar, and moved to the archaeological museum. Cantera and Millás hypothesize that they once constituted
part of the lateral faces of a tomb; the text corresponds to lines 11–16 and 30–37 of
Shadal's inscription no. 10 (= Cantera no. 99). The fuller transcription preserved
by the anonymous copyist is an ornate prose and verse epitaph for the famed rabbinic scholar Menahem ben Zerah, who died in 1385.[29]

Another ten fragments or larger stones in granite or clay do not correspond
to any of the inscriptions. Two consist of entire trapezoidal stones: one is the
tomb of Moses ibn Abi Zardil (d. 1354), secretary of the chancellery to Alfonso
XI; and the other is too eroded to identify.[30] These are beyond the reach of this
study, but they do confirm the characteristic "truncated pyramid" form of the
tombstones unique to the Toledo cemetery.

Of seventy-six inscriptions, twenty-eight describe deaths due to plague between 1349 and 1352. One additional epitaph commemorates a physician who
died in the next plague epidemic in 1362, Joseph son of Abraham Makhir (Shadal no. 37 = Cantera no. 96). Following some general remarks, I would like to
focus closely on a representative sample. The eight epitaphs that I have chosen
provide opportunities for comparison and contrast: two are for women, six are
for men; three are for Jews belonging to old aristocratic families in Toledo, and
five are for descendants of the towering religious leader Ashkenazi-born Rabbi
(R.) Asher b. Yehiel (known as the "Rosh"). Seven of the victims died in 1349,
one the following winter; and seven died at home in Toledo, one on the road to
Seville. My annotated translation of all twenty-eight epitaphs may be found in
an appendix to this book.

In total, nearly thirty epitaphs mark deaths from plague over a two- to
three-year span beginning in the Jewish month of Nisan (approximately April)
1349, steadily peaking through the months of Sivan and Tamuz (June–July),
and then tapering in Av (August), with three deaths in the winter month of Marheshvan 1350 and one in Iyar 1352.[31] Several general observations may be made
about this set. Significantly, they are individual graves, graced with individual

memorials. The (Christian) plague cemetery recently unearthed in Barcelona (to the east in Catalonia) is a mass grave, as are the Jewish graves in Tàrrega and Valencia and, for that matter, other plague burial grounds across Europe.[32] Whatever the experience of plague was in Toledo in 1349, it apparently unfolded without the massive mortality, disruption, or unrest that characterized other locations.[33] Jewish law prescribes a waiting period between burial and the erection of a tombstone; nonetheless, each of these Toledo Jewish worthies found an individual resting place to await commemoration. Likewise, the biographical detail on many of the inscriptions testifies to the familiarity of the writer, or those who prompted him, with the life and activities of the deceased. Those memorial texts that are comparatively scanty may testify to the disruptive effects of a prolonged pandemic. The presence of only one epitaph from the second round of plague in 1362 may equally testify to its harsher impact in Toledo; I shall return to this epitaph below.

Thus, one yield of these texts, long ignored by historians and scholars of literature, is greater knowledge of the effects of the plague in Castile. As other sources and studies have tentatively posited, the impact of the Black Death may have been less severe in urban Castilian settings like Toledo, and more devastating in the countryside.[34] The use of individual graves, the evidence for elaborate and individualized tombstones, and the continuity of literary conventions for eulogizing the dead indicate that however terrible the years of 1349–52 were for Castilian Jews, they did not perceive the pandemic as a rupture with "ordinary" experience. It was an order of catastrophe that forced no break with preexisting conventions for commemoration and no unparalleled sense of loss. This is a markedly different landscape from that found farther to the east or south.

Some of the formal features of the epitaphs deserve mention. Their dating conventions vary. Out of twenty-eight epitaphs for the first wave of plague (1349–52), five list only the year (1349) and no month; seventeen list the month and year but no day; and six record day, month, and year of death. Three of the six epitaphs that include precise dates belong to members of the Rosh's family: two for his adult sons, Jacob and Judah, who died on the twelfth and seventeenth of Tamuz, respectively, and one for Judah's son Solomon, who died on the fifteenth of Av.[35] Dating topoi specific to plague deaths may have taken time to solidify. Most of the plague epitaphs convert the Hebrew year 5109 (1349 c.e.) into a word or phrase whose numerical equivalent is 109, sometimes leaving it to the reader to add the millennial count. Several stock phrases dominate, chiefly the Hebrew word for "rest" (מנוחה) or "perish" (לגוע), the latter pulling along with it the biblical expression "Behold, we perish" (האם תמנו לגוע) from the biblical plague story of Num. 17:34. A few texts simply record the year, 109 = קי; the possibility exists that these deaths were not due to plague. All three of the 1350 deaths inscribe the year as קטב, "destruction" or "pestilence," probably from Ps. 91:6; the single death in 1352 cites the biblical verse "by the right hand of my righteousness" (Isa. 41:10), indicating the year with the first word, בימין. The 1362 epitaph simply spells out the year with no acronym.

The strolling copyist was selective, so we must be wary of drawing demographic conclusions from his list.[36] For instance, only three of our group commemorate women, and two of those three were, respectively, the first and second wives of Judah ben (i.e., the son of) the Rosh. The third, Sitbona, was also distinguished by marriage and pedigree. In addition to the copyist's celebrity bias, the topography of the now-lost cemetery may have posed hurdles to extracting demographic data. Recent research has suggested that medieval Jewish burial practices in Toledo may also have limited the use of headstones to the wealthy or prominent. The dead were arranged in rows, but as the copyist's transcription sequence suggests, they were also clustered by extended family, more or less extending the neighborhood arrangements that they had enjoyed in life.[37] The cemetery was located almost a mile from the Jewish quarter, beyond the medieval walls, in the vicinity of Cerro de la Horca.[38] In 2008, bones were discovered in the area, and the following year, during preliminary construction of a new high school, more than a hundred graves were unearthed. Archaeologists identified the grave sites as Jewish, with remains dating from the twelfth to fifteenth centuries. Subsequent protests by Orthodox Jewish groups, many arriving from outside Spain, successfully blocked further exploration. The remains were reburied in or near the original site, and the Azarquiel High School rose above them, so that, depending on the quality of its construction, the souls of the dead will wait safely for another millennium before receiving new visitors.[39] Until then, we can say almost nothing about the graves of those Jews of Toledo who did not amass fortune or fame in their lifetimes and who were buried in other parts of the cemetery. As for the evidence of the inscriptions, its chief value lies in other sorts of meaning.

The inscriptions do not always indicate ages; and when they do, it is often to emphasize youth and an untimely end. The youngest among the plague victims was fourteen and the son of Judah ben haRosh. None of the seventy-six inscriptions commemorates a young child, suggesting that it was not customary to provide them with tombstones.[40] Hayim, the fourteen-year-old son of Judah ben haRosh, may have been exceptional because of his illustrious family.[41] The next youngest plague victim commemorated was Asher son of Yosef ben Turiel. Asher was fifteen but had celebrated his wedding shortly before his death, and was recalled as an avid scholar.[42]

Asher, for that matter, is recalled with some of the same encomia that appear in another inscription, this one for the eighteen-year-old Isaac son of Solomon ibn al-Masudia.[43] Both are described as learned youths who are as wise as eighty-year-old men. Asher was a pampered or favored child (ילד שעשועים) who was "pure in knowledge" (תמים דעים). Isaac, too, was a darling son and pampered or favored (בן נחמד ונעים וילד שעשועים), beloved by his friends and also "pure in knowledge" (תמים דעים). Isaac died of plague on the fourth of Tamuz, at the height of the pandemic, and he is described as the son of a sage. Asher also died in Tamuz, but we do not know the day. He had studied with his father, and learned biblical and rabbinic texts. Fifteen-year-old Asher had married "just days before his death," and left behind him a grieving family. The concluding verses of his epitaph turn away from Asher and toward the survivors, petitioning God to bring consolation and future children to Asher's grief-stricken father. The father is described in a clever expression as "pained and pining"—וישב אב נכאב ונדאב—a thudding sequence of closed rhymes that echoes the father's choked grief. However, the same expression appears in Shadal's epitaph no. 27, which is not for a plague victim but for the twenty-seven-year-old Judah ben Nahmias, who died in 1240.[44] The image of Judah's grieving father leads off the thirteenth-century epitaph, which begins אב נכאב בלב נדאב—"a father pained with a pining heart." So, too, young Abraham son of Samuel of the Sasson dynasty, who died in 1354, left a father who was an אב נכאב ונדאב, a pained and pining father, while the deceased Abraham, who had not yet married, was also a favored child of incommensurate wisdom.[45]

In other words, this genre poses challenges. Like all occasional poetry, these gravestone inscriptions rely on encomia, conventional expressions that soften the distinctive edges of human personality. Many of the attributes that adorn the memories of the dead in the Toledo epitaphs appear in more than one of them. Some, as in the case of the grieving father, are not exclusive to victims of plague. On the one hand, we learn that conventions for heaping honor upon the dead and his or her family had evolved among the Toledo Jewish elite long before the Black Death. On the other hand, it is striking how little the existing conventions required emendation in the face of that event. A youth's untimely death was routinely described in terms of a truncated scholarly trajectory and wisdom beyond his years, and his loss in terms of his parents' suffering. Likewise, all dead children turn out to have been their parents' favorites.

And yet, when we carefully compare these chiseled texts, we also discern how tiny variations, additions, or deletions can animate cliché. Abraham son of Reb

Moses ibn Falcon also died young—young enough that he merited the conventional comparison of his wisdom to that of a man of eighty.. His was one of the early deaths from plague, in Sivan 5109 (May–June 1349). He was chosen, or select, among sons—another favorite child but enlisting a different idiom. In three unmetered but rhyming lines, he is described as having been plucked, snatched, and plucked again from the world of the living; the epitaph concludes that "he died while his father *and mother* were still living."[46] Why is Abraham Falcon uniquely mourned by two living parents? The answer cannot be that the other mothers were indifferent to the deaths of their sons. Nor can we argue that the convention was not yet in place, as it is documented in the thirteenth-century epitaph for Judah ben Nahmias. Something about Abraham Falcon's parents may be different. Perhaps Abraham's mother had some visibility in the community that the epitaph subtly acknowledges. Or, for reasons lost to history, the poet who composed the epitaph may have wished to draw on a set of affective tropes that sentimentalized maternal as well as paternal grief. The beautiful epitaph for Joseph son of Reb Meir Abul'afia haMerari, in contrast, invokes *only* his mother; the father must be dead. The dead son, Joseph son of Reb Meir, was another newlywed. He is recalled in language that invokes none of the tropes that constitute common currency among the greater collection. His epitaph is also a work of consummate artistry whose author may have spurned the usual conventions.[47]

Cliché and prooftext can be subtly manipulated to suggest biographical detail that the author could not announce explicitly. Sitbona's epitaph describes her important father, "one of the lords of the land," who defended the Jewish community against some unspecified political or financial threat. (The father "stood in the breach for God's people," another stock phrase that surfaces in other epitaphs for men who had access to Christian kings and courts.) Her husband, Meir, is also described as a bulwark of the people. What is lacking in this long epitaph is any mention of Sitbona and Meir's own children and their remarkable achievements. Instead, the concluding verses of the text summon phrases from Isa. 54:2, which the biblical prophet addressed to "the barren one" (Israel awaiting redemption), and from Jer. 31:16 and 31:25 (the elegiac passage depicting the exiled Rachel weeping for her lost children). In this way, the author subtly tells us without offending her memory that at the time of her death, Sitbona was childless. In this case, the familiar tropes of biblical passages permit later readers to read between the lines of the memorial text.

Recent studies by Rami Reiner dedicated to the honorifics found in the epitaphs for medieval Würzburg Jews have attempted to sift and sort the various kinds of titles attached to the names of the deceased. Reiner identified several categories of honorifics referring to professional roles, personal status or piety. A fourth category bestowed social respect and status.[48] The Toledo epitaphs, although fewer in number, offer a richer panoply of honorifics. As in Würzburg, the title "Reb" is used much like our English "Mister," a generic term of respect that does not indicate particular religious or secular status. Other phrases, such as the expression "to stand in the breach," indicate a professional status or role by means of a descriptive phrase rather than a specific title. These phrases also predate the plague period. Two plague victims, R. Meir haLevi Abulafia (ben Solomon ben al-Lauwee) and the youthful R. Samuel haLevi ben R. Samuel haLevi Abulafia, are described as a "princely scion" (חוטר משרה). The expression, from Isa. 11:1, may allude to a specific function or simply to aristocratic status. Overall, the epitaphs offer a generous selection of adjectives and apposite descriptions of valiant, pious, generous, humble, learned, charitable, faithful, glorious, honorable, noble, pure, modest, splendid, discrete, wise, intelligent, accomplished, righteous, honest, and beloved men, who had the fortune to marry wives or to father daughters who were honest, pious, great, righteous, talented, charitable, humble, gracious, modest, and pure. But this, too, tells us something about the public face of privilege in fourteenth-century Toledo, at least as it saw itself. Service to the community, protection of its learning and wealth, book-learning, diplomacy, good lineage, and generosity were attributes associated with an elite, but remembered for their public value. And what of the private lives of these men and women, lost in one of the cataclysmic and wrenching traumas of the fourteenth century? A closer look at several epitaphs suggests the degree to which we can answer that question.

The Epitaphs: Select Readings

Shadal No. 1 (= Cantera No. 71): Sitbona, Daughter of Judah b. Sahwan, Wife of Meir haLevi

The first epitaph transcribed by the Toledo tourist was for a woman, and he prefaced the text with the words "On the headstone, this is what was written for this woman."[49] The epitaph opens with a dramatic command to the mourners and later visitors to clear the path to the cemetery and to sanctify the plot where Sitbona lies buried; the poet may be alluding to a formal procession and circuit. These opening verses draw on Isa. 62 and Exod. 3, the former proclaiming redemption and the latter proclaiming proximity to the divine. The application of this language to a woman is striking. The woman herself is named only after a drumroll of apposite praises:

That goodly plot where a noble and aristocratic woman is buried,
a great woman,
She is Madam Sitbona. (lines 4–6)[50]

The name Sitbona, which baffled Luzzatto and Almanzi, is documented in another Toledo epitaph not belonging to the plague set. Cantera and Millás parsed it as a combination of the Arabic *sit* (lady) and the female name Bona. As Sitbona's gravestone has survived, we can see that the text of the inscription fills all five sides of the trapezoidal granite stone. The inscription begins on top, with three even lines inscribed lengthwise, and then continues onto the inclined facet directly below. Each of the four sides holds three evenly spaced lines, which are read as a wraparound text: it would be necessary to circle the stone three times to read the whole inscription. Moreover, the "line breaks" do not correspond to breaks in phrasing or meaning but are subordinated to the visual geometry, producing a chiseled surface that is completely regular and includes no blank area.

Yet the text has its own internal structure and propulsion, which emerge when it is printed. The mourners are commanded to clear the way for Sitbona, a great and noble lady. She is great and noble—first, because she is descended from the aristocratic Sahwan dynasty; her father is recalled as a lord of the land and benefactor "who stood in the breach for God's people." Sitbona's husband, Meir haLevi son of Reb Isaac haLevi, was a great man who defended the community. The phrase used to describe. Meir, *hoshen yeshu'ot umigdal*, a stalwart of

FIGURE 2. Sitbona's tomb. Granite tombstone in the form of a truncated pyramid, with inscription in Hebrew characters, 1349. Museo Sefardi, 0007/001. Photograph by Rebeca García Merino. Courtesy of the Ministry of Education, Culture and Sport, Spain.

salvation and fortress, is uncommon in this collection. The first two words come from Isaiah 33:6, and many modern translations note that their combined meaning is unclear. The medieval glossators Rashi and Radaq understood the phrase to mean that the people's faith and ritual observance might serve as a bulwark in a time of trial. If our poet understood the phrase this way, he implies that R. Meir has lived an exemplary life of piety that has somehow served his community in a time of stress.

Literally circled by these figures of male authority, Sitbona reappears. She died of the plague in June 1349, the "year of REST," and a righteous life prepared her for her heavenly journey and merited her a spacious resting place for eternity. The last and third line of circling text anticipates the End of Days and Sitbona's future resurrection. First the poet, and then God, addresses Sitbona directly:

> At the end of days, He will raise you up and compensate your actions.
> There is hope for your future with the resurrection of His pious few.
> He will say to you, "Do not grieve!
> Shake off the dust! Arise and return!"[51]

As noted above, several of the closing verses allude to passages in Isaiah and Jeremiah that suggest that Sitbona was childless at the time of her death. Even the choice of the verb *da'av*, echoing Jer. 31:25 (24), reminds us of the epitaphs' generic trope for a bereaved father, *av nid'av*. The elegant shift in speaker from the poet to God, executed in the penultimate line, was a standard feature of the popular *muwashshah* lyrics, hinging the body of the song to its concluding *kharja*, often spoken by a different character in the song. Its appearance here is a sign that the author of this inscription was familiar with the cultural forms and attitudes that characterized upper-class Jewish tastes in Castile. Finally, the conclusion of the text executes a pleasing circle thematically, moving from its opening command to the procession to clear the path to God's intimate command to Sitbona. The first call is to the living who accompany the dead woman to the grave; the second call is to Sitbona, as she continues her journey alone.

The Family of the Rosh: Epitaph Nos. 3, 4, 5, 6, and 42 (= Cantera Nos. 76, 75, 84, 11, and 42)

The fame achieved by R. Asher ben Yehiel in his lifetime did not fade with his death, and he remains a monumental presence among scholars of halakha as well as rabbinic decisors today. Born in the heart of Ashkenaz, he was the leading student of R. Meir of Rothenburg, whose death in prison may have contributed to

R. Asher's decision to emigrate. In the early years of the fourteenth century, he
made his way from Cologne through Provence to Barcelona. By 1306, the year of
the great expulsion of French Jewry, he had found a mission and new home in Toledo, the capital of Old Castile, where the Jewish community appointed him rabbi
of Toledo and head of the local Jewish academy.[52] Whether the Rosh, as he is
called, ever fully acclimated to the more freewheeling atmosphere in Toledo is de-
batable. He sought to impose a systematic, austere, and Ashkenazi brand of piety
on the Jews of Toledo and beyond, although over time he seems to have tempered
the public formulations of some of his religious views.[53] R. Asher fathered eight
sons and two daughters, some born in Germany. Yehiel, the eldest, was praised for
his brilliance, but died young.[54] The second son, Solomon "the pious," led an eco-
nomically precarious life characterized by extreme piety. Despite his poverty, he
married the daughter of an established family in Toledo, and died shortly after his
father.[55] The third son, Jacob, was a prolific author; among his enduring works on
ritual and religious law was the *Arba' Turim* (Four Columns). He, too, left Germany as a child with his father. Like his brother Solomon, he struggled to make
ends meet but had a formidable scholarly reputation. His epitaph stresses his religious learning and writings.[56]

According to Jacob's epitaph, he also suffered from poor health, and died in
pain on the twelfth of Tamuz. He was buried in the family tomb that his father
had erected and to which he refers in his will, the fifth of the sons to join the
Rosh there, "two to his right and three to his left."[57] Scholars Freimann and
Havatselet thought that he had died in 1343.[58] As for the family tomb, it is mentioned in the Rosh's final testament and suggested by the tight cluster of family
epitaphs in the copyist's transcriptions. Noteworthy in Jacob's epitaph, too, is an
expression that we have seen already in Sitbona's: the Lord will call to the Rosh
and his sons to "ascend the sacred path" to their heavenly destination. Once
again, the physical journey from the walled city to the cemetery becomes a lim-
inal passage traveled, however temporarily, by inhabitants of both worlds; it is a
"sacred path."[59]

Judah, the fourth son, was not initially encouraged to seek a scholar's life. A
childhood illness damaged his vision, and a woman practitioner nearly blinded
him. A second (Jewish) woman managed to restore some of young Judah's eyesight, but she unfortunately died before the treatment was complete, leaving
him with poor eyesight for the rest of his life.[60] Nonetheless, it is Judah who
would go on to inherit his father's mantle, assuming his post as Toledo's chief
rabbi and directing the school that he had founded there for over two decades
after his father's death. Although he was never a prolific scholar, his surviving

writings include a last will and testament written prior to his death in 1349. He was married twice, first at the age of fifteen, to a daughter of his brother Yehiel's, and then to Miriam, the daughter of his brother Solomon.[61] The remaining brothers were Eliakim, a scholar and financier; Moses (who died sometime before his brother Jacob); Eliezer, who managed the family charitable trust; and Simon (d. 1341). Two daughters were married in Toledo: one to Judah Cresp, who later left Toledo; and one to Isaac Aldabi, "the Hasid of Toledo." The daughters' names are lost to history.[62]

R. Asher (the Rosh)'s family tomb housed most of his sons..[63] A second cluster of family members found themselves in a different cemetery "neighborhood." Together, their epitaphs testify to the toll exacted by the plague, with five family members succumbing over a three-month period. Jacob's son Solomon died in Nisan (April–May). Judah's wife Miriam and son Hayim died in Sivan (June) and Judah himself in Tamuz (July). Hayim was only fourteen, Solomon a year older. Judah was seventy-nine at the time of his death.[64] The addendum to Judah's will dated Sivan 5109 (1349) refers repeatedly to financial decisions that Judah makes in his and his wife's names, so she was still living at this point.[65] Another of Judah's sons, Solomon, died in Av (July–August).

The family epitaphs constitute a natural group; given the proximity of the deaths, the same author, perhaps even Judah, may have been responsible for composing them. Their stolidity contrasts sharply with the more literary exemplars. It is, however, consistent with the religious values upheld by R. Asher and his sons, who were determined to bring Ashkenazi rigor to what they judged to be a laxer piety among Toledo's Jewish elite. Whoever composed these epitaphs had a sense of the family's historical importance. More than elegant turns of phrase or stylistic motifs, he has opted to insert biographical details into his texts, emphasizing also the preeminence of the family patriarch R. Asher, whose shining attributes were exemplified in the lives of his sons. I begin with the epitaph for Judah's second wife, Miriam, daughter of his older brother Solomon (Shadal's epitaph no. 3 = Cantera no. 76).

Miriam's identity is refracted through her husband's, and she is chiefly recalled for her wifely virtues. Her epitaph opens with praise for a "gracious woman" (*eshet hen*) whose industry and modesty brought honor to her household. The epitaph consists of nineteen lines, short bursts of unmetered verse that achieve poetic weight by means of rhyme and syntactical anaphora. The rhyme pattern (*aaa bb cc dd eee ff g h ii j*) is irregular but dominated by couplets. The first rhyming triplet emphasizes the deceased's energetic virtue with a string of active and transitive verbs: this "gracious woman" attained [virtue], set [table], poured [wine]. The second tercet links this activity to its chief beneficiary, her husband, Judah, and, by extension, the people; the lines rhyme *te'udah, Yehudah, Yehudah* (the Law, the territory, the people/man). Between the two tercets, three couplets inform us that this woman was humble and modestly veiled. She is "Madam Miriam," daughter of Solomon ben haRosh and wife of his brother Judah, who illumined the mysteries of the Torah until God's wrath fell upon the community. As the husband's honor was reflected in the modest concealment of his wife, now his shame is revealed with his people's uncovering.[66] The double echo of "Judah" points to the husband as well as the eponymous nation. Plague has come to punish a straying people, and the diligent Madam Miriam has preceded her husband to find a secure resting place. In the final couplet, the husband journeys to a front-row seat in paradise while the wife accompanies him faithfully. The epitaph ends with a rabbinic proverb, "the wife of a friend is accounted a friend."[67]

In his will, Judah ben haRosh recommended to his sons that they marry in the family. He married his brothers' wives, he explained, because they had been raised among scholars and were familiar with the rigors of scholarly life: these women knew how to care for their husbands without making undue demands.[68] These are, in fact, the attributes that the epitaph celebrates in Miriam, honoring her personal stature and reputation for piety. The concluding proverb derives from a discussion of whether one must stand in the presence of a scholar's wife, just as would be done in the presence of her husband. The Talmud argues in favor of extending to the spouse the gesture of respect accorded to the scholar. Ironically, a medieval debate over whether this principle derived from Written or Oral Law (Torah or rabbinic custom) had already drawn the Rosh's attention. According to Miriam's grandfather and father-in-law, the precept was rabbinic and lacked scriptural authority. Does this undercut the final compliment bestowed upon her by the inscription on her tomb? Or is it a straightforward acknowledgment by men (both as mourners and as later readers) that this woman's labors on behalf of their teacher and friend had earned her respect as their friend as well? The reader must decide.

Judah's will and testament, an ethical will that included a family history, autobiography, and advice to his sons, were drawn up in November 1342; an addendum dealing with practical distribution of his assets and a trust fund for his descendants is dated a month prior to his death. The ethical will mentions the early death of one son.[69] The plague would take two of Judah and Miriam's remaining four children: Hayim and the eldest son, Solomon. Hayim died on the nineteenth of Sivan (June 6), in the same month as his mother. He was fourteen and presumably living under his parents' roof. Four lines survive of his epitaph; either the fuller inscription was illegible to the copyist, or this was all that was written. Despite its brevity, this epitaph ignored the rapidly emerging topoi of the genre. Hayim's father is described with an abbreviated honorific, ה"הר (H"HR), perhaps "the exalted sage" (He-hakham HaRam) or "the brilliant and exalted" (Ha-muvhaq veHaRam), since similar formulations are spelled out in other epitaphs. Since the meaning is not certain, I have left it untranslated. The entire text reads:

> He died in the storm at the age of fourteen
> Reb Hayim son of H"HR Rabbi Judah ben haRosh, may his memory be a
>   blessing
> On the nineteenth of Sivan in the year LIFE IS HIS [= [5]109]
> He ascended to the light in the Light of life.[70]

One other plague epitaph also refers to death in a storm, Shadal's no. 44 (= Cantera no. 79), for David son of Joseph ben Nahmias, who died in Tamuz (July–August) "in [the] storm and tempest" of plague that "ravaged the land and left it waste and totally consumed." The storm in question may be metaphorical or an allusion to violent weather conditions (which, in turn, may have been associated with the corrupt air assumed to cause pestilence). In Hayim's case, the numerical value of "LIFE IS HIS" supplies the plague year; the eulogist devised this unique expression to highlight Hayim's name, which means "life." The final pun on the "light of life" also alludes to Hayim.

The epitaph for Hayim's father, Judah ben haRosh, is consistent with the eulogist's preference for emphasizing patriarchal lineage and biography over literary flourishes.[71] Judah's epitaph gives the year of his death, "109," without mentioning the plague. Technically, we cannot be sure that plague was the cause of his death, even though the date falls in the middle of the pandemic. Judah was seventy-nine in 1349, and had lost a wife and child in the preceding weeks; he could have died of many things. However, I include him here as part of the plague group because he died amid these losses and, directly or indirectly, with some relation to them. The epitaph begins in the voice of the memorial stone calling attention to itself:[72]

> I stand as a sign and memorial
> That under me is buried
> The body of the man Judah ben haRosh.[73]

The next four lines are devoted to Judah's father, R. Asher ben Yehiel (the Rosh) and his journey from Ashkenaz to Toledo, after which the text returns abruptly to chronicle Judah's life:

> He married the daughter of his brother Rabbi Yehiel on the eve of Sukkot
>   5066
> After Rosh Hashanah his wife died and was laid in the dust.[74]
> Then he remarried
> The daughter of his brother Rabbi Solomon
> God granted him the people's favor
> So that he held his father's post immediately upon his death
> And for twenty-one years directed the academy of his fathers
> He died on the seventeenth of Tamuz in the year [5]109.[75]

This is plain language. Judah's first marriage is described literally as "after the Day of the Throne, his house came to be buried in the dust / Then he built himself a firm house." The euphemistic use of "house" (*bayit*) for "wife" is rabbinic and barely metaphor for a religious Jew. So, too, the "Day of the Throne" would have been a familiar expression for the New Year, the Day of Judgment (God on His throne). Both expressions are standard rabbinic idioms. Where Judah's eulogist did exert himself was in the epitaph's final few lines, which begin with a proverb and conclude with three loosely connected images:

> A son brings joy to a wise father
> And in his place, the fruit of the righteous will flourish [like] a tree of life[76]
> Let him find shelter and rest in the shade of the God of Israel in whom he
>   trusted and had faith
> And may he rest until he stands in his allotted place at the End of Days.[77]

Judah's work would please his father. His "fruit" (progeny) will flourish like a tree—not any tree, but the tree of life whose fruits bestow immortality upon men. Judah himself will find shade in God—extending the tree imagery—and rest there until he rises at the end of time, a messianic reading of Dan. 12:3. This epitaph tells us how Judah wished to see the long arc of his life. If he did not draft it himself, whoever did compose it was familiar with the autobiographical section of his will, which enlists some of the same phrases.[78] Compared with Sitbona's epitaph, Judah's is prosaic; his distrust for "foreign" knowledge apparently embraced poetry as well as philosophy and science.[79]

Judah's epitaph is followed by a brief epitaph for his nephew, Solomon the son of Jacob. Solomon died in "the year of REST," the term frequently used to indicate the year 5109 (1349), based on the numerical value of the Hebrew word for "rest" (109 = מנוחה). The entire epitaph reads:

> Torah Piety Humility
> The lot and the portion
> Of Solomon son of Jacob ben haRosh, may his memory be a blessing.
> He came to his ancestors in Nisan in the year of REST.[80]

The biblical expression "lot and portion " (חלק ונחלה) appears four times in the Hebrew Bible, always in connection with the Levites, who must be provided for because their role as cultic functionaries deprives them of land. The phrase also appears in Gen. 31:14, where Jacob's wives, Rachel and Leah, complain that their father has failed to provide for them because he is jealous of Jacob's prosperity. Thus the eulogist delicately implies that Solomon son of Jacob ben haRosh was dedicated to religious learning or piety but poor and supported by others.

One final plague epitaph belongs to a member of the Rosh's family who was buried among "the rabbis," a section of the cemetery that also included the Rosh's son, Simon, and Judah the son of the Rosh's son Eliakim.[81] Shadal's epitaph no. 42 mourns Judah ben haRosh's eldest son, Solomon, who died on the fifteenth of Av (July 29) in 1349, after his parents and brother Hayim.[82] From a literary perspective, the text is richer than others commemorating family members who died of plague. It begins with a reference to the stone that originally bore the inscription:

> Touchstone and precious hewn stone
> A beautiful crown and glorious diadem
> For beneath it is buried the sapling of understanding and wisdom
> The branch of the tree of knowledge and cunning
> The most splendid among young men
> Who walked in the way of his Lord and ever applied himself
> To read the laws and ordinances and precepts
> He is Rabbi Solomon, may he rest in paradise.[83]

The opening lines gesture to the granite marker that stands like a crown over Solomon's grave, a young man distinguished by his love of learning. The text consists of rhyming, unmetered couplets, perhaps better described as rhymed prose. As we have already seen in several of the family epitaphs, the middle section is dedicated to the father of the deceased, here R. Judah ben haRosh, "the sage, the great rabbi, the breath of our nostrils, the star of our dawns, the light of our eyelids, chief among the exiles of Ariel."[84] And since R. Judah is the son of R. Asher the Rosh, this must also be noted. The text then turns back to Solomon, concluding:

> He died of the plague on the fifteenth of Av in the year of REST
> He went up from his territory
> To see the beauty of the Lord and to visit God's Temple in His heavenly
>   heights.[85]

The first line, describing Solomon's "ascent" to heaven from earth, cites 1 Sam. 6:9, a biblical plague account, and perhaps reminds the mourners of the altitude of the burial ground;[86] the second line alludes to Ps. 27:4, where the psalmist asks that he be permitted to dwell in God's House forever, beholding "the beauty of the Lord" and seeking His Temple.

To summarize, these epitaphs are relatively plain by comparison with others in the corpus. The prose is stolid, and the encomia emphasize piety and zeal for religious law. The group demonstrates the tight cohesion of the Rosh's family and the centrality that he held in their lives—mimetically represented by his centrality in the longer epitaphs. The unmetered texts make sparing use of rhyme and frequently conclude with a biblical verse or rabbinic proverb that either uses the name of the deceased or celebrates him or her for a particular virtue. How different this sternly pious approach was from that of other elite Toledo Jews may be glimpsed in the epitaph for Sitbona. To draw the distinction more sharply, I look at two more examples. One is the epitaph for young Joseph son of Reb Meir Abulafia, who died of the plague shortly after his marriage, at the age of fifteen. The second is for a later victim, Joseph haLevi Abulafia, who died in October–November 1350.

Joseph son of Reb Meir Abulafia haMerari, Shadal No. 17 (= Cantera No. 66)

> Who are you here, O groom,
> Who has built an eternal dwelling place?
> Behold you are shut in the cleft of the rock
> Why did you hasten to leave
> With the woman you loved?[87]

The composer of this epitaph has left us a poignant lament for a young man's untimely death. The text opens with a direct address to the dead youth. The burial stone does not gesture to itself ("here I stand," "beneath this stone is buried," or some such expression) but is gestured to by the speaker, who asks the dead man why he is shut up in the rock of his tomb. We learn immediately that the recently married Joseph died with his young wife. The introductory verses rhyme *aaabbcc*, where the *b* rhyme is an internal rhyme mimetically "burying" the youth in the "buried" rhyme of the verse: *ve-hinkha 'atzur beniqrat hatzur.* The epitaph continues with another tercet leading to couplets, unmetered but built on grammatical stress patterns that create a rhythmic effect. We have already seen this technique of playing rhyming tercets off couplets, where triple rhymes inaugurate a section of text. In this epitaph, a second tercet introduces a new thematic section, in which the deceased Joseph tells us his story.

> I am the man
> Who has seen desolation and destruction
> Blood and pestilence
> The days of my youth were cut short
> Suddenly, in the prime of my life,
> Young and tender in years,
> Evil, unending illnesses snatched me away. (vv. 6–12)[88]

The dead youth tells us that he was cut down in the prime of youth amid great devastation. In quick succession, he alludes to Lam. 3:1, and then to Isaiah's and Jeremiah's evocations of "desolation and destruction" (*shod ve-shever*). The allusion to Jer. 48:3, describing the destruction of Moab, specifically refers to the wailing of the kingdom's youth. The cause of this man's death was a harsh and lasting illness—here the poet cites Deut. 28:59, in which God threatens to punish Israelite disobedience with conquest, famine, and sicknesses that are "evil and unending." The medieval commentators Rashi, Ibn Ezra, and Rashbam gloss the odd expression as referring to "plagues" that have not been seen before and that do not go away, readings that surely resonated for this epitaph's readers.

The dead boy describes his fate. Illness and pain drove him to abandon home and inheritance, including his recent bride. His abandoned "house" is described in the words of Jer. 12:7, where God's destruction falls upon livestock and land; his desolate household echoes Jeremiah 44, where God threatens the Israelites in Egypt with sword, famine, and plague that will annihilate young and old. The youth laments that he was struck down before he had any heir "to inherit from me and recall my name / among my people" (v. 23). Instead, he must recall himself:

> It is I who must say, here I am!
> And let the one who hears what befell me have pity on me
> Joseph son of Reb Meir, may his rest be honorable, known as Abulafia
>   haMerari
> That is my name forever and this is my memorial. (vv. 25–28)[89]

Joseph belonged to the prominent Abulafia dynasty, although his particular identity, as he feared, has been lost to time.[90] He describes himself as "haMerari," referring to one of the sons of the biblical Levi (Exod.6:16) but perhaps intended for its lexical association with bitterness.[91] Joseph's plea to be remembered bares the reciprocity of the bond between the mourners and the mourned. It was a bond that would be succeeded over time by a reciprocity less raw but still powerfully linking the worlds of living and dead, first in the pilgrimage of family and friends who knew the deceased, and later in the visits from those who never had but who might earn a connection as they circled and read. Elliot Horowitz has noted the queasiness of religious authorities confronted with cemetery practices that seemed to encourage praying *to* the dead. In his words, "the channels between the living and the dead could never be hermetically sealed," and Horowitz traces an intractable belief in the power of the dead to intercede on behalf of the living.[92] Even Judah ben haRosh, he observes, referred in his will to visiting the graves of the *tsaddikim* (righteous ones), where he offered a prayer that he passes on to his children—a prayer that Horowitz describes as "cautiously worded," to avoid the outright impression that the dead are being asked to do something on his behalf.[93]

In contrast, Joseph's epitaph reminds us that the dead also needed help. Plaintively, the dead young man beseeches his visitors to pray for him. Not only has he no children to fulfill this solemn task, but his father must have predeceased him, too; when the epitaph swivels finally to the trope of parental grief, only Joseph's mother appears, a mother "afflicted and distraught," bitterly weeping and alone. The biblical subtexts stretch finely from the opening through this final section of the text to embrace the figure of the grieving mother, a kind of pièta whose image must have been familiar in the streets of Toledo. "Distraught and desolate" comes from Isa. 54:11, where it refers to the feminized image of the people Israel, "afflicted and distraught and unconsoled." But the second half of the verse is God's promise to set carbuncles as their "building stones" and sapphires as their foundation, a corollary promise that the reader would have understood to be signified materially in the chiseled stone before him. The disconsolate mother who has lost her son Joseph has "sent off" her daughters before him, so that she remains alone. Shadal thought that the poet referred to daughters who must have married and left the home, and Cantera supposed that they were dead. We will never know who was correct; the terrible image of the solitary, grieving mother is what lingers. She is, moreover, "bereft and barren," in the words of Isa. 49:21, another biblical promise that lost children shall be restored. In 1349, that was a promise that demanded superhuman faith.

Several themes, all of them reinforced by an artful web of biblical prooftexts, elevate this text beyond its affecting surface narrative. Some of these prooftexts allude to biblical stories in which plague befell the Israelites in punishment for their sins. Other prooftexts, primarily from Jeremiah and Isaiah, describe devastation and plague that have wrought destruction on agricultural land and livestock as well as humans; depopulated city and countryside; and are accompanied by famine. Many of these biblical verses also locate this devastation in Egypt, a rich and bounteous land to which Israelites have fled in search of security and wealth. Together, these subtexts offer a commentary on the pandemic that violently stripped young Joseph of his future and life. They "make sense" of the plague as a rebuke to the laxity of Jewish life in a comfortable exile, a punishment for straying from the path laid out for them of old. Some of the contours of their punishment correspond to those suggested by the documents assembled by Cabrillon, Callico, and others—neglected land and livestock, food shortages, and famine. What the gap was between the death of Joseph son of Meir and the composition of this epitaph is impossible to say, but if the stone was not erected until the following year, some of the economic and environmental impacts of the plague would have been amply in evidence. Others had been a fact of life in the years preceding the pandemic.

Equally important is that the author of this epitaph wrote fluidly and well, tapping old and new conventions to bring to life the voice of a young man whose real life had abruptly ended. The simple lines, the shift from the opening tercets to effortless couplets, the careful insertion of the date and cause of death, pose a stark contrast to the angular, tense prose of the Rosh family compositions. Yet even among the wealthy and cultured Jews to whom the Rosh struggled to sell his version of religious piety, it was possible to believe that the plague was a rebuke for the worldliness of their lives. That view was not the sole possession of some mythical "popular" stratum of Jewish society, as if only the uneducated feared God's wrath in the wake of devastation. Very few men and women who lived through the plague years of 1348–50 were willing to dismiss the role of an almighty and angry God in unleashing it upon them. Even physicians were reluctant to abandon this view, as seen in Chapter 3. (The sole Toledo epitaph from the epidemic of 1361–62 invokes this belief, too.)

But, again, how many of the hallmark features of this epitaph are new? Beyond the dating conventions, the answer is that they are not new at all. For instance, as noted in the beginning of this chapter, Shadal's epitaph no. 27 also memorializes a young son and grieving parent. In this case, the young man, Judah ben Nahmias, was twenty-seven years old—hardly a child, and yet depicted through his father's eyes as:

His youngest son and delight of his eyes
The most beloved among children
Young in years
Greater than elders in understanding.[94]
The father bewails his loss:
I am the man who has seen affliction
For I shall go down mourning to Sheol to my son
To make my tomb beside him while I live,
For when my time shall come.

And so the father spoke in bitterness of heart
My son my son
Wait until my turn comes
Rest in sweet sleep
Your father will come see you
My tomb beside your tomb
In the grave I have dug for myself.[95]

The epitaph concludes with the anticipated details of name and date: Judah son of Moses ben Nahmias died on the twenty-second of Tevet 5000 (= 1240 C.E.). The family is one of the old elite families of Jewish Castile; several of its fourteenth-century members are documented among the plague epitaphs. The pathos of the inscription, with the overpowering image of Judah's grief-stricken father, summons familiar biblical prooftexts from Lam. 3:1 (the same verse put into the mouth of young Joseph son of Reb Meir), Gen. 37:35, and 2 Sam. 19:1. The Genesis passage describes Jacob mourning at the falsely reported death of his youngest son, Joseph, while the 2 Samuel context is that of King David mourning his beloved son

Absalom. In Judah ben Nahmias's epitaph, the father's speech also directs the reader's attention to the physical placement of a family plot, with two tombs side by side. The formulation "my tomb beside your tomb" (*ve-etzel qevuratkha qevurati*) finds an alliterative response in the "tomb" and "hewn" that follow (*be-qivri asher kariti li*). The former expression plays on the loyal Naomi's words to her mother-in-law in the book of Ruth (Ruth 1:16), inverted now so that the parent must follow the child. The sentimentality in Judah's thirteenth-century epitaph, like the artful mix of poetry and prooftext, are echoed in the epitaph written a century later for Meir's son Joseph. In other words, the memorialist for the plague victim felt no need to invent new ways to commemorate the dead; nor did he seem to struggle with the idioms at his disposal. Minimally, this suggests that the catastrophe represented by the Black Death in Castile in 1349 was not perceived in the cataclysmic terms that found expression to the east. Or perhaps, we might equally say that the death of a child is its own cataclysm, and the scale of surrounding catastrophe has nothing to do with it.

Joseph haLevi, Son of Rabbi Solomon haLevi al-Lauwee Abulafia, Shadal No. 22 (= Cantera No. 91)

To further illustrate my point that the poetic conventions utilized in the Toledo epitaphs are conventions of continuity more than rupture, let me conclude our sample with an inscription from the tail end of the pandemic, Marheshvan 5111 (= October–November 1350). The deceased was Joseph haLevi, son of R. Solomon haLevi of the al-Lauwee Abulafia family. Joseph died in Seville, a long way from Toledo, but was brought home for burial. The route between Toledo and Seville—the respective capitals of Old and New Castile—was well trafficked, and Jewish courtier-bankers acting as diplomats or financiers, as well as Jewish physicians, would have found it a familiar journey. Another brief plague epitaph from this collection commemorates a young physician from the famed Sasson (or Shushan) family who also died "on the border of Seville" at the age of twenty-five.[96] Seville, an early frontier city of the Reconquest, had grown to rival Castile in prominence. Interestingly, it had its own Jewish burial ground, but it must have been important to these Toledo families to bring their loved ones home.[97]

Joseph haLevi performed some diplomatic function for the king. The opening lines of his epitaph, with their motifs of aromatic spices and compounds, may hint that he had some medical training. The lines also gesture to the physical tombstone: Joseph is buried in a northern plot—invoking Gen. 33:13—stirred by a breeze that wafts perfumed scents over his grave. The stone marker is hewn from a "helping stone," used by women in childbirth but also referring to the biblical site Even haEzer, encountered in 1 Sam. 5:1 and 7:12. Under the stone lies Joseph, who is described in a long series of encomia and paired attributes. These are followed by a series of parallel constructs that etymologically, homophonically, or thematically bind subject and verb, so that, for example, "Privilege is privileged" or "honor is graced."

This long middle section constitutes the bulk of the epitaph. The rhetorical pairs have no biblical source, although the use of personified pairs appears throughout Hebrew Scripture, and a popular late antique hymn enlists just this technique and may have echoed in the writer's mind.[98] The medieval author felt free to compose a series of these doublets untethered to sacred text. The passage reads:

> Lineage and rank are his stewards
> Humility and Greatness his merchants. . . .
> Generosity is glorified
> And Humility resplendent
> Splendor is evident
> And Honor is graced
> Aptitude and Deed take pride.
> How can a book contain his praise? (vv. 8–18)[99]

The contrast with the Rosh family epitaphs is striking: where the Rosh family epitaphs emphasize genealogy over self-promotion, and biographical data over elegant encomia, the epitaph before us does the opposite. Its interest in historical fact is minimal: Joseph's epitaph includes his name, his father's name, and the date and place of his death. The year is spelled קטב, whose numerical value is [5]111, meaning "pestilence" or "destruction." The epitaph's concluding verse incorporates the name of the deceased, here "in Joseph's tent" (Ps. 78:67). It is an eerie allusion, as Psalm 78 contains a lengthy recounting of biblical history, seen as repeated cycles of Israelite straying and divine punishment, culminating with the election of David as king. The eulogist may simply have wished to signify Joseph's final resting place, or he may have read the verse like Rashi, who glossed "tent of Joseph" as Shiloh in the hills of Ramatah, hence an allusion to the rocky ascent to the grave.

What might we know of Joseph b. Meir when we completed circling his tomb? We would know his name and family and that he had risen to prominence as one of the elite courtier Jews who served the Castilian king. We would know that he died in Seville, perhaps on a diplomatic or medical mission, and that his body was returned to Toledo for a distinguished burial. We could, moreover, recognize that his family wished to eulogize him in language characterized by rhetorical grace, style, and a sustained tension between poetic license and sacred tether. Certainly, the cultured milieu of an old Sephardic family has shaped this text and the way contemporary readers were supposed to respond to it. The same courtly tone characterizes the stately epitaph for Madam Sitbona, whose gender and widowed status encouraged the writer to stress personal virtue more than aristocratic tastes. In contrast, a sterner vision of what constituted good living—and death—speaks to us from the plague epitaphs belonging to family members of the Rosh. Yet in their own way, the writers of these inscriptions also recognized conventions of the genre and adapted them for their clients and needs.

Significantly, there is very little indication that the nearly thirty epitaphs commemorating plague deaths of 1349–50 felt a need to break with received conventions as they are represented among the other inscriptions preserved by the anonymous copyist. Likewise, there is little suggestion that the formal expressions of mourning and praise underwent any evolution as the plague continued to rage. In this context, it is useful to conclude with a look at the sole epitaph preserved in this collection that memorializes a victim of the next plague outbreak in 1361–62. The dark tone of this epitaph is a product of its biblical allusions, which create a subtext of disease and suffering and imply a divine source for the plague that ended a physician's life. The result is not so much a startling divergence from the 1349–50 epitaphs as a reprise of their plaintive elegance in a minor key. Shadal's epitaph no. 37 (= Cantera no. 96) is for Joseph son of Abraham Makhir. From its very first words, the text echoes the biblical Job describing his lamentable physical degradation to his friends and begging them to comfort him instead of accusing him. Job's wish that his words might be engraved in iron for eternity open Joseph's epitaph, followed by allusions to the finely wrought metalwork of the priestly ephod, and the psalmist's wry and weary assurance that the rich die as well as the poor, despite their wealth and property. The reference to the finely engraved work of the priestly ephod was also exploited by the writer of Shadal's epitaph no. 37 (= Cantera no. 96), for Joseph son of Reb Abraham ben Makhir. The writer of the 1362 epitaph twists the meaning of the verse from Ps. 49:12 to have the dead man wish for his "names" to be read "across the lands"—I think a wish for the engraved text to be legible from afar:[100]

> If only my words might be written
> Carved forever in stone
> Engraved in fine relief
> So that their names are legible across the lands (vv. 1–4)

Joseph,a physician, was a faithful practitioner. A " jar of manna" and a "balm of Gilead" allude to medical learning that he had acquired from his father, Abraham, also a physician, and would hopefully pass on to future generations. The epitaph thus nods to a dynastic legacy—as indeed it was, for the Makhir physicians were known from their origins in Montpellier prior to the 1306 expulsion. This passage constitutes the core of the text, which then gives Joseph's full name and the date of his death (in the month of Kislev 5122 = December 1362). Joseph was "gathered to his people" (Num. 27:13), and "departed from his place" (Jer. 4:7), to "go up on the way to his own land" (1 Sam. 6:9) to God's heavenly Temple. As we have seen in earlier examples, the phrases suggest a procession and journey that the deceased must complete on his own. But in this case, the terse formulas carry other meanings: the brief citation from Numbers alludes to Moses' inability to enter the Promised Land, the clipped allusion to Jeremiah 4 comes in the context of a ravaging "lion" (for Jeremiah, the king of Babylonia) who will descend from the north and lay the land waste, and the final phrase from 1 Samuel 6 is taken from a description of a plague outbreak that has befallen the Philistines for having taken the Israelite Ark. The Philistines send the Ark back on the road toward their Israelite enemies, reasoning that "if it goes up on the way to its own land," the plague that they are suffering must be an act of God. If the Ark veers and travels in another direction, the plague was merely due to "chance." By tapping these allusions, the writer elegantly eulogizes the dead Joseph, while managing to allude to suffering and illness, perhaps in the line of duty, and death by plague that was explicable only as an act of God. The same idiom, in fact, appeared in one of the earlier epitaphs, Shadal's no. 57 (= Cantera no. 86), for R. Meir son of Abraham ben Sasson, who may also have been a physician and was certainly a high-ranking Jew in his community. Even the concluding image of the dead Joseph ascending the road to God's Temple alludes, so Rashi tells us, to King David at the end of his life. Taken together, the tautly phrased verses seem grimmer than the exemplars from 1349–50. Of the two phrases found in earlier texts, the description of the finely wrought engraving on the tomb was attested among the pious Rosh family epitaphs; the other expression ("jar of manna") was arguably a conventional accolade for a physician. Neither carryover, in other words, marks continuity of a theological doctrine or a valorized moral attribute beyond that of continued respect for the prominent dynasties of Jewish physicians. Here, however, the physician's fate is analogized to Job's, both in terms of a progressively debilitating and disfiguring illness and an ultimate recognition that his condition is divinely ordained. As a source for comparison, one epitaph is not much to go on, and certainly some of our earlier epitaphs made one or both of these points. At the same time, there is a weariness to the consolations proffered by the later eulogist that may suggest a grimmer epidemiological and social context to his text—speculation, to be sure, but worth considering.

Generally, the range of imagery and narrative formats in the Toledo epitaphs was wider than those found among recently excavated tombstones in Würzburg, which remind us more of the austere piety found in the epitaphs for Judah ben haRosh and his kin. The Toledo epitaphs also maintain their individuality and elegance even as they grapple with multiple deaths among families and friends—perhaps an indication that the mortality levels in the city were lower than those found elsewhere. Here, too, the paucity of 1362 epitaphs may suggest that this second plague wave struck the community harder and with greater disruption to commemorative institutions. In the 1349–50 epitaphs, the preservation of biographical details is sometimes meager and may reflect some lack of information among survivors pressed by crisis and sorrow. Nonetheless, the production of graceful epitaphs that express a range of religious and cultural outlooks, the traces of ritual processions and customs that presume regular access to the Jewish cemetery, and an ongoing connection to those who are dead— all these things testify less to physical and psychological shattering and rupture than they do to resilience and a presumption that life and the living resume and go on. Significantly, not a single one of the Toledo plague epitaphs commemorates a victim of anti-Jewish violence.

In Aragon and Catalonia, in contrast, the Black Death was inseparable from the experience of devastating violence, so much so that the memory of violence would outweigh that of the plague. We turn to that story in Chapter 5. It is hard to say what etched this moment so lightly in Castilian Jewish memory— the milder impact of the pandemic, the later shock of violence in 1391 and the early fifteenth century, or a combination of these and other factors. But it is worth noting that among the exiles from Spain who would scatter across Europe, North Africa, and the New World, it was the Castilians whose identity and memory would come to be identified with the world of "Sepharad." The hegemonic stamp of Castile on postexilic Iberian identities meant that after 1492, the narratives, voices, and traumas of other Iberian communities would be buried under the ruins of Castilian Jewish history. I will return to these thoughts in conclusion.

Chapter 5

Bones and Poems: Perpetrators and Victims

> You have seen how difficult it is to decipher the script with one's eyes,
> but our man deciphers it with his wounds.
> —Kafka, "In the Penal Colony"

> E si quisieres saber el mi nombre abierto
> Sépas que Mosé Azàn me llaman por cierto
> Vecino de Tàrrega, un pequeño lugar
> Et de mui nobles gentes et omes de prestar
> Et es noble lugar, ordinado e puesto
> Et poblado de mucho ome limpio e honesto.
> —Moses Nathan

TÀRREGA IS A small town of 16,500 people, approximately seventy miles due west of Barcelona, about an hour and a half by car. Medieval travelers knew the route, which also passed through Cervera, seven miles before reaching Tàrrega, and continued on to Lleida. The medieval town, far smaller in population, outstripped its modern descendant in importance.[1] Linking the fertile Ebro Valley to the coast, Tàrrega was on the route used by shepherds and their flocks migrating annually from their summer pastures in the Pyrenees to their winter homes outside Tarragona. By the late thirteenth century, the town was an important source of royal revenues and centrally located for weekly markets and fairs.[2] In the mid-fourteenth century, it was governed by a Consell General consisting of three or four *paers*, a Consell Particular (ten *prohoms*, or councillors), and heads of household. In theory, this arrangement afforded representation to all "hands" or classes of citizens, although in practice a small number of wealthy, powerful families dominated the *paers* and local politics. A royal deputy or mayor, the *batlle*, was Tàrrega's chief officer.[3]

As for its Jewish residents, the Tàrrega *aljama* (the legal designation for the community) was not particularly venerable. There are no documentary references to it prior to 1278, but it remarkably survived the pogroms of 1391, when its Jews were not attacked. The community first achieved independent status as an *aljama* in 1325.[4] It was governed by a council constituted to mirror its municipal counterpart: a maximum of fifteen councillors represented the upper, middle, and lower "hands" of the community, and these councillors elected two or three leaders.[5] In the first half of the fourteenth century, the period of its greatest prosperity, the Jewish community counted several hundred men and women. Some were of notable wealth and others considerably less so, but they had their own Jewish quarter, or *call*, a bakery, and a cemetery, the last located outside the city walls, approximately 900 meters from the Jewish quarter. During the 1340s, the community was still growing and had begun work on a new synagogue.[6] At mid-century, despite challenges of climate and economy, the community was doing well.

In the summer of 1348, the same medieval roads that carried humans, sheep, and merchandise transported plague-bearing fleas. Along with the fleas, the roads carried rumors blaming the pestilence on the Jews. Beginning with Barcelona on May 17, Jewish communities to the west were savagely attacked. In many cases, municipal authorities acted to stem the violence, sometimes more successfully than others. In Tàrrega, they did not. According to a contemporary Jewish chronicle, the death toll reached three hundred—a figure that may be inflated but that preserves a local sense of shock. It was, in fact, the worst outbreak of plague-inspired violence in Iberia. This chapter reexamines the sources from Tàrrega to explore and refine the representations of Jewish victims and Christian perpetrators.

The chief Hebrew source for this incident comes from Hayim Galipapa, in nearby Huesca, who described the uprisings against the Jews of Cervera, Solsona, and Tàrrega. As an independent text, Hayim's chronicle disappeared, but a copy must have made its way to Italy, perhaps with Spanish exiles of 1492. There, Joseph haCohen excerpted Galipapa's narrative in his own better-known chronicle of Jewish persecutions, the *Emeq haBakha*, and again in his history of Jewish communities under European and Ottoman monarchs. This account has been analyzed by Tzafrir Barzilay, who juxtaposed the two versions to extract Galipapa's narrative.[7] Supplementing Galipapa's account, historians have mined the royal archives and correspondence, which include a recapitulation of the attack by survivors in two documents, the first a petition to Pere III of Catalonia (also known as Pere IV of Aragon) seeking restitution for damages, and the second a set of intra-communal regulations adopted by a consortium of

Catalonian *aljamas* in 1354.[8] Other royal records shed spotty but illuminating light on the dramatic events of the summer.[9] Local archives have been more erratically exploited and, in the case of Tàrrega, contain critical gaps.[10] In 2007, the written sources were augmented by the discovery of six communal grave pits containing the remains of Jewish victims. Finally, at least one Jewish survivor of the attack, the financier and writer Moses Nathan, composed a lament that I believe responds to this incident. The survival of a traditional liturgical lament fittingly returns us to the themes and preoccupations of Chapters 1 and 2 and provides a useful means of concluding while circling back to earlier concerns.

This chapter looks at these old and new sources to focus on the impact of violence on Jewish survivors and Christian perpetrators. Both groups prove to be complex, though that complexity is often suppressed by the conventions of the literature that represents them. Disaggregation of the Christian attackers opens the door to asking—even if there are ultimately no answers—about perpetrator trauma in the wake of the assault, a subject alien to most considerations of medieval anti-Jewish violence. Surprisingly, as Moses Nathan's commemorative lament illustrates, the resilience of literary conventions and psychological tropes for responding to tragedy attests to the resilience of those who wrote and used them. The combined blows of plague and violence did not fundamentally alter the worldview of Christians or Jews in Tàrrega: the ways people sought to make sense of what had happened to them remained pretty much the same before and after the pandemic. I conclude with a return to this study's overarching questions of commemoration, catastrophe, and plague.

*   *   *

General studies of the Black Death in Aragon map the progress of the plague from east to west along the route from Girona to Barcelona, Cervera, Tàrrega, Lleida, and then moving northwest through towns like Solsona, Monzón, and Barbastro, all of which experienced attacks on their Jews.[11] These studies conclude that the plague struck hard in Catalonia, although not entirely evenly, its impact exacerbated by drought, famine, and civil war. In Barcelona, the *call* was attacked on May 17, leaving nineteen dead and causing extensive damage. Alarmed, King Pere III in July ordered reinforcements of the battered *aljama* and punishment of those who had participated in the attack. On May 29, the king sent letters to the governors to the west, ordering them to protect Jewish lives and property.[12] But as the plague spread westward, so did the violence. In Cervera, municipal authorities averted tragedy, sheltering frantic Jews in a castle;

as a result, although the quarter was attacked, there were few casualties. In Tàrrega, a vicious assault on the *call* took place in early July, on the tenth of the Jewish month of Av.[13] When news of the uprisings reached the king, he wrote urgently to the municipal authorities in Lleida to protect their Jews. This command was futile, as Lleida and its Jewish satellite neighborhoods were also attacked.[14] According to the 1349 petition later submitted by local Jews, "certain individuals" in Tàrrega incited "the people" to break down the gates to the *call* with axes and other arms, after which the mob proceeded to vent its wrath. With a cry of "death to the traitors!" (*Muyren los traydors*), they entered Jewish homes with "spears, stones, and arrows" (*lanceis, lapidibus, et sagitis*), looting property, as well as shredding and burning financial accounts:

> Et plures judeos ipsius aljame inaniter occiderunt et quosdam alios atrociter percusserunt et etiam vulnerarunt et plura alia dampna gravia et immensa, injurias, ofensas, raubarias molestias et violentias ipsis judies fecurunt.

> And they senselessly murdered many Jews in this community, and others were beaten mercilessly and were wounded, and they inflicted many terrible evils, grave injuries, offenses, robberies, harms, and atrocities on these Jews.[15]

Hayim Galipapa, in nearby Huesca, recalled the attack succinctly:

> ויקומו גם יושבי טאריגה ויכו ביהודים ואבד יותר משלוש מאות נפש ויסחבום אל בור רק ובביזה שלחו את ידם. והנשארים ברחו לנפשם אל בית מכיריהם במתן בסתר עד עבור הזעם וישארו ערומים מכל קנינם ולא יתבוששו ביום הנמהר ההוא.

> And the people of Tàrrega also rose up and struck their Jews, and more than three hundred souls were lost. They dragged them to an empty cistern and looted their goods. Those who survived fled for their lives to the homes of (Christian) acquaintances and stayed hidden until the fury had passed. On that rash day, they were left naked (stripped) of all they owned but without shame.[16]

Chancery documents repeat the estimate of three hundred casualties, which may incorporate the tolls of neighboring towns.[17] The king's designated prosecutor, Gilabert de Corbera, was appointed a month after the attacks, and authorized to punish the perpetrators of anti-Jewish violence in Barcelona, Cervera, Tàrrega, and Lleida. Gilabert rapidly found himself stymied: he imprisoned the *batlle*, Francesc Aguiló, without bail, and sentenced Ramon Folquet, from a powerful merchant family, to a stiff fine and two-year exile.[18] A few exemplary penalties were meted out on participants with fewer connections.[19] By the next summer, Francesc's case was under appeal. Ramon's sentence was reduced in March 1350 to time served and his 5,000-sous fine reduced, with an extended term for payment.[20] Another powerful local, Berenguer de Corteilles, was released on bond when his 1,000-sous fine was fronted by a local physician.[21] The murder of a Targarin Jew in 1349 further infuriated the representatives of the Jewish *aljamas*, who complained of Gilabert's inaction. After six months at his post, Gilabert was recalled by the king and replaced with another investigator, Atarn de Tallarn.[22] Not long afterward, in 1350, Francesc Aguiló, Ramon Folquet, and, indeed, the entire city (*tota la universitat*) received a remission for their crimes. The city was fined 20,000 sous and ordered to rebuild the *aljama*. Most of the money was never paid.[23]

With exquisite patience, Josep Muntané has combed the records to reconstitute the backdrop to the 1348 assault on the Tàrrega *call*. Why was this particular attack characterized by a level of viciousness and brutality surpassing that of other towns? What was the meaning of the mob's rallying cry, *Muyren los traydors* ("Death to the traitors")?[24] Perhaps most important, why, in other nearby towns like Cervera, did local authorities act to protect their Jews while in Tàrrega they turned against them? Muntané traces a complex web of decisions, policies, and developments that deepened the rift between Tàrrega's Christian and Jewish populations. Both segments of the city were thriving in the early fourteenth century, as evidenced in a number of ambitious public-works projects and a reorganization of the municipal government that relegated power to the *paers* and *prohoms*. By the first half of the fourteenth century, if surrounding towns are representative, the *aljama* may have accounted for 5 percent of the town's population.[25] Accompanying this boom, however, were signs of tension. The Jewish cemetery was vandalized, and the *call* (or its gate) was stoned on Holy Week. At the same time, municipal debt was mounting, its finances increasingly entangled with those of the *aljama*. The powerful families that constituted Tàrrega's general council were personal borrowers on Jewish credit. The poor harvests and civil warfare that characterized the 1330s and early 1340s and aggravated debt are attested in a series of suits and countersuits between mighty Christian borrowers and Jewish brokers. The brothers Moses and Solomon Nathan appear frequently in the Consell accounts of 1342–44 as the target of Christian accusations of usurious interest rates and pleas for renegotiated terms of repayment. The Consell acknowledged its ballooning debt, desperation, and resentment in other ways, too, investigating the *aljama* for concealing assets; prohibiting Jews (and pimps, prostitutes, and lepers) from touching bread, fruit, or meat products in the market; and compelling Jewish butchers to sell meat at lower prices than their Christian counterparts.[26]

The period of 1347–48 was also one of political turmoil, and much of this territory was in open revolt against the king. In 1347, the king had removed his brother James, the powerful count of Urgell, from his position as procurator for the region. In defiance, Count James based himself in Lleida, a stronghold of rebel support.[27] According to Muntané, David Nirenberg's claim that all the anti-Jewish attacks during the plague took place in royal towns, where antiroyalist sentiment ran high, is not entirely accurate but generally true. Still, he notes, this cannot be the sole explanation for the ensuing brutality, as Jewish lending was hardly restricted to royal townships.[28] The plague itself exacted a frightening toll in the area, affecting local governments and the daily operation of courts, hospitals, cemeteries, farmland, and businesses. Jewish and Christian interests were thus deeply intertwined and increasingly at odds in the years leading up to the Black Death. Simultaneously, royal policies that guaranteed Jewish protection and privilege accelerated the growing severance of Jewish prosperity and life from municipal control. The same factors that had spurred growth in the city were now, ironically, fueling the bifurcation of two communities that had previously coexisted, or had at least shared a perception of their interdependence. The more the *aljama* sought protection from the king, or the king sought to protect his income from the *aljama*, the less the municipality had access to its wealth in the form of taxation or constraints on lending.[29] As the municipality struggled with soaring taxation and debt, that lack of control rankled more.

*   *   *

In the immediate aftermath of the assault, those survivors who could fled for nearby towns; they are documented over the next decade in Cervera, Balaguer, Lleida, and as far away as Barcelona. The fact that they surface in the records is already an indication that these were men of means—or had been, as, along with life and limb, one of the goals of the Tàrrega attack was the destruction of Jewish ledger books and debt records. Subsequent to the tragic events of the summer, we find these survivors scrambling to collect loans for which they have no paperwork, a failed undertaking even with several royal interventions and assistance in documenting outstanding debt.[30] All of this scrambling was done from afar, in contrast to the situation in Barcelona, where survivors of the May attack on the *aljama* filed their petitions in that city. Clearly an atmosphere of fear persisted. That the

Targarin Jewish memory of the July assault lingered long and deeply is attested by the apprehension that characterizes a letter written by some of their representatives when the plague returned in 1362. Recalling the terrible events of 1348, the Jews of Tàrrega appealed to the king to protect them lest they should again prove vulnerable to their enemies.[31] Fear is also evident in the trouble the city had in persuading survivors to return or new Jewish immigrants to settle there. Surribas Camps's genealogical reconstruction documents a number of marriages between the daughters of survivors and men of other cities. This may not have been out of the ordinary and may represent a desire to reinvigorate family holdings with exogamous ties. Alternatively, the spike in marriage arrangements that reached beyond the remnants of the community may hint that young women who were exposed to shame or assault were more marriageable beyond the arena of violence.[32] In sum, the evidence for lingering Jewish trauma is abundant even in records whose primary motive is not to preserve it.

Christian memory also endured—not in the key of remorse, however, so much as in a rankling resentment that the bloody outburst against the Jews was still being held against them. Thus, Muntané reconstructs the clash over the gallows erected outside the town for the exemplary executions of a few Tàrrega Christians who were condemned for participation in the attacks. Although the condemned seem to have been singled out more because they lacked the wealth or political connections of higher-ranking suspects than because of spectacular acts of brutality, the towering gallows on which they concluded their earthly lives served as a daily reminder of the reach of royal wrath. Significantly, Pere III promised the Jews that those gallows would stand as a memorial forever.

"Forever" lasted not quite six years. In early 1354, the king acceded to a request from municipal officers in Tàrrega that the gallows be removed.[33] For the ruling class, apparently, it was not the memory of inciting and perpetrating a massacre that was traumatic but the memory of subsequent humiliation and punishment. The sources do not say whether this attitude ran down the social ladder to the "people" who had been stirred to or tolerated frenzied acts of violence. The tendency to paint the punished with one brush may have been a political convenience, but it distorts social reality. Galipapa's account of the episode explicitly notes that some Christians sheltered Jews, and the size of the Christian town makes it improbable that all Targarins, whatever their sympathies, physically participated in the attacks.[34] Tàrrega was a town of 2,500 to 6,000 people, of whom some three hundred were Jews. If the sixty-nine occupants of the mass graves are a low-end estimate of the casualties, how many men, at most, could have killed them? Using Galipapa's high-end figure of three hundred casualties, the attacking forces could not have numbered into the thousands. Studies of modern intercommunal violence note that perpetrators of mass killings tend to outnumber their victims greatly, in part to reinforce a sense of corporate complicity that shields individual perpetrators from prosecution or even guilt.[35] Even so, many Targarins, as the same case studies suggest, probably opted to stay safely in their homes.[36] This does not mean that they were sympathetic to the Jews. It does mean that a significant percentage of the town's population did not actively participate in killing. Many were sick or dying; they were struggling with their own woes.

Muntané's careful parsing of the archival records convincingly elicits different groups among the attackers: a few men of power, like the mayor, Francesc Aguiló, and the municipal *paers* and *prohoms*; a generic "populace" whom these leaders are described as inciting; and an insignificant handful of outsiders from Cervera and elsewhere, convenient for later scapegoating but inconsequential in terms of numbers or influence. References to these groups in official documents are augmented by levies of fines and ascriptions of guilt to *tota la universitat de la vila*, a corporate assignment of guilt with weighty financial consequences for the town.[37] The defiance of Aguiló and his men is evident. Muntané emphasizes the striking coincidence of the fact that the city's notarial records are missing for 1344–61—most of the recent scholarship has relied on royal archives—a gap that cannot entirely be explained by disruptions caused by the Black Death. Rather, Muntané suspects that the implication of ruling families and officers in the inquests following the assault motivated a willful destruction of those documents by someone in power.[38]

In 2007, a story built on documentary traces acquired a material witness. That year, a team of archaeologists commenced excavating a site slated for construction of a new housing development in Tàrrega. Irrigation work several decades earlier had already unearthed graves in the area, and new construction in 2000 disclosed more of them. Ironically, the human remains were initially assumed to belong to victims of the Spanish Civil War, and they were quietly reburied in the municipal cemetery. Despite what would turn out to be a five-hundred-year error, the discovery earned the zone protection as a site of potential historical value. When new remains were uncovered in 2006, a team of historians and archaeologists was assembled to investigate what they suspected was the location of Tàrrega's medieval Jewish cemetery.[39]

From February through the summer of 2007, at the site known as Les Roquetes, archaeologists excavated 158 individual graves and six communal burial pits containing the remains of at least sixty-nine individuals, many bearing signs of lethal trauma. Included in the communal graves were a variety of personal objects ranging from coins, amulets, and utensils to pottery, buttons, buckles, a thimble, and jewelry, including a ring with a Hebrew inscription. The coins permitted a firmer dating of the remains to the mid-fourteenth century, and the historians concluded that the occupants of the communal graves were the victims of the 1348 assault.[40]

Tàrrega lies in the province of Lleida. When notified of the finds, Lleida officials duly contacted the umbrella organization for Lleida's present-day Jewish community, known as Tarbut Sefarad de Lleida. Tarbut Sefarad de Lleida had no objection to letting the archaeologists continue their work, asking only that the remains be reinterred after they had been studied. As word of the excavation spread, however, Jewish institutional voices from Barcelona and farther afield voiced their own opinions. The Barcelona-based Commission for Jewish Heritage in Catalonia, founded in 2006, represented several Jewish constituencies of liberal to Orthodox affiliation. Their leadership turned to a group called Zakhor, a relatively recent arrival on the Jewish organizational stage, with some relationship to Spain's progressive congregation, ATID. These groups moved swiftly to pressure the Catalonian government to halt the excavation.[41] By the end of May 2007, ATID had also joined forces with the Lubavitch center of Barcelona and approached local officials in Tàrrega as well as the Director General for Cultural Heritage, soon expanding its reach to the Catalonian Department of Cultural and Communications Media. These groups demanded an immediate halt to the excavation, which posed the threat of "irreversible damage to the burial ground and an offense to the Jewish communities of this country."[42] Jewish tradition and law should govern the fate of the dead, they felt, and the ancient cemeteries were witnesses to a Jewish "historical memory" that transcended that of Tàrrega; they should be considered sacred ground.[43] None of the American Jewish experts who advised the Barcelona Commission for Jewish Heritage had historical or professional ties to the area, but they invoked transhistorical Jewish interests in making their claims.[44] Later, the archaeologists would challenge that transhistorical construct:

> [T]he claim by some groups of exclusive rights over the "ancient dead" raises
> legal, ethical, and scientific questions. Can the norms that regulate the
> current funerary practices of a religious group prevail over the general law
> that regulates the scientific study of archaeological remains from seven
> centuries ago? Do the convictions of a community suffice to demand that
> knowledge be sacrificed against the general rights? Can a minority prohibit a

whole nation access to its past? Nowadays, do the Catalan Jews, without any family links to the victims of 1348, have any "particular right" over these ancient deaths? In contrast, would it not be better for the "rights" of possible descendants of the converts who remained in Tàrrega after the edict of expulsion in 1492 to prevail, currently unaware of their Jewish origins but potentially linked, from the genealogic point of view, to the defunct in the Jewish necropolis of Les Roquetes?[45]

By late June, representatives from the Jewish groups began showing up at the excavation site to disrupt the archaeologists at work. An emergency meeting convened in late July elicited a new complaint from the Federation of Jewish Communities in Spain, alleging that the archaeologists were failing to handle the human remains properly.[46] On July 27, the Department of Culture ordered the return of remains that had been transferred to the Autonomous University of Barcelona for study. Before the archaeologists had time to react, the remains were removed for burial to the modern cemetery of Collserola, outside Barce-lona.[47] The archaeologists filed their own complaint, while the Jewish commu-nity seems to have been divided; a sense of their disenfranchisement from the "solution" purportedly negotiated on their behalf comes through the sources.[48] Ultimately, the Department of Culture softened its stand to permit the excava-tion to proceed through the end of the year. In the meantime, the victims of the 1348 assault on the Tàrrega *aljama*, after a brief return from the repressed mem-ory of Spaniards and Jews, descended into darkness again. During the brief time that they found themselves unexpectedly among the living, the dead of Tàrrega tried to tell us about themselves and the neighbors who killed them. The re-mainder of this chapter seeks to recover their voices.[49]

*   *   *

Trauma theorists often speak of a human triad of victims, perpetrators, and by-standers or witnesses. Those whose perspective and categories are drawn from humanitarianism or human rights theory sometimes add the category of benefi-ciary, whether in the form of later generations who have benefited from past in-justice that they themselves deplore, or as the class of readers or listeners whose empathic identification with the victim's narrative provides a moral "benefit" relative to others.[50] In many cases, the categories of perpetrator and victim are an unstable binary: perpetrators are also witnesses, and, in certain contexts, they are victims.[51] As Riera i Sans observed in his study of anti-Jewish violence associated with the Pastoureaux bands crossing Provence and Aragon in 1320, neither the perpetrators nor the victims of that violence were monolithic blocs; the former included urban nobility and officials as well as rural "shepherds," each faction with its own history of grievances against royalty and Jews. The Jewish victims, for their part, were also divided by class and access to privilege and power. For Jews and Christians—in the markets, fairs, fields, or court-rooms, as physicians and patients, lenders and debtors, midwives and wet nurses, craftsmen and neighbors—interaction was a fact of daily life.[52] At the same time, local tensions were also real, and conflicts could be and sometimes were rendered in the affective language of sacred history and symbols that high-lighted identification with prior suffering or traumatic violence.

So, too, traumatic events do not affect all victims equally, not only because each human being is different, but also by virtue of the cumulative experiences that have shaped them prior to a catastrophic encounter and the resources avail-able to them in its aftermath. Unfortunately, the psychological literature, which is reflected in popular usage, often tends to assume that terrible events have a universal and predictable impact upon all those who experience them. At the same time, the medical and psychological definitions of "trauma" have largely evolved from a focus on individual sufferers. This has made it difficult to draw on the classic theory for situations of collective trauma, and in general, the at-tempt to shift from individual to collective models has been unsatisfactory and theoretically weak. In contrast, some of the psychological literature has rejected the emphasis on event-based trauma (assuming that "trauma" is the inevitable consequence of exposure to a singularly shocking event) as well as the emphasis on Western idioms of distress that emphasize psychological disorder at the ex-pense of political and social context. These authors can be helpful in looking at medieval settings and asking about the repercussions of social violence and how communities sought to cope with them.[53]

For sociologists, anthropologists, and political scientists, who are interested in the behavior of groups, the parallel corrective to overgeneralization has been an emphasis on the "micro" in studies of ethnic and communal violence. Perhaps it is fair to say that where the psychological literature looks at the aftereffects of vio-lence, these other disciplines seek to illuminate the preconditions to its eruption as well as the shape of post-violence equilibrium. Local memory and history shape perpetrators, victims, and bystanders, none of whom is a passive tool of outside influences and forces, but each of whom inherits a worldview and cultural idioms that are continuously tested against daily reality and adapted for use. Local mem-ory can loom large in times of stress. Many of the same Jewish communities that experienced attacks during the Black Death had also been terrorized by the Pastoureaux nearly thirty years earlier. Some may have remembered the experience. One of the victims whose remains were unearthed in the Tàrrega excavations, labeled UE 1215, suffered a particularly brutal assault: the forensic study tallied twenty-two traumatic lesions to this individual, a dozen to the head and ten to the lower extremities. One injury had long preceded the injuries that killed him, a blow to the leg that had improperly healed and left him lame. Notably, excavations in Valencia, where mass Jewish graves have been uncovered and where many of the remains testify to violent death, document the same phenomenon: approximately 2 percent of the individuals studied in Valencia bore traces of earlier violence as well.[54] These individuals could have been injured in any number of ways. But among the possibilities, Pastoureaux violence is a real option, meaning that some percentage of Jewish victims in 1348 had lived with the memory of an earlier episode of violence. Was that an enduring trauma? If so, what kinds of memory or distress persisted among their attackers? For surely, if even a small percentage of victims had survived the Pastoureaux attacks of 1320, the perpetrators may have counted a few men or women who had witnessed or participated in that earlier assault. This possibility, too, may add some depth and complexity to their ranks.

*   *   *

In their own language, the bones of Tàrrega tell a story. The forensic analysis of the traumatic injuries to the skeletal remains points to weapon types that range from stones and axes to swords—swords that would not have been the possessions of the simple commoners or "rabble" described by some of the sources. The account preserved by the gashes and fractures to the bones is one in which fleeing men, women, and children were either struck down by blows to the legs and finished off with multiple head wounds, or struck down from above, perhaps from horseback, by blows to the head, and then repeatedly struck in the head and legs. The mayor, Francesc Aguiló, and his men may have been among the crowd, perhaps dealing the initial blows: only they would have had the swords whose traces remain on the bones of the victims. An ax handle through the head was a contribution from further down the social ladder.[55] If the *batlle* and his friends felt no regret or fear at what they had unleashed, there is little way to know if the same was true for those common men and women who committed most of the violence and then contemplated the deadly results. However, studies of ethnic, religious, and genocidal violence increasingly reject the notion of a small and cunning elite inciting blind obedience among the masses. Local actors also pursue their own agenda, "that may have little to do with communal antipathies per se."[56] An emphasis on local agency likewise undermines the argument that violence between groups was inevitable because of essentialist, enduring characteristics of those groups. What victims and perpetrators perceive as eternal marks of difference may surface in the performance of traditional, religious, or mythic "scripts" that are enlisted in moments of conflict.[57] So, too, the widespread nature of the violence in Tàrrega, as well as the subsequent condemnation of *tota la universitat de la vila*, suggests that deliberately or by happenstance, the slaughter linked bystanders to actual perpetrators of violence in corporate complicity.

The emphasis on local agency also usefully reminds us that from top to bottom, the Christians of Tàrrega—those who participated in the murder of Jews, those who were bystanders, those who were neutral, and those few who actively resisted—made individual decisions and had individual reactions in the immediate and long-term aftermath of the attack. Alas, the documentary record is not constructed to preserve them. What the documents do preserve is the king's fury and the subsequent difficulty that royal officials had in prosecuting those responsible, some indication that local sympathy for the attackers was strong (or fear of their retribution). Nonetheless, although royal power may have been too slow to save the *aljama*, it eventually bore down heavily. This is evident in the municipality's struggle to comply with royal demands despite ongoing hardships, in the surly back-and-forth over the iconic gallows, and in the absence of subsequent attacks against Targarin Jews.

In Cervera, the assertion that outsiders had instigated most of the violence appears to have had some truth, and there the town authorities followed royal orders and sheltered Jews within the castle. But in Tàrrega, leaders of the violence were precisely the men who had been charged with protecting the Jews; they were men of authority, from powerful families. In Tàrrega's defense, they, too, were recovering from the devastation wrought by a combination of plague, civil war, and years of drought and poor harvest. Were they sorry for having murdered their Jews? Muntané notes that in the years after the Black Death, the city hired Jewish physicians and dutifully encouraged Jewish settlement.[58] Does the absence of subsequent (collective) violence against Tàrrega's Jews, even in 1391 when such violence was ubiquitous, argue that they had learned tolerance? I suspect that it is unlikely. Caution, certainly, and a wary sense of self-preservation. Shame also counted—not merely the shame that lingered in the smoldering ruins of the *aljama* but the shame that squirms with ritual, judicial, and social humiliation. From the perspective of Tàrrega's elite, moreover, violence had failed to deter

further royal incursions, even if it had temporarily harnessed disaffected elements at home. From a psychological perspective, it is harder to say what lingering impact the summer episode had. If nightmares or insomnia, intrusive
memories, emotional outbursts, or strange physical symptoms—the suffering of
the perpetrator—had unusual currency, no one thought to record this.

At least, not intentionally. The remains of their victims speak of things that
the textual record could not or would not put into words.[59] I return, then, to the
language of the bones.

*   *   *

The Tàrrega excavation uncovered approximately 150 individual and six communal graves.[60] Due to the topographical constraints of the dig and the hasty conclusion of their work, the full extent of the medieval cemetery could not be excavated;
additional burial pits and graves may remain unidentified.[61] References to the Jewish cemetery in Tàrrega date only to the early fourteenth century, although some
of the individual graves reflect older burial practices. The communal graves, which
are at the western end of the burial ground, do not reflect normative Jewish practice; the mere presence of these graves indicates that extreme circumstances characterized death, burial, or both. This assumption is reinforced by the awkward
shape of the graves, which are generally quite cramped along the head-to-toe axis,
so that bodies were often bent to fit the contours of the space.[62] The smallest of the
communal pits, FS 54, yielded the remains of at least five individuals; the largest,
FS 164, contained at least twenty-five. Two pits, FS 161 and FS 163, yielding ten and
eight individuals, respectively, may have once constituted a single grave. Together,
the six communal graves unearthed in 2007 contained some sixty-nine individuals ranging in age from a perinatal infant to adults in their sixties. The majority of
the remains (67 percent) belonged to adults. Some 32 percent were identified as
"subadult," meaning under the age of twenty. The age of the remaining 1 percent
was unidentifiable. Of the sixty-nine individuals, 31 percent were male, 50 percent
female, and 19 percent of indeterminate sex.

Anna Colet and her fellow archaeologists emphasize that these sixty-nine individuals were buried with care. In conformity with Jewish practice, they are ori-
ented so that their heads are at the west and their feet at the east, and caution was
exercised to avoid the overlapping of bodies. Thus it seems likely that these Jews
were buried by other Jews, who were anxious to observe ritual requirements while
working with some haste.[63] The studies also distinguish between primary and secondary deposits, both documented in the communal graves.[64]

Like communal burials, secondary burials are highly unusual in Judaism, and these examples are characterized by greater disarticulation as a result of decomposition prior to reburial. We recall Hayim Galipapa's description of the dead being dragged to a cistern or tank. This could have been done by fellow Jews or by their attackers, although it is hard to imagine the terrified survivors emerging to perform this task. The plague was also raging. Medical and sanitary concerns might have recommended removal of the bodies from open air, especially in the heat of summer. (Recall that medical theory explained plague as a result of corruption of the air, a condition that could be aggravated by putrefaction.)[65] Alternatively, callousness and cruelty could have motivated the unceremonious disposal of the dead. In either case, the relatively damp interior of a cistern or pit would have accelerated decomposition. By the time survivors returned to bury the dead, perhaps accompanied by representatives of the communities that had harbored them, the bodies would have decomposed considerably. Many of the skeletal remains were found with flexed arms and legs, suggesting that they were carried and hoisted into place.[66] Describing a similar phenomenon in Valencia, Matías Calvo Gálvez has speculated that at least two men would have transported the bodies to their new burial site, probably by means of a stretcher. Either the dead were tied at the wrists and feet to facilitate their transfer, or lifted under the arms and by the feet and swung into their graves.[67]

There is more evidence that the dead were buried hastily and in unusual circumstances. Jewish burial practice calls for the body to be garbed only in a shroud and unaccompanied by personal possessions. Yet these individuals were clothed at the time of burial, and a fascinating trove of objects was recovered with their remains, including coins and buttons, buckles and jewelry, a thimble, and the cover of a decorative box.[68] The coins, which helped to date the remains, were found clustered near parts of a body where they may have once rested in a pouch or purse. Amulets accompanied the remains of one small child found in FS 163, which Colet calls the "most peculiar" of all the common graves because of its punishing shape and the high degree of disarticulation among its eight occupants. The skeletal analysis of the child, UE 1185, revealed a malformation in his legs that explains his mother's bid for supernatural protection.[69] Bits of pottery, nails, a key, and a knife also tell a story of death that came unexpectedly and was followed by a delayed burial that did not observe all proprieties.

As visible from the photographs, many of the victims lack feet, particularly in graves FS 161, FS 54, and FS 162. There is no evidence of amputation prior to or at the time of death, and all the examples belong to skeletons that were fully extended in their graves. Individuals whose legs were flexed still retain their feet.

The archaeologists have suggested various possibilities, from a desire to recycle footwear in a time of scarcity; the need to fit decomposed bodies into the straitened formation of the pit; or an act of post-burial malice. In the first case, it is difficult to imagine why either looters or survivors would salvage shoes but not clothing and jewelry items. In the second case, it is difficult to imagine Jewish survivors who otherwise demonstrate concern for burial rites but were willing to profane the bodies of the dead. For the third case, Colet and her colleagues reject the possibility of more recent acts of vandalism to wonder if sometime after reburial, Christians deliberately removed the feet of the dead as a symbolic way of hobbling their journey to the afterworld. In this context, we may recall the common trope found in the Toledo epitaphs that depicts the path or road taken by the dead.[70] If their Christian neighbors shared this belief in a path between worlds, such a profanation would be especially vengeful, a sign that over the interval between the murder of these Jews and their reburial, their tempers had not cooled.[71]

Even more telling are the signs of violence on the bones themselves. The overall pattern suggests not only the ferocity of the attackers but the indiscriminate nature of the attack. Thirty-seven of the sixty-nine individuals found in the communal graves bear marks of traumatic violence: ten children and twenty-seven adults; twelve males, fifteen females, ten of indeterminate sex. Those remains that do not bear the signs of traumatic violence may still have been its victims, but felled by injuries to organs and soft tissue.[72] For the thirty-seven, 155 bone lesions were tallied, all of them visible to the naked eye.[73] Of that sum, 105 were cranial blows, one was to the spine, eleven to the arms, and thirty-eight to the legs. Several Tàrrega victims had limbs amputated, one was killed by a blunt instrument, and another's skull had been crushed by a heavy object (perhaps a stone, as the petition described); in one startling case, mentioned earlier, an ax or sword handle penetrated the skull with such force that the rectangular outline of the handle cleanly cut through the bone. There are two decapitations: one ended the life of the individual tagged UE 1221, a young woman twenty to twenty-five years of age.[74] UE 1221's head was severed at the second cervical vertebra by a heavy blow to the back of her neck; her skull retains the marks of six cranial blows, and she was felled by a blow to the legs. UE 1221 was positioned in the exact center of FS 164, one of the larger communal graves and never completely excavated. The section of the grave that was exposed contained the remains of at least twenty-five individuals and a cache of buttons, coins, and nails, one of which served as a bolt or key, possibly to a chest or strongbox. Signs of violence are visible on twenty-three of the twenty-five individuals.

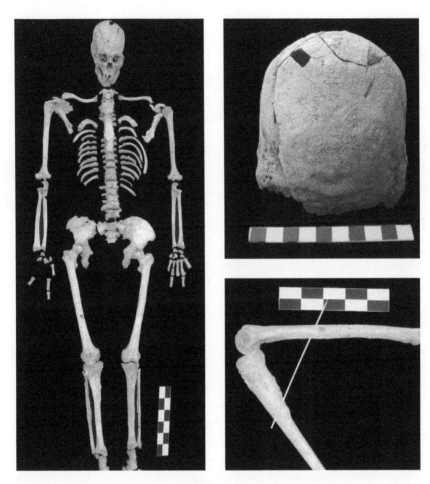

FIGURE 3. The remains of UE 1215, with details of the skull and leg, at the site of the medieval Jewish cemetery in Les Roquetes, Tàrrega. Courtesy of the Museu Comarcal de l'Urgell-Tàrrega.

This grave also contains the remains of UE 1215, the adult male with twenty-two traumatic lesions, twelve to the head and ten to the legs, including one old leg injury that left him lame. UE 1215's age has been estimated between thirty and thirty-five, and the osteomyelitis caused by his earlier injury is often associated with juvenile bones.[75] Thus it is possible—there is no way to know for sure—that UE 1215 was the victim of an earlier assault when he was a child, perhaps when the Pastoureaux passed through the region. Whatever the cause of his childhood injury, he was unable to flee his pursuers in 1348 and was vulnerable

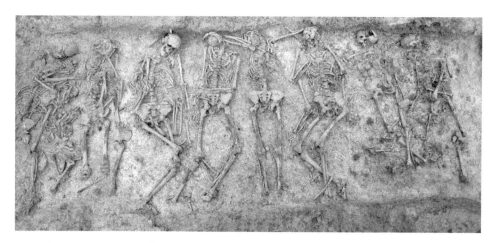

FIGURE 4. Communal grave FS 164 at the site of the medieval Jewish cemetery in Les Roquetes, Tàrrega. Note the remains of the young adult woman, UE 1221, in the center with her arms outstretched. Courtesy of the Museu Comarcal de l'Urgell-Tàrrega.

to their wrath. Perhaps his pursuers were particularly interested in targeting him. After all, how does a lame man earn a living? Perhaps lending money or keeping accounts. But if that is the case, how to explain UE 1221? Was she a moneylender also, whose clients knew deserved to lose her head? For that matter, another occupant of FS 164 is a little girl estimated to be about six. This child, UE 1200, was felled by nine cranial injuries and one blow to the legs. Indeed, FS 164 contains the remains of a number of small children, with violence writ large upon nearly every one. Why did they merit special fury? As for UE 1215, who was lamed in his youth: maybe after all, he was a tailor or a scribe. Other victims who appear to have been young and robust may have been sick with plague, which would have weakened them considerably.

The desire to diversify the dead and render them as individuals may be especially modern, or Western, but it is also hard to resist. In the same communal resting place, FS 164, a handful of coins lay among the remains of UE 1141, an adult male, who may have been carrying them in a pouch or purse at the time of his death. A nail or clasp for the money pouch was found with them. EU 1211 and EU 1201, respectively male and female, were wearing clothes with brass buttons; the clothing disintegrated, but the buttons still remain. Another individual, of indeterminate sex, was wearing a slender copper ring engraved with an eight-leaved flower. A thimble was among the bodies buried in FS 164, worn or carried by its owner when death surprised her. Each tiny object makes its claim to an owner and to the shared biography of human and material things. In the archaeologists' photographs, UE 1221, the young decapitated woman, lies in the center of FS 164, her arms raised above her head as if hovering protectively over the adult skeletons to her right and left. Did she know them? Were they family? Did the buriers try to group families or friends? The awkward angle of the woman's arms has been explained by the theory that she and others like her must have been hoisted into the grave. Nonetheless, when considered with the spectacular brutality of her death, the woman's centrality and gesture of protectiveness seem purposeful—an illusion, but eerie.

The same distribution of lesions found at Tàrrega characterizes the only other known communal Jewish burial associated with plague violence: in Valencia, where 30 percent of the forty individuals uncovered showed signs of lethal traumatic injury, 76.3 percent cranial and 23.4 percent to the extremities. As in Tàrrega, the victims were buried clothed, so that a variety of objects—a ring, nails, ceramics, and coins—were found with them. However, the Valencia victims also testify to violence that targeted adult males, not to the indiscriminate fury of the Tàrrega attack, and they were buried in atypical positions, so that their bones would later mingle, in a north-south orientation, contrary to Jewish law.[76] The infliction of mortal blows in Valencia was executed with a variety of sharp, cutting instruments and an up-down motion that led Matías Calvo Gálvez to posit a scenario in which the victims were either knocked to the ground and then attacked from above, or struck from above by men on horseback. (The options are not exclusive.)[77] Based upon the blade diameter, type, and force of blow, the Valencia and Tàrrega studies insist that some wounds were inflicted by swords—hardly a commoner's weapon.

Thus, we have additional proof that the instigators of the attacks were not lowly ruffians, artisans, or peasants but men of higher social standing, men who had horses and swords. It would be easy to conclude that these men were responsible for what followed, inciting others to a bloodthirsty frenzy, men who also had sharp implements in abundance, blunter but wielded with "energy and skill."[78] However, as studies of ethnic violence have concluded, "the picture of receptive masses whipped up by an unscrupulous leader is not quite true to life."[79] Local factors and local ties matter, a sense that violence will be tolerated and bring some gain. So, too, a sense of existential threat, even an apocalyptic threat, is common to all the cases—and what else was the plague? At the same time, even though many studies of modern violence invoke this theme, it is unwise to characterize the perpetrators as a mob of disaffected and angry young men. In her study of the Rwandan genocide, Lee Ann Fujii has powerfully documented that most of the low-level participants in violent attacks were "ordinary members of their communities," adult men who were married with children.[80] For the most part, these men were not even aware of the "extremist ideas that elites propagated" about their Tutsi neighbors. Jan Gross makes a similar point in his study of anti-Jewish violence in Jedwabne, Poland, during World War II.[81]

The weapons that have left their mark on these remains further disaggregate the perpetrators. The attackers came with axes, lances, stones, and arrows, as grimly transcribed from the 1349 petition submitted by stunned remnants of the *aljama* to the king.[82] The blows that delivered death to Tàrrega's Jews indicate a mix of classes: men with swords; men who could wield large knives, axes, or other bladed objects; and men, women, and children who could throw stones and loot houses, tear books, and set fires. The force necessary to slam an ax or a sword handle through UE 1215's skull testifies to the rage of a very strong man. The high percentage of oblique gashes to victims ranging from the age of two into their sixties testifies also, as Muntané emphasizes, to single-minded and murderous intent. One of the archaeological studies even wonders whether the victims' missing feet might have been expertly and posthumously removed by a butcher, someone with the skill to avoid cutting the bone. Butchers, for that matter, were frequently in conflict with their Jewish counterparts, and Tàrrega's butchers were no exception.[83] They worked close to the *call* and perhaps even shared workspace with their Jewish counterparts. Centuries later, it may be that the language of their fury is discerned on these bones.

* * *

The notion that trauma as an experience and as a theoretical concept might metaphorically represent the human condition inflated theoretical sails in the 1990s. It was an argument that capitalized on deconstructive and postmodern foundations to emphasize a dialectic of knowing and not knowing, language and silence, unassimilated drives, experiences, or memories, and their creative evasion or repression. Caruth described trauma as speaking from the wound, the "story of a wound that cries out, that addresses us in the attempt to tell us of a reality or truth that is not otherwise available."[84] The focus of this school of theory is predominantly on the traumatized survivor and her therapeutic redemption through narrative. Of necessity, this approach cannot speak for the dead: trauma theory as a narrative of psychological assault cannot describe their experience.[85] Trauma may or may not characterize the experience of survivors, who display a gamut of responses to catastrophic disease and danger.

In the case of Tàrrega, we can follow a few survivors, most—if not all—of them wealthy and powerful men, occasionally with family. That is true both for survivors among the Christian perpetrators and survivors among their Jewish victims. Among the perpetrators, no sense of remorse or compunction shadows the records of their deeds. The powerful figures whose names Muntané has painstakingly resurrected were defiant before the story began, and their defiance does not seem to have abated quickly. Men like Francesc Aguiló and Ramon Folquet had a history of resisting royal meddling in the town's affairs, and so did the council. The difficulties encountered by the royal procurator point to a degree of solidarity among these men and their peers. The same men had been ratcheting up tensions with the Jewish community for years prior to the appearance of the plague. After the plague and Jews had vanished, their problems still remained. Labor was in short supply throughout Catalonia, wages were high, and government functioned haltingly. Rebuilding the *aljama* incurred new financial obligations that were passed downwards in taxes on basic subsidies. And as if the repeated humiliation of taxation, rebuilding, and repaying Jewish debt were not enough, there were those gallows, which the municipality did not succeed in demolishing until 1354. Muntané has signaled a striking gap in the city's notarial records between 1344–61, a gap that cannot be entirely explained by plague-related disruptions. He argues convincingly for the implication of ruling families in the destruction of these documents.[86] None of these actions signals great regret.

But the royal penalty meted out to the mayor, the *paers*, and *prohoms* of the General Consell included the entire *universitat*—the townspeople as a whole. Like a haze, an aura of corporate complicity surrounds the summer's violence, which unfolded in public view and communal venues and enlisted silence and fear as much as active collaboration. But the indictment was also strategic on the part of the Crown and deliberately obscures distinctions of degree. Some Christians hid and saved Jews during the tumult, a testimony to ties across confessional divides. Some Christians may have been intimidated and afraid; they learned to live with what they had or had not done. What can we say about these men or women of Tàrrega, the butchers and shoemakers, shopkeepers and bakers, the tailors, greengrocers, clerics, students, beggars, and friars? Did they wake up from nightmares or suffer from outbursts of anxiety or rage? Did they forget or remember, repeat or repent? We simply do not know. The longer *durée* also played its part, the devastating cycles of famine and drought, daily violence, corrupt officials, political instability, and chronic war. And then the plague, which came in the summer of 1348, returned less than ten years later, and in irregular intervals after that. From a certain perspective, history stretched out in an endless spiral of human sin and divine punishment, sickness of crops and cattle and humans, sickness in the water, and sickness in the air. The wars of kings and noblemen were part of this sickness, too—Jacme d'Agramont in nearby Lleida singles them out in his plague tract's chapter on moral pestilence. And in Aragon and Catalonia, the kings were not only fighting local noblemen but constantly fighting Muslims while defending the treachery of their Jews.[87]

Unfortunately, what the language of documents enlists and preserves is not the language of private sentiment. Oddly, the situation is similar for the victims, and Moses Nathan is a striking example. Moses was one of a handful of Jewish men of finance whose capital and hence influence stretched across the kingdom. He had family in Barcelona and Cervera as well as in Tàrrega, and his brother, the Targarin financier Solomon Nathan, appears frequently in the archives (often as a result of his conflicts with Christians and Jews).[88] The municipality was mired in debt to him, and the king was among his personal borrowers. Moses was also a man of letters, some of whose writings in Catalan and Hebrew have survived.[89] A curious poem condemning gambling (excluding chess!) has been tentatively attributed to him. A lengthy collection of Moses' didactic proverbs was published by Lonzano in the seventeenth century, with several later reprintings; the bilingual text recently merited a critical edition under the title *Qüestions de vida*, by Josep Muntané. The proverbs were composed prior to the Black Death, around 1341. Seven years later, one wonders if Moses winced to recall the sense of place and pride that had attached him to his home:

> E si quisieres saber el mi nombre abierto
> Sépas que Mosé Azàn me llaman por cierto
> Vecino de Tàrrega, un pequeño lugar
> Et de mui nobles gentes et omes de prestar
> Et es noble lugar, ordinado e puesto
> Et poblado de mucho ome limpio e honesto

> If you wish to know my name
> Know that Moses Azan is what I claim
> From Tàrrega, a little town
> Of very noble people and men of renown
> It is a noble place, tidy and neat
> With clean and honest men replete.[90]

Like other prominent Jews who signed the 1354 accord, Moses never said how he
had managed to escape the frenzied slaughter of July 1348. Most likely, one or more
of his noble Christian friends intervened to help him. Somehow he escaped, first
to Bellpuig and from there to Barcelona.[91] He was in Barcelona for some years,
struggling to collect on unpaid loans without his destroyed account books, and
lobbying on behalf of himself and the shattered *aljama*. According to his own account, he never recovered his wealth, and he spent his final years in poverty.

Moses Nathan also composed liturgical verse. His lament, "Mi gam bakhem,"
was written for inclusion among the laments recited on the Ninth of Av, the
great commemorative fast of Jewish historical tragedies from the Destruction of
the Temple through modern times. In 1348, as noted earlier, the Ninth of Av fell
on a Saturday. Since observance of the Sabbath supersedes a day of mourning,
the fast day was commemorated on the tenth that year—a detail that Hayim
Galipapa remembered because it was the day that the *call* was attacked. "Mi gam
bakhem" survived in several liturgies from Italy and the Comtat Venaissin. One
fifteenth-century Paduan liturgy has squeezed it into the margins of an anthology of laments. A late fourteenth-century Vatican manuscript appends this
hymn and a few others to the text of Lamentations that follows a huge compendium of laments and penitential hymns. The Vatican manuscript was copied in
1389, before the 1391 pogroms that might have displaced it. A third Provençal
example is a miscellany that includes a lexicon for the book of Job and two collections of laments for the Ninth of Av.[92] One of those collections was copied in
the fourteenth century, the other a century later. Moses Nathan's lament found
a home in the fifteenth-century collection.

"Mi gam bakhem" does not overtly mention plague, although it alludes abundantly to the ecological catastrophes that preceded and accompanied it, specifically invoking urban ruin and drought.[93] No irrefutable proof links this text's
composition to 1348. It is possible that it was composed earlier, but that in the
wake of the *call*'s destruction, it was retroactively identified with that event and
enlisted (or believed) to commemorate it.[94] Nonetheless, there are a number of reasons I believe that this hymn was composed in the aftermath of the summer's violence. Its inclusion in an anthology of laments associated with authors from
Aragon and the Midi is one clue that it belonged to the local memory and history
of these Jews. It lacks concrete descriptions of an attack, but Moses could not have
supplied such details even if he had wished to, as he had escaped the slaughter and
did not witness the violence. Moreover, even a lament composed to recall the
1348 tragedy could not have been *recited* for another year, when the great fast day

was marked again. By that time, Moses was in Bellpuig and perhaps inclined to subordinate local detail to evocative generality. Even without that impulse, a list to generality was ubiquitous in Hebrew laments, especially from Iberia. In Ashkenaz, the custom of marking specifics of time and place in commemorative laments appeared early, in the wake of 1096 violence. In contrast, local detail is not a feature of Iberian laments until the late fourteenth century. Thus, for Iberian Jews, whose mythic origins reached to the Roman destruction of Jerusalem, the conflation of ancient and present catastrophe was instinctive. Nonetheless, Moses' lament layers its generic allusions with not-quite-generic details that suggest the traces of recent experience. While the result may not have been memorable as literature, it was memorable as memory and is testimony to the ongoing power of the liturgy to interpret historical tragedy.

Here is the text and my translation. In the Hebrew, the meter is irregular but dominated by five stresses per hemistich, alternating schemes of ten and eleven syllables per line. Counting hemistich rhymes, each stanza rhymes *aA* /*aB* /*aB*. The pattern is suited to antiphonal recitation, with the final *aB* verse of the first stanza possibly serving as a refrain at the end of succeeding stanzas. My translation follows the text, and then my case for this lament's relevance to the Tàrrega attack:[95]

מִי גַם בָּכֶם וְיִסְגּוֹר דְּלָתַיִם / מִי הוּא זֶה לֹא יִזַּל מִדְּלָיָו מַיִם
מִי לֹא יִבְכֶּה עַל שׁוֹד יְרוּשָׁלַם / עִיר עַלִּיזָה הָעִיר רַבָּתִי עָם:
הֵילִילוּ הָהּ וְסִפְקוּ עַל כַּפַּיִם / עַל כֶּתֶם פָּז אֵיכָה זָהָב יוּעַם:

שַׁאֲגַת אַרְיֵה וְקוֹל שַׁחַל שָׁמַעְתִּי / יוֹם מִקְרִיָּה הַמְעֻשִּׁירָה נָסַעְתִּי
הוֹלֵךְ יָחֵף בִּנְתִיבוֹת לֹא יָדַעְתִּי / בְּחוֹסֶר כֹּל בְּרָעָב וּבְצָמָא:
בֵּית תִּפְאַרְתִּי כַּרְמֵי שֶׁלִּי לֹא נָטַרְתִּי / זָרִים אוֹכְלִים אוֹתָהּ וּשְׁמָמָה:

הַשְׁקִיפָה צוּר כִּי מִקְדָּשֶׁךָ הֶחֱרִיבוּ / וּבְטִירוֹתַי מְכוֹן שִׁבְתָּם הִרְחִיבוּ
כָּל מַעְיָן טוֹב וְכָל חֶלְקָה הִכְאִיבוּ / הֵיכְלֵי מֶלֶךְ וְחַדְרֵי מַשְׂכִּיּוֹת
שָׁמוּ עִיִּים הִשְׁחִיתוּ וְהִתְעִיבוּ / מִגְדַּל דָּוִד בָּנוּי לְתַלְפִּיּוֹת

נוֹסַף שֶׁבֶר כִּי אֵין אִישׁ אָן וְאָנָה / יָשִׂים עַל לֵב יוֹם אִישׁ אֶת אָחִיו אָנָה
מָלְאָה מוּטָה קִרְיָה נֶאֱמָנָה, / אֵין דָּן בֵּין דִּין לָדִין בֵּין דָּם לְדָם
וְיָתוֹם לֹא יִשְׁפּוֹט וְרִיב אַלְמָנָה / כִּי פַסּוּ אֱמוּנִים מִבְּנֵי אָדָם

תַּמּוּ סָפוּ יוֹדְעֵי לְרַצוֹתָךְ / גּוֹדְרֵי גֶדֶר מְשִׁיבֵי עֶבְרָתָךְ
שְׁבִי תָּשִׁיב אֶל פִּנַּת יְקָרָתָךְ / אֶל בֵּית אִמִּי וְאֶל חֶדֶר הוֹרָתִי
שׁוּב וַעֲשֵׂה לְמַעַן צִדְקוֹתָיךְ / סְלַח חוֹבִי וְתִמְחוֹל חַטָּאתִי

נַחֲמוּ נַחֲמוּ כִּי עוֹד תִּהְיֶה הָרְוָוחָה / שָׂשׂוֹן יֵסַף וְנָסוּ יָגוֹן וַאֲנָחָה

צֹאן מַרְעִיתִי מֵעִיר וּמִמִּשְׁפָּחָה / אֶסוֹף כִּי מִצִּיוֹן תֵּצֵא תוֹרָה

שִׂישׂוּ אִתָּהּ מָשׂוֹשׂ שָׂשׂוֹן וְשִׂמְחָה / יִמָּצֵא בָהּ תוֹרָה וְקוֹל זִמְרָה

נשלמה

1. If only one of you would shut the doors, whose bucket does not overflow,

2. Who does not weep for the destruction of Jerusalem, the joyous city of multitudes.

3. Wail and beat your hands for the finest gold, how pure gold has dimmed.

4. I heard the lion's roar and the voice of the cub on the day I left the prosperous town

5. Going barefoot on unknown paths, hungry, thirsty, and penniless.

6. I failed to tend my splendid house, my very own vineyard; strangers consumed it and laid it waste.

7. Look, O Rock, for they have destroyed Your Sanctuary, and taken possession of my towers.

8. They have [filled] spring and land [with stones]. The king's palace and his storerooms

9. They have turned into rubble. They have ruined and polluted David's fortress, which was built for defense.

10. The destruction was worse because there was no one anywhere to pay heed when men tormented their brothers.

11. The faithful city was filled with injustice. There was no one to judge between claims or blood.

12. The grievances of orphans and widows were not judged, for trustworthy men were gone.

13. My familiars have ceased supplicating You—those who protect us and turn back Your wrath.

14. Return me from captivity to Your cornerstone, to my mother's house, my parent's room.

15. Do this once more for the sake of Your righteousness: forgive my debt and erase my sin.

16. Take comfort, take comfort, for relief will come. Joy will increase; sorrow and sighing will flee.

17. *"Gather the flock of My pasture from city and kin, for Torah shall come forth from Zion."*

18. Rejoice with her in joy and gladness: in her are found Torah and
   sounds of song.

Notes. 1. *If only one of you*—Mal. 1:10. The prophet wishes that someone would shut the doors to the Temple to prevent abuse of the sacrifices. *Whose bucket does not overflow*—Num. 24:7, from Balaam's prophecy of abundance for Israel but here a metaphor for unstoppable weeping. **2.** Isa. 22:2, 32:13 (alluding to drought and famine). I have transcribed as written, ירושלם; as Naoya Katsumata indicates, it is impossible to insert the extra vowel (*ḥiriq*) for the full spelling, ירושלים, but it must have been pronounced. **3.** Ezek. 30:2; Lam. 2:15, 4:11; Cant. 5:11. **4.** Job 4:10. **5.** *Going barefoot*—the expression is used three times in Isaiah 20 (vv. 2, 3, 4) and once in 2 Sam. 15:30 (David mourning for Absalom). *Unknown paths*—perhaps echoing Isa. 42:16, which, in turn, evokes drought and blight. *Naked and lacking all*—Deut. 28:48, a plague verse. I have translated "lacking all" as "penniless." **6.** Cant. 1:6; Isa. 1:7. **7.** Deut. 26:15. **8.** 2 Kings 3:19—again a context of drought and the revolt of a tribute kingdom. *King's palace*—Prov. 30:28. *And his storerooms*—Ezek. 8:12, where the biblical expression is actually חדרי משכיתו, which Moses alters to משכיות for the rhyme. The Tosafist compilation *Metzudat Zion* glosses the expression as "where they hide the treasure." **9.** Ps. 79:1; Jer. 26:18; Cant. 4:4. **10.** Exod. 2:12, 32:17. The verb *'-n-h*, which I have translated "tormented," can mean to vex, annoy, or cause trouble but also has a strong range of usage referring to commercial deceit or cheating. The echo may be intended to suggest that the Jews were deceived in some way (promised protection?), or that bad business dealings fueled Christian resentment. **11.** Isa. 1:26; Deut. 17:8. *Filled with injustice*—cf. Ezek. 9:9; and thank you to Naoya Katsumata for his comments on this verse. **12.** Isa. 1:23; Ps. 12:2. *Trustworthy men* (אמונים) may refer to the *aljama*'s councillors, called נאמנים. **13.** Ps. 73:19. *Protect us*—literally, those who build fences (גודרי גדר); see Ezek. 22:30. These are the men whose piety may also turn back God's wrath. **14.** *Your cornerstone*—Isa. 28:16. This expression gains interest with the accrued associations of the glosses. Rashi reads the expression to refer to a messianic leader who will be the "cornerstone" of rebuilding. Qimhi (Radaq), however, says that it refers to a king, "who is compared to a large stone ... and cornerstones are made from large stones to support the building." The Tosafist compilation, *Metzudat David*, interprets the expression as a strong foundation stone visible from all sides. The royal analogy might imply that Moses associated rebuilding of the community with an assertion of royal power. *To my mother's house, my parent's room*—Cant. 3:4. **15.** No biblical source, but cf. the very similar verse in Emanuel's lament (Chap. 2): ומחות לחובם והעבר חטאים—"erase their debt and remove [their] sins." **16.** Isa. 40:1; Exod. 8:11; Isa. 35:10. **17.** Ps. 79:13 (the expression "flock of My pasture" also appears elsewhere; cf. Jer. 23:1; Ezek. 34:31; Mic. 4:2. This verse is pronounced by God. **18.** Isa. 66:10. *Joy and gladness*—a common pair (Ps. 51:10; Isa. 51:3, 10, 11, 22:13; Esther 8:17; and more). The expression also appears in the traditional wedding benedictions. It is linked firmly to the use in Isaiah 51, however, by the next phrase, *sounds of song* (literally, sound of song) —Isa. 51:3, where the entire verse describes God's compassion for the ruined city (Zion) and His promise to restore it to Edenic glory.

Moses (or, more technically, the speaker) has had to flee a home ransacked and ruined by strangers, escaping via an unknown route. In stanza 2, the "lion's roar" belongs to the authorities, and the cub is their offspring, perhaps the *paers* and *prohoms*, perhaps the townsfolk. Alternatively, the expression simply describes the rapacious attackers (see Gen. 49:9). The expression "hungry, thirsty, and lacking all" is borrowed from Deut. 28:48, a list of catastrophes that will requite Israelite disobedience—notably, accompanied by plague. This passage is frequently cited in plague tracts.[96] Moses describes the widespread destruction of the place that he called home:

> They have [filled] spring and land [with stones]. The king's palace and his
>   storerooms
> They have turned into rubble. They have ruined and polluted David's
>   fortress, which was built for defense. (vv. 8–9)

The language of 2 Kings 3:19, a tale of drought and rebellion, might easily evoke the rubble of the *aljama* and the defiance of royal authority implicit in the municipality's incitement or endorsement of the attack. The collapse of the built landscape is mimetically captured by the run-on line, which, in turn, taps Ps. 79:1: "The nations have come upon your inheritance, polluted Your holy Temple, turned Jerusalem into rubble." The psalm describes the destruction of Jerusalem, the dead unburied and food for wild beasts. The medieval glosses understood *'iyyim*, an uncommon word, to refer to heaps of stones. The twelfth-century Spanish exegete Abraham Ibn Ezra adds that the word can describe "a place unfit for habitation, or that they dug up Jerusalem looking for hidden wealth." This image, too, is reinforced by the reference to the "king's palace and storerooms," a phrase drawn from Ezek. 8:12 and glossed by the Tosafists as "where they hide the treasure."[97]

Yes, on the surface, Moses laments the destruction of the ancient sanctuary in Jerusalem. But he has selected his allusions cunningly: in 1348, his house was destroyed and so were his ledgers, technically royal "treasure."[98] We know from other cases, too, that valuable pledges like jewelry, books, textiles, and even sacred objects were often seized by rioters; cellars or floors might have been dug up looking for hidden valuables. One of the prize finds in the recent discovery of the medieval Jewish quarter in Regensburg was a cache of several hundred gold coins hidden for safekeeping in one owner's cellar; they had escaped detection for five hundred years.[99]

Moses explicitly condemns the absence of royal authority and justice for the violence. "There was no one anywhere to pay heed," his lament continues, "when men tormented their brothers," and "no one to judge between claims or blood" (vv. 10–11). Coauthored by Moses Nathan, Crescas Solomon, and Judah Eleazar, the 1354 accords commented bitterly, "when they began to cry out in anguish, no one saved them, and those who heard their cries did not come to their aid."[100] Moreover, the Jewish leaders who might be expected to advocate for their people are gone (v. 13), another point that the accords reiterate, bemoaning the loss of those who might have negotiated relief for their communities, now left "like sheep without a shepherd, people like insects with no ruler, like fish caught in a net."[101] The speaker in the lament prays to be restored to his "mother's house and the room of my parent" (Cant. 3:4), yearning for God's "cornerstone" (Isa. 28:16). Rashi understood Isaiah to refer to a messianic return (to the Land of Israel), but for Radaq (David Qimhi), the cornerstone was a metaphor for royal power. Whether Moses specifically intended to embed these associations into his poem is not the point so much as that they were part of the conscious and unconscious baggage that he himself had inherited with the biblical text. When those associations ring frequently enough in a single text—as do these evocations of failed royal power—they must be given weight.

The speaker pleads with God to "forgive my debt and erase my sin." We have seen very similar phrasing elsewhere, in the lament by the poet Emanuel discussed in Chapter 2; Emanuel concluded his poem with a plea to God to "erase their debt and remove [their] sin" (למחות חובם והעבר חטאים). The shared language invokes a shared worldview and perhaps indicates that Emanuel, like the better-documented Moses, was a man of finance as well as a poet. In any event, it was a financial metaphor that might have echoed widely among Moses' peers. Abruptly, a facile promise of consolation concludes the hymn. It, too, envisions restoration in the language of Jerusalem. Surely, like every good Jew, Moses hoped for that city's rebirth. But his verses remind us of Tàrrega, too. Even the clichéd last verse seems deliberate: "Rejoice with her [Jerusalem] in joy and gladness. / In her are found Torah and sounds of song."

The promise of future redemption taps well-known phrases from Deutero-Isaiah and the Psalms. But the final words, a liturgical commonplace, send us to Isa. 51:3, where joy and song mark the rebirth of a city in ruins. Cliché, yes. But as an image of consolation, it was also local and real. Could it have still been composed earlier and acquired its evocative timeliness after the fact? Although this is certainly possible, the concentration and cumulative force of Moses' allusions would be uncanny as well as troublingly prescient for a man who elsewhere found his neighbors so exemplary. There is a better case, I think, for the claim that this lament was written after the devastating events of the summer the plague arrived.

Moses, of course, was lucky, a beneficiary of privilege, good friends, and good health. His lament says something about the experience of shocking violence and mourning as it might be expressed by a public man. As befits his perspective, Moses focuses on the failure of authority and institutions; the loss of home and property; repentance as the path to restoration. The same sentiments characterize his proverbs, written years before the plague. Before and after the catastrophe, Moses remained a king's man, and he continued to turn to royal officials to recuperate what he had lost. So, too, his foes were not necessarily defined by their faith: Christians likely saved him, and not all Jews were his friends. The 1354 accords that Moses helped to author devote considerable space to stifling dissent and "informers" within Jewish communities, suggesting that intra-communal differences characterized Jewish victims in ways commemorative poetry suppresses. A similar conclusion applies to Francesc Aguiló and his friends: violence and plague did not shatter them, and their actions and outlook before and after the plague are essentially unchanged. Perhaps surprisingly, the plague itself figures minimally in their anxieties or concerns, even though its effects were severe.

In sum, what is at stake in this study and what does it add to the picture drawn in the preceding chapters? Most generally, the Tàrrega sources confirm the great variability that characterized the experience of the Black Death in Iberian communities. Both as an epidemiological phenomenon and as a social, cultural, spiritual, and political phenomenon, the impact of the 1348 plague varied across the peninsula. In some regions, mortality was high; in others, it was lower. In some regions, the plague befell communities already struggling with famine and shortages, drought, and civil unrest; in others, the years of famine had been less severe, and the conflicts of kings and noblemen fewer. In Tàrrega, a perfect storm of dreadful possibilities was realized, and the worst of all outcomes—disease and violence—came to pass. The studies by Josep Muntané trace a clear evolution of the burgeoning growth of Tàrrega as a medieval town and the role it played in plans to harness the kingdom's towns and resources—among them the Jews—for royal gain. The "slow violence" of Targarin Christian-Jewish relations is as illuminating as its day of terror, inasmuch as it also highlights the decision of Jewish leaders to align themselves with royal power at the risk of their growing alienation from their neighbors. This was a policy commitment that remained essentially unchanged after the disaster, too, testifying to an intact set of assumptions about survival despite near-annihilation. It would be unfair to imply that Jewish communities had many other options. The long evolution of relations between Crown and town and Jews and long-ingrained patterns of prejudice had acquired their own kind of naturalness; for the Jewish elite especially, fortune and security were intricately dependent upon royal protection. Could Moses Nathan have imagined jettisoning his familiar protectors for the kindness of Francesc Aguiló and his men? Not, at least, in 1348.

The evidence of the bones enriches this picture. Perhaps most important, it allows us to ask about Tàrrega's victims as well as perpetrators, groups we tend to consider monolithically when writing about the Jewish past. Some of the perpetrators were men of rank and power; others were common men or women with their own resentments and agendas. If their blades converged on their victims, their signatures were distinctive, and the archival records confirm that their rewards and punishments varied greatly. So, too, the Jewish victims were not a bloc. Those who died testify to indiscriminate violence, but some of the most privileged escaped. They, too, speak in distinct voices, in chronicles, letters, ordinances, and liturgy. But movingly, they speak of continuity. Some Targarin survivors must have been among the Jewish delegation that returned to the city to rebury the slaughtered victims. A decade later, the municipality would hire a Jewish physician, and slowly the *aljama* returned to life. For its own part, Moses' lament testifies to the ongoing production of liturgical poetry, validating institutions and beliefs that reigned before the plague and continued to find value after it.

Tàrrega's victims cannot be embraced by current theories of trauma, although contemporary theory's preoccupation with perpetrator trauma highlights, by contrast, the lack of attention paid to this category in medieval settings of anti-Jewish violence. But neither the self-perception of the medieval survivors (Jewish or Christian) nor the evidence for their responses suggests that they saw themselves as victims. They may have felt betrayed by powers greater than they, they may have felt chastised by God or by civil or religious authorities. Their world may have been shattered by pestilence, war, famine, and fear. But they did not cease thinking in terms of community and rebirth.

This human complexity rarely features in analyses of medieval anti-Jewish violence. Some of the fault lies with our sources: the literary conventions of medieval chronicles, liturgical laments, or legal judgments prefer two-dimensional portraits of friends and foes. Some of the fault lies with us. When, retrospectively, our sympathies are keenly tuned to the fate of the victims, we do not always probe those conventions deeply. But this focus can flatten readings of the victims and of the men and women who rose and killed them. Even in Tàrrega, a worst-case scenario, where the survivors' literature attests to an experience of unimaginable horror and loss, it does not imply the collapse of their way of making sense. It is important to recognize how much Moses Nathan and his fellow survivors proved resilient. Other men and women may have been more fragile, but their traces do not survive.

Finally, the forms of traditional commemoration whose dearth was the catalyst for this book must have remained viable, too. Moses Nathan's lament, like Emanuel ben Joseph's, testifies to the ongoing production of liturgical poetry of commemoration and consolation. Even more fascinating, perhaps, is the fluidity we can observe in the movement between collective and personal idiom, the way phrases move from verse to legal text to tombstone and to personal inscription with their own forms of resilience and vitality. The individual survivor—male, to be sure, and belonging to an intellectual or political elite—was still willing to describe himself and his loved ones, his home, and his dreams of eternal reward—in the language of communal honor and dignity, order, and meaning. It would take other kinds of blows, recurring waves of plague and violence, new kinds of terror, and heartbreaking loss to render that language inoperable. Strange to say, but in 1348, 1349, and into 1350, even when she came armed with sword as well as sickle, the Black Death did not do it.

Appendix

The Toledo Plague Epitaphs: Translations

THE HEBREW TEXTS of the seventy-six epitaphs from the medieval Jewish cemetery in Toledo have been published several times. Their story and the relevant bibliography appear in Chapter 4, which treats the twenty-eight epitaphs commemorating plague deaths of 1349–50 and one later epitaph from the next plague outbreak, in 1362. Following are my translations of the Toledo plague epitaphs, based on two editions: Shadal (Samuel D. Luzzatto)'s 1841 publication of his friend Joseph Almanzi's copy of the original transcriptions; and the 1956 edition with Spanish translations by Cantera and Millás. Shadal retained the order of the epitaphs in Almanzi's copy, and that is the number I have indicated first. Cantera and Millás reordered the texts; especially because their version is easier to access than Shadal's, I have also indicated their numeration. The full citations for both editions are: F. Cantera and J. M. Millás, *Las inscripciones hebraicas de España* (Madrid: C. Bermejo, 1956); Samuel David Luzzatto, *Avnei zikkaron* (Prague: J. Landau, 1841).

A note on abbreviations: The honorifics that prefix the names of the (male) deceased in the Toledo epitaphs are not so easy to translate. As is suggested by the case of Hayim, the fourteen-year-old grandson of the famed scholar known as the Rosh, the prefix ר cannot intend the scholarly title of "rabbi." Close scrutiny of the entire set of these epitaphs confirms that, as Rami Reiner has shown for epitaph inscriptions in Ashkenaz, the *resh* prefix should be translated as "reb," a lay title of respect like our "Mr." This is not the translation found in Cantera and Millas but I have adopted it here. Compound prefixes pose another problem, which is that the initials may stand for different attributes. This, too, can be confirmed by examining the epitaph collection where occasionally the phrases are spelled out in full. Thus, the prefix ה"הר (H"HR) could be read as הרב המובהק והרם (Harav Hamuvhaq vehaRam, in Shadal's epitaph 18, meaning "the brilliant and exalted rabbi") or הרב החכם (Hehakham HaRav, Shadal's nos.

3, 42, meaning "the sage, the rabbi"). Because a multiplicity of options is available, I am hesitant to select one over the other. In such cases, I have left the acronym transliterated. The reader may refer to the following list of possibilities:

ר' = Reb (Mr.) or, when following honorifics indicating scholarly or
    religious status, Rabbi.

ב'ר = Ben reb (the son of Mr.) (Shadal nos. 1, 15, 17, 29, 30)

בה"ר = Ben haRav (the son of Rabbi) (Shadal no. 5)

ה"הר = Harav Hamuvhaq vehaRam (the brilliant and exalted rabbi);
    or Hehakham HaRav (the sage, the rabbi). (Shadal no. 4)

Finally, regarding בן = Ben (son of), I have sometimes left this word transliterated rather than translated. Where the name is dynastic—Ben Sahwan, for instance, or Ben Sasson, Ben Nahmias, also Ben haRosh—I have considered it part of the proper name. In cases where direct parentage is the point, I have translated "son of." So, for instance, a grandchild of the Rosh appears as Hayim son of Judah ben haRosh.

> **Shadal no. 1, pp. 5–6 (Cantera no. 71, pp. 119–22)**
> **Sitbona, daughter of Judah b. Sahwan, wife of Meir haLevi**
> Clear, oh clear the path[1]
> That goes up to the House of the Lord
> Remove your shoes in the fields of offerings and chariot[2]
> And let it be called a sacred way
> That goodly plot where a noble and aristocratic woman is buried
> A great woman
> She is Madam Sitbona, daughter of one of the lords of the land
> Who stood in the breach for God's people,[3]
> Reb Judah the son of Reb Petachia, may he rest in honor, ben Sahwan.
> [And she is] the wife of the great man
> A stalwart and fortress of salvation[4]
> Reb Meir haLevi the son of Reb Isaac haLevi, may he rest in honor.
> She died of the plague in the month of Sivan in the year of REST [= 5109].
> A benefactor's daughter
> Happy are you and happy your lot[5]
> For your piety and righteousness were abundant
> And you have provided well for yourself on your journey[6]
> From your skillful acts[7]

And the rectitude of your charity and deeds[8]
Find a spacious place in the garden of paradise[9]
At the end of days, He will raise you up and compensate your actions.[10]
There is hope for your future with the resurrection of His pious few.[11]
He will say to you, "Do not grieve![12]
Shake off the dust! Arise and return!"[13]

Shadal no. 2, pp. 6–7 (Cantera no. 77, pp. 129–30)
Samuel the son of Joseph ben Mazah
Buried in this tomb is the champion
Who girded his loins in strength
To stand in the breach for God's people
Against all the Gentiles of the land
The glory and splendor of the community
He came and went on its behalf[14]
He sat among the elders[15]
And rendered justice to the poor
He would rouse himself to help his people
And did not turn back[16]
He is Reb Samuel, son of the honorable Rabbi Joseph ben Mazah
He died of the plague in the month of Tamuz in the year of REST [= 5109]
To dwell in the shade of his Lord and to be serene and tranquil
His leaf was fresh
No taint will come near his tent
For [so] He will command His angels[17]
For his booth and his dwelling are concealed [beneath] the wings of his Rock
He has returned to Ramatah, for there lies his home.[18]

Shadal no. 3, pp. 7–8 (Cantera no. 76, pp. 128–29)
Miriam, daughter of Solomon ben haRosh, wife of Judah ben haRosh
A gracious woman who attained honor[19]
With righteousness, she set her table
With aptitude, she mixed her wine[20]
In humility, she wrapped her shawl
And tied her scarf with ribbons of purity.[21]

She is Madam Miriam, daughter of Solomon ben haRosh, may he be
    remembered for a blessing,
And the wife of the sage, Rabbi Judah ben haRosh, may he be remembered
    for a blessing—
Who reached the essential mysteries and secrets of the Torah[22]
And illuminated them
Until the Law cut them off
And God grew angry with Judah and Israel
And uncovered Judah
And God's people were left to stray
Like sheep that have no shepherd[23]
In the plague during Sivan in the year of REST [= 5109]
She went to find her foot a resting place[24]
And her husband followed after her into the foremost section [of paradise]
Just as she had stayed with him faithfully
Behold, the wife of a friend is considered a friend.

Shadal no. 4, p. 8 (Cantera no. 75, pp. 127–29)
Hayim son of Rabbi Judah ben haRosh
He died in the storm at the age of fourteen
Reb Hayim son of HH"R Rabbi Judah ben haRosh, may his memory be a
    blessing
On the nineteenth of Sivan in the year LIFE IS HIS [= 5109]
He ascended to the light in the light of life.[25]

Shadal no. 5, pp. 8–10 (Cantera no. 84, pp. 138–40)
Judah ben haRosh
I stand as a sign and memorial
That under me is buried
The body of the man Judah son of the Rosh
The son of Rabbi Yehiel ben [Rabbi Uri ben] Rabbi Eliakim ben Rabbi
    Judah[26]
Who was born in Ashkenaz on Tuesday toward evening on the ninth of Av.[27]
He left there on Sunday the twenty-second of Tamuz in a ship [= 5063]
    that he encountered[28]
And came to Toledo on Friday on the first day of Iyar[29]
He married the daughter of his brother Rabbi Yehiel on the eve of Sukkot
    5066[30]

After Rosh Hashanah his wife died and was laid in the dust.
Then he remarried[31]
The daughter of his brother Rabbi Solomon
God granted him the people's favor
So that he held his father's post immediately upon his death[32]
And for twenty-one years directed the academy of his fathers
He died on the seventeenth of Tamuz in the year [5]109.
A son brings joy to a wise father
And in his place, the fruit of the righteous will flourish [like] a tree of life[33]
Let him find shelter and rest in the shade of the God of Israel in whom he
     trusted and had faith
And may he rest until he stands in his allotted place at the End of Days.

Shadal no. 6, p. 11 (Cantera no. 70, p. 119)
Solomon, son of Jacob ben haRosh
Torah Piety Humility
The lot and the portion
Of Solomon, the son of Jacob ben haRosh, may his memory be a blessing
He came to his ancestors in Nisan in the year of REST [= 5109].

Shadal no. 15, p. 21 (Cantera no. 83, p. 138)
Judah haLevi son of Reb Meir haLevi Abulafia
Buried in this tomb is Reb Judah haLevi, son of Reb Meir haLevi, may he
     rest in paradise
Named Abulafia
He died on the fourteenth of Tamuz in the year 5109 since Creation.[34]

Shadal no. 17, pp. 21–23 (Cantera no. 66, pp. 114–16)
Joseph son of Reb Meir Abulafia haMerari
Who are you here, O groom,
Who has built an eternal dwelling place?[35]
Behold, you are shut in the cleft of the rock.[36]
Why did you hasten to leave
With the woman you loved?
I am the man[37]
Who has seen desolation and destruction[38]
Blood and pestilence
The days of my youth were cut short

Suddenly, in the prime of my life,
Young and tender in years,
Evil, unending illnesses snatched me away.[39]
When my pain grew great and my illness grew graver
I left my home, I abandoned my inheritance.[40]
Causing dismay, the plague cut off[41]
The groom from the bride
Before a year had passed
And left my house a waste and desolation.[42]
It did not leave me in peace and quiet[43]
Or purify my household for a year
But upon my death came briars and thorns[44]
And destroyed the house.
I have no son to inherit from me and recall my name
Among my people.
It is I who must say, here I am!
And let the one who hears what befell me have pity on me
Joseph the son of Reb Meir, may his rest be honorable, known as Abulafia
    haMerari
That is my name forever and this is my memorial.
I died of the plague in the year "BEHOLD, WE PERISH" plus five
    thousand[45] [= 5109]
And I left behind a mother afflicted and distraught.[46]
She remains in her bitter weeping[47]
And before she died in grief and sorrow
She sent off her daughters[48]
Remaining bereft and barren
Just she alone.[49]

Shadal no. 20, pp. 26–27 (Cantera no. 89, pp. 147–49)
Meir haLevi Abulafia haLevi son of Samuel haLevi ben al-Lauwee
Written on this tombstone in clear script
So that the reader will rush toward it
"You shall engrave them like a seal"[50]
So that all shall know that buried beneath it is the crown and diadem of
    his day
Its crowning glory
The necklace of what is precious and its ornament[51]

The tree of good lineage and its fruit
Splendid among men
The glory and pride of the descendants of Levi
Of the descendants of Hebron and Uzziel
The nobility of Israel
And a faithful witness
A merciful treasurer[52]
He loved to walk in God's ways
And he judged Israel
He is Reb Meir haLevi, may he rest in paradise, called Abulafia haLevi
The son of the honorable Rabbi Samuel haLevi, may God guide him, ben
     al-Lauwee
And he died in the month of Marheshvan in the year of
     DESTRUCTION plus five thousand [5112 = 1352] from Creation
His life ascended on high
And his soul yearned for his Lord
To stand watch in His House
And do His work.[53]
His soul also yearned and ached[54]
To serve in God's dwelling in His holy place
To be a light in the light of life
Like all his brothers the Levites
To bear his holy utensils
For holy service is required of them
And seven days before his death
He sent forth the dove from him[55]
To find a place of rest
And she found rest for her foot[56]
Then her husband followed her
At the End of Days when the bones of the sleeping are stirred
May God give light to the eyes of them both.

Shadal no. 22, pp. 28–29 (Cantera no. 91, pp. 150–52)
Joseph haLevi son of Solomon haLevi ben al-Lauwee Abulafia
It is a northern plot
Whose scents are stirred by the northern wind
Wafting its nard and cinnamon.
It is hewn from a "helping stone"[57]

Under which lies buried the Law and the Crown
The man whom the king wished to honor[58]
On whom he placed the golden necklace[59]
Lineage and Rank are his stewards
Humility and Greatness his merchants
Generosity and Honor his friends.
Privilege is privileged
And greatness is greatened
Generosity is glorified
And Humility resplendent
Splendor is evident
And Honor is graced
Aptitude and Deed take pride.
How can a book contain his praise?
The man who possesses all of these
Is Reb Joseph haLevi, may he rest in paradise,
The son of the honorable Rabbi Solomon haLevi—may the Blessed One
    guide him—ben al-Lauwee called Abulafia.
He died in Seville
In Marheshvan in the year of DESTRUCTION plus five thousand [= 5111]
He ascended to the House of the Lord
Among those who sit in the foremost section
In the kingdom on high
And his soul in the highest heavens
Walks among angels[60]
He yearned to live on high in the shadow of Shaddai[61]
In Joseph's tent.

Shadal no. 29, p. 35 (Cantera no. 67, pp. 116–17)
Solomon son of Reb Samuel ben al-Naqawa
Pure in thought, pleasant, and fair,
He died in the plague with his wife and children and all that he had.
No remnant is left in his tent[62]
Except a small daughter, and she is all.
He is Reb Solomon son of Samuel, may he rest in paradise, ben al-Naqawa
In the year WE ARE DOOMED TO PERISH [= 5109].[63]

Shadal no. 30, p. 35 (Cantera no. 78, p. 131)
Joseph son of Samuel ben al-Naqawa[64]

A pure and righteous man known to all peoples
Humble of spirit and modest
Neither prideful nor arrogant[65]
He gave widely to the poor[66]
His food and drink will ever be ready[67]
Reb Joseph son of Reb Samuel ben al-Naqawa
He died in the month of Tamuz in the year of REST [= 5109].

Shadal no. 35, p. 38 (Cantera no. 65, pp. 113–14)
Isaac son of Meir Rofé

Hidden in this grave is Don Isaac the Physician
The son of Meir the Physician, may he rest in paradise, ben Sasson.
He died at the border of Seville at the age of twenty-five
Of plague in the year of REST [= 5109].

Shadal no. 42, pp. 44–45 (Cantera no. 87, pp. 144–45)
Solomon son of Judah ben haRosh

Touchstone and precious hewn stone
A beautiful crown and glorious diadem[68]
For beneath it is buried the sapling of understanding and wisdom
The branch of the tree of knowledge and cunning
The most splendid among young men
Who walked in the way of his Lord and ever applied himself
To read the laws and ordinances and precepts[69]
He is Rabbi Solomon, may he rest in paradise,
The son of the sage, the great rabbi, the breath of our nostrils, the star of
    our dawns, and the light of our eyelids[70]
Chief among the exiles of Ariel[71]
The eyes of all Israel
Rabbi Judah, may the memory of a righteous man be for blessing, ben
    haRosh, may his memory be a blessing
He died of the plague on the fifteenth of Av in the year of REST [5109 =
    1349 C.E.]
He went up from his territory[72]
To see the beauty of the Lord and to visit God's Temple in His heavenly
    heights.[73]

Shadal no. 43, pp. 44–45 (Cantera no. 85, pp. 140–42)
Dona, daughter of Solomon ben al-Bagal, wife of Abraham son of Moses ben Sasson

Let her be called a woman
Let her be called Sought After[74]
She was honest on earth[75]
And pious in heaven
She is Madam Dona, daughter of Reb Solomon, may he rest in paradise, ben al-Bagal
The wife of Reb Abraham bar Moses, may he rest in paradise, ben Sasson
She died in the month of Av in the year 5109 since Creation.

Shadal no. 44, pp. 45–46 (Cantera no. 79, pp. 131–33)
David son of Joseph ben Nahmias

Under a foundation stone
Beloved David hides in the strongholds.[76]
Of the stock of the pious ones
Of the seed of noblemen
The princes of high lineage, the men of discretion[77]
Whose names have been designated[78]
Whose fathers were among the exiles from Ariel[79]
The elite of Israel
He is Reb David, may he rest in glory, son of the honorable Rabbi Joseph, may God's spirit guide him, ben Nahmias
He died of the plague in storm and tempest
In the month of Tamuz in the year WE ARE DOOMED TO PERISH plus five thousand [= 5109]
When the destruction came[80]
It ravaged the land and left it waste and totally consumed.[81]
He ascended from earth
To find shelter in the shade of the Lord in his heavenly dwelling
He and his three sons
He went higher and higher[82]
To [his] rest and inheritance[83]
Prepared beforehand beneath the wings of the Rock his salvation[84]
To David and his descendants
Let us say Amen.

Shadal no. 45, pp. 46–47 (Cantera no. 88, pp. 145–47)
Reb Judah son of Rabbi Eliakim ben haRosh
Let the stones be a memorial for the names of the children of Israel
So that the last generation will know
Their names and history
Engraved in fine relief
According to their families on their fathers' side
Proclaim their names across the land
These men who were distinguished
This is for Judah
That it may be a witness
Among the community
That beneath it is buried the most splendid of youths
The glory of young and old
A rare spirit, a man of understanding[85]
One who has knowledge and understanding
His soul is clean
His spirit holds no deception
A shoot [planted] by the saints and the righteous
Who cling to God's laws
The rams of justice, the learned sages
God's portion above and Shaddai's inheritance from heaven
Those who hold fast to the Torah and know the Lord
The elite among the children of Israel
They showed no arrogance or contempt for their studies
And had no quarrel with fellow men.
He is the darling and pleasant Reb Judah, may he rest in paradise,
The son of the revered rabbinic elder, Rabbi Eliakim, God grant him
    consolation
Ben haRosh, may his memory be a blessing
He submitted to his fate and went up
On the path that ascends to the House of the Lord
He set his path to find REST [with the] Almighty
Judah went down from his brothers.[86]

Shadal no. 50, pp. 51–52 (Cantera no. 80, pp. 133–34)
Asher ben Turiel
This stone is a memorial
So that the last generation may know
That a beautiful flower is hidden beneath it
A pampered child[87]
Pure in knowledge
He would read in the Torah
And recite Mishnah and Gemara.
He learned from his father what his father had learned from his teachers
God's laws and precepts.
He was fifteen years old
But wise as a man of eighty.
Blessed among children, Asher, may paradise bring him rest,
The son of Joseph ben Turiel, may God console him.
He died of the plague in the month of Tamuz in the year [5]109.[88]
Just days before his death
He had married.[89]
Then the voice of the bride and groom
Became a voice of weeping,
And a father is pained and pining.[90]
God of the heavens, grant him consolation.
Restorer of souls,[91] [grant him] progeny.[92]

Shadal no. 53, pp. 53–54 (Cantera 74, p. 127)
Abraham son of Reb Moses ibn Falcon
Buried in this tomb is the elect among sons
Intelligent as a man of eighty
Abraham son of Reb Moses ibn Falcon. He was snatched
And brought away in the month of Sivan in the year 5109 since Creation.
   He was still in his prime when he was plucked
For it was the season of trial and he was snatched[93]
And died while his father and mother still lived.

Shadal no. 57, p. 57 (Cantera no. 86, pp. 143–44)
Meir son of Abraham ben Sasson[94]
This stone and memorial
Was hewn from a beautiful mountain

For beneath it is buried the light of [our] eyes
Myrrh wafting to all noses
Oil compounded of joy
His nard gave forth its fragrance
He rose and was borne up
He prospered and accomplished
He was stationed at honor's head
And stood before kings
He is Reb Meir, may he rest in paradise, son of the honorable Rabbi
    Abraham, my God guide him, ben Sasson
He died of the plague in the month of Av in the year of REST [= 5109].
He departed the earth [when it was] waste and totally consumed.[95]
He ascended from earth
On the way to his land[96]
For his destined portion.

Shadal no. 69, p. 65 (Cantera no. 68, pp. 117–18)
Solomon son of Samuel ibn al-Harb
In the year 5109 from Creation
A year of wrath and ire and sorrow
The year of the plague
That consumed and ravaged the yield of the land[97]
Uprooted mountains in a deluge[98]
He was cut down in the decree "[who] makes the thunderstorms"[99]
An understanding, intelligent man, a youth like the cedars
In him were gathered all the pathways
Of rectitude and good qualities
Reb Solomon son of Reb Samuel, may he rest in paradise, ben al-Harb
Ascended to rest
He will awaken at the End of Days with the appointed ones
Inscribed for eternal life.

Shadal no. 70, pp. 65–66 (Cantera no. 82, pp. 135–38)
Jacob son of Reb Isaac the Sarqastan (Saragossan?)
Buried in this grave
Is a man of intelligence and wisdom
Honest and pure
Full of glory and wisdom

Knowledge and skill
A councillor and craftsman[100]
Pleasing to God and to people.
He healed souls of their sicknesses
And was a descendant of saints/martyrs.
His name is Reb Jacob son of Reb Isaac, may he rest in paradise, the
　　Sarqastan[101]
He strove all his days
To love the Lord and cling to Him[102]
When He caused an outbreak[103]
Among the holy ones in the land
And the plague broke out among them[104]
He was gathered to his people[105]
He left the earth and rose to dwell in the heavens
On the twelfth of Tamuz in the year of REST [= 5109], God's hand came
　　upon him[106]
To turn back Jacob unto Him
To grant him a hand(?) among His pious ones and to pass by at their
　　head[107]
And God said to Jacob, Arise, go to Beth-El and dwell there,
And Jacob went on his way to see the face of Him who dwells in radiance.
And God's angels met him.

Shadal no. 71, p. 66 (Cantera no. 69, p. 118)
Solomon son of Reb Isaac ibn Israel
Hidden in this tomb is Reb Solomon bar Isaac, may his rest be in paradise,
　　ibn Israel
Whose goal was to occupy himself with Torah
And he died in the year of REST [= 5109].

Shadal no. 73, pp. 67–68 (Cantera no. 81, pp. 134–35)
Isaac son of Solomon ibn Masudia
Can we find another like him?[108]
Hidden in this tomb
Is a dear and pleasing son and favored child
Beloved among companions, pure of thought
When he was yet a youth
He was removed from the earth

Reb Isaac, may his paradise be restful, son of the sage Rabbi Solomon, may
  his soul be wrapped in the bonds of life, ibn al-Masudia
He went and turned away
He was eighteen years old
Short-lived
But his heart's grasp like a man of eighty
He died of the plague
On the fourth of Tamuz in the year WE ARE DOOMED TO PERISH
  [= 5109].

Shadal no. 37, p. 40 (Cantera no. 96, pp. 156–57)
Joseph son of Reb Abraham Makhir[109]
If only my words would be written
And carved in rock forever[110]
Engraved in fine relief[111]
So their names would be legible far and wide[112]
This stone that I have placed as a gravestone[113]
Is inscribed with an iron pen and lead[114]
For hidden beneath it is a loyal physician
A jar of manna[115]
The balm of Gilead he inherited from his parents[116]
For himself and his descendants after him
He is Reb Joseph the physician son of Abraham Makhir the physician,
  may his Eden be pleasant,
He was gathered to his people[117]
And departed from his place[118]
In the month of Kislev the year 5122 of Creation
He went up on the way along his land[119]
To see God's beauty and visit His Temple.[120]

Notes

Introduction

Note to Caslari epigraph at beginning of chapter: MS Leiden Cod. Or. 4778, fols. 115b–116a; and see Chap. 3.

1. The first pandemic, also known as the Justinian Plague, has also merited a spike in recent attention. See Lester Little, ed., *Plague and the End of Antiquity: The Pandemic of 541–750* (New York: Cambridge University Press, 2006). The third pandemic began in the late nineteenth century and lingers today. Until quite recently, it was associated with relatively isolated Southeast Asian and South American locations, but is now documented again in regions as far-flung as the American Southwest, Libya, the Democratic Republic of the Congo, Uganda, and Iran. There has been some evidence of its use in biological warfare arsenals, a trend that we hope fails to flourish. See Michelle Xiegler, "The Black Death and the Future of the Plague," *Pandemic Disease in the Medieval World: Rethinking the Black Death, The Medieval Globe* 1.1 (2014): 259–83, esp. 265.

2. See the works cited in notes throughout the following chapters. For a convenient and recent collection of essays, see Monica Green, ed., *Pandemic Disease in the Medieval World: Rethinking the Black Death, The Medieval Globe* 1.1 (2014).

3. Jean-Noël Biraben, *Les hommes et la peste en France et dans les pays européens et méditerranéens*, 2 vols. (Paris: Mouton, 1975); Ole Benedictow, *The Black Death 1346–1353: The Complete History* (Suffolk, U.K.: Boydell Press, 2004).

4. Bruce Campbell, *The Great Transition: Climate, Disease and Society in the Late-Medieval World* (Cambridge: Cambridge University Press, 2016), chap. 1. See also Fabian Crespo and Matthew B. Lawrenz, "Heterogeneous Immunological Landscapes and Medieval Plague: An Invitation to a New Dialogue Between Historians and Immunologists," *The Medieval Globe* 1.1 (2014): 229–54.

5. The studies are inconclusive when it comes to breaking down mortality by age and gender. In some regions, there does seem to be greater or lesser immunity among a specific age or gender demographic. This could be a factor linked to immune suppression associated with environmental or social factors. The tentative observations in this regard must, at best, be limited to local experience. See, e.g., Sharon DeWitte, "The Anthropology of Plague: Insights from Bioarcheological Analyses of Epidemic Cemeteries," *The Medieval Globe* 1.1 (2014): 97–125; or idem and Philip Slavin, "Between Famine and Death: England on the Eve of the Black Death: Evidence from Paleoepidemiology and Manorial Accounts," *Journal of Interdisciplinary History* 44.1 (2013): 37–60.

6. John Masson Smith, "Mongol Campaign Rations: Milk, Marmots and Blood?,"
Journal of Turkish Studies 8 (1984): 223–28. Monica Green's overview essay notes that several
hundred animal species have now been recognized as potential plague carriers, in addition
to "a variety of fleas, ticks and lice." Monica Green, "Taking Pandemic Seriously: Making
the Black Death Global," *The Medieval Globe* 1.1 (2014): 32–33.

7. E.g., the important essay by Ann Carmichael, "Plague Persistence in Western Europe: A Hypothesis," *The Medieval Globe* 1.1 (2014): 157–92.

8. From the classic by Anna Montgomery Campbell, *The Black Death and Men of
Learning* (New York: Columbia University Press, 1931), to, e.g., Christine M. Boeckl, *Images
of Plague and Pestilence* (Kirksville, Mo.: Truman State University Press, 2000); Justin Stearns, "New Directions in the Study of Religious Responses to the Black Death," *History
Compass* 7.5 (September 2009): 1363–75. There is room for a lot more work on cultural, literary, visual, and musical responses.

9. "Black Death," entry by Richard Gottheil and Joseph Jacobs, *Jewish Encyclopedia*
(1906 ed.), www.jewishencyclopedia.com/articles/3349-black-death.

10. Adolphe Crémieux, "Les juifs de Toulon au Moyen Age et le massacre du 13 avril
1348," *Revue des Études Juives* 89 (1930): 33–72; 90 (1931): 43–64. For a recent local study, see,
e.g., Cordelia Hess, "Jews and the Black Death in Fourteenth-Century Prussia: A Search for
Traces," in idem and Jonathan Adams, eds., *Fear and Loathing in the North: Jews and Muslims in Medieval Scandinavia and the Baltic Region* (Berlin: Walter de Gruyter, 2015),
109–26.

11. In alphabetical order by author, see Klaus Bergdolt, *Der Schwarze Tod in Europa:
Die Grosse Pest und das Ende des Mittelalters* (Munich: C. H. Beck, 2017); Samuel K. Cohn,
Jr., "The Black Death and the Burning of the Jews," *Past & Present* 196 (August 2007):
3–36; Adolphe Crémieux, "Les Juifs de Toulon au Moyen Âge et le massacre du 13 avril
1348," *Revue des Études Juives* 89 (1930): 33–72; 90 (1931): 43–64; František Graus, *Pest—
Geissler—Judenmorde* (Göttingen: Vandenhoeck & Ruprecht, 1988); Alfred Haverkamp,
"Die Judenverfolgungen zur Zeit des Schwarzen Todes in Gesellschaftsgefüge deutscher
Städte," *Zur Geschichte der Juden in Deutschland* (Stuttgart: Anton Hiersemann, 1981),
27–93; David Nirenberg, *Communities of Violence* (Princeton, N.J.: Princeton University
Press, 1996); Joseph Shatzmiller, "Les juifs de Provence pendant la Peste Noire," *Revue des
Études Juives* 133 (1974): 457–80. This is not an exhaustive list but representative of works
that have attempted to generalize their conclusions over wider geographical or cultural
terrain.

12. Carmichael, "Plague Persistence in Western Europe."

13. See, e.g., Melanie Shirk, "The Black Death in Aragon," *Journal of Medieval History*
7 (1981): 357, 365, who makes this point explicitly regarding that region.

14. David Mengel, "A Plague on Bohemia? Mapping the Black Death," *Past & Present*
211 (May 2011): 27.

15. Ron Barkai, "Jewish Treatises on the Black Death (1350–1500): A Preliminary Study,"
in Roger French et al., eds., *Medicine from the Black Death to the French Disease* (Aldershot:
Ashgate, 1998), 6–25, and chap. 5, pp. 112–36, in Susan Einbinder, *No Place of Rest: Jewish Literature, Expulsion, and the Memory of Medieval France* (Philadelphia: University of Pennsylvania

Press, 2009), which analyzes a memorial tract written by a Jewish physician in Avignon for his daughter, who died of plague in 1382. Gerrit Bos and Guido Mensching have edited and published two Hebrew plague tractates.

16. H. Pinkhof, *Abraham Kashlari, over Pestachtige Koortsen* (Amsterdam, 1891), 51–35 (pagination backward to accommodate Hebrew order); MS Leiden Cod. Or. 4778.

17. In fact, the violence had begun even earlier, before the plague reached Caslari's home in Besalú. In April 1348, the entire Jewish community in Toulouse (Provence) was massacred, and violence against other Jewish communities in Provence preceded the plague's advance into Catalonia, where a cascade of attacks on Jewish calls (quarters) took place in Barcelona, Cervera, Tàrrega, and elsewhere. See Shirk, 357–67; J. Gautier-Dalché, "La Pesta Negra dans les états de la Couronne d'Aragon," in *Mélanges offerts à Marcel Bataillon* (Bordeaux: Fèret, 1962), 65–80; Amada López de Meneses, "Una consecuencia de la Pesta Negre en Cataluña: El pogrom de 1348," *Sefarad* 19 (1959): 92–131, 321–64.

18. Samuel David Luzzatto, *Avnei zikkaron* (Prague: J. Landau, 1841).

19. While often neglected as a genre, epitaph poetry has crossed the radar of recent Jewish studies scholarship, and a number of studies enrich our reading of the Toledo sample. See, e.g., Tzvi Avineri, "Hebrew Inscriptions from the Middle Ages," PAAJR 33 (1965): 1–33; Avriel Bar-Levav, "Another Place: Cemeteries in Jewish Culture" [Hebrew], *Pe'amim* 98–99 (2002): 5–37; J. A. Brombacher, "Poetry on Gravestones: Poetry by the Seventeenth-Century Portuguese Rabbi Solomon de Oliveryra," *Dutch Jewish History* 2 (1985): 153–65; David Malkiel, "Poems on Tombstone Inscriptions in Northern Italy in the Sixteenth and Seventeenth Centuries" [Hebrew], *Pe'amim* 98–99 (2004): 120–54; idem, "Christian Hebraism in a Contemporary Key," *JQR* 96.1 (Winter 2006): 123–46. See also Rami (Avraham) Reiner on the ongoing excavations in Würzburg, e.g., "Shard Drawn to Shard: Discoveries from the Jewish Cemetery in Würzburg" [Hebrew], *Zemanim* 95 (2006): 52–57; "Inscribed on a Stone: Descriptions of the Deceased on the Gravestones from the Würzburg Cemetery, 1147–1346" [Hebrew], *Tarbiz* 78.1 (2008): 123–52.

20. Michele Hamilton, *Beyond Faith: Belief, Morality and Memory in a Fifteenth-Century Judeo-Iberian Manuscript* (Leiden: Brill, 2014), 205–48. See also Marcelino V. Amasuno, "La medicina y el físico en la Dança general de la muerte," *Hispanic Review* 65.1 (1997): 1–24.

21. Smelser cites an essay by Arthur G. Neal that asserts: "The enduring effects of a trauma in the memories of an individual resemble the enduring effects of a national trauma in collective consciousness." There is no justification for this extrapolation given, and this is merely one of many examples. See Neil Smelser, "Psychological and Cultural Trauma," in Jeffrey Alexander et al., eds., *Cultural Trauma and Collective Identity* (Berkeley: University of California Press, 2004), 38. Caruth's treatment of Freud's Moses and Monotheism astonishingly ignores the way that Freud casually posits a similar, mythical leap, so that, in Caruth's words, "the essence of [Jewish] history is the repression, and return, of the deeds of Moses." Cathy Caruth, *Unclaimed Experience* (Baltimore: Johns Hopkins University Press, 1996), 14 and throughout chap. 1.

22. This is what Leys refers to as the "anti-mimetic" strand of trauma theory, which Leys says is attractive to its proponents in part because it salvages individual autonomy; in

the "mimetic" model, which analogizes the trauma victim to a person under hypnosis, the individual is unconscious of the event and unconscious of her need to repeat it later. See Ruth Leys, *Trauma: A Genealogy* (Chicago: University of Chicago Press, 2000). Ironically, when applied to a mass of individuals, the event model actually subordinates individual agency to the production of identical affect among all the exposed victims. For Leys's critique of Caruth's (and Freud's) readings, see chap. 8, esp. 274–80, 284–86. Claire Stocks also treats the argument for collective and transgenerational trauma in her "Trauma Theory and the Singular Self: Rethinking Extreme Experiences in the Light of Cross-Cultural Identity," *Textual Practice* 21.1 (2007): 71–92, esp. 81–82. The literature on secondary trauma is huge. In Israel, the *dor sheni* ("second generation" of Holocaust survivors) have their own psychiatric label and support organizations.

23. For the first term, see Jeffrey Alexander, "Toward a Theory of Cultural Trauma," in idem et al., *Cultural Trauma and Collective Identity*, 1–30. For the second, see Wulf Kansteiner, "Finding Meaning in Memory: A Methodological Critique of Collective Memory Studies," *History & Theory* 41.2 (2002): 79–97. From a sociological perspective, "a cultural trauma differs greatly from a psychological trauma in terms of the mechanisms that establish and sustain it"; Smelser, 38–39.

24. Dori Laub and N. Auerhahn, "Knowing and Not-Knowing Massive Psychic Trauma: Forms of Traumatic Memory," *International Journal of Psychoanalysis* 74.2 (1993): 287–302; Henry Greenspan et al., "Engaging Survivors: Assessing 'Testimony' and 'Trauma' as Foundational Concepts," *Dapim* 28.3 (2014): 190–225.

25. Derek Summerfield, "A Critique of Seven Assumptions Behind Psychological Trauma Programmes in War-Affected Areas," *Social Science and Medicine* 48 (1999): 1456 describes this focus on "spectacular groups," particularly women and children, in the mobilization of "trauma experts."

26. Kansteiner, whose overly positivist approach also has its critics, observes correctly that "even the cultural critics who acknowledge essential conceptual differences between individual and collective states of mind tend to construct cultural trauma as a process that somehow runs parallel to the development of actual psychological trauma." Wulf Kansteiner, "Genealogy of a Category Mistake: A Critical Intellectual History of the Cultural Trauma Metaphor," *Rethinking History* 8.2 (2004): 207. For a critique, see Robert Eaglestone, "Knowledge, 'Afterwardsness,' and the Future of Trauma Theory," in Gert Buelens, Sam Durrant, and Robert Eaglestone, eds., *The Future of Trauma Theory* (New York: Routledge, 2014), 13–14. In the same volume as Eaglestone's essay, Durrant notes the problematic conflation of collective and individual trauma models, which he suggests would be better addressed by a focus on the "role of the state in . . . subjectification"; see "Undoing Sovereignty: Towards a Theory of Critical Mourning," 92.

27. For critiques of trauma theory's failure to justify its application of a theoretical, individual-centric and psychological model of trauma to collectivities, see, among others, Summerfield; Ian Hacking, "Memory Sciences, Memory Politics," in Paul Antze and M. Lambek, eds., *Tense Past: Cultural Essays in Trauma and Memory* (New York: Routledge, 1996), 67–89; Susannah Radstone, "Trauma Theory: Contexts, Politics, Ethics," *Paragraph* 30.1 (2007): 9–29. One massive, supposedly definitive, volume on trauma published by a

Dutch researcher never even mentions the concept of collective trauma or trauma-related conditions. See Ellert Nijenhuis, *The Trinity of Trauma: Ignorance, Fragility and Control* (Göttingen: Vandenhoeck & Ruprecht, 2015). For the sociological position—that "collective trauma" is a construct of "culture carriers" or "memory makers" who do their work after the event—see, e.g., Jeffrey Alexander, *Trauma: A Social Theory* (New Haven, Conn.: Polity, 2012), 1–30; and Kansteiner, "Genealogy of a Category Mistake," as well as the discussion in Chapter 2 in this volume. The citation is from Summerfield, 1456.

28. Summerfield, 1456, 1458.

Chapter 1

1. Jean de Saint-Victor, in Georges Passerat, *La croisade des Pastoureaux* (Cahors: La Louve, 2006), French translation of the Latin on 88 (*et comme le bois et les pierres vinrent à leur manquer ils jetèrent leurs enfants à la place des pierres*); Latin on 120, *Cum autem eis ligna et lapides defecissent, pueros loco lapidum projecerunt.*

2. The very forgotten-ness of these experiences in the literature seemed curious, almost a case of collective repressed memory in itself, but the problem may be more historiographic than traumatic. Most of the violence took place in Provence, off the bipolar Ashkenaz-Sepharad map that has defined medieval European Judaism for several centuries. Those Jews who survived the worst attacks soon ended up in other places where competing tales of hardship and persecution surrounded them. Cf. Shahid Amin, *Event, Metaphor, Memory: Chauri Chaura 1922–92* (Los Angeles: University of California Press, 1995), 3.

3. Richard Rechtman, "L'enquête sur la condition de victime," *Études* 414 (2011): 176; Didier Fassin and Richard Rechtman, *Empire of Trauma: An Inquiry into the Condition of Victimhood* (Princeton, N.J.: Princeton University Press, 2009), 25–39; Stef Craps, *Postcolonial Witnessing: Trauma Out of Bounds* (New York: Palgrave Macmillan, 2013); Summerfield. These are critical views. For a weighty expression of the maximalist view (that trauma is ubiquitous and universal), see the recent work of Nijenhuis.

4. See the introduction and essays in Gert Buelens, Sam Durrant, and Robert Eaglestone, eds., *The Future of Trauma Theory: Contemporary Literary and Cultural Criticism* (New York: Routledge, 2014).

5. Devon S. Hinton and Roberto Lewis-Fernandez, "Idioms of Distress Among Trauma Survivors: Subtypes and Clinical Utility," *Culture, Medicine and Psychiatry* 34.2 (June 2012): 215. See also Bessel van der Kolk, *The Body Keeps the Score: Mind and Body in the Healing of Trauma* (New York: Viking, 2014). For a critique, see Leys, *Trauma*, 229–65. According to Fassin and Rechtman, it is the only psychological disorder embraced by those who receive the diagnosis. Fassin and Rechtman, *Empire of Trauma*; Richard Rechtman, "Être victime: Généalogie d'une condition clinique," *Evolutionary Psychiatry* 67 (2002): 775–95.

6. Jaume Riera i Sans, *Fam i fe: L'entrada dels pastorells (juliol de 1320)* (Lleida: Pages Editors, 2004), 21; Passerat, *La croisade des Pastoureaux*, 71ff. See also Malcolm Barber, "The Pastoureaux of 1320," *Journal of Ecclesiastical History* 32 (1981): 143–66; Joachim Miret y

Sans, "Le Massacre des juifs de Montclus en 1320," *Revue des Études Juives* 53 (1907): 255–66; Dominique Paladilhe, "Les Pastoureaux contre les juifs," *Historia* 410 (January 1981): 116–24; and the bibliography below.

7. William C. Jordan, *The French Monarchy and the Jews* (Philadelphia: University of Pennsylvania Press, 1989), 242–44.

8. Nirenberg, *Communities of Violence*. This is a motif that continues to surface in analyses of plague-related attacks, as noted in the following chapters.

9. Passerat, *La croisade des Pastoureaux*. See also idem, "Les derniers juifs du pays toulousain victimes des émeutes populaires," in Gilbert Dahan, ed., *L'expulsion des juifs de France, 1394* (Paris: Cerf, 2004), 69–77.

10. Riera i Sans, *Fam i fe*. On the Gascon origins of the shepherds, 24–25, 103.

11. See the essays by John Tolan and Robin Mundhill in Tolan, ed., *Expulsion and Diaspora Formation* (Leiden: Brepols/RELMIN, 2015). Significantly, the pro-English bailiffs who hold Pastoureaux prisoners in Gascon territory (under English sovereignty) refuse to remand them to France for prosecution.

12. Barber.

13. J.-M. Vidal, "L'émeute des Pastoureaux en 1320," in *Lettres du pape Jean xxii: Déposition du juif Baruc devant l'inquisition* (Rome: Ph. Cuggiana, 1898); Solomon Grayzel, "Confession of a Medieval Jewish Convert," *Historia Judaica* 17 (1955): 89–120.

14. Cf., e.g., Amin; or, for a medieval context contemporary to the Pastoureaux, William TeBrake, *A Plague of Insurrection: Popular Politics and Peasant Revolt in Flanders 1323–28* (Philadelphia: University of Pennsylvania Press, 1993).

15. See Paul Freedman, *Images of the Medieval Peasant* (Palo Alto, Calif.: Stanford University Press, 1999); Stephen Greenblatt, "Murdering Peasants: Status, Genre and the Representation of Rebellion," *Representations* 1 (1983): 1–29.

16. Riera, 106–19.

17. Passerat, *La croisade des Pastoureaux*, 107.

18. Ibid., 66.

19. For a later illustration (1348) following plague-inspired violence against Jews in Toulon, see Crémieux, "Les juifs de Toulon au Moyen Age et le massacre du 13 avril 1348," *Revue des Études Juives* 89 (1930): 65.

20. Nirenberg, *Communities of Violence*, 84.

21. I am using Riera's dates. See Riera, 28, 38, respectively.

22. Gary Dickson, "The Advent of the *Pastores*," *Revue Belge de Philologie et d'Histoire* 66 (1988): 249–67. On Bourges, Passerat, *La croisade des Pastoureaux*, 38. On the identification of the lament, see Simon Bernfeld, *Sefer haDema'ot* (Berlin: Eshkol, 1925), 2:67–69; Leopold Zunz, *Literaturgeschichte der synagogalen poesie* (Berlin, 1865), 349.

23. Passerat, *La croisade des Pastoureaux*, 106.

24. See Chapter 5.

25. Susan Einbinder, "Anti-Jewish Violence and the Pastoureaux: The Case for Medieval Trauma," in Wendy Turner, ed., *Medieval Trauma* (Leiden: Brill, forthcoming).

26. Indeed, the same royal registers that are scoured to reconstruct the movements of the Pastoureaux and their local supporters as well as the effectiveness or ineffectiveness of

royal officials in deterring them are peppered with references to domestic conflicts among the king's Jews—a remission to a Jew accused of murdering his wife, and permission to another to marry two at once.

27. Riera thinks that this delegation was too big to have been merely seeking permission to rebury the dead in Montclus; see Riera, 139–40. See Jean Régné, *History of the Jews in Aragon: Regesta and Documents 1213–1327*, ed. Yom Tov Assis (Jerusalem: Magnes Press, 1978), doc. nos. 3133, 3138, 3156, 3188, 3189 (pp. 577–79, 582, 587–89).

28. K. N. Triplett et al., "Post-Traumatic Growth, Meaning in Life and Life Satisfaction in Response to Trauma," *Psychological Trauma: Theory Research Practice Policy* 4 (2012): 400–410. The more the external event, as opposed to intrapsychic factors, becomes determinative, the more this surfaces as a problem.

29. This convention goes back at least to the Hebrew chronicles and laments written in the wake of the Rhineland slaughters of the First Crusade. Repeatedly, the Hebrew texts describe Jewish communities "responding with one voice" or "responding as one." These texts also feature the motif of the mingled blood of the dead. For the chronicles, see Eva Haverkamp, *Hebräische Berichte über die Judenverfolgungen während des Ersten Kreuzzugs* (Hannover: Hahnsche, 2005).

30. Arthur Kleinman and Joan Kleinman, "The Appeal of Experience: The Dismay of Images: Cultural Appropriations of Suffering in Our Times," *Daedalus* 125.1 (Winter 1996): 9 (where he is referring to photography, not *piyyut*!).

31. Douglas Hollan, "Coping in Plain Sight: Work and Trauma," *Transcultural Psychiatry* 50.5 (October 2013): 730, citing Obeyesekere. Indeed, if this liturgical outlet is to work, it must provide an adequate "match" for what Obeyesekere refers to as the "expression and containment" of individual distress.

32. In *Beautiful Death*, I argued similarly that the image of beloved teachers and communal leaders crying out at the stake might be converted to the redemptive image of revelation at Sinai. There is an actual shard of memory that is incorporated into the text to signify terror and promise, in language that any moderately literate male Jew would recognize. See Susan Einbinder, *Beautiful Death: Jewish Poetry and Martyrdom from Medieval France* (Princeton, N.J.: Princeton University Press, 2002).

33. MS Hamburg Heb. 41a, fol. 76r. The poem was published once, by Jacob Ettinger, in *Shomer Tsiyon haNe'eman* (1846–56), 369b. My thanks to Marilyn Krider of the Hebrew Union College Klau Library for a scanned copy of the Ettinger publication.

34. It appears in the liturgy surrounding the reading of the Torah for the fast day.

35. Mitchell B. Merback, *Pilgrimage and Pogrom: Violence, Memory and Visual Culture at the Host-Miracle Shrines of Germany and Austria* (Chicago: University of Chicago Press, 2012), 33, 35. On collective memory as a social construct, see, e.g., Smelser.

36. Note the melodic indication at the beginning of Emanuel's lament, tentatively transcribed by Bar-Tikva as לנהי עלוני. The lament would be chanted to a melody associated with familiar *qinot*.

37. See, e.g., Dean Ajdukovic, "Social Contexts of Trauma and Healing," *Medicine, Conflict and Survival* 20.2 (2004): 120–35.

38. MS Oxf. Opp. Add. QU 37.

39. For a recapitulation of the debate over the accuracy of witness testimony, see Ruth Leys, *Trauma: A Genealogy*, chap. 7.

40. MS Vatican Heb. 247.

41. I avoid the term "traumatic memory." On the invention of this concept, see Allan Young, "Suffering and the Origins of Traumatic Memory," *Daedalus* 125.1 (Winter 1996): 245–60; Kerwin L. Klein, "On the Emergence of Memory in Historical Discourse," *Representations* 69 (2000): 127–50; Leys, *Trauma*.

42. For a contemporary illustration of the same process, see Joseph Goldstein, "From Pariah to Martyr After Death in Kabul," *New York Times*, March 30, 2015, about the death by stoning of a young Afghani woman erroneously accused of burning a Qur'an. According to the article, the family of the victim, whose name was Farkhunda, at first complied with police requests that they say the daughter was mentally ill. Terrified, the family was even prepared to flee. The reversal of the public narrative and the embrace of their daughter as a devout Muslim who had been decrying corruption at a local mosque led the family instead to "proudly [take] her name as their surname." Communal validation, especially in traditional societies, has real force.

43. For a few examples, drawn from Ephraim Urbach, *Ba'alei haTosafot* (Jerusalem: Mosad Bialik, 1955), 128–29: Jacob haQadosh, Menahem haQadosh; 179: Isaac bar Yoel Halevi of Mainz haQadosh; 219: Shlomo bar Yehuda of Dreux haQadosh; 317: Joseph ben haQadosh. Also see the Toledo gravestones published by F. Cantera and J. M. Millás, *Las inscripciones hebraicas de España* (Madrid: C. Bermejo, 1956), 36–38; and Luzzatto, *Avnei zikkaron*.

44. In our own context, martyrological proximity works quite differently: our collateral martyrs embody national, not religious, sacrifice. At the same time, contemporary readings of trauma assume that it has a leveling effect on its victims, whose particular virtues or vices, strengths or weaknesses, matter less than the simple fact of having lived through the event. More than any other twentieth-century moment, the Holocaust raised the problem of collective trauma for practitioners and theorists, accelerating a trend toward emphasis on "exposure to the event" as the signal criterion for predicting traumatic response. At the same time, traumatic events now demanded a moral as much as a medical response, an empathic identification with the victims as a gesture toward repair of the social or political conditions that led to or might repeat further abuse. Caruth, *Unclaimed Experience*; Dominick LaCapra, *Writing History, Writing Trauma* (Baltimore: John Hopkins University Press, 2001). For the critics of this trend, see Leys; Fassin and Rechtman.

45. In contrast, modern culture, at least in the West, has preferred the notion of witness. Those who bear witness to terrible things derive traumatic "charge" by their proximity to those who have undergone them. In this view, even those who hear the story from others—e.g., therapists, or health-care workers—are "infected" by a secondary form of trauma. This theory has even been extended to argue that the text (or film, TV show, or video) constitutes a kind of witness, whose secondary victim becomes the reader or viewer. See Caruth, *Unclaimed Experience*, esp. 10–24; and Leys, in critique, 266–97.

46. See Susan L. Einbinder, "Seeing the Blind: The Lament for Uri haLevi and Hysterical Blindness Among Medieval Jews," *Jewish Studies Quarterly* 20.1 (2013): 9–32.

47. Since the Vietnam War, this, too, has been an interest of modern trauma theory and treatment. Indeed, a glance at the table of contents of any of a dozen new(ish) English-language journals dedicated to trauma studies confirms that a significant percentage of their published articles concern perpetrator trauma, chiefly among U.S. veterans of the wars in Iraq and Afghanistan. Modern-day soldiers (even more than medieval ones) are men and women trained to commit and endure violence. Studies of perpetrator trauma among civilians have been less popular, and their conclusions have been divergent: Gross's much-publicized study of the role of Polish Christians in the town of Jedwabne in the slaughter of their Jewish neighbors strongly implied that the participants felt little to no regret for their actions. See Jan Gross, *Neighbors: The Destruction of the Jewish Community in Jedwabne, Poland* (Princeton, N.J.: Princeton University Press, 2000). Fujii's study of Hutu killings of Tutsi in Rwanda, in contrast, emphasized the diversity of the participants as well as the fact of non-participants, i.e., the many Hutu who refused passively or actively to turn against Tutsi neighbors. See Lee Ann Fujii, *Killing Neighbors: Levels of Violence in Rwanda* (Ithaca, N.Y.: Cornell University Press, 2010). Shahid Amin's analysis of the Chauri Chauri massacre likewise differentiates among the participants and their motives. See Amin.

48. Daniel Baraz, *Medieval Cruelty: Changing Perceptions, Late Antiquity to the Early Modern Period* (Ithaca, N.Y.: Cornell University Press, 2003).

49. Anthony Bale, *Feeling Persecuted: Christians, Jews and Images of Violence in the Middle Ages* (London: Reaktion, 2010).

50. Passerat, *La croisade des Pastoureaux*, 102–3 and n. 78. Passerat identified this man with the "Jacob Alaman" listed among the preaching friars in Gascony and surmises that Baruch's friend may have been a convert himself.

51. Ibid., 100.

52. Ibid., 103.

53. Ibid., 100.

54. Nirenberg, *Communities of Violence*, 64.

55. Cf. Amin's observation that local villagers referred ubiquitously to "the day the thana was burnt," and not to the day twenty-two policemen were first locked inside. Amin notes, with a nod to Natalie Davis, that invoking the building rather than the people "could well be a way by which members of a face-to-face society escape remembering the actual killing of local watchmen who were familiar figures in the villages." Amin, 152.

56. See Tzafrir Barzilay, "The Black Death in Aragon: Notes on a Jewish Chronicle" [Hebrew], *Hayo Haya* 8 (Winter 2011): 55.

57. See Anna Colet et al., "The Black Death and Its Consequences for the Jewish Community in Tàrrega: Lessons from History and Archeology," *The Medieval Globe* 1.1 (2014): 63–96; and, most recently, Maria Jose Surribas Camps, *Destruction of the Jewish Community of Tàrrega in 1348 and Its Reconstitution* (Jerusalem: International Institute for Jewish Genealogy and Paul Jacobi Center, JNUL, 2015).

58. Josep Muntané, "Metges jueus contractats pel govern municipal de Tàrrega durant els segles XIV i XV," *Urtx* 26.1 (2012): 135–47.

59. See, e.g., Fujii, *Killing Neighbors*; Kalyvas, *The Logic of Violence in Civil War*; and the relevant bibliography in Chapter 5 below.

60. See, e.g., Mitchell B. Merback, *The Thief, the Cross and the Wheel* (Chicago: University of Chicago Press, 1999); Esther Cohen, *The Modulated Scream: Pain in Medieval Culture* (Chicago: University of Chicago Press, 2010).

Chapter 2

1. See Ezra Fleischer, *Shirat haQodesh ha'Ivrit byemei habeinayyim* (Jerusalem: Magnes, 1975); Elisabeth Hollender, "Narrative Exegesis in Ashkenas and Zarfat: The Case of *Piyyut* Commentary," in Judit Targarona Borrás and Angel Saenz-Badillos, eds., *Jewish Studies at the Turn of the Twentieth Century* (Leiden: Brill, 1999), 429–35; Ephraim Kanarfogel, *The Intellectual History and Rabbinic Culture of Medieval Ashkenaz* (Detroit: Wayne State University Press, 2012); Susan Einbinder, with Samuel N. Rosenberg, "Exegesis and Romance: Revisiting the Old French Translation of Kallir," in Elisheva Baumgarten and Judah D. Galinsky, eds., *Jews and Christians in Thirteenth-Century France* (New York: Palgrave Macmillan, 2015), 235–49 and appendix 249–59. In an essay tracing, among other things, the history of funeral orations from Sepharad, Eleazer Gutwirth notes the rich attention to funerary and lament forms in late medieval Spain; see his "Penso's Roots: The Politics and Poetics of Cultural Fusion," *Studia Rosenthalia* 35.2 (2001): 276–77.

2. Technically, beginning with the First Crusade, the laments for historical persecutions found a home in three distinct genres of liturgical poetry: the *qinah*, the *selihah*, and the *zulat*. Each genre belonged to its own liturgical setting: the *qinah* collections to the Ninth of Av; the *selihah* to communal penitential liturgies, Rosh Hashanah, and Yom Kippur; and the *zulat* to the morning Sabbath liturgy of the month of Iyar. See Avraham Gross, "Liturgy as Personal Memorial for the Victims in 1096," in Stefan Reif, Andreas Lehnardt, and Avriel Bar-Levav, eds., *Death in Jewish Life: Burial and Mourning Customs Among Jews of Europe and Nearby Communities* (Berlin: De Gruyter, 2014), 156–57.

3. LaCapra, *Writing History*; Caruth, *Unclaimed Experience*. While earlier studies invoking this term emphasized modernist and postmodern techniques of aporia and atemporality, more recent work has challenged this perspective, often on grounds of its Western-centric bias: Craps, *Postcolonial Witnessing*; Roger Luckhurst, *The Trauma Question* (New York: Routledge, 2008); Eaglestone, "Knowledge, 'Afterwardness,' and the Future of Trauma Theory."

4. In fact, none of the extant plague laments is interested in the plague itself. It was the combination of pestilence and the brutality of their neighbors that merited poetic attention and explanation within a meaningful framework. The lament discussed in Chapter 5, by Moses Nathan, also survived in some Italian and Algerian liturgies, but never attracted the attention of later anthologists.

5. Ephraim of Bonn's lament, "Le-mi oy le-mi avoy," has been included in a number of anthologies and is still recited today. For an excerpted Hebrew text with English translation, see T. Carmi, *The Penguin Book of Hebrew Verse* (New York: Penguin, 1981), 384–85, or my full translation in "The Martyrs of Blois," in Thomas Head, ed., *Medieval Hagiography: A Sourcebook* (New York: Routledge, 2000), 537–61. I treat the text in Einbinder, *Beautiful*

Death, Chap. 2. The powerful lament by Isaac bar Shalom, "Ein kamokha ba'ilmim," also appears in full translation and discussion in Jakob Petuchowski, *Theology and Poetry: Studies in the Medieval Piyyut* (London: Routledge, 1978), 71–83.

6. Smelser, "Psychological and Cultural Trauma," 38. Alexander, "Toward a Theory of Cultural Trauma," defines the concept of "culture carriers" who are responsible for giving voice to collective traumas. As Smelser and Alexander emphasize, collective or cultural trauma is therefore inherently a social construct. It takes time to construct, its construction may be contested, and its traumatic value must be "actively sustained and reproduced" (see Smelser, 38–39). These features distinguish it from individual or psychological trauma.

7. See Alexander and Smelser.

8. See Mishnah Ta'anit. The Mishnah is commonly considered to have been completed by the early third century.

9. Thus, many unique copies of martyrological hymns come to us from the penitential hymns for fast days like the Ninth of Av or the Seventeenth of Tamuz. On the other hand, hymns that treat the annual stoning of the gate or wall to a Jewish quarter are preserved in liturgies for the seventh night of Passover, not a fast-day liturgy at all but close in time to the Easter holiday. See Susan Einbinder, "Hebrew Poems for 'the Day of Shutting In': Problems and Methods," *Revue des Études Juives* 163.1–2 (January–June 2004): 111–35.

10. Surprisingly, these hymns have never been collected for treatment.

11. IMHM, F 13090 (vol. 2), listed with F 13085 (vol. 1).

12. Fol. 102a, beginning... אנא ה' אלהינו ואלהי אבותינו האל הגדול הגבור והנורא העזיז והאמיץ

13. This can be established from Christian documentation, such as the letters from Pere (Pedro) IV of Aragon to the municipal governments of these towns, ordering them to protect their Jews, and from the sole Hebrew chronicle account of Hayim Galipapa, excerpts of which survived in the sixteenth-century chronicles of Joseph haCohen. See Chapter 5 for more on these sources. Galipapa's chronicle has been recently treated by Barzilay, "The Black Death in Aragon."

14. See Einbinder, "Hebrew Poems for 'the Day of Shutting In.'"

15. We shall meet Shadal again in Chapter 4, as he was also responsible for publishing a transcription of medieval epitaphs from Toledo that include a number of texts describing death from the plague.

16. Lazar Landshuth, *'Amudei ha'avodah* (Berlin: G. Bernstein, 1857), appendix, xxvi; Bernfeld, *Sefer haDema'ot*, 2:108–10.

17. For more on this incipit, see the discussion later in this chapter.

18. Or German Jewish authors who had spent time in northern French schools, such as the brothers Ephraim and Hillel of Bonn, who both composed narrative laments for the victims of an auto-da-fé in Blois in 1171. See Einbinder, *Beautiful Death*, chap. 2; idem, "Signs of Romance: Hebrew Poetry in the Twelfth-Century Renaissance," in Michael A. Signer and John van Engen, eds., *Jews and Christians in Twelfth-Century Europe* (Notre Dame, Ind.: University of Notre Dame, 2001), 221–34. See also Einbinder, "Exegesis and Romance."

19. Cathy Caruth, *Listening to Trauma: Conversations with Leaders in the Theory and Treatment of Catastrophic Experience* (Baltimore: Johns Hopkins University Press, 2014), xiii.

20. Gautier-Dalché, "La Peste Negra dans les états de la Couronne d'Aragon"; Richard F. Gyug, "The Effects and Extent of the Black Death of 1348: New Evidence for Clerical Mortality in Barcelona," *Mediaeval Studies* 45.1 (1983): 385–98; Shirk, "The Black Death in Aragon 1348–1351"; López de Meneses, "Una consecuencia de la Peste Negra en Cataluña; idem, *Documentos acerca de la Peste Negra en los dominios de la Corona de Aragón* (Zaragoza: Imprenta Heraldo de Aragón, 1956).

21. It may be that the term נכאים, usually referring to "crippled," alludes to the poor motor control of those stricken by plague; cf. Abraham Caslari's catalog of symptoms, discussed in Chapter 3.

22. As we might, e.g., say, "Timbuktu," not in reference to the actual place in Africa but to a place "really far away."

23. As Smelser notes, "the 'active' or 'inactive' status of cultural trauma is . . . contingent on forever changing and ongoing social and political conditions. . . . The very status of 'indelibility' . . . is itself subject to constantly changing historical circumstances." Smelser, 51.

24. Summerfield, "A Critique of Seven Assumptions Behind Psychological Trauma Programmes in War-Affected Areas," 1449–62. Summerfield describes clinical conditions and theory; my observation can be extended to literary works that, in effect, perform the theoretical clichés that, in turn, claim to find them.

25. Hannes Fricke, *Das hört nicht auf: Trauma, Literatur und Empathie* (Göttingen: Wallstein, 2004); see also Craps, *Postcolonial Witnessing*, chap. 3; Luckhurst, *The Trauma Question*; Eaglestone, "Knowledge, 'Afterwardness,' and the Future of Trauma Theory," 11–23, for reprises on the insufficiencies of a "trauma aesthetic" limited to techniques of temporal disjunction, narrative gaps, and split forms of discourse. Like many of the antiphonal laments that would have surrounded it, Emanuel's *qinah* served as what Feldman has described as a "cultural tool for collectivizing truth claims." Emanuel's lament does produce a victim—and with them, an enemy—but no sense of the "debilitating blockage or disability of traumatization." See Allen Feldman, "Memory Theaters, Virtual Witnessing and the Trauma-Aesthetic," *Biography* 27.1 (Winter 2004): 178. For a contrasting, far more naive, perspective, see Caruth, *Unclaimed Experience*.

26. See Bernfeld, *Sefer haDema'ot*, 2:106–54. The first lament begins משוד עניים אנקת אביוני, 106; it is followed by Emanuel's lament, and then אני הוא הקונן קינה of Baruch bar Yehiel, 111–21; ציון אריוך / בכי אשר נוך by Israel bar Joel Zusselin, 121–42, and עם קדושים נפלו by Akiva ben Eleazar, 142–54.

27. Israel Yuval, "Vengeance and Curse, Blood and Libel: From Saints' Stories to the Blood Libel" [Hebrew], *Ziyyon* 58 (1993): 33–90.

28. From its early articulation in Freud and Breuer's essay on hysterical neurosis, "language" was one means of abreacting the excess stimulation that the authors posited characterized situations of trauma. According to their theory, the brain in "normal" conditions could process a surge in stimuli by means of physical response (including violence), anger, grief, and speech. In the case of trauma, excess stimulation was not processed but "stored" unprocessed, out of reach of memory and speech. Until the unprocessed memory (in a sense, pre-memory) was recovered, the experience that belatedly expressed itself in the intrusive symptoms and somatic "conversions" defining trauma could not be related as narrative and

"cured." While this theory has undergone considerable tinkering since its first appearance in 1895, Freud's basic model—with, as Ruth Leys points out, all its inherent contradictions—has remained largely intact. Josef Breuer and Sigmund Freud, "On the Psychical Mechanism of Hysterical Phenomena: Preliminary Communication (1893)," in *Freud and Breuer: Studies on Hysteria* (New York: Avon, 1966), 37–52; Leys, *Trauma*, 18–41.

29. Caruth, *Unclaimed Experience*; and see Leys's critique in *Trauma*, chap. 8.

30. Edwin Seroussi, "The Songs of Grief and Hope: Ancient Western Sepharadi Melodies of Qinot for the 9th of Av," *Yuval* 7 (2002): 201–32.

31. Susan Einbinder, "*Muʿāraḍa* as a Key to the Literary Unity of the *Muwashshaḥ*" (Ph.D. diss., Columbia University, 1991); and idem, review of Joachim Yeshaya, *Poetry and Memory in Karaite Prayer* (Leiden: Brill, 2014), *The Medieval Review*, TMR 15.09.31.

32. עינינו לך תלויות עד שתחננו ותסיר דבר ומגפה ומשחית היום מעלינו קדוש

33. Jeffrey Alexander, *Cultural Trauma: A Social Theory* (Cambridge: Polity Press, 2012). See Smelser, "Psychological and Cultural Trauma," 31–59; Smelser observes that "a claim of traumatic cultural damage . . . must be established by deliberate efforts on the part of cultural carriers—cultural specialists such as priests, politicians, intellectuals, journalists, moral entrepreneurs, and leaders of social movements" (38). Moreover, to maintain its status as collective trauma, an effort is necessary so that this status is "continuously and actively sustained and reproduced" (ibid.). Emanuel's lament suggests that at some point in time, this process collapsed.

34. Shatzmiller, "Les juifs de Provence pendant la Peste Noire," 462–63. Shatzmiller describes "toute la communauté massacré." See also the recent invocation of this incident and Shatzmiller's reconstruction in Carlo Ginzburg, *Threads and Traces: True False Fictive* (Berkeley: University of California Press, 2012), 82–96.

35. See, e.g., Petrarch's letter to his brother, e.g., in translation in George Deaux, *The Black Death 1347* (New York: Weybright & Talley, 1969), 92–94.

36. Summerfield, 1453.

Chapter 3

1. From its initial landing point in Marseilles, the plague had by April arrived in Perpignan, where it continued to rage through the end of June. In Barcelona, the fevers made their entrance in mid-May; Girona, close to Besalú, was struck at the same time. By mid-July, the pandemic had reached Lleida to the west and Cervera and Tàrrega to the southwest. Castile, which Abraham mentions as one of the regions affected, did not really feel the impact of the pestilence until the spring and summer of 1349, hence the necessity to date Abraham's work no earlier than that time. Christian Guilleré, "La Peste Noire à Gérone (1348)," *Annals de l'institut d'estudis Gironins* 27 (1984): 104–6; Colet et al., "The Black Death and Its Consequences," 65–67; Richard F. Gyug, "Clerical Mortality in Barcelona," *Mediaeval Studies* 45 (1983): 389–90; López de Meneses, "Una consecuencia de la Peste Negra en Cataluña," docs. 5–8; idem, *Documentos acerca de la Peste Negra en los dominios de la Corona de Aragón*, 298, no. 8, documenting the attack on the Jewish *call* of Barcelona on May 17, 1348. As for the

production of plague tractates, Anna Montgomery Campbell lists seventeen composed during 1348–50; according to Lori Jones, there are twenty-four extant treatises, a count that does not include the Hebrew exemplars; personal e-mail, May 2016. See A. Campbell, *The Black Death and Men of Learning*, chap. 2.

2. As I have generally opted for Catalan spellings throughout this chapter and Chapter 5, I use the Catalan Lleida, as opposed to the more familiar Spanish Lérida.

3. For Jacme's treatise, see C. E. Winslow and M. L. Duran-Reynals, "Jacme d'Agramont and the First of the Plague Tractates," *Bulletin of the History of Medicine* 22 (1948): 761; idem, their edition of the text, "Regiment de Preservacio a Epidimia o Pestilencia e Mortaldats," *Bulletin of the History of Medicine* 23 (1949): 57–89 (hereafter Duran-Reynals and Winslow). An edition with facing Catalan translation appeared in 1998; see Jon Arrizabalaga, Luis García-Ballester, and Joan Veny, eds., *Jacme d'Agramont: Regiment de preservació de pestilència (Lleida, 1348)* (Lleida: Universitat de Lleida, 1998), 24. I had completed this chapter when I learned of a newer edition: Joan Veny and Francesc Cremades, eds., *Regiment de preservació de pestilència (1348): Jacme d'Agramont* (Barcelona: Universitat de Barcelona, 2015) (hereafter Veny and Cremades). References to the text have been adjusted to incorporate this edition. See also Jon Arrizabalaga, "Facing the Black Death: Perceptions and Reactions of University Medical Practitioners," in Luis García-Ballester et al., eds., *Practical Medicine from Salerno to the Black Death* (Cambridge: Cambridge University Press, 1994), 240. On the history of the university, which was founded in 1300, see Michael McVaugh and Luis García-Ballester, "The Medical Faculty at Early Fourteenth-Century Lérida," *History of Universities* 8 (1989): 1–25.

4. The term "universal pestilence" sometimes implies that a large geographical area is affected (what we refer to today as a pandemic). See Ann Carmichael, "Universal and Particular: The Language of Plague, 1348–1500," in Vivian Nutton, ed., *Pestilential Complexities: Understanding Medieval Plague* (London: Wellcome Trust, 2008), 17–52.

5. Guilleré, 104.

6. See, e.g., Colet et al., "The Black Death and Its Consequences"; Guilleré; Gautier-Dalché, "La Peste Negra dans les États de la Couronne d'Aragon"; Yitzhak Baer, *A History of the Jews in Christian Spain* (Philadelphia: Jewish Publication Society, 1966), 2:24–26; Nirenberg, *Communities of Violence*, 231–45.

7. Some studies do refer to anti-Jewish violence in Girona, but this does not seem to be accurate. See, e.g., Valdéon, who mentions "la ola antisemita" that struck the calls of Cervera and Tàrrega, and, "to a lesser extent, those of Lérida and Girona": Julio Valdéon, "La muerte negra en la Península," *Historia* 16.56 (1980): 60–66. López de Meneses refers to "continued hostility" toward the Jews of Girona in 1352; see *Sefarad* 19.2, doc. 32, letter of August 18, 1352. Guilleré's study is clear that there was no violence in Girona in 1348, although in 1350 there is some Easter week trouble with stoning of the Jewish quarter; Guilleré, 54.

8. Guilleré, 18.

9. For historical/biographical details on the family, see Michael McVaugh, *Medicine Before the Plague: Practitioners and Their Patients in the Crown of Aragon, 1285–1345* (Cambridge: Cambridge University Press, 1993); Joseph Shatzmiller, *Jews, Medicine, and Medieval Society* (Berkeley: University of California Press, 1994); Einbinder, *No Place of Rest*;

idem, "Literature, Memory and Medieval French Jews," *JSQ* 15.3 (2008): 225–40; idem, "God's Forgotten Sheep: Jewish Poetry and the Expulsion from France (1306)," *Masoret haPiyyut* 4 (2008): 55*–82* (English sec.).

10. Manuel Grau i Montserrat, "Metges Jueus del Vell Comtat de Besalú," *Gimbernat: Revista Catalana d'història de la medicina i de la ciència* 8 (1987): 84, 87.

11. Guilleré, 18.

12. I am grateful to Michael McVaugh for sharing his notes from the archives. For the thirty-year exemption, see Canc. 483, 69, for 1333; for the contract with the Infante, see Canc. 393, 93–94. E-mail correspondence, October 5–6, 2006. According to McVaugh, *Medicine Before the Plague*, 59, Abraham provided medical care to at least three of Jaume II of Aragon's children in the 1320s and 1330s. His daughter's name, for that matter, suggests that the second marriage was the one that survived. Jaume II of Aragon was succeeded by Alfonso IV in 1327, and Alfonso by Pere (Pedro) IV in 1336. See William Jordan, *Europe in the High Middle Ages* (London: Penguin Press, 2001), 341.

13. The "Alei ra'anan" (Fragrant leaves) can be dated by the author's colophon preserved in a fourteenth-century copy of the text, MS Parma 1952 (= de Rossi 946) (IMHM F 13107); Caslari says there that he composed the work at the request of a friend. At least nine other copies of the text are extant, most fifteenth-century copies in Provençal, Sephardic, or Italian hands.

14. For the movement of the Black Death through this region, see Gautier-Dalché; Shirk, "The Black Death in Aragon 1348–1351"; Gyug, "Clerical Mortality in Barcelona"; and idem, *The Diocese of Barcelona During the Black Death: The Register Notule Communium 15 (1348–49)* (Toronto: PIMS, 1994); Guilleré, 87–161; López de Meneses, *Documentos*; idem, "Una consecuencia de la Peste Negra"; Valdéon, "La muerte negra en la Península." Benedictow, *The Black Death*, is a concise survey, as, from a different perspective, is Paul Freedman, *The Origins of Peasant Servitude in Medieval Catalonia* (Cambridge: Cambridge University Press, 1991), 154–78. The classic work of Biraben also covers Iberia, although not in great detail; see *Les hommes et la peste en France et dans les pays européens et méditerranéens*.

15. The tractate discussed in this chapter, *Ma'amar beqaddahot divriyyot uminei qaddahot* (Tractate on pestilential and other types of fevers), survives in one copy, MS Leiden OR 7/4778 (IMHM microfilm F 17378). The Institute for Microfilmed Hebrew Manuscripts lists two additional sources—MS Leeuwarder, Provinciale Bibliotheek van Friesland BA Fr. 19 (IMHM F 3479); and MS Berlin Or. Qu 836 (Berlin Staatsbibliothek Preussischer Kulturbesitz) (IMHM F 1787)—that do not correspond to this work but to the anonymous tractate published by Gerrit Bos a few years ago: "The Black Death in Hebrew Literature: *Ha-Ma'amar be-Qaddahot ha-Dever* (Treatise on Pestilential Fever)," *European Journal of Jewish Studies* 5.1 (2011): 1–52. Apparently, a critical edition of Abraham's tractate is under preparation by Jessica Kley in Cologne; I was unable to obtain access to this work.

16. Hayim Schirmann, ed., and notes by Ezra Fleischer, *Toldot Hashirah ha'ivrit biSefarad uveDrom Tzarfat* (Jerusalem: Magnes, 1997). On the poem, see 242n80 and 478n34; for the poetry contest, 484n61. See also Einbinder, *No Place of Rest*, 91; N. S. Doniach, "Abraham Bedersi's Purim Letter to David Kaslari," *Jewish Quarterly Review* n.s. 23 (1932–33): 63–69; Israel Davidson, "Abraham Bedarshi's Purim Letter," *Jewish Quarterly Review* n.s. 23.4 (1932–33): 349–56.

17. McVaugh, *Medicine Before the Plague*, 58; idem, e-mail of January 14, 2014, citing archival records that refer to Abraham's "late father" in 1315–16.

18. For the Jewish tractates, see Gerrit Bos and Guido Mensching, "The Black Death in Hebrew Literature: Abraham Ben Solomon Hen's *Tractatulus de pestilentia*," *JSQ* 18.1 (2011): 32–63; Gerrit Bos, "The Black Death in Hebrew Literature: *Ha-ma'amar beqaddahot ha-dever* (Treatise on Pestilential Fever)," *European Journal of Jewish Studies* 5.1 (2011): 1–52. For the 1362 treatise of Isaac b. Todros, see David Ginzburg, "*Be'er Lehi*: The Plague Tract of Isaac ben Todros" [Hebrew], in Curatorium der Zunz-Stiftung, eds., *Tef'eret Seivah* (*Jubelschrift zum Neunzigsten Geburtstag des Dr. L. Zunz*) (Berlin: Louis Gerschel, 1884), 91–126. For a recent discussion and edition of a late fifteenth-century tractate authored by a *converso* physician, see Efrén de la Peña Barroso, "Un *Regimen Sanitatis* contra la peste: El tratado del licenciado Vázquez," *Asclepio* 44.2 (2012): 397–416.

19. Barkai, "Jewish Treatises on the Black Death."

20. Arrizabalaga, "Facing the Black Death," 241. Lori Jones reminds me that Arrizabalaga's list is limited to university-based physicians, and other plague tracts appeared also. Personal correspondence (e-mail), May 2016. .

21. Melissa Chase, "Fever, Poisons and Apostemes: Authority and Experience in Montpellier Plague Treatises," *Annals of the New York Academy of Sciences* 441 (1985): 154–55. See also Arrizabalaga, "Facing the Black Death," on this point, 245–46.

22. Chase, 155–56.

23. A diagnosis of non-pestilential fever is also made by Alfonso de Córdoba in Avignon and Giovanni della Penna in Italy. The secondary literature on the Black Death is now gigantic, but see, e.g., A. Campbell, cited above, or the bibliography cited inter alia below.

24. Guilleré, 29. But note that the percentages are unevenly distributed among the various professional categories that he investigates, ranging from 25 percent of the city's jurists to 50 percent of its notaries. He has no data on physicians but concludes that, in general, the elite fared better than other groups in the city or elsewhere, 30–34.

25. Carmichael, "Universal and Particular."

26. Arrizabalaga et al., *Jacme d'Agramont*, 22.

27. Arrizabalaga, "Facing the Black Death," 240.

28. A similar idea may be found in Gentile da Foligno's final tractate, which draws a connection between pestilence and war—because the disorderly behavior of humans in wartime generates corrupting humors and because the "fertility which usually follows on the famine provoked by war" generates its own humoral surplus, from which putrefaction may result. Arrizabalaga, "Facing the Black Death," 245.

29. Ibid.

30. Ibid., 256. Sam Cohn's formidable essay on plague-inspired violence against Jewish communities focuses on central and eastern Europe, but there, too, he identifies municipal officials, local nobility, and clergy as instigators of the attacks. In Tàrrega, discussed in Chapter 5 of this volume, the mayor is arrested and fined after the attacks. While it seems to have been a standard ploy to blame outsiders or riffraff for the violence and looting, the evidence points to trouble far higher up the social scale. Thus, e.g., Morey's insistence that the 1348 violence against the Jews in the Franche-Comté was entirely economical in motivation

does not really hold with the findings of more recent studies. See Cohn, "The Black Death and the Burning of the Jews"; Colet et al., "The Black Death and Its Consequences"; Muntané, "Metges jueus contractats"; J. Morey, "Les juifs au Franche-Comté au XIVe siècle," *Revue des Études Juives* 7 (1883): 1–39.

31. Arrizabalaga et al., *Jacme d'Agramont*. Arrizabalaga also notes that d'Agramont describes Montpellier as a region where plague was, in fact, deliberately engineered, suggesting that he was aware of Alfonso de Córdoba's writings. Arrizabalaga, "Facing the Black Death," 236–37.

32. Art. 2, pt. 1, chap. 2. For the Catalan, see Arrizabalaga et al., *Jacme d'Agramont*, 56; or Veny and Cremades, 54. The English translation is my adaptation of Duran-Reynals and Winslow, 65.

33. Joan Veny i Clar, ed., *"Regiment de Preservació de Pestilència" de Jacme d'Agramont* (Tarragona: Excelentisima Diputación Provincial, 1971), 40. Curiously, Veny observes that the manuscript history of the work does not demonstrate wide diffusion. It is not cited by other physicians (to whom it was not, in any event, addressed). Only one copy is extant, and it was discovered in an ecclesiastical archive in Solsona in the early twentieth century. See the introduction to the 1971 ed. just cited, 38–40; and Veny and Cremades, 21–23.

34. Gautier-Dalché mentions that some local authorities began banning the peal of church bells for the dead, one of Jacme's recommendations. Jacme also makes this recommendation (see below), but it is not necessarily his regimen that is the source of the practice. Gautier-Dalché, 71, citing a 1350 document.

35. Winslow and Duran-Reynals, "Jacme d'Agramont and the First of the Plague Tractates," 754. They note that a copy of Pinkhof's "pamphlet" was "read for us" by a colleague, presumably from the Dutch.

36. ולכן כתבתי בקצרה מה ירצה באמרי דבר ודבר בגדרים ואבאר סבותיהם ואותותיהם והנגהתם והנהגותיהם האלה בקדחות סברתי אודיע ואחר. Pinkhof, *Abraham Kashlari, over Pestachtige Koortsen*; p. 50 = MS Leiden Cod. Or. 4778, fol. 115b.

37. In the regimen for true pestilence, Pinkhof 45 = MS Leiden 119a, the physician is cautioned to avoid feeding his patients lamb or pork "for those who eat it": ולא בכבשים וירחקו החזיר אוכליו.

38. This was not an unusual option (or tactic). Maimonides also never refers to Avicenna by name, even when he is citing him directly, although it may be that in Maimonides' case, he encountered Avicenna's works, particularly his philosophical ones, via other writers. Gad Freudenthal and Mauro Zonta, "Avicenna Among Medieval Jews: The Reception of Avicenna's Philosophical, Scientific and Medical Writings in Jewish Cultures, East and West," *Arabic Sciences and Philosophy* 22 (2012): 236, 280. Other writers, Jewish and Christian, sometimes chose to conceal the names of the authors they embedded in their works.

39. Luis García-Ballester, Michael McVaugh, and Agustín Rubio-Vela, *Medical Licensing and Learning in Fourteenth-Century Valencia* (Philadelphia: Transactions of the American Philosophical Society, 1989), 79, pt. 6; Joseph Shatzmiller, "On Becoming a Jewish Doctor in the High Middle Ages," *Sefarad* 43 (1983): 239–50.

40. McVaugh, *Medicine Before the Plague*; idem and Luis García Ballester, "Jewish Appreciation of Fourteenth-Century Scholastic Medicine," *Viator* 23 (1990):

201–13; García-Ballester, McVaugh, and Rubio-Vela, *Medical Licensing and Learning in Fourteenth-Century Valencia*. I say "possible," but the obstacles must also be noted. They included outright bans on Jewish study at the universities, such as that decreed in Aragon in 1329, and bans on loaning medical books to Jews; see Hagar Kahana-Smilansky, "The Commentaries by Medieval Jews on Avicenna's Canon of Medicine: A Hypothesis," unpublished lecture, IAS-Hebrew University, May 10, 2007. Ironically, in 1300 the first professor of medicine at the fledgling University of Lleida demanded and received some of his reference library with a royal order impounding the texts from local Jews.

41. Nancy Siraissi, *Taddeo Alderotti and His Pupils: Two Generations of Italian Medical Learning* (Princeton, N.J.: Princeton University Press, 1991).

42. This is why, Freudenthal and Zonta note, the first Hebrew translations appeared in Italy, where the "Arabophone" legacy was limited or nonexistent. Freudenthal and Zonta, 270. Among Arabic-speaking Jews, copies of the Canon written in Arabic but transcribed in Hebrew characters were also common. Freudenthal and Zonta count twenty-two extant copies today, none of them complete. Ibid., 236.

43. Haim Rabin, "A History of the Translation of the Canon into Hebrew" [Hebrew], *Melilah* 3–4 (1950): 132–47.

44. Benjamin Richler, "Manuscripts of Avicenna's Kanon in Hebrew Translation: A Revised and Up-to-Date List," *Korot* 8.3–4 (1982): 145*–168* in English sec.; 137–43 in Hebrew. Freudenthal and Zonta tally "at least seven" full or partial translations. See Freudenthal and Zonta, 270.

45. Richler, "Manuscripts of Avicenna's Canon."

46. Ibid. More recently, Freudenthal and Zonta have raised the count to more than 150 manuscripts containing all or parts of the Canon in Hebrew, making that work "the most widely disseminated medieval Hebrew work of science." They also count more than thirty known Hebrew commentaries on the Canon. Freudenthal and Zonta, 271.

47. Apparently, readers in general found this a critical section, as indicated by the fact that these pages have been torn out of the Countway Library's copy of the 1491 print edition, presumably for personal use (one hopes, not a modern scholar's!).

48. For book 4 alone, Richler counted thirty-eight manuscript copies of Nathan haMe'ati's translation and six copies of four anonymous translations. Among the Me'ati listings, no fewer than nine are fourteenth-century "Spanish" copies. Of the six remaining copies, four are fourteenth-century Italian works, one is from fourteenth-century Ashkenaz, and one fifteenth-century Spain. While the distribution attests to the widespread appeal of the Canon among Jewish readers, it also indicates the heavy interest in this work among Iberian Jewish physicians. Richler, "Manuscripts of Avicenna's Kanon."

49. Kahana-Smilansky, 9.

50. Naples 1491 ed., bk. 4, fen 1, intro. Cf. Harvard University Countway Library of Medicine, MS Ballard 11, fol. 5a,־מתלקח ברוב [!] ויצמח ממנו במצוע הרוח והדם בשרייינים והעור קים בכל הגוף.

51. Pinkhof 49 = MS Leiden Cod. Or. 4778, fol. 116b.

52. Pinkhof 47 = MS Leiden Cod. Or. 4778, fol. 118a.

53. Duran-Reynals and Winslow, 61 (art. 1, chap. 1).

54. Pinkhof 47 = MS Leiden Cod. Or. 4778, fol. 117b.

55. Pinkhof 43 = MS Leiden Cod. Or. 4778, fol. 121a.

56. From the Me'ati translation of the 1491 Naples ed., n.p. bk. 4, Fen 1, art. 4, chap. 3. The version in Countway MS Ballard 11 (listed in Richler's study as Heb. 2, IMHM microfilm F 41333), fol. 41ab, is slightly different. The codex is a Sephardic semi-cursive script copy in mixed hands; the section containing bk. 4 of the canon is dated to 1463. אגסים may derive from the Arabic *ajashsh*, which refers to a hoarse or screeching voice. The manuscript version includes the image of rodents and reptiles "in a panic and fleeing so that they are visible" and, oddly, describes the stork as "clean-natured" rather than "bad/evil-natured." It also uses שרצים for insects, not רמשים. Otherwise, the texts are almost identical.

57. Jacme, art. 2, pt. 2, chap. i, ii and iii, in Duran-Reynals and Winslow, 68–71; Veny and Cremades, 57–61.

58. Duran-Reynals and Winslow, 68, art. 2, pt. 2, chap. 1: "specialment noguers que han proprietat special de corrompre l'àer e semblant proprietat ha la figuera"—Veny and Cremades, 57.

59. Duran-Reynals and Winslow, 69–70, art. 2, pt. 2, chap. i.

60. Pinkhof 50, 49, 42 = MS Leiden Cod. Or. 4778, fols. 116a, 116b, 121a, respectively.

61. See Avicenna, Canon, bk. 4, fen 1, art. 4, והכנת הגוף למה שאנחנו בו מהההתפעלות שיהיה מלא ליחות רעות... כמו אותם שהרבה המשגל והגופים רחבי הנקבים רבי הרחיצה... And cf. the slightly different version in Countway, MS Ballard 11, 41a, where, instead of the print version's description of people with an excess of bad humors, "like those who indulge in sex, and people with large pores or who bathe too much," the manuscript refers to "people who indulge in sex, and people who are broad-chested and who bathe too much": ויתפשט... בגוף ותהיה קדחת דבריית. ויעמס רבים מהאנשים לחום ג"כ בנפשים בגבולות הכנה בו הפעל אחד אם יגיע ולא יהיה הנפעל מוכן לא יתחדש פועל ומתפעלות. והכנת הגוף למה שיקיף בו ואנחנו? מהההתפעלו' כשיהיה מלא ליחות רעות .. כמו אותם שהרבו המשגל והגוף רחבי החזה החלים רבי הרחיצה... Harvard, Countway, MS Ballard 11, 41a.

62. Arrizabalaga notes that variable susceptibility to disease was "unanimously recognized among late medieval university physicians." Arrizabalaga, "Facing the Black Death," 261.

63. Pinkhof 46 = MS Leiden Cod. Or. 4778, fol. 118b.

64. והארציות יהיה משכונת העפושים מפסידים האויר כשכונת בעלי הגדמות והצרעות והנשד'. פים והחרחורים המתעבר הפסדם לאויר והפעולות.... לפי מה שהסכימו עליו המנסים והמקשים See further discussion of this line below. Pinkhof, 49 = MS Leiden Cod. Or. 4778, fol. 116b.

65. Ibid., וכן יראה בבחירה בתאנה ואגוז וכ"ש בעת נפילתו נבלת עליהם. I do not find this specification in Avicenna, so it seems likely that both men are taking it from another shared source.

66. Duran-Reynals and Winslow translate this list as "leprosy, or scabies, phthisis and opthalmia, pestilential fever, smallpox and measles and skin diseases," art. 2, pt. 2, chap. 1: Duran-Reynals and Winslow, 69; Veny and Cremades, 58. I am not so sure about their retrospective diagnosis. See, on this hazard, Jon Arrizabalaga, "Problematizing Retrospective Diagnosis in the History of Disease," *Asclepio* 54.1 (2002): 51–69.

67. Pinkhof 48 = MS Leiden Cod. Or. 4778, fol. 117b; see also Pinkhof 50 = MS Leiden Cod. Or. 4778, fol. 116a. The reading in MS Leiden 4778 is וקרבתם מהמות, "The heart and

brain are close to death, so that," etc. Avicenna considers the reading of pulse and urine for different fever conditions. A "normal" pulse and urine can be signs of an ephemeral fever, which perhaps would not give the physician undue cause for alarm. In differentiating between pestilential and humoral-pestilential fevers, Avicenna notes that it is easy for physicians to be confused: ולפעמים יקרה מן הקדחות הדבריות האלו מה שלא יחוש בה . . . ולא ישתנה הדפק ולא השתן שנוי רב. ועם זה תהיה המיתה במהרה ויבהל הרופא בעניינה. (Occasionally, the symptoms of these pestilential fevers will not be perceptible . . . [T]he pulse and urine will not change much. Nonetheless, death will come suddenly and the physician will be stunned by it.) Canon, bk. 4, fen 1, art. 4, Harvard Countway, MS Ballard 11, 41a. The uncharacteristic behavior of pulse and urine in the case of plague must have become familiar to physicians over subsequent outbreaks, as one later reader of the Countway copy of the Hebrew print edition, MS Ballard 160, has written in the margin next to Avicenna's description of "good" pulse and urine indicating ephemeral fever: וקדחת העפוש הוא ההפך, i.e., "pestilential fevers are the opposite." Canon, bk. 4, fen 1 art. 1, chap. 6, marginal note. The same diagnostic problem is noted by another Jewish physician at the end of the fifteenth century, a Spanish-born Jew known alternatively as Elijah ben Abraham or Ilyas ibn Ibrahaim al-Yahudi al-Isbani. Elijah/Ilyas's Arabic-language tractate, dedicated to the Ottoman ruler, also notes that doctors are confounded by plague patients whose heartbeat and urine are normal but who suddenly die. Barkai, 15–16.

68. Cf. similar recommendations in Ibn al-Jazzar's *Book on Fevers*, e.g., in the section on fevers originating in the blood, where putrefaction also travels via veins and arteries to the heart and other organs. Ibn al-Jazzar recommends "oil of roses with rose-water, juice of Egyptian willow, unripe, sour grapes or purslane" or "juice of chamomile and violet blossoms" daubed on the forehead and temples, and soaking or massaging feet in herbal baths containing violets and chamomile. Ibn al-Jazzar's tenth-century work on fevers was translated into Latin by the eleventh century and was included among the texts of the Articella, the medical compendium that was a staple of Salernitan and Montpellier curricula; it was translated into Hebrew three times and was well-known to Jewish practitioners. Gerrit Bos, ed., *Ibn al-Jazzar on Fevers* (New York: Kegan Paul, 2000), v and 125. Caslari's leg bath includes myrtle, chamomile, and grape leaves (Pinkhof 41 = MS Leiden 122a). Avicenna recommends the same solution of violet and rose waters, chamomile, and anesthetic herbs for compresses to treat headaches associated with acute fevers. See the Canon, bk. 4, fen 1, art. 2, chap. 24.

69. Most of these recommendations from Pinkhof, 39–41, MS Leiden Cod. Or. 4778, fols. 122a–123b. This particular one refers to a drug called פוליפודי, which targets all humors and contains no toxins: שזה המשלשל כול הליחות כלנה . . . [ו] אין בו סם משלשל בעל איכות רעה ולא ארסיית, Pinkhof 41= MS Leiden Cod. Or. 4778, fol. 122a.

70. The same preference for familiar foods and locavore diet is documented in the 1327 Esther romance composed by Israel Caslari (no relation to Abraham), where the Judaeo-Occitan version of the romance indicates that the guests at Ahashverus's feast drank wine "as each would have drunk in their homes/ that did not go to their heads." See Einbinder, *No Place of Rest*, 99.

71. E.g., Pinkhof 40 = MS Leiden Cod. Or. 4778, fol. 123a. Avicenna, too, differentiates between the affect and treatment of fever in children, so it is hard to say whether Abraham's deference to this category reflects experience.

72. Carmichael, "Universal and Particular."

73. Pinkhof 51 = MS Leiden Cod. Or. 4778, fol. 115a.

74. וכמעט שנעלמו מן הרופאים מיני הקדחות האלה ולערבוב אותותיהם רבים יפשטום דבריים
Pinkhof 51 = MS Leiden Cod. והנהיגום בהנהגת קדחות דבריות... וראיתי שנהג זאת ההנהגה ומת
Or. 4778, fol. 115a–b.

75. See the lovely piece by Joseph Ziegler, "Bodies, Diseases, and the Preservation of
Health as Foci of Interreligious Encounters in the Middle Ages," in L. Berlivet et al., eds.,
Médecine et religion: Compétition, collaboration, conflit: Cas de figures (Rome: École française de Rome, 2013), 37–57. For contemporary women practitioners, see A. Cardoner
Planas, "Seis mujeres hebreas practicando la medicina en el reino de Aragón," *Sefarad* 9
(1949): 441–45. Five of the six are documented chiefly in the decades after 1348, which suggests that they are filling a gap created by physician mortality.

76. Pinkhof 48 = Leiden Cod. Or. 4778, fol. 117b.

77. Pinkhof 43 = MS Leiden Cod. Or. 4778, fol. 120b ולפי האותות לא יספק אחד מן החכמים
...כשאינן דבריות אמתיות... וכאשר עייניתי בהם באישים רבים הן להיות מעורבבות לא פשוטות

78. Pinkhof, 51, 50 = MS Leiden Cod. Or. 4778, ffol. 115b–116a.

79. Pinkhof 50 = MS Leiden Cod. Or. 4778, fol. 115b.

80. ואפשר שהיתה סבת הקדחות האלה חמריות ר"ל מרוע הנהגת המזונות בכמותם ואיכותם כי
היתה יוקר ומעוט המצא מזונות הנהוגים בחמשת מיני התבואה ואכלו רוב העם לחם גרגרים וזרעים בלתי
נהוגים חרצין וערמן ואלונים; Pinkhof 42 = MS Leiden Cod. Or. 4778, fol. 121a.

81. Ibid.

82. Pinkhof 42 = MS Leiden Cod. Or. 4778, fol. 121b.

83. Arrizabalaga, "Facing the Black Death," 257.

84. McVaugh and Garcia-Ballester identify Jacme's colleagues on the medical faculty of
Lleida as an Englishman, Walter de Wrobruge(!), a Paduan, and a Castilian. I do not know
where they were trained. Michael McVaugh and Luis Garcia-Ballester, "The Medical Faculty
at Early Fourteenth-Century Lerida," *History of Universities* 8 (1989): 4–5.

85. Pinkhof 48 = MS Leiden Cod. Or. 4778, fol. 117a.

86. Pinkhof 48 = MS Leiden Cod. Or. 4778, fol. 117b.

87. Pinkhof 43 = MS Leiden Cod. Or. 4778, fol. 120b. The passage referring his reader
to other works on humoral fevers precedes this citation, on the same page and folio.

88. Guilleré's study of the plague in nearby Girona offers a breakdown of mortality
rates among the various professions. Regrettably, he does not include physicians. However,
the dramatic spike in fatalities among those professionals who had frequent and close contact with the sick suggests that physicians were also at risk. On the high mortality rate of
notaries, see also the classic study by Richard Emery, "The Black Death of 1348 in Perpignan," *Speculum* 42 (1967): 611–21.

89. I thank Lori Jones for informing me that most Christian plague tractates avoided
biblical language and precedent. E-mail comments, May 2016.

90. A few writers who composed belletristic literature and authored or translated scientific prose maintained an elegant sense of style even in the latter. I am thinking of men like Judah al-Harizi, Solomon Ibn Falaquera, and Qalonymos b. Qalonymos. They are exceptional cases. For a recent look at some of the issues, see the essays in Resianne Fontaine and Gad Freudenthal, eds., *Latin-into-Hebrew: Texts and Studies* (Leiden: Brill, 2013).

91. Duran-Reynals and Winslow, 63 (art. 2, pt. 1, chap. 2), Veny and Cremades, 52–53.

92. Duran-Reynals and Winslow, 65 (art. 2, pt. 1, chap. 2).

93. Ibid., 69 (art. 2, pt. 2, chap. 2), Veny and Cremades, 58; and 72 (art. 3, chap. 1), Veny and Cremades, 63.

94. Duran-Reynals and Winslow, 88–89 (art. 6), Veny and Cremades 85–87.

95. In support of this view, see Ziegler.

96. Arrizabalaga, "Facing the Black Death," 250.

97. In contrast, Jacob b. Solomon, writing after the plague outbreak of 1382 in Avignon, argued that the plague was sent by God as a trial of faith. See Einbinder, *No Place of Rest*, chap. 5, and idem, "Theory and Practice: A Jewish Physician in Paris and Avignon," *Association for Jewish Studies Review* 33.1 (April 2009): 135–54.

98. Five times on one page—Pinkhof 42 = MS Leiden 121a–b.

99. In more recent terms, a generation's immune system was compromised and more vulnerable to the plague bacillus. William C. Jordan, *The Great Famine: Northern Europe in the Early Fourteenth Century* (Princeton, N.J.: Princeton University Press, 1996), 186–87; DeWitte and Slavin, "Between Famine and Death."

100. Luis García-Ballester, Lola Ferre, and Eduard Feliu, "Jewish Appreciation of Fourteenth-Century Scholastic Medicine," *Osiris* 6 (1990): 85–117.

101. Pinkhof 51 = MS Leiden Cod. Or. 4778, fol. 115a, [ה]שגבו ועיר קריה היתה לא מקדחות.

102. Other scapegoated groups, which included foreigners and pilgrims, would not be described as native to the land, although foreigners, pilgrims, "Lombards," and lepers were also targets of plague-related violence. Gautier-Dalché, 70–71; Cohn, "The Black Death and the Burning of the Jews," 11.

103. Galipapa indicates that his chronicle has five parts, the fifth dedicated to the effects of the Black Death among the Jewish communities of Aragon. That section is now lost, except for the identified excerpts in haCohen. See Barzilay, 55; and Hayim ben Avraham Galipapa, "*Sefer Emeq Refaim* and Several Responsa by R. Hayim Galipapa" [Hebrew], in Shaul Israeli et al., eds., *Sefer yuval likhvod . . . Rabbi Yosef Dov haLevi Soloveitchik* (Jerusalem: Mossad haRav Kook, 1984), 1211–59.

104. Barzilay, 56. My translation.

105. Pinkhof 49 = MS Leiden Cod. Or. 4778, fol. 116b.

106. The modern Hebrew meanings of the words diverge from their biblical origins: flu and fever, virus and gangrene, desolation, blight and mildew(!).

107. In Chapter 2, the poet Emanuel ben Joseph also invoked the term *herev* to describe the double plight of the Jews destined for the sword and "desolation." Given Abraham's more technical usage, it is tempting to reread Emanuel's verse to refer to agricultural disaster, so that the Jews are consigned to slaughter and starvation.

108. See above, p. 63.

109. See Arrizabalaga, "Facing the Black Death," 255. Again, much of the list is drawn directly from the Canon, bk. 4, fen 1, art. 4.

110. This view persisted for quite some time. Arrizabalaga mentions a fifteenth-century treatise, Enrique de Villena's *Tratado de la lepra*, in which the author argues that the condition begins with corrupted humor (the *colera negra*) and spreads to other members of the body; it is contagious not only to other humans but to nearby animals and minerals and also houses. Jon Arrizabalaga, "La enfermedad y la asistencia hospitalaria," in Luis García-Ballester, ed., *Historia de la ciencia y de la técnica en la Corona de Castilla* (Valladolid: Junta de Castilla y León, 2001), 1:607.

111. The passage enumerates a list of familiar recommendations for fumigations and scented air fresheners, applied outdoors and indoors, as well as along the stone foundations of houses. Abraham claims that these remedies are especially necessary at night, when the body is less able to combat the corrupting elements in the air. Because of this, he recommends that the sick should not be allowed to sleep long, referring specifically to those who are "toxic, who have poisonous abscesses, those who are struggling to breathe and who are at the fever's onset." ‏ולזאת הסבה תמנע השינה הארסיים לבעלי המורסות הארסיות ולמחנקים ובהת־ חתה עונות הקדחת‎, Pinkhof 45 = MS Leiden Cod. Or. 4778, fol. 119a.

112. In contrast, Ephraim Shoham-Steiner has argued that European Jews' status as a "pariah minority" gave them an increased sensitivity to the plight of other vulnerable groups. See his "An Ultimate Pariah: Jewish Social Attitudes Toward Jewish Lepers," *Social Research* 70.1 (2003): 237–68; idem, "Pharaoh's Bloodbath: Medieval European Jewish Thoughts About Leprosy, Disease and Blood Therapy," in Mitchell Hart, ed., *Jewish Blood: Reality and Metaphor in History* (New York: Routledge, 2009), 99–115; and idem, *On the Margins of a Minority: Leprosy, Madness, and Disability Among the Jews of Medieval Europe* (Detroit: Wayne State University Press, 2014). If Shoham-Steiner were correct, however, African-Americans would not attack Korean grocers in Harlem, or Israelis attack Sudanese refugees in Israel, etc.

113. Nirenberg, *Communities of Violence*, chap. 4.

114. Caslari writes in his introduction that he has composed his tractate at the behest of "wise and learned men" who wished him to record his opinion about the proper treatment of these fevers: ‏ואחשוב שאחזתי ענינים ולתועלת כללי כתבתי סברתי מאי זה מין הם ואיך הונהגה‎ ("and I think that I have grasped [these] matters, and on behalf of the common good I have written my opinion of what kind they are and how they should be treated"). Pinkhof 50 = MS Leiden 115b. Jacme writes that he has composed his tract for the "honorable Aldermen and Councillors of the City of Lleida," as official representatives of the city and those who can implement its recommendations, which are "for the common and public good." Duran-Reynals and Winslow, 58 (preface), Veny and Cremades, 42: "car lo tractat aquest es feyt principalment a profit del poble. . . . Lo damondit tractat . . . sie feyt a utilitat comuna e publica."

115. Naama Cohen-Hanegbi, "A Moving Soul: Emotions in Late Medieval Medicine," *Osiris* 31 (2016): 46–66.

116. Naama Cohen-Hanegbi, "Mourning Under Medical Care," *Parergon* 3.2 (2014): 39.

117. Naama Cohen-Hanegbi, *Caring for the Living Soul: Emotions, Medicine and Penance in the Late Medieval Mediterranean* (Leiden: Brill, 2017), 39.

118. Arrizabalaga, "Facing the Black Death," 273, 279–80; A. Campbell, 7–77.

119. Duran-Reynals and Winslow, 84–85, V, pt. 2, chap. vi.

120. Bos and Mensching, 44, sec. 18, which says ראוי להתענג בששון ובשמחה כי זאת העלה נושאה הרוח החיוב.

121. Bos, "The Black Death in Hebrew Literature"; my translation from the Hebrew, sec. 19 on pp. 18–19.

122. The edition of this text is shaky, but it's what we have. See Ginzburg, *"Be'er Lehi,"* 114: השישית בתנועות הנפשיות השמר לך ושמור נפשך מאד מהפעליות הנפשיות כמו היגון והכעס והדמיונות מהדברים המחייבים הפחד והדאגה והשמר מהלאות הכח השכלי ואל תטריחהו במעמיק העיון במה שיטריחך אבל במה שיושג בנקלה והמין מן העיון אשר תשמח בו והיית אך שמח . . .

123. Thus, e.g., quotidian fevers caused by anger are treated in bk. 4, fen 1, art. 1, chap. 15, and their treatment in the following chapter, which recommends calming the patient with happy things, stories and good news and laughter, lukewarm baths and oils, and keeping them from drinking wine. Chap. 22 combines fevers caused by fear and their treatment, which depends on reassuring the patient about the cause of his fear and bringing him good tidings, etc.

124. Bos, *Ibn al-Jazzar*, 10, 105.

125. Pinkhof 47 = MS Leiden Cod. Or. 4778, fol. 118a.

126. פחד ואימת מות, Pinkhof 48 = MS Leiden Cod. Or. 4778, fol. 117b.

127. Pinkhof 43 = MS Leiden Cod. Or. 4778, fol. 120b.

Chapter 4

1. Nicolás Cabrillana, "La crisis del siglo XIV en Castilla: La Peste Negra en el opisbado de Palencia," *Hispania* 28 (1968): 247; J. Callico, "La Peste Negra en la Peninsule Iberica," *Anuario de estudios medievales* 7 (1970–71): 88. More recently, see Arrizabalaga, "La enfermedad y la asistencia hospitalaria." As Arrizabalaga notes, the lack of documentation and the lack of research make it difficult to determine the exact dates for the plague's arrival and duration in Castile. Arrizabalaga, 610. For the available data on Aragon, see Shirk, "The Black Death in Aragon 1348–1351," and the recent study of B. Campbell, *The Great Transition*, with references scattered throughout (for post-plague blows to labor, wages, and population, see, esp., 376–80).

2. Cabrillana, 254–56; Callico, 86.

3. Cabrillana, 255; and Joseph F. O'Callaghan, *The Gibraltar Crusade: Castile and the Battle for the Strait* (Philadelphia: University of Pennsylvania Press, 2011).

4. Cabrillana, 256. See also Pilar León Tello, "Judíos toledanos víctimas de la Peste Negra," *Sefarad* 37 (1977): 333–37; and Arrizabalaga, "La enfermedad y la asistencia hospitalaria," which summarizes the effects of the Black Death in the different regions of Iberia. Arrizabalaga's material for Castile draws on the same studies that I cite here (chiefly Cabrillana and Callico); see 604, 609–11.

5. See Nina Melechen, "The Jews of Medieval Toledo: Their Economic and Social Contacts with Christians from 1150 to 1391" (Ph.D. diss., Fordham University, 1999), for an overview of context and earlier scholarship. As Melechen notes, by the late thirteenth century, Toledo hosted the "largest and wealthiest" Jewish community in Castile (18), constituting about 15–20 percent of the city's population (45). Until the 1350s, there is little evidence of systemic hostility toward the Jews, and "no evidence, whether from epitaphs, memoirs, chronicles, or official reactions, of the Christians of Toledo attacking Jews as a reaction to outbreaks of the Black Death" (304).

6. Luis García-Ballester, *La búsqueda de la salud: Sanadores y enfermos en la España medieval* (Barcelona: Peninsula, 2001); idem and C. Vázquez de Benito, "Los médicos judíos castellanos del siglo XIV y al galenismo árabe," *Asclepio* 42.1 (1990): 119–47.

7. Maya Soifer Irish, *Jews and Christians in Medieval Castile: Tradition, Coexistence, and Change* (Washington, D.C.: Catholic University Press, 2016), 8. Increasingly, as Soifer Irish documents, Castilian Jews would find themselves caught between "centralizing tendencies of the Crown and the town councils' attempts to preserve local *fueros* (charters) and privileges" (173–74); the civil war of the 1360s saw the Jews notoriously scapegoated by the rebel prince, Enrique Trastámara (see, e.g., 219, 227). In 1348, the seeds of these terrible years were just beginning to pierce the soil. See also Maya Soifer Irish, "Beyond *Convivencia*: Critical Reflections on the Historiography of Interfaith Relations in Christian Spain," *Journal of Medieval Iberian Studies* 1.1 (2009): 21.

8. Rachel Greenblatt, "The Shapes of Memory: Evidence in Stone from the Old Jewish Cemetery in Prague," *Leo Baeck Institute Year Book* 47 (2002): 44. Greenblatt refers to "the relationships between the living and the dead, and the ways the living remembered the dead."

9. Some of those came quickly. By 1360, the king's half-brother, Enrique Trastámara, was fomenting rebellion and encouraging vicious anti-Jewish rhetoric and physical violence; see Soifer Irish, *Jews and Christians in Medieval Castile*, 219, 227.

10. Some of the flurry attends recent excavations of medieval Jewish cemeteries in Würzburg and Mainz. A special issue of the journal *Pe'amim* was dedicated to Jewish cemeteries; see *Pe'amim* 98–99 (2002). See also Avineri, "Hebrew Inscriptions from the Middle Ages"; Bar-Levav, "Another Place"; Elliot Horowitz, "Speaking to the Dead: Cemetery Prayer in Medieval and Early Modern Jewry," *Journal of Jewish Thought and Philosophy* 8 (1999): 303–17; David Roskies, "A Revolution Set in Stone: The Art of Burial," in idem, *The Jewish Search for a Usable Past* (Bloomington: Indiana University Press, 1999), 120–45. See, esp., the slate of recent publications by Reiner on the ongoing excavations in Würzburg, e.g., "Shard Drawn to Shard"; "Inscribed on a Stone." A recent anthology of essays on "Jewish archaeology" contains several on topics related to cemeteries (none on epitaphs); see the essays by Vismara, Schütte, Anna Colet et al., Riquelme Cantal and Ortega, Silberman, Wallislova, Taboada, Blanchard, and Georges (a third of the total!), in Paul Salmona and L. Sigal, eds., *L'Archéologie du judaïsme en France et en Europe* (Paris: La Découverte, 2011). Among the publications on non-Jewish cemeteries and epitaphs, see Armando Petrucci, *Writing the Dead: Death and Writing Strategies in the Western Tradition* (Palo Alto, Calif.: Stanford University Press, 1998); Thomas Laqueur, *The Work of the Dead: A Cultural History of Mortal Remains* (Princeton, N.J.: Princeton University Press, 2015). Both Petrucci

and Laqueur take sweeping views of their subject matter, with uneven results. Another recent and elegant survey of this terrain is Hillel Halkin's *After One Hundred and Twenty: Reflecting on Death, Mourning and the Afterlife in the Jewish Tradition* (Princeton, N.J.: Princeton University Press, 2016). On the travails of archaeologists who work with these artifacts—particularly ancient Jewish remains, see Chapter 5 in this volume.

11. Neil Asher Silberman, "Qui doit se soucier des morts? Droits religieux et responsabilité citoyenne," in Salmona and Sigal, 225–34; Anna Colet Marcé and Oriol Saula Briansó, "La influència de l'element religiós en l'excavació del fossar dels jueus de Tàrrega," in Renée Sivan et al., eds., *La intervencio arqueològica a les necropolis historiques: El cementiris jueus* (Barcelona: Museu d'Història de Barcelona, 2012), 44–51.

12. Malkiel, "Poems on Tombstone Inscriptions in Northern Italy"; idem, "Christian Hebraism in a Contemporary Key"; Richard Barnett, Philip Wright, and Oren Yoffe, eds., *The Jews of Jamaica: Tombstone Inscriptions 1663–1880* (Jerusalem: Ben-Zvi Institute, 1997); Brombacher, "Poetry on Gravestones"; F. J. Hoogewood and Falk Wresenmann, "Sephardic Cemeteries: A Selective Bibliography," in Henriques de Castro, ed., *Keur von Grafstenen: Selected Gravestones from the Dutch Portuguese Jewish Cemetery* (Ouderkerk aan de Amstel: 1999), 17–23; Stefan Reif et al., eds., *Death in Jewish Life: Burial and Mourning Customs Among Jews of Europe and Nearby Communities* (Boston: De Gruyter, 2014); Marian Sárraga and Ramón F. Sárraga, "Early Links Between Amsterdam, Hamburg and Italy: Epitaphs from Hamburg's Old Sephardic Cemetery," *Studia Rosenthaliana* 34 (2000): 23–55; idem, "Sephardic Epitaphs in Hamburg's Oldest Jewish Cemetery: Poetry, Riddles and Eccentric Texts," *AJSR* 26 (2002): 53–92; Karlheinz Müller, Simon Schwarzfuchs, and Avraham Reiner, eds., *Die Grabsteine vom jüdischen Friedhof in Würzburg aus der Zeit vor dem Schwarzen Tod* (Würzburg: Monumenta Germaniae Historica, 2012). See also the relevant poetic texts transcribed and edited by Dvora Bregman, *Tzror zehuvim: Sonetim ivriyim metekufat harenesans vehabarok* (Jerusalem: Ben-Zvi Institute, 1997); idem, *Esa et Levavi: Shirim me'et Moshe Zakut* (Jerusalem: Ben-Zvi Institute, 2009), esp. 309–434; idem, "Now You Shall Be Housed in Stone: The Epitaph Poems of Moses Zacuto" [Hebrew], in Jonathan Decter and Michael Rand, eds., *Studies in Arabic and Hebrew Letters in Honor of Raymond P. Scheindlin* (Piscataway, N.J.: Gorgias Press, 2007), Hebrew sec., 13–21. Several pages of Anania Coen's old *Saggio di Eloquenza Ebrea* (Florence: Coen, 1827) are also dedicated to epitaph poetry, although no medieval examples are included (see "Dello stile Lapidario," lesson 23, 102–11).

13. The following account draws primarily on Cantera and Millás, *Las inscripciones hebraicas de España*, 36–38, and Luzzatto, *Avnei zikkaron*, 3–4. See also the introduction to the responsa of Judah ben haRosh, in Abraham Joseph Havatselet, A. I. Goldmintz and Yoel Qatan, eds., *Zikhron Yehuda: Lerabbenu Yehuda ben haRosh* (Jerusalem: Makhon Shlomo Oman, Makhon Or haMizrah, Makhon Yerushalayim, 2005); and Abraham Hayyim Freimann, *Rabbenu Asher bar Yehiel ve-Tze'etze'av* (Jerusalem: Rav Kook, 1986). The transcriptions of the epitaphs are found in Cantera and Millás, 40–167, with notes, some illustrations, and translations into Spanish, and in Luzzatto, 5–70, with notes.

14. Havatselet, Goldmintz, and Qatan refer to an anecdotal report passed on by the chronicler Joseph haCohen, whose parents were among the 1492 exiles; according to this

account, the rabbis of Toledo decreed that the tomb of the Rosh should be destroyed before they left, lest the Christians desecrate it. Havatselet, Goldmintz, and Qatan, introduction, 37. It is true that the curious copyist did not include an inscription from the Rosh's tomb, although he provided us with the epitaphs of a number of other members of the family.

15. Cantera and Millás, 36. The owner was Fernán Rodriguez de Aguilar.

16. Benjamin Richler, *Guide to Hebrew Manuscript Collections*, 2nd rev. ed. (Jerusalem: Israel Academy of Sciences and Humanities, 2014), 215. The library is now called the Biblioteca Nazionale Universitaria.

17. Cantera and Millás, 37.

18. Valpergo died in 1815, so the collection must have been designated for the library in his will. See Chiara Pilocane, "I manoscritti ebraici della Biblioteca Nazionale di Torino," *Materia Giudaica: Bollettino dell'Associazione italiana per lo studio del giudaismo* 9 (2004): 184.

19. Almanzi (b. 1801, d. 1860) was from Padua, where an elite and generous education left him with an avid taste for literature and manuscripts. His personal library, collected over years of travel and acquisition, would continue to have a global life. Originally cataloged after his death by his friend Shadal, it made its way to a book dealer, Frederik Mueller, in Amsterdam, who sold the contents in 1868; most of the manuscripts were bought by the British Museum, and some of the rare books went to Temple Emanu-El in New York. The transcriptions are not in either batch. In 1892, the Reform synagogue gave its collection to Columbia University as a gift; the correspondence retained by the Columbia Rare Book and Manuscript Library indicates that the gift was in appreciation of Columbia's willingness to admit Jewish students at a time when other Ivy League institutions were reluctant to do so. On Almanzi, see *Encyclopaedia Judaica* ("Joseph Almanzi," online ed., Thomas Gale, 2007); for the Columbia/Temple Emanu-El correspondence, see the Columbia University trustee minutes of June 5, 1892, p. 173, which also cite the letter from Temple Emanu-El dated May 19, 1892. My thanks to Michelle Chesner at Columbia University Libraries for her help in retracing this citation.

20. B. Peyron, *Codicus Hebraici Manu Exarati Regiae Bibliothecae quae in Tauriensis* (Turin: Fratres Bocca, 1880), entry 119, listed as A.IV.37, pp. 111–18. The entry describes a 200-page miscellany containing a number of works popular among the philosophically minded intellectuals of Italian, Provençal, and Iberian lands, notably dominated by the Provençal author Yedaiah Bedersi (haPenini), Joseph Ezobi, Gaqatilla, Menahem ben Zerah, and others. The anonymous transcription of the Toledo epitaphs appears second-to-last in this collection, at fol. 181, pp. 116–18.

21. Richler, *Guide to Hebrew Manuscript Collections*, 216, and Pilocane. Cantera and Millás seem to think that the fire occurred shortly after Almanzi made his copy—a more romantic narrative, to be sure, but unjustified. See Cantera and Millás, 37. Notices of the fire appeared in several publications not long after it occurred; see, e.g., Giovanni Gorrini, *L'incendio della R. Biblioteca Nazionale di Torino* (Turin: Renzo Stregio, 1905); Albert Shaw, "The Loss to Literature by the Turin Library Fire," *American Monthly Review of Reviews* 30 (1904): 234–35. Shaw's post refers to condolence letters in Latin(!) sent from Oxford and Cambridge to Paolo Boselli, author of the report of the Turin fire. He summarizes the loss to various collections, noting that of 31,511 volumes known to be in the library's

possession before the fire, only 6,800 remained afterward. Shaw, 234. Pilocane, 183, notes that renewed restoration efforts have focused on the remains of the Hebrew collection since 2001. Gorrini's photographs of the early restoration efforts, as well as photographs of mutilated manuscripts, are still poignant.

22. See, e.g., Giuseppe Veltri and Gianfranco Miletto, *R. Judah Moscati and the Jewish Intellectual World of Mantua* (Leiden: Brill, 2012), 287; Cristina dal Molin, "Recovery of Some Unedited MSS by Leone de' Sommi at the National Library in Turin," in Ahuva Belkin, ed., *Leone de' Sommi and the Performing Arts* (Tel Aviv: Tel Aviv University, 1997), 101–17; Mayer Gruber, "Floating Letters," in Steven L. Jacobs, ed., *Maven in Blue Jeans: A Festschrift in Honor of Zev Garber* (Lafayette, Ind.: Purdue University Press, 2009), 44–45.

23. Richler, *Guide to Hebrew Manuscript Collections*, appendix 1, no. 41, p. 309.

24. Cantera and Millás, 37. The full slabs are for Shadal no. 70 (= Cantera no. 82, pp. 135–38).

25. Cantera and Millás have reordered the inscriptions, following their early re-edition by Moïse Schwab, whose arrangement they describe as "more logical." See p. 37, and Moïse Schwab, *Rapport sur les inscriptions hébraïques de l'Espagne* (Paris: Imprimerie Nationale, 1907). As far as I can tell, the arrangement produced by the copyist reflects the topography of the tombs, as he walked among them; see below. Cantera and Millás's rearrangement is chronological by date of death. While their ordering has some usefulness, its value is undercut by the loss of spatial arrangement preserved in the original. For this reason, I list Shadal's numbering first; and Cantera and Millás in parentheses.

26. Cantera and Millás, 135–38.

27. See Lucia Raspe, "Sacred Space, Local History and Diasporic Identity: The Graves of the Righteous in Medieval and Early Modern Ashkenaz," in Ra'anan Boustan, Oren Kosansky, and Marina Rustow, eds., *Jewish Studies at the Crossroads of Anthropology and History* (Philadelphia: University of Pennsylvania Press, 2011), 147–63. I have found one popular website that refers to circumambulation of the grave as a "Sephardic" custom, without documentation. "Sephardic" in this context must mean "Castilian" and may indicate a survival of this custom. As for the trapezoidal stones, the geometrical term refers to the three-dimensional construction of slabs that would have lain over the grave: viewed from the top, the cross-section is rectangular, but the top rectangle is smaller than the base, and all four lateral facets are trapezoidal. The word "trapezoidal" is sometimes used to describe the shape of medieval Jewish coffins, wider at the head and narrower at the feet, but this essentially "anthropomorphic" design is not what I designate by the term. See, e.g., David Romano, "Restos judíos en Lérida," *Sefarad* 20.1 (1960): 50–65.

28. Cantera and Millás, 141, citing the 1865 catalog of the Toledo archaeological museum.

29. Cantera and Millás, 160–66. Menahem ben Zerah was a child of the French expulsion of 1306, born to exiles in Navarre in 1308. An heir also to violence and loss in Navarre— his parents and four siblings were killed in a riot in 1328—he eventually reached Toledo, where his *Tzedah laDerekh* would achieve him enduring fame.

30. Cantera and Millás, 54, 58 (inscription nos. 23 and 24). The second stone yields the name Moses and a death year of 1357, but little more.

31. There is one epitaph for the month of Nisan 1349 (no. 6), six for Sivan, nine for Tamuz, and three for Av. For Marheshvan (October–November) 1350, there are three, all from the same family, the aristocratic haLevi Abulafia's (nos. 20, 21, 22). Inscription no. 72 is dated Iyar (April) 1352. Regarding the 1362 epitaph, see below.

32. See Julia Beltrán de Heredia Bercero, "El primer testimoni arqueologic de la Pesta Negra a Barcelona: La fossa comuna de la basílica dels sants màrtirs just i pastor," *Quaderns d'arqueologia i historia de la Ciutat de Barcelona (QUARHIS)* 2.10 (2014): 164–79; José Angel Montanés, "Staring Black Death in the Face in Barcelona," *El País* [English], August 15, 2014, http://elpais.com/elpais/2014/08/15/inenglish/1408097721_483831.html. For Valencia and Tàrrega, see Chapter 5 in this volume.

33. Kacki and Castex note that the remains of several individuals from single burials tested positive for aDNA with the antigen for *Yersinia pestis* in graves excavated at Saint-Laurent-de-la-Cabrerisse, where there is a combination of multiple and single graves. Their conclusion is that not all crises of mortality led to a rupture in normal burial practices, including the preference for single burials. See Sacha Kacki and D. Castex, "Réflexions sur la variété des modalités funéraires en temps d'épidémie: L'exemple de la Peste Noire en contexts urbain et rural," *Archéologie Médiévale* 42.1 (2012): 9, 13.

34. In some ways, this is counterintuitive. The prolonged effects of famine, drought, or other factors may explain the differences in climate and altitude, access to food sources, etc. For the series of bad harvests in parts of Iberia through the 1330s, see B. Campbell, 149.

35. See Shadal's epitaph nos. 5, 7, and 42 (= Cantera nos. 84, 56, and 87).

36. We cannot even say whether the entire cemetery was accessible when the copyist decided what to copy. It would seem that at least parts of it had already been uprooted. According to Gómez Menor, sale of the stones was authorized by the Catholic monarchs. José Carlos Gómez Menor, "Algunos datos sobre el cementerio judío de Toledo," *Sefarad* 31.2 (1971): 363–73.

37. See Arturo Ruiz Taboada, "Comments on Muslim, Jewish and Christian Burial Practices in Medieval Toledo (Spain)," *Journal of Islamic Archaeology* 2.1 (2015): 60; and idem, "La nécropole juive de Tolède: Type, construction et distribution des tombes," in Salmona and Sigal, 287–300.

38. Ruiz Taboada, "Comments on Muslim, Jewish and Christian Burial Practices," 59–60, for the 1,200-kilometer estimate, and idem, "La nécropole juive de Tolède," 291, for the 2-kilometer estimate. The necropolis was at the high point of the cemetery. It was quite extensive, which may account for the variance in estimates.

39. We shall encounter this problem again in Chapter 5, with the Tàrrega excavation. On Toledo, see Ruiz Taboada, "La nécropole juive de Tolède," 299–300. Several articles appeared in the popular press on this excavation and the struggle for control of the remains; see, e.g., "School Built on Cemetery Provides Lesson in History," www.nytimes.com/2009/07/02/europe/02Toledo.html?_r=0, repr. in *Toledo Journal*, July 1, 2009; and the notice in *Archaeology* posted June 26, 2013, "Excavation Complete at Medieval Jewish Cemetery," www.archaeology.org/news/1027-130626-toledo-spain-medieval-jewish-cemetery.

40. Ruiz Taboada reports that most of the graves excavated hastily in 2009 were single graves but that there were occasional instances of double or triple burials; his examples are

for an adult (mother) and child. Ruiz Taboada, "La nécropole juive de Tolède." According to Reiner, Ashkenazi communities did not provide small children with headstones, and he notes that the traditional Ashkenazi *memorbuchen* refer to them anonymously. See Reiner, "Inscribed on a Stone."

41. Shadal no. 4 (= Cantera no. 75).

42. Shadal no. 50 (= Cantera no. 80); in my opinion, this is one of the most beautiful inscriptions of the whole set.

43. Shadal no. 73 (= Cantera no. 81).

44. Shadal no. 27 (= Cantera no. 27). The Ibn Nahmias dynastic was one of Toledo Jewry's elite families and goes back to the eleventh century. Their early wealth seems to have been connected to vineyards, but they soon rose to leadership roles in the community. See Melechen, 53–54, 266–68.

45. Shadal no. 34 (= Cantera no. 93). The (Ben) Sasson, or Ibn Shushan, family is documented in Toledo archives by the twelfth century, where they already are prominent. Abuomar Yucef Ibn Shushan (d. 1205) was Alfonso VIII's tax collector and amassed considerable land holdings as well as royal privileges. In the mid-thirteenth century, his great-grandson or great-nephew was royal tax collector for Fernando III, and this Shushan's three sons also played important financial and diplomatic roles into the fourteenth century. See Melechen, 53, 57, 82–83, 265–66.

46. Shadal no. 53 (= Cantera no. 74): וימת בחיי אביו ואמו

47. See the discussion below, and for the Hebrew text, Shadal no. 17 (= Cantera 66). Strikingly, we can draw a straight line from this trope to the unusual lament of Moses Rimos, written in anticipation of his own death (by execution) in Italy in the 1370s. The Rimos family came from Provence or Aragon, where the name appears as Rimoch. Moses' lament concludes with a wrenching appeal to his grieving mother and father. See Susan Einbinder, "Moses Rimos: Poetry, Poison and History," *Italia* 20 (2010): 67–91.

48. Reiner, "Inscribed on a Stone," 125–26, and elaborated with examples in the rest of the article.

49. על האבן הראשה כתוב זאת על זאת האשה. Shadal and Almanzi mistakenly drew the last three words of the incipit into the epitaph text. Cantera's edition corrects them.

50. חלקת הטובה אשר שם קוברה גברת ואצילה / אשת גדולה / היא מרת סתבונה.... Cantera, 121, translates slightly differently: "la heredad de la ventura (o bondad) dónde está la sepultura etc."

51. ולקץ הימין יקימך לשלום תגמול פעולותיך / ויש תקוה לאחריתך בהחיות מתי חסידיך / יאמר לך אל תדאבי / התנערי מעפר קומי שבי

52. Havatselet, Goldmintz, and Qatan, 26. Galinsky understand the term *rav ha'ir* to extend this official's authority beyond the city proper, including Jewish settlements in New Castile such as Seville and Guadalajara. See Judah Galinsky, "On the Legacy of R. Judah ben haRosh, Rabbi of Toledo: A Chapter in the History of Responsa Literature from the Sages of Christian Spain" [Hebrew], *Pe'amim* 128 (2011): 177–78, 180.

53. On the Rosh, see Freimann; Havatselet, Goldmintz, and Qatan, and, in addition to the essay cited in the preceding note, other recent studies by Judah Galinsky. According to Havatselet, Goldmintz, and Qatan, the Rosh never deviated from the French/German training of his youth. More subtly, Galinsky discusses the gap between R. Asher's private

opinions and public rulings, as well as his curious decision to hire an astronomy teacher during his early years in Toledo, in a rich essay, "An Ashkenazic Rabbi Encounters Sephardic Culture: R. Asher b. Jehiel's Attitude Towards Philosophy and Science," *Simon Dubnow Institute Yearbook* 8 (2009): 191–211. By the same author, see also "Of Exile and Halakha: 14th Century Halakhic Literature and the Works of the French Exiles Aaron b. haKohen and Jeruham b. Meshulam," *Jewish History* 22 (2008): 81–96; this essay treats the Rosh briefly in the larger context of the impact of French exiles on intellectual life and production in Iberia. My thanks to the author for his comments, corrections, and suggested sources and approaches.

54. Yehiel died before the Rosh composed his will. Havatselet, Goldmintz, and Qatan, 20.

55. Havatselet, Goldmintz, and Qatan, 21, accept Freimann's date of 1327 for R. Asher's death; Galinsky, "An Ashkenazic Rabbi Encounters Sephardic Culture," 192, prefers an earlier date of 1320–21, which would mean that Solomon might still have been alive.

56. Shadal, pp. 11–12, no. 7 (= Cantera no. 56). אמרתו כטל תזל / מפי ספרים אשר חבר בשפה ברורה / פירוש לפסקים ולתורה / ופסקים לשלשה סדרים / ומלאכת ארבע טורים / אבן העזר וחשן משפט לנכשלים חיים וארחות דעה יורה / לנחשלים. I have translated שפה ברורה as "lucid prose"; more literally, it means "clear language." Almanzi was not sure what to make of פירוש לפסקים ולתורה, and suggested either emending to read פיורש לפסוקים לתורה (as I have translated above, "commentary to verses of Torah") or as commentary on "novellae and verses of Torah."

57. Luzzatto, *Avnei zikkaron*, 12.

58. Freimann, 121–24.

59. As with the replication of dynastic "neighborhoods" in the configuration of the cemetery—what Laqueur calls "necro-geography"—the references to procession or passage illustrate Laqueur's point that the rituals of transition that bring the dead from the world of the living to their final resting place perform the social role of "creating, recreating and representing the social order." Thomas Laqueur, "The Deep Time of the Dead," *Social Research* 78.3 (2011): 799.

60. Judah relates this story in the beginning of his ethical will. The will is included in the edition of his response, Havatselet, Goldmintz, and Qatan, 173.

61. Havatselet, Goldmintz, and Qatan, 22–24 and 36–37. The second marriage took place when Judah was 35; the bride may have been twenty years younger.

62. Freimann, 204; Havatselet, Goldmintz, and Qatan, 27, think that Cresp may have been the grandfather of the poet Isaac Ahdav.

63. Yehiel was also not living in Toledo at the time of his death, and may have been buried elsewhere.

64. This means that he was sixty-five at the time of Hayim's birth, and there is no telling if Hayim was the youngest of his children. If Miriam was fourteen or fifteen at the time of her marriage, she would have been in her forties when Hayim was born and in her mid-fifties at her death.

65. Havatselet, Goldmintz, and Qatan, *Zikhron Yehuda*, 182–83. The editors think that the codicil was added (to the literary testament) after Hayim's death but before Miriam's, i.e., between June 6 and the middle of the month in 1349, approximately a month before Judah's own death. *Zikhron Yehuda*, 199.

66. Mark Cohen has elaborated at length on this trope in the "begging letters" of the Geniza. The letter writers also frequently invoke the language of being "covered" (*mastur* in Arabic) as desirable; to be "uncovered" is to be exposed to shame. As this epitaph illustrates, the image had currency in Sephardic Hebrew contexts as well. See Mark R. Cohen, *Poverty and Charity in the Jewish Community of Medieval Egypt* (Princeton, N.J.: Princeton University Press, 2005).

67. אשת חבר הרי היא כחבר .b. Shavuot 30b.

68. The women in the Rosh family, Judah wrote, הורגלו עם לומדי תורה ונכנסה ההבתהן הורגלו עם לומדי תורה ובעליהן לקיים תלמודיהם בידיהם, ועוד שלא הורגלו בהוצאות יתירות ולא יבקשו מבעליהן "מותרות . . . , Havatselet, Goldmintz, and Qatan, 36. Elsewhere in his testament, Judah repeats this sentiment, telling his sons that they should have no complaint to lodge against him on account of their marriages, הלא אתם נשואים ממשפחתכם, אשר לא יבקשו גדולות מכם אדרבה להחזיק אתכם בלימוד יחזיקו ידיכם ("for you have married within the family, [to those] who will not make great demands on you; on the contrary, they will support you in your studies"), *Iggeret Tokhahat*, 174.

69. Freimann, 199.

70. Shadal no. 4 (= Cantera 75). נפטר בסופה בן י"ד שנים / ר' חיים בן הה"ר ר' / יהודה בן הר"אש ז"ל / בי"ט בסיון שנת ל*ו ה*חיים / עלה לאור באור החיים, where the asterisk indicates the dots over the marked words that should be numerically converted for the year.

71. Havatselet, Goldmintz, and Qatan, 36, note that רבינו תשא ברמה את שם אבותיו, והשתבח בשבחיהם (Our rabbi vaunted the name of his forefathers, and took praise in their praises).

72. Reiner describes a number of these topoi as he has found them in the Würzburg cemetery. Those epitaphs begin in one of four conventional ways, all derived from biblical verses: (1) "This stone, which I placed as a tombstone . . . "; (2) "This mound shall be a witness and this pillar . . . "; (3) "This marker was raised . . . "; and (4) "This is the monument on the grave of. . . ." The Toledo epitaphs tap a wider variety of opening options, but some do correspond to Reiner's categories. It may be no accident that the epitaph for Judah ben haRosh begins with a formula similar to those found in Ashkenaz, the place of his birth and the source of his religious learning and values. See Rami (Avraham) Reiner, "Epitaph Style of Tombstones from Würzburg Cemetery, 1147–1346," in Müller et al., *Die Grabsteine*, 263–95.

73. Shadal no. 5 (= Cantera no. 84). אני הנצבת לאות ולמזכרת / שתחתי נקברת / גויית איש יהודה בן הרא"ש

74. Havatselet, Goldmintz, and Qatan, 37–38, point out that the absence of a year for the first wife's death does not mean that it necessarily occurred on the New Year following their marriage; it could have been some years later.

75. ונשא את בת אחיו הר' יחיאל ערב סכות שנת הס"ו / אחר יום הכסא בא ביתו ובעפר נטמן / ובנה לו בית נאמן / בת אחיו ר' שלמה / ויתנהו ה' לחן בעיני עמו / וישב על כסא אביו תכף עת פטירתו / ויחזק בא"ך שנים בישיבת אבותיו / ונפטר בי"ז בתמוז שנת ק"ט

76. I am not happy with this line. ותחתיו פרי צדיק עץ חיים יצמח. Cantera and Millás translate it as if it read פרי צדק, "y en su lugar, como fruto justo un árbol de vida crece," 139.

אב חכם בן ישמח / ותחתיו פרי צדיק עץ חיים יצמח / יחסה ויתלונן בצל אלהי ישראל אשר בו .77 בטח והאמין / וינוח ויעמוד לגורלו לקץ הימין

78. See, e.g., וישב על כסא אביו in the epitaph, and ועל כסא א"א הושיבוני in the will, 173.

79. On the Rosh's antipathy toward logic, philosophy, and astronomy, otherwise much cherished among Toledo Jewish intellectuals, see Galinsky, "An Ashkenazic Rabbi Encounters Sephardic Culture." In an e-mail exchange, Professor Galinsky offered the possibility that Judah had written his own epitaph before his death, as the style is similar to that found in his will. E-mail, January 11, 2016. If he is right, a family member or members may have been responsible for the family epitaphs, which would account for their relatively austere style and need to emphasize the life and achievements of R. Asher, the family patriarch.

80. Shadal no. 6 (= Cantera 70). תורה יראה ענוה / חלק ונחלה / לשלמה בן הר' יעקב בן הר"אש ז"ל / בא אל אבותיו בניסן שנת אל המ*נוחה

81. Simon's epitaph is inscription no. 41 in Shadal (= Cantera no. 60); he died in 1342. Judah b. Eliakim's is no. 45 in Shadal (= Cantera no. 88); it does not list a date of death and is extremely poetic, compared with the others.

82. Shadal no. 42 (= Cantera no. 87).

83. אבן בחן פנה יקרה / לעטרת צבי וצפירת תפארה / כי נגנז תחתיה שתיל הבינה והחכמה / וענף עץ הדעת והמזמה / תפארת בחורים / הלך בדרך אלהיו ומשתקד תמיד לקרות / החקים והמשפטים והתורות / הוא ר' שלמה מ"ב

84. Cf. Job 3:9 for two of the three encomia. The word 'af'af may refer either to eyelids or to the rays of the sun. "The exiles of Ariel" refers to R. Judah's Ashkenazic origins; the term is also applied to French exiles and, in one epitaph, to an immigrant from Portugal. See Shadal's epitaph nos. 12, 26, 42 (this one), 44 (= Cantera nos. 33, 54, 87, and 79, respectively).

85. ונפטר במגפה בט"ו באב שנת מנו"חה / עלה דרך גבולו / לחזות בנעם ה' ולבקר בהיכל אלהים / לשמי מרומו

86. Ruiz Taboada, "La nécropole juive de Tolède," 294: "L'étude de documents photographiques et cartographiques permet de situer avec certitude la nécropole fouillée à la limite sud-ouest du cimitière, dans une de ses parties les plus hautes."

87. מי לך פה חתן / כי שמת מושבך איתן / ומאסת שכון טירות וביתן / והנך עצור בנקרת הצור / ומדוע הלוך מהרת / עם האשה אשר אהבת?

88. אני הגבר / ראיתי שוד ושבר / ודם ודבר / וקרצו ימי עלומי / ויחטפוני פתאום בדמי ימי / נער / ורך שנים / חליים רעים ונאמנים

89. אני הוא המדבר הנני / ושומע קורותי יתנני / יוסף ב"ר מאיר מ"ב הנקרא אבולעפייא המררי / זה שמי לעולם וזה זכרי

90. Also one of the premier Jewish families of Toledo, with roots predating the Christian conquest. See Melechen.

91. Cantera and Millás, 116, write: "alusión al triste destino de Yosef, por lo que se le llama el amargado."

92. E. Horowitz, 312.

93. Ibid.; and on the prayer of Judah ben haRosh, 309.

94. Shadal no. 27 (= Cantera no. 27), vv. 6–9. קטן-בניו מחמד עיניו / אהוב מבניו / נער בשנים / מבין מזקנים

95. אני הגבר / ראה עני / כי ארד אבל שאולה אל בני / להכין אצלו קברי בימי חלדי / לעת בוא מועדי / וכה אמר בלב מר / בני בני / הוחל עד בוא זמני / ושכבת וערבה שנתך / ובא אביך לראותך / ואצל קבורתך קבורתי / בקברי אשר כריתי לי

96. Shadal no. 35 (= Cantera no. 65); the young man, Isaac the physician, is the son of Meir ben Sasson, also a physician, who succumbed to the plague in 1349 and whose epitaph is Shadal's no. 57 (= Cantera no. 86).

97. Cantera and Millás, 175–80, discuss the sole extant Hebrew gravestone inscription from Seville, belonging to the physician Solomon ben Ya'ish, who died in 1345. The reconstituted fragments of the partial inscription display long lines of page-like text, so that the stone was not in the trapezoidal shape favored by Toledo Jews. See illustration 9, p. 177. On the rivalry between Seville and Toledo, see Melechen, 20.

98. For biblical examples, "heaven and earth" (Deut. 32:1), or "goodness and mercy" (Ps. 23:6). For the late antique hymn, see Peter Cole, *The Poetry of Kabbalah* (New Haven: Yale University Press, 2012), "Awe and Adornment," p. 9. For the Hebrew text, see his appendix for the poem, האדרת והאמונה p. 2.

99. / המשרה משתררת / והנדיבות והכבוד מכיריו / והענוה והגלה סוחריו / היחס והמשרה ציריו
יכיל מהללו / ואיך ספר / והכבוד יתנאה / ההוד יתראה / והענוה מתהדרת / והנדיבות מתפארת / והגדולה מתגברת

100. Jonathan Ray refers to at least one instance of a Castilian Jew granted actual villages by Pedro III. These could be a form of "lands" that bear the owner's name, too, but the context of the epitaph rules against such a reading here. See, however, Jonathan Ray, "Beyond Tolerance and Persecution: Reassessing Our Approach to Medieval *Convivencia*," *Jewish Social Studies* 11.2 (2005): 11n32.

Chapter 5

Note to Moses Nathan epigraph at beginning of chapter: N. Antonio, *Bibliotheca Hispana Vetus* (Madrid, 1788), vol. 2, bk. 9, chap. 3, p. 141, cited by Josep Muntané, in Anna Colet, Jordi Ruíz Ventura, and Eulàlia Subirà, *Tragedia al call* (Tàrrega: Museu Comarcal de l'Urgell, 2014) (henceforth MCUT 2014), 383–84. My thanks to Anna Colet for providing an online version of the catalog, personal e-mail communication, October 30, 2015.

1. Population estimates vary for fourteenth-century Catalonian cities and towns and are based on extrapolations from hearth tax (*fogatge*) and census records, none earlier than 1357. It is assumed that populations prior to the Black Death were higher than those afterward. Estimates for the entire population of fourteenth-century Catalonia, including Rousillon and Cerdagne, range between 300,000 and 365,000. McVaugh estimates the population of Lleida, a much bigger city than Tàrrega, as 8,000 in the 1340s; Tàrrega may qualify as one of the next tier of smaller towns, which he gauges at 2,500–6,000. See Robert S. Smith, "Fourteenth-Century Population Records of Catalonia," *Speculum* 19.4 (October 1944): 494–501; McVaugh, *Medicine Before the Plague*, 35–37; Gregory B. Milton, *Market Power: Lordship, Society and Economy in Medieval Catalonia 1276–1313* (New York: Palgrave Macmillan, 2012), chap. 1.

2. MCUT 2014, 365–66, sec. 1.2.

3. MCUT 2014, by Miquel Àngel Farré Targa, 367–68.

4. It had previously been incorporated into the Lleida *aljama*. Perhaps not coincidentally, in the same year, the municipality also achieved independent status as an ecclesiastical

diaconate, severing it from its previous incorporation in the diaconate of Cervera. See Miquel Àngel Farré Targa, "Consolidation of the Town," MCUT 2014, 367.

5. MCUT 2014, by Muntané, sec. 3.1, 377–78.

6. Josep Muntané i Santiveri, "Aproximació a les causes de l'avalot de Tàrrega de 1348," *Tamid: Revista Catalana Anual d'Estudis Hebraics* 8 (2012): 121. The new synagogue was a source of conflict within the Jewish community and with the municipality, some of whose officers sided with one Jewish faction and some with another. The conflict is evidence of routine cross-confessional alliances between Christians and Jews in everyday business and even politics.

7. Barzilay, "The Black Death in Aragon."

8. Josep Muntané i Santiveri, "Itinerari pels documents relatius a l'assalt del call de Tàrrega de l'any 1348," *Urtx* 23 (2009): 163, and "Aproximació a les causes," 105; full text in Bert Pieters, *De Akkoorden van Bercelona (1354)* (Barcelona: Promociones y Publicaciones Universitarias, 2006). The text of the 1349 letter appears in López de Meneses, *Documentos acerca de la Peste Negra*, no. 14; Colet et al., "The Black Death and Its Consequences," appendix, 71.

9. Many of the royal documents were gathered and published by López de Meneses, "Una consecuencia de la Peste Negra en Cataluña; and idem, *Documentos acerca de la Peste Negra*.

10. See p. 124.

11. For the general studies, which are few, see Chapter 3. See also Shirk, "The Black Death in Aragon 1348–1351"; Gautier-Dalché, "La Peste Negra dans lets états de la Couronne d'Aragon"; Grau i Montserrat, "Metges Jueus del Vell Comtat de Besalú"; Gyug, "The Effects and Extent of the Black Death of 1348"; idem, *The Diocese of Barcelona During the Black Death*; Biraben, *Les hommes et la peste en France et dans les pays européens et méditerranéens.*

12. Colet et al., "The Black Death and Its Consequences," 66: letters to Montblanc, Tàrrega, Vilafranca del Penedès, and Cervera. For the text of the letter, see López, *Documentos acerca de la Peste Negra*, no. 9 (pp. 20–300), May 29, 1348.

13. Based on Hayim Galipapa's assertion that the attack took place on the tenth of Av, a penitential fast day observed traditionally on the ninth, unless the ninth falls on a Sabbath. Barzilay dates the attack to July 3–6; Barzilay, 62. Muntané uses a July 6 date; Muntané, "Aproximació a les causes," 111, apparently revised from an earlier estimate of no later than July 24; Muntané, "Itinerari pels documents," 162. Colet et al. say "probably around 6 July"; Colet et al., "The Black Death and Its Consequences," 67.

14. Colet et al., "The Black Death and Its Consequences," 67n12; Muntané, "Aproximació a les causes," 110–12.

15. Colet et al., "The Black Death and Its Consequences," appendix, doc. 1, excerpted from López, *Documentos acerca de la Peste Negra*, no. 14. English translation is theirs. As they note, the cry of the mob is recorded in Catalan, not Latin. See also Muntané, "Itinerari pels documents," 163n14 and 169, and "Aproximació a les causes," 112, 115.

16. Barzilay cites haCohen's use of Galipapa in two chronicles, the *Emeq haBakha* and the *Divrei hayamim kemalkei Tzarfat uveit Otoman ha-Tugar* [Chronicle of the Kings of France and the Ottoman Empire]. I have included the former version, which is almost identical to the second. Where the version above has "all their possessions"—מכל קנינם—the *Chronicle of the Kings of France and the Ottoman Empire* has מכל אשר להם (everything they

owned). Where the *Emeq haBakha* has "they were not ashamed on that hasty day" (‏ולא הת·‏
‏בושש ביום הנמהר ההוא‏), the royal chronicle has "they were not ashamed" (‏ולא התבוששו‏). See
Barzilay, 57. Colet et al. cite the *Emeq haBakha* version, "The Black Death and Its Consequences," appendix, doc. 2, 72.

17. Muntané, "Itinerari pels documents," 165, and "Aproximació a les causes," 112–13,
which notes that the confirming chancery account uses the figure to describe the casualties
in Barcelona, Cervera, and Tàrrega. Since the first two incidents did not number that many
victims, the Tàrrega count remains high. Yom Tov Assis notes that the Jewish cemetery in
Lleida was so full after 1348 that in 1353, the *aljama* was allowed to expand into an additional
plot; some of the unanticipated burials may have been due to plague, but the dead may also
have been victims of violence. According to Assis, the Jews of Cervera did not have their own
cemetery, which means that they might have added to the Lleida toll. See Yom Tov Assis, *The
Golden Age of Aragonese Jewry* (London: Littman Library of Jewish Civilization, 1997), 232.

18. Muntané points out that Ramon Folquet had "political ambitions and a history of
rebelling against royal power." MCUT 2014, 389; and see discussion below.

19. According to Muntané, the executed men were not from families connected to
those in power but "must have been people of lowly origins." MCUT 2014, 397.

20. Muntané, "Aproximació a les causes," 113nn30, 31; López, "Una consecuencia de la
Peste Negra en Cataluña," nos. 11, 12, 15.

21. Muntané, "Itinerari pels documents," 169. Berenguer is an interesting case, as his
family ties were better suited to a pro-royalist position. Like Ramon Folquet, he came from a
big merchant family but not a local one; the family was also involved in collection of royal
tributes. Muntané, MCUT 2014, 389.

22. Muntané, "Itinerari pels documents," 167–68.

23. Muntané, "Aproximació a les causes," 114.

24. Muntané cannot really answer this question. Was the battle cry a reference to local
perceptions and specific acts recalled as perfidious? Or default to an ancient script honored
by their faith? Ibid., 115.

25. Milton estimates that Santa Coloma had 300–320 households (1,500 inhabitants),
thirty of which were Jewish, a much higher percentage than McVaugh's 5 percent figure for
the region. Milton; McVaugh, *Medicine Before the Plague*, 37.

26. Muntané, "Aproximació a les causes," 119–20; MCUT 2014, 386. Interestingly,
García Biosca notes that the king canceled the investigation of Jewish tax fraud, which had
been directed by his brother, Count James d'Urgell, at the same time that he was negotiating
a personal loan with Moses Nathan. Joan E. García Biosca, "The urbanism of the medieval
town," MCUT 2014, 387–88.

27. Muntané, MCUT 2014, 390. This further illuminates the alignment of factions
over the 1342–43 investigation of the *aljama* for tax fraud. The municipality sought the investigation, and the count was handling it. The king's intervention protected "his" Jews and
was a rebuke to his brother's authority.

28. Ibid., 390, offering the counterexamples of Valencia, Monzón, Huesca, and Solsona.
See Nirenberg, *Communities of Violence*; idem, *Anti-Judaism: The Western Tradition* (New
York: Norton, 2013), 183–216.

29. "[M]algrat que l'aljama era una part de la vila cada vegada més visible físicament i més influent econòmicament, tanmateix, a l'hora de la veritat, no podia ser considerada com a tal. Per als paers, la missié dels quals dins del municipi ja estava ben consolidada des de principis dels anys quaranta, l'ajama era una realitat que els estava vedada, els fugia de les mans, un cos estrany que, en el cas de Tàrrega, havia adquirit unes dimensions i un pes incòmodes de tolerar." Muntané, "Aproximació a les causes," 122.

30. Muntané, "Itinerari pels documents," 166, 170–71; Surribas Camps, *Destruction of the Jewish Community of Tàrrega*, 13. Muntané writes that despite the fact that some of the first demands of the king following the attack were concerned with reconstituting these records, two years later the Targarin lenders were still unable to recuperate unpaid debt; moreover, they were clearly afraid to do so without royal muscle behind them. Four years after the attack, they were still seeking royal help in pressing their debtors. See docs. 14 (December 23, 1349); 27 (January 18, 1352); and 31 (July 1, 1352), in López, "Una consecuencia de la Peste Negra."

31. Muntané, "Itinerari pels documents," 169, citing doc. 150 in López, *Documentos acerca de la Peste Negra*, dated January 12, 1362 ("iterator dampnificari, depredari et interfici et immaniter prout prius"). See also Colet et al., "The Black Death and Its Consequences," 69.

32. Surribas Camps, *Destruction of the Jewish Community of Tàrrega*. Surribas Camps lists the names of residents who were living in the *call* prior to 1348 and after. She is not interested in the phenomenon that I am noting. In another context altogether, Lemos invokes studies on the Rwanda genocide that emphasize sexual violence as a response to long-felt humiliation among the perpetrators; see Tracy M. Lemos, "Dispossessing Nations: Population Growth, Scarcity and Genocide in Ancient Israel and Twentieth Century Rwanda," in Saul Olyan, ed., *Ritual Violence in the Hebrew Bible* (New York: Oxford University Press, 2016), 35 and nn. 62, 63.

33. Muntané, "Aproximació a les causes," 104–5.

34. As one recent study of the Rwandan genocide notes, most people opt for neutrality in similar conflicts and try to avoid being drawn into violence. See Fujii, *Killing Neighbors*, introduction. See also the discussion below.

35. Fujii, introduction and chap. 6.

36. This point is emphasized by Fujii for the case of Rwanda and by Kalyvas in his study of communal violence in Greece.

37. Muntané, "Itinerari pels documents," 168.

38. Ibid., 161: "Però aquells llibres d'actes s'han perdut. I sospito el perquè: davant del trist episodi que va tenir lloc contra el segment jueu de la població targarina, en què es van veure involucrades diverses personalitats cristianes de la vila i del qual forçasament se'n devia parlar. Durant les reunions del Consell amb la manifestiació de noms i cognoms de gent implicada, algú prou influent va fer desaparèixer el tesimoni incrimant d'aquells anys contra si mateix, la seva familia o amics. Tinc la sospita que darrere d'aquest buit en la sèrie de llibres d'actes del Consell, hi ha la voluntat deliberada d'exonerar culpables." The claim is repeated in Muntané's "Aproximació a les causes," 114.

39. Colet Marcé and Saula Briansó, 44.

40. See Muntané, "Aproximació a les causes," and "Itinerari pels documents," 79; idem, "Proposta d'ubicació del fossar dels jueus de la vila de Tàrrega a partir dels testimonis documentals continguts en els libres d'estimes (1501–1510)," *Urtx* 20 (2007): 103–18. The recent collaborative publication in English summarizes the historical and archaeological findings; see Colet et al., "The Black Death and Its Consequences," 63–96. The museum catalog also includes a number of impressive contributions by Joan García Biosca and Miquel Àngel Farré Targa. See MCUT 2014. The online catalog includes descriptions of the material artifacts found in the graves, 414ff.; images are accessible at http://museutarrega.cat/download/pdf/English%20 version%20%22Trage%CC%80dia%20al%20call.%20Ta%CC%80rrega%201348%22.pdf.

41. The Barcelona commission's two leaders quickly aligned themselves with Zakhor and its claims to speak for the "way in which Jewish history and cultural heritage were research [sic], evaluated and presented in modern Spain." Samuel D. Gruber, "Lessons from Medieval Jewish Center Discoveries," Jewish Heritage Report, *International Survey of Jewish Monuments* (ISJM) online newsletter, August 27, 2008, http://www.isjm.org/SitesMonuments/Europe/Spain/tabid/134/Default.aspx. See also the account by José Luis Lacave, "Antiguos cementerios judíos en España," *Raíces revista judía de cultura* 78 (2009): 76–78. According to Laia Colomer, Zakhor usually acts in league with the ultraorthodox Atra Kadisha; Colomer argues that all these groups assume a Western (U.S.) concept of cultural heritage as "property." See Laia Colomer, "The Politics of Human Remains in Managing Archaeological Medieval Jewish Burial Grounds in Europe," *Nordisk Kulturpolitisk Tidskoff [Nordic Journal of Cultural Politics]* 17.2 (2014): 168–86.

42. Colet Marcé and Saula Briansó, 15: "exigiren . . . la immediate paralització de les excavacions—i aquí cal remarcar que la zona on es troba el jaciment són terrenys urbanitzables de propietat privada." The archaeologists may have hoped that the developers' interests would have exerted greater force on their behalf, but they are oddly absent from the entire account of subsequent events. Samuel D. Gruber's triumphal account also acknowledged that the developers could have stymied them and hints that this was one reason for a focus on the remains, rather than the site, as "it is hard to stop excavation, though removal or [*sic*] bones is somewhat easier to negotiate since archaeologists have less power than banks." Gruber.

43. Colet Marcé and Saula Briansó, citing the May 31, 2007, filing with the Ajuntament de Tàrrega.

44. Gruber.

45. MCUT 2014, xx.

46. Lacave points out that prior to this episode, the practice had been to permit study of human remains. Lacave, 77.

47. The transfer took place three days after the publication of the order, but on the same day, it was delivered to the workers in Tàrrega. Ibid., 16–18. The order was based on a 1992 law that assumed that there was no scientific or historical value to further study of the remains. The archaeologists saw matters differently. Certainly, it would have been of historical value to determine whether any of the remains contained plague antigens, and a more extensive forensic analysis of traumatic lesions would have been informative for a number of reasons that I address below. Lacave's brief essay, while expressly identified with the interests of

Zakhor, is a plaintive call for dialogue among the various constituencies, who, he felt, were inadequately represented by their official representatives.

48. Ibid., 19.

49. The archaeological and historical studies produced by the Tàrrega researchers, many cited above, are often moving pieces of scholarship, impeccably documented and painstakingly reaching into the nooks and crannies of the city's medieval past. Most of what has been published has been in Catalan, limiting its circulation; the museum catalog contains an impressive anthology of linked studies with English translations, and the summative piece in *The Medieval Globe* is also in English. The English-language study of Surribas Camps clearly draws on the work of her Spanish colleagues but problematically retrofits their findings for a lachrymose emplotment.

50. See Robert Meister, "Human Rights and the Politics of Victimhood," *Ethics and International Affairs* 16.2 (2002): 91–108; Christopher Patrick Miller, "A Just Grammar: Unspeakable Speech in Robert Meister," *Qui Parle: Critical Humanities and Social Sciences* 22.1 (2013): 203–22; Susannah Radstone, "Trauma Theory: Contexts, Politics, Ethics," *Paragraph* 301.1 (2007): 9–29.

51. But, as Rechtman observes, the willingness to view the perpetrator as victim is primarily motivated by politics, not psychology: "our" soldiers may be traumatized perpetrators, but "theirs" are not. Rechtman, "Enquête sur la condition de victime": "Enfin, la catégorie du 'bourreau victim de traumatisme' n'est pas requise dans toutes les situations. Elle concerne les bourreaux dont on ne veut pas dire qu'ils sont des monstres. Cela s'applique parfaitement bien pour les soldats américains pendant la guerre du Vietnam, pour les soldats français pendant la guerre d'Algérie, mais cela ne s'applique pas aux terroristes et aux combattants d'Al Qaida," 179.

52. Riera i Sans, *Fam i fe*; and see Chapter 1 in this volume. For a classic overview of Jewish-Christian relations in medieval Aragon, see Assis, *The Golden Age of Aragonese Jewry*; the local studies cited throughout Chapter 5 confirm the high degree of exchange and contact among Targarin Christians and Jews. For more contemporary attempts to render the complexity of perpetrator (and victim) groups in the context of massacres, see Fujii; Amin; Charles King, "The Micropolitics of Social Violence," *World Politics* 56.3 (April 2004): 431–55; Kalyvas, *The Logic of Violence in Civil War*.

53. See an early exemplar in Arthur Kleinman and Robert Desjarlais, "Ni patients ni victimes: Pour une ethnographie de la violence politique," *Actes de la recherche en sciences sociales* 104 (1994): 56–93. Fassin and Rechtman, Radstone, Summerfield, and others stress the political and social context of traumatic violence and, like Kleinman, the troubling implications of the "medicalization" of what now falls under the umbrella of "trauma," a shift that has pathologized suffering and obscured the social context of collective violence; cf. Kleinman and Desjarlais, 58.

54. Matías Calvo Gálvez, "Necrópolis judía de Valencia: Nuevos datos," in Ana María Álvarez, *Juderías y sinagogas de la Sefarad medieval* (La Mancha: Universidad de Castilla la Mancha, 2003), 599; idem, "Peste Negra y pogrom en la ciudad de Valencia: La evidencia arqueológica," *Revista de arqueologia* 19.206 (1998): 56.

55. Descriptions of the Rwandan genocide are again strikingly similar. The Hutu attackers carried "massues [nail-studded clubs], swords, axes, spears, hammers"; Fujii, chap. 6.

Descriptions that account for military and paramilitary violence add grenades and firearms: "grenade, gun, machete, impiri [club], sword, knife, drowning, arson, stick, rock and bare-handed assault"; Scott Strauss, "How Many Perpetrators Were There in the Rwandan Genocide? An Estimate," *Journal of Genocide Research* 6.1 (2004): 88. In the Rwandan case, too, a mix of local elements were involved in the attacks, and the newer studies emphasize the need to "disaggregate the masses"; see Fujii, e.g., chap. 5. The Rwandan testimonies also refer to the role frequently played by Hutu women in looting homes after their owners had been murdered; two perpetrators specifically note that their own wives refused to participate in the looting. See Fujii, chap. 5. The gendered dimension of participation is one that is never raised in readings of medieval anti-Jewish violence, but in Tàrrega could easily have paralleled the Rwandan model.

56. See the thoughtful summary and analysis of James Fearon and David Laitin, "Violence and the Social Construction of Ethnic Identity," *International Organization* 54.4 (Autumn 2000): 855, and referring to the work of Kalyvas. See also Stathis Kalyvas, "The Paradox of Terrorism in Civil War," *Journal of Ethics* 8.1 (2004): 97–138, and "The Ontology of Political Violence: Action and Identity in Civil Wars," *Perspectives on Politics* 1.3 (2003): 475–94.

57. The essentialist argument is called "primordialist" in the political science literature. Fearon and Laitin, 846–48, 857–58; Fujii, intro. See also Smelser, 51, who rejects "the notion of a repressed, highly charged, under-the-surface force ready to break into the open at all times." Smelser does, however, describe moments of cultural "forgetting" or "repression."

58. Muntané, "Metges jueus contractats."

59. Fleming has put this eloquently: "the bones...tell us things about life and death...that texts rarely do—intimate things, the kinds of things that we know from our own experience make or break individual lives." Robin Fleming, "Bones for Historians: Putting the Body Back into Biography," in David Bates, Julia Crick, and Sarah Hamilton, eds., *Writing Medieval Biography: Essays in Honour of Professor Frank Barlow* (Woodbridge, U.K.: Boydell Press, 2006), 30.

60. Moving from the farthest west to the east, the pits were labeled FS 161, FS 163, FS 54, FS 162, FS 164, and FS 166.

61. The forensic studies and data have appeared in several articles, most of which overlap but which were clearly composed in an effort to maximize publication of the archaeologists' work. I will try to cross-reference them as much as possible. The Catalan study is by Anna Colet et al., "Les fosses communes de la necropolis jueva de les Roquetes, Tàrrega," *Urtx* 23.1 (2009): 103–23 (in English, Colet et al., "The Black Death and Its Consequences"). The Tàrrega Museum catalog contains a restatement of the findings in Catalan and in English by Anna Colet, Jordi Ruíz Ventura, and Eulàlia Subirà; I will cite from the English sec., MCUT 2014. Finally, the separate study by Jordi Ruíz Ventura and Eulàlia Subirà de Galdacàno, "Reconstrucció antropològica del pogrom de 1348 a Tàrrega," *Urtx* 23.1 (2009): 126–37 (hereafter, Ruíz et al.).

62. The widths, on an east-west axis, can be 1.5 meters or less, so that heads and legs are bent to accommodate the narrow space.

63. Colet et al., "The Black Death and Its Consequences," 80; idem, "Les fosses communes de la necropolis jueva," 104.

64. Primary deposits refer to bodies that remained untouched from the time of their burial until their recent discovery; secondary deposits refer to bodies that were deposited

somewhere else soon after death, and then reburied in the communal graves. The five individuals in FS 54 were primary burials. FS 163 and FS 166, in contrast, contained individuals who were moved to these graves after a lapse of time. FS 161, 162, and 164 contained a mixture of primary and secondary burials, with primary deposits in the center and other individuals added later at the ends.

65. Oddly enough, a recent article describes the victims of gang killings in El Salvador who are routinely deposited in rural wells. See Óscar Martínez, "Our Bottomless Well," *Nation*, March 21, 2016, 13–16. These victims are apparently killed one at a time and concealed in wells. In Tàrrega, the concern seems not to have been concealment but containment of a huge number of corpses exposed to July heat.

66. Colet et al., "The Black Death and Its Consequences," 85; idem, MCUT 2014, 400–401; Ruíz et al., 130.

67. See Calvo Gálvez, "Necropólis judía de Valencia: Nuevos datos," *Juderías y sinagogas de la Sefarad medieval* (Cuenca: Ediciones de la Universidad de Castilla—La Mancha, 2003), 583–610.

68. Colet et al., MCUT 2014, 414ff., is a special section of the catalog describing the material artifacts found in the graves. For images, see Colet et al., "The Black Death and Its Consequences," and Figures 3 and 4.

69. Colet et al., "The Black Death and Its Consequences," 76; idem, "Les fosses communes de la necropolis jueva," 115–16; Ruiz et al., 129. Fleming's study concerns much earlier (seventh-century) remains but notes, in that context, the evidence that children were generally "unhealthy" in the medieval period. Moreover, the growth of urban centers—like Tàrrega's—was often "about sick children, fast-moving illness and early death." Fleming, 47. In this context, the prevalence of periodontal disease among the Tàrrega victims attests to years of nutritional stress that might be expected in a time of shortages or famine.

70. See Chapter 4 in this volume.

71. Muntané and the archaeologists have since walked back from this view in favor of disarticulation prior to reburial. Personal e-mail, March 15, 2017.

72. Colet et al., "The Black Death and Its Consequences," 86–87; Ruíz et al., 133.

73. The study included only macroscopic analysis; Ruíz et al., 127–28.

74. Colet et al., "The Black Death and Its Consequences," 86–90; idem, MCUT 2014, 399–402; Ruíz et al., 130–35.

75. Fleming, 33, notes that periostitis, an "inflammatory response to infection or injury," is an especially common stress marker in medieval bones, often in the shin area, where circulation is poor. See also Charlotte Roberts and Keith Manchester, *The Archaeology of Disease*, 3rd ed., (Ithaca, N.Y.: Cornell University Press, 2007), 169–71.

76. Calvo Gálvez, "Nécropolis judía de Valencia," 589–601. The Valencia attack is not recorded in any documents thus far known, so it is important in its own right. The Tàrrega studies reference the Valencia analogue in several places, e.g., Colet et al., "The Black Death and Its Consequences," 81; idem, "Les fosses communes de la necropolis jueva," 120; idem, MCUT 2014, 400.

77. Calvo Gálvez notes that 89.2 percent of the blows were oblique, 7.3 percent glancing (tangential), and 3.5 percent perpendicular, inflicted by something with a smooth continuous

blade of 4–5mm width, which he characterizes as a sword. Calvo Gálvez, "Nécropolis judía de Valencia," 600.

78. Colet et al., "The Black Death and Its Consequences."

79. King, 439, paraphrasing Horowitz. See Donald L. Horowitz, *The Deadly Ethnic Riot* (Berkeley: University of California Press, 2001). For the same point, see Mahmoud Mamdani, *When Victims Become Killers* (Princeton, N.J.: Princeton University Press, 2001), 7, where Mamdani observes that the Rwandan genocide was "neither a conspiracy from above . . . nor . . . a popular *jacquerie* gone berserk."

80. Fujii, chap. 5. Fujii is interested in local violence, i.e., murderous and mass violence perpetrated by everyday people against other everyday people. She is not interested in the paramilitary or military death squads that also functioned in Rwanda and that were, in fact, dominated by disaffected young men, a reality also in interethnic violence in the Sudan and the Balkans. Fearon and Laitin, 869–70.

81. Gross, *Neighbors*; and see the responses collected in Antoni Polonsky and Joanna Michlic, eds., *The Neighbors Respond: The Controversy over the Jedwabne Massacre* (Princeton, N.J.: Princeton University Press, 2003).

82. Muntané, "Itinerari pels documents," 162–63; Colet et al., "The Black Death and Its Consequences," 71–72, citing López, "Una consecuencia de la Peste Negra," doc. 14.

83. William C. Jordan, "Problems of the Meat Market of Béziers 1240–1247: A Question of Anti-Semitism," *Revue des Études Juives* 135 (1976): 31–49; Nirenberg, *Communities of Violence*; Susan L. Einbinder, "The Libel and the Lamb," plenary talk, International Congress of Medieval Studies, Western Michigan University, Kalamazoo, 2014. Remember that the 1347 legislation prohibiting Jews from touching bread, vegetables, or meat in the markets came with a corollary demand that Jewish butchers sell their meat for lower prices than the Christian competition, a sign that tension in the meat markets was flaring just prior to the attack.

84. Cathy Caruth, *Unclaimed Experience*, 4. She then can make her equally cited claim that "history, like trauma, is never simply one's own, that history is precisely the way we are implicated in each other's traumas," 24.

85. Michael Rothberg, "Beyond Tancred and Clorinda: Trauma Studies for Implicated Subjects," in Buelens et al., *The Future of Trauma Theory*, xiv, makes this point strongly in a nod to a series of horrendous factory fires that killed hundreds of garment workers in Pakistan and Bangladesh: "[T]rauma is not a category that encompasses death directly but rather draws our attention to the *survival* of subjects in and beyond sites of violence and *in proximity* to death. The dead workers are not the victims of trauma, and thus trauma theory can only partially reckon with their death."

86. Muntané, "Itinerari pels documents," 161; idem, "Aproximació a les causes," 114.

87. For Jacme, see Chapter 3 in this volume.

88. In 1331, Queen Elinor absolved Solomon Nathan and three Christian accomplices for causing three deaths and multiple injuries to plaintiffs in Vilagrassa. The following year, one of Solomon's sons and his daughter-in-law were pardoned in the killing of her husband, Solomon's brother. Solomon paid a 70,000-sous fine for the pardon—a stupendous sum. For comparison, consider the 20,000-sous fine levied upon the entire municipality of

Tàrrega for the assault on the *aljama*, which they were unable to pay. MCUT 2014, 378 and 383–84.

89. Modern scholarship has treated them as facile but not particularly creative exemplars of the genre, testimony to the immersion of the Jewish elite in Aragon-Catalonia in wider cultural trends. See Schirmann with Fleischer, Toldot *haShirah ha'Ivrit biSfarad haNotzrit uve-Drom Tzarfat*, 569–70; MCUT 2014, 383–84; Josep Muntané, *Moixé Natan: Qüestions de vida / Tots'ot hayim* (Barcelona: Institut Món Juic, Pormociones y Publicaciones Universitarias, 2010). A few of the Hebrew proverbs were also included in Hayim Schirmann's classic anthology *HaShirah ha'ivrit biSfarad uveProvans* (Jerusalem: Mosad Bialik; Tel Aviv: Dvir, 1956, 1960), 4:541–44. The *piyyutim* have not received any treatment prior to now.

90. N. Antonio, *Bibliotheca Hispana Vetus* (Madrid, 1788), vol. 2, bk. 9, chap. 3, p. 141. Cited by Muntané in Colet et al., MCUT 2014, 383–84. The English translation is tweaked from the one in the catalog (my tweaking).

91. Josep Muntané, *Regest dels documents de l'Arxiu Parroquial de Verdú relatius als jueus (1265–1484)*, citing his reference to APV, doc. 3945, dated March 1349. My thanks to Professor Muntané for this important reference.

92. Vatican MS Heb. 553, fol. 88a; Parma Biblioteca Palatina Cod. Heb. 1883 (= De Rossi 485), fol. 19a; Budapest MS Kaufman A 370, fols. 721–23 in margins; a fourth listing for the text locates it in British Library Add. 27200–27201, fol. 115b, described as a thirteenth-century copy of the Mahzor Vitry with liturgical and halakhic additions. As a number of the paytanim listed are known figures from the fourteenth and fifteenth centuries, the catalog is not entirely correct.

93. See verses 2, 5, 8, 9, 14 and my analysis of the poetic text.

94. This is not a strange concept. When the British played an old folk tune, "The World Turned Upside-Down," as they acknowledged defeat to the new American nation in 1776, they did not need to write a new song: the old, familiar lyrics were understood to reflect a contemporary historical moment. When Lady Gaga sang "This Land Is Your Land," an old American folk song immortalized by Woodie Guthrie, at the 2017 Super Bowl halftime show, the political remapping of the lyrics to the context of the new Trump administration's exclusionist, anti-immigration policies, was obvious. Moses Nathan's lament plausibly commemorates the attack on the *call* in 1348, but even if it had been written before that tragedy, its survival in the liturgy suggests that it was identified with that event later on.

95. Transcription from MS Parma 1883 = de Rossi 485, fol. 19a (IMHM Microfilm F 13048). Other copies of the text are in MS Vat. Heb. 553, fol. 88 (F 557, F 72286); Budapest, MS Kaufman A370 (BUD 370 = IMHM F 15136); and MS British Library Add. 27200–27201 (IMHM F 5872, 5873), 2 vols., after fol. 115b of vol. 2.

96. See Jacme d'Agramont's and Abraham Caslari's plague treatises, discussed in Chapter 3, and Emanuel's lament, in Chapter 2.

97. *Metzudat Zion*.

98. A percentage of Jewish loans was royal income.

99. "624 Goldmünzen bestehende Schatz des ausgehenden 14. Jahrhunderts"—see the museum website for images, http://www.regensburg.de/kultur/museen-in-regensburg/alle-museen/document-neupfarrplatz.

100. Pieters, *De Akkorden*, from the Hebrew text, 128: ואם היא תחיל תזעק בחבילה ואין
מושיע לה, ולא ירדו השומעים קולה להצילה ...

101. Ibid., 129: וראינו כי כאשר איש אין בארץ לדבר הזה ישעה. עדר ה' כצאן אשר אין להם רועה.
והנה העם כרמש לא מושל בו כדגים במצודה נאחזימת רי המניגים וראשיהם החוזים חוזים ...

Appendix

1. Isa. 62:10 (and cf. Isa. 57:14).

2. Exod. 3:5; 2 Sam. 1:21.

3. E.g., Ezek. 22:30 and Ps. 106:23; and see elsewhere in these epitaphs.

4. Cf. Isa. 33:6, where the modern translations note that the meaning of the phrase
והיתה עתים חוסן ישועות is unclear. For Rashi and Radaq, the people's faith and ritual observance in days past serve as a bulwark for them in times of trial.

5. E.g., Ps. 128:2; Deut. 33:29; Eccles. 10:17.

6. Gen. 42:25, 45:21.

7. Eccles. 4:4.

8. I am translating צדקה here as "charity" rather than "righteousness," as three lines above.

9. Isa. 54:2.

10. Ps. 116:12, 142:8.

11. Jer. 31:16.

12. Jer. 31:25 (24).

13. Isa. 52:2.

14. Lit., "in all its work."

15. Lit., "he sat in the seat of the elders."

16. Cf. Isa. 1:4.

17. Ps. 91:10–11.

18. 1 Sam. 7:17.

19. Prov. 11:16.

20. Prov. 9:2.

21. Cf. Judg. 8:21, 26; Isa. 3:18.

22. Cf. Obadiah 6. Cantera translates מצפוניה as "treasures."

23. Num. 27:17 = 1 Kings 22:17 = 2 Chron. 18:16.

24. Gen. 8:9.

25. Job 33:30; Ps. 56:14.

26. "R. Uri ben"—elided in Schechter's emended text, published in Freimann, 185.

27. Following Schechter/Freimann, emending יום ששי (Friday) to יום שלישי (Tuesday).

28. 1 Kings 9:27 and perhaps echoing also Jon. 1:3. Schechter/Freimann read: באני
שמ"ג. Shadal reads באני שמצא. I follow Schechter/Freimann. Shadal's extensive notes explain that the Rosh did not initially set out for Toledo but wandered from place to place. He
left Ashkenaz in 5063 and reached Castile two years later. Luzzatto, 9n1.

29. Following Schechter/Freimann, who emend Shadal's "Tuesday, [when they recited]
Hallel on the first day of Iyar," for "Friday, the first of Iyar."

30. Following Schechter/Freimann and emending Shadal's 5046 = המ"ו. As Shadal notes, this is impossible. He suggests emending המ"ו (51) to הס"ו or המ"ן. I do not know where Cantera gets 56 from המ"ו but he also notes that the transcription must be in error and makes the same suggestions for emendation, without counting the initial ה in his tally.

31. The Hebrew idiom is hard to translate. The wife is his "house" or "household." The first "house" falls into the dust, and the second is firmly built. Shadal notes (my translation): Two wives of R. Judah are mentioned here, the first the daughter of his brother R. Yehiel and the second the daughter of his brother R. Solomon; there is no mention at all [of the fact] that he also married the daughter of R. Jacob the author of the Tur (according to the *Sefer Yuhasin*)."

32. Following Schechter/Freimann's emendation of עת to עם.

33. The Hebrew is convoluted.

34. Perhaps the brother of Shadal no. 17? Note that here we have a precise date of death but not much text, whereas in no. 17 we have an extremely poetic and elaborate text with no precise date. Since no. 17 just mentions sisters of the deceased, these two may not be brothers.

35. Num. 24:21.

36. Exod. 33:22.

37. Lam. 3:1.

38. Isa. 59:7, 60:18; Jer. 48:3.

39. Deut. 28:59. Rashi glosses, plagues unlike those seen before and that are *ne'emanim*—that won't go away. The reading is echoed by Abraham ibn Ezra and the Rashbam.

40. Jer. 12:7 (also echoed in 2 Kings 21:14).

41. 1 Kings 13:14; Exod. 23:23; and more.

42. Jer. 44:6. I have switched the order of this line with the preceding to make sense in English.

43. Isa. 30:15; and see Rashi and Radaq.

44. Isa. 7:23.

45. Num. 17:34 = RSV 17:12.

46. Isa. 54:1.

47. Lam. 1:16.

48. Shadal thinks that the phrase means that she "married off" her daughters; Cantera and Millás read the expression to mean that they have died.

49. Isa. 49:2.

50. Exod. 28:11.

51. Shadal has חלי הזמן ועדיו; Cantera, הלי הזמן ועדיו. The word must be a synonym for "crown" or "ornament."

52. Avraham Reiner points out the relative infrequency of the term *parnas* among the Würzburg tombstones, concluding that it refers to a communal function filled by a specific individual. See Reiner, "Epitaph Style of Tombstones from the Würzburg Cemetery, 1147–1346," in Karlheinz Müller et al., *Die Grabsteine vom jüdischen Friedhof in Würzburg aus der Zeit von dem Schwarzen Tod* (Würzburg: Monumenta Germaniae Historica, 2012), 263–95.

53. These lines and the following few lines evoke the biblical role of the Levites, who carried the holy utensils and served in rotations in the work of the Holy Sanctuary. See the description in Numbers 3.

54. Ps. 84:3.

55. His wife.

56. Gen. 8:8–9.

57. See 1 Sam. 5:1.

58. Esther 6:6, 7:9, 7:11.

59. Ezek. 16:11.

60. חיות; cf. Ezekiel 1 throughout.

61. הסתופף; Ps. 84:11.

62. Cf. Job 20:26.

63. Num. 17:28.

64. Another brother to nos. 28, 29. Abraham b. Samuel ben al-Naqawa, memorialized in no. 28, died in 1360 with a long epitaph that suggests that he was the victim of a violent intrigue. Abraham built a school and an inn for travelers, and was murdered on Yom Kippur eve.

65. Lit., "he did not raise his heart or lift up his eyes."

66. Ps. 112:9; the same phrase is used in no. 48 for someone with a scholarly career. Here the deceased is chiefly distinguished by his charitable acts.

67. Isa. 33:16.

68. Isa. 28:5.

69. 2 Chron. 33:8.

70. Job 3:9.

71. I.e., from Ashkenaz/France; cf. inscriptions 12, 26, 44.

72. 1 Sam. 6:9.

73. Ps. 27:4.

74. Isa. 62:12.

75. Ps. 24:4.

76. Combining Ps. 54:2 and 1 Sam. 23:19.

77. Cf. Prov. 8:12 and elsewhere. David must have been a diplomat or councillor.

78. Num. 1:17; 1 Chron. 12:31; Ezra 8:30; and more.

79. I.e., Ashkenaz or northern France. See nos. 12, 26, 42.

80. Jer. 46:20.

81. Isa. 10:23, 28:22; Dan. 9:27.

82. Deut. 28:43.

83. Deut. 12:9.

84. Cf. Ruth 2:12.

85. Prov. 17:27, reading יקר is read as קר—cool of spirit.

86. Gen. 38:1.

87. Jer. 31:20.

88. July–Aug 1349.

89. Lit., "built his house."

90. Jer. 31:12, 25.

91. Cf. Isa. 58:12.

92. 1 Sam. 1:11.

93. The Hebrew reads: כי עתי הבדק ונחטף. Shadal says that the line is incomprehensible and must be corrupt; he leaves it untranslated. Cantera has *pues llegó el tiempo de la prueba y fué arrebatado*. There is no other instance in this collection where the author was so at a loss for words that he repeated himself in a rhyme; I am inclined to agree with Shadal that there is something amiss in the text.

94. Apparently, the father of no. 35, Isaac b. Meir Sasson. Father and son are described as physicians in epitaph no. 35, so the reference in no. 57 to compounded spices may allude to Meir's pharmaceutical or medical activity.

95. Cf. the same phrase in no. 44; and see Isa. 10:23, 28:22 and Dan. 9:27.

96. 1 Sam. 6:9, implying that the plague is an act of God.

97. Cf. Judg. 6:4.

98. Cf. Ps. 69:3.

99. Zech. 10:1.

100. Isa. 3:3. Rashi and Radaq gloss חרשים as mental acumen. If this is the way the poet understood the phrase, it could be translated "a skilled councillor." The phrase recurs in a number of the inscriptions, see, e.g., Shadal nos. 28, 36, 48.

101. Cantera and Millás suggest "Saragossan."

102. Deut. 11:22, 30:20; Josh. 22:5; and the liturgical verse from the ואהבת.

103. Cf. Judg. 21:15; 2 Sam. 6:8; Gen. 38:29.

104. Ps. 106:29.

105. Gen. 49:29.

106. Many examples: Neh. 2:18; Ezra 8:22; Ezek. 1:3, 3:22, 37:1, 40:1; 2 Kings 3:15.

107. Cf. Mic. 2:13.

108. Gen. 41:38.

109. The deceased was a victim of the next plague outbreak (1361–62). This is the only epitaph in the collection from this second plague wave.

110. Job 19:23.

111. Exod. 39:6.

112. Ps. 49:6.

113. Gen. 28:22.

114. Job 19:24.

115. Exod. 16:33.

116. Jer. 8:22 and elsewhere.

117. Num. 27:13.

118. Jer. 4:7.

119. 1 Sam. 6:9.

120. Ps. 27:4.

Bibliography

Ajdukovic, Dean. "Social Contexts of Trauma and Healing." *Medicine, Conflict and Survival* 20.2 (2004): 120–35.

Alexander, Jeffrey C. *Cultural Trauma: A Social Theory*. Malden, Mass.: Polity Press, 2012.

Alexander, Jeffrey C. "Toward a Theory of Cultural Trauma." In Jeffrey Alexander et al., eds., *Cultural Trauma and Collective Identity*. Berkeley: University of California Press, 2004, 1–30.

Algazi, Gadi. "Forget Memory: Some Critical Remarks on Memory, Forgetting and History." In Sebastian Scholz, Gerald Schwedler, and Kai-Michael Sprenger, eds., *Damnatio in Memoria: Deformation und Gegenkonstruktionen von Geschichte*. Vienna: Böhlau, 2014, 25–34.

Amasuno, Marcelino V. "La medicina y el físico en la Dança general de la muerte." *Hispanic Review* 65.1 (1997): 1–24.

Amin, Shahid. *Event, Metaphor, Memory: Chauri Chaura 1922–92*. Los Angeles: University of California Press, 1995.

Arrizabalaga, Jon. "La enfermedad y la asistencia hospitalaria." In Luis García-Ballester, ed., *Historia de la ciencia y de la técnica en la Corona de Castilla*. Valladolid: Junta de Castilla y León, 2001, 1:603–27.

———. "Facing the Black Death: Perceptions and Reactions of University Medical Practitioners." In Luis García-Ballester et al., eds., *Practical Medicine from Salerno to the Black Death*. Cambridge: Cambridge University Press, 1994, 237–88.

———, Luis García-Ballester, and Joan Veny, eds. *Jacme d'Agramont: Regiment de preservació de pestilència (Lleida, 1348)*. Lleida: Universitat de Lleida, 1998.

Assis, Yom Tov. *The Golden Age of Aragonese Jewry*. London: Littman Library of Jewish Civilization, 1997.

Avineri, Tzvi. "Hebrew Inscriptions from the Middle Ages." *Proceedings of the American Academy for Jewish Research (PAAJR)* 33 (1965): 1–33.

Bale, Anthony. *Feeling Persecuted: Christians, Jews and Images of Violence in the Middle Ages*. London: Reaktion, 2010.

Baraz, Daniel. *Medieval Cruelty: Changing Perceptions, Late Antiquity to the Early Modern Period*. Ithaca, N.Y.: Cornell University Press, 2003.

Barber, Malcolm. "The Pastoureaux of 1320." *Journal of Ecclesiastical History* 32 (1981): 143–66.

Barkai, Ron. "Jewish Treatises on the Black Death (1350–1500): A Preliminary Study." In Roger French et al., eds., *Medicine from the Black Death to the French Disease*. Aldershot: Ashgate, 1998, 6–25.

Bar-Levav, Avriel. "Another Place: Cemeteries in Jewish Culture" [Hebrew]. *Pe'amim* 98–99 (2002): 5–37.

Barnett, Richard, Philip Wright, and Oren Yoffe, eds. *The Jews of Jamaica: Tombstone Inscriptions 1663–1880*. Jerusalem: Ben-Zvi Institute, 1997.

Barzilay, Tzafrir. "The Black Death in Aragon: Notes on a Jewish Chronicle" [Hebrew]. *Hayo Haya* 8 (Winter 2011): 53–72.

Beltrán de Heredia Bercero, Julia. "El primer testimoni arqueologic de la Pesta Negra a Barcelona: La fossa comuna de la basílica dels sants màrtirs just i pastor." *Quaderns d'arqueologia i historia de la Ciutat de Barcelona (QUARHIS)* 2.10 (2014): 164–79.

Benedictow, Ole. *The Black Death 1346–1353: The Complete History*. Suffolk, U.K.: Boydell Press, 2004.

Bergdolt, Klaus. *Der Schwarze Tod in Europa: Die Grosse Pest und das Ende des Mittelalters*. Munich: C. H. Beck, 2017.

Bernfeld, Simon. *Sefer haDema'ot*. 4 vols. Berlin: Eshkol, 1925–34.

Biraben, Jean. *Les hommes et la peste en France et dans les pays européens et méditerranéens*. 2 vols. Paris: Mouton, 1975.

Bolton, J. L. "Looking for *Yersinia Pestis*: Scientists, Historians and the Black Death." In *The Fifteenth Century XII: Society in an Age of Plague*, ed. Linda Clark and Carole Rawcliffe. Woodbridge, Suffolk UK: Boydell & Brewer, 2013, 22:15–38.

Bos, Gerrit. "The Black Death in Hebrew Literature: *Ha-Ma'amar be-Qaddahot ha-Dever* (Treatise on Pestilential Fever)." *European Journal of Jewish Studies* 5.1 (2011): 1–52.

———, ed. *Ibn al-Jazzar on Fevers*. New York: Kegan Paul, 2000.

———, and Guido Mensching. "The Black Death in Hebrew Literature: Abraham Ben Solomon Hen's *Tractatulus de pestilentia*." *Jewish Studies Quarterly* 18.1 (2011): 32–63.

Bregman, Dvora. *Esa et levavi: Shirim me'et Moshe Zakut*. Jerusalem: Ben-Zvi Institute, 2009.

———. "Now You Shall Be in Verses of Stone: The Epitaph Poems of Moses Zacuto" [Hebrew]. In Jonathan Decter and Michael Rand, eds., *Studies in Arabic and Hebrew Letters in Honor of Raymond P. Scheindlin*. Piscataway, N.J.: Gorgias Press, 2007, Hebrew sec., 13–21.

———. *Tzror zehuvim: Sonetim ivriyim metekufat harenesans vehabarok*. Jerusalem: Ben-Zvi Institute, 1997.

Breuer, Josef, and Sigmund Freud. "On the Psychical Mechanism of Hysterical Phenomena: Preliminary Communication (1893)." In *Freud and Breuer: Studies on Hysteria*. New York: Avon, 1966, 37–52.

Brombacher, J. A. "Poetry on Gravestones: Poetry by the Seventeenth-Century Portuguese Rabbi Solomon de Oliveryra." *Dutch Jewish History* 2 (1985): 153–65.

Cabrillana, Nicolás. "La crisis del siglo XIV en Castilla: La Peste Negra en el opisbado de Palencia." *Hispania* 28 (1968): 245–58.

Callico, J. "La Peste Negra en la Peninsule Iberica." *Anuario de estudios medievales* 7 (1970–71): 67–102.

Calvo Gálvez, Matías. "Necróplis judía de Valencia: Nuevos datos." In Ana Maria Alvárez, *Juderías y sinagogas de la Sefarad medieval*. Cuenca: Ediciones de la Universidad de Castilla—La Mancha, 2003, 583–610.

———. "Peste Negra y pogrom en la ciudad de Valencia: La evidencia arqueológica." *Revista de arqueologia* 19.206 (1998): 50–59.

Campbell, Anna Montgomery. *The Black Death and Men of Learning.* New York: Columbia University Press, 1931.

Campbell, Bruce. *The Great Transition: Climate, Disease and Society in the Late-Medieval World.* Cambridge: Cambridge University Press, 2016.

Cantera, F., and J. M. Millás. *Las inscripciones hebraicas de España.* Madrid: C. Bermejo, 1956.

Cardoner Planas, A. "Seis mujeres hebreas practicando la medicina en el reino de Aragón." *Sefarad* 9 (1949): 441–45.

Carmichael, Ann. "Plague Persistence in Western Europe: A Hypothesis." *The Medieval Globe* 1 (2014): 157–93.

———. "Universal and Particular: The Language of Plague, 1348–1500." In Vivian Nutton, ed., *Pestilential Complexities: Understanding Medieval Plague.* London: Wellcome Trust, 2008, 17–52.

Caruth, Cathy. *Listening to Trauma: Conversations with Leaders in the Theory and Treatment of Catastrophic Experience.* Baltimore: Johns Hopkins University Press, 2014.

———. *Unclaimed Experience: Trauma, Narrative, and History.* Baltimore: Johns Hopkins University Press, 1996.

Certex, Dominique. "Identification and Interpretation of Historical Cemeteries Linked to Epidemics." In Didier Raoult and Michel Drancourt, *Paleomicrobiology: Past Human Infections.* Berlin: Springer, 2008, 23–48.

Chase, Melissa. "Fever, Poisons and Apostemes: Authority and Experience in Montpellier Plague Treatises." *Annals of the New York Academy of Sciences* 441 (1985): 153–70.

Cohen, Esther. *The Modulated Scream: Pain in Medieval Culture.* Chicago: University of Chicago Press, 2010.

Cohen, Mark R. *Poverty and Charity in the Jewish Community of Medieval Egypt.* Princeton, N.J.: Princeton University Press, 2005.

Cohen-Hanegbi, Naama. *Caring for the Living Soul: Emotions, Medicine and Penance in the Late Medieval Mediterranean.* Leiden: Brill, 2017.

———. "Mourning Under Medical Care: A Study of a Consilium by Bartolomeo Montagnana." *Parergon* 3.2 (2014): 35–53.

———. "A Moving Soul: Emotions in Late Medieval Medicine." *Osiris* 31 (2016): 46–66.

Cohn, Samuel K., Jr. "The Black Death and the Burning of the Jews." *Past & Present* 196 (August 2007): 3–36.

———. *The Black Death Transformed: Disease and Culture in Early Renaissance Europe.* London: Oxford University Press, 2002.

———. "Popular Insurrection and the Black Death: A Comparative View." *Past & Present* 195, supplement 2 (2007): 188–204.

Colet, Anna, et al. "The Black Death and Its Consequences for the Jewish Community in Tàrrega: Lessons from History and Archeology." *The Medieval Globe* 1.1 (2014): 63–96.

Colet, Anna, Jordi Ruíz Ventura, and Eulàlia Subirà. *Tragèdia al call.* Tàrrega: Museu Comarcal de l'Urgell, 2014.

Colet Marcé, Anna, and Oriol Saula Briansó. "La influència de l'element religiós en l'excavació del fossar dels jueus de Tàrrega." In Renée Sivan et al., eds., *La intervenció arqueològica a les necròpolis històriques: Els cementiris jueus.* Barcelona: Museu d'Història de Barcelona, 2009, 44–51.

Colet, Anna, et al. "Les fosses communes de la necropolis jueva de les Roquetes, Tàrrega." *Urtx* 23.1 (2009): 103–23.

Colomer, Laia. "The Politics of Human Remains in Managing Archaeological Medieval Jewish Burial Grounds in Europe." *Nordisk Kulturpolitisk Tidskoff (Nordic Journal of Cultural Politics)* 17.2 (2014): 168–86.

Craps, Stef. *Postcolonial Witnessing: Trauma Out of Bounds.* New York: Palgrave Macmillan, 2013.

Crémieux, Adolphe. "Les juifs de Toulon au Moyen Âge et le massacre du 13 avril 1348." *Revue des Études Juives* 89 (1930): 33–72; 90 (1931): 43–64.

dal Molin, Cristina. "Recovery of Some Unedited MSS by Leone de' Sommi at the National Library in Turin." In Ahuva Belkin, ed., *Leone de' Sommi and the Performing Arts.* Tel Aviv: Tel Aviv University, 1997, 101–17.

Davidson, Israel. "Abraham Bedarshi's Purim Letter." *Jewish Quarterly Review* n.s. 23.4 (1932–33): 349–56.

de la Peña Barroso, Efrén. "Un *Regimen Sanitatis* contra la peste: El tratado del licenciado Vázquez." *Asclepio* 44.2 (2012): 397–416.

DeWitte, Sharon, and Philip Slavin. "Between Famine and Death: England on the Eve of the Black Death: Evidence from Paleoepidemiology and Manorial Accounts." *Journal of Interdisciplinary History* 44.1 (2013): 37–60.

Dickson, Gary. "The Advent of the *Pastores.*" *Revue Belge de Philologie et d'Histoire* 66 (1988): 249–67.

Doniach, N. S. "Abraham Bedersi's Purim Letter to David Kaslari." *Jewish Quarterly Review* n.s. 23 (1932–33): 63–69.

Durrant, Sam. "Undoing Sovereignty: Towards a Critical Theory of Mourning." In Gert Buelens, Sam Durrant, and Robert Eaglestone, eds., *The Future of Trauma Theory.* New York: Routledge, 2014, 91–110.

Eaglestone, Robert. "Knowledge, 'Afterwardness' and the Future of Trauma Theory." In Gert Buelens, Sam Durrant, and Robert Eaglestone, eds., *The Future of Trauma Theory.* New York: Routledge, 2014, 11–22.

Einbinder, Susan. "Anti-Jewish Violence and the Pastoureaux: The Case for Medieval Trauma." In Wendy Turner, ed., *Medieval Trauma.* Leiden: Brill, forthcoming.

———. *Beautiful Death: Jewish Poetry and Martyrdom from Medieval France.* Princeton, N.J.: Princeton University Press, 2002.

———. "Exegesis and Romance: Revisiting the Old French Translation of Kallir." In Elisheva Baumgarten and Judah D. Galinsky, eds., *Jews and Christians in Thirteenth-Century France.* New York: Palgrave Macmillan, 2015, 235–49 and appendix 249–59 (bilingual translation in collaboration with Samuel N. Rosenberg).

———. "God's Forgotten Sheep: Jewish Poetry and the Expulsion from France (1306)." *Masoret haPiyyut* 4 (2008): 55*–82* (English sec.).

———. "Hebrew Poems for 'the Day of Shutting In': Problems and Methods." *Revue des Études Juives* 163.1–2 (January–June 2004): 111–35.

———. "The Libel and the Lamb." Plenary talk, International Congress of Medieval Studies, Western Michigan University, Kalamazoo, 2014.

———. "Literature, Memory and Medieval French Jews." *Jewish Studies Quarterly* 15.3 (2008): 225–40.

———. "Moses Rimos: Poetry, Poison and History." *Italia* 20 (2010): 67–91.

———. *No Place of Rest: Jewish Literature, Expulsion, and the Memory of Medieval France.* Philadelphia: University of Pennsylvania Press, 2009.

———. "Theory and Practice: A Jewish Physician in Paris and Avignon." *Association for Jewish Studies Review* 33.1 (April 2009): 135–54.

Emery, Richard. "The Black Death of 1348 in Perpignan." *Speculum* 42 (1967): 611–21.

Fassin, Didier, and Richard Rechtman. *Empire of Trauma: An Inquiry into the Condition of Victimhood.* Princeton, N.J.: Princeton University Press, 2009.

Fearon, James, and David Laitin. "Violence and the Social Construction of Ethnic Identity." *International Organization* 54.4 (Autumn 2000): 845–77.

Feldman, Allen. "Memory Theaters, Virtual Witnessing and the Trauma-Aesthetic." *Biography* 27.1 (Winter 2004): 163–202.

Fleming, Robin. "Bones for Historians: Putting the Body Back into Biography." In David Bates, Julia Crick, and Sarah Hamilton, eds., *Writing Medieval Biography 750–1250: Essays in Honour of Frank Barlow.* Woodbridge, U.K.: Boydell, 2006, 29–48.

Freedman, Paul. *Images of the Medieval Peasant.* Palo Alto, Calif.: Stanford University Press, 1999.

———. *The Origins of Peasant Servitude in Medieval Catalonia.* Cambridge: Cambridge University Press, 1991.

Freimann, Abraham Hayyim. *Rabbenu Asher bar Yehiel ve-Tze'etze'av.* Jerusalem: Rav Kook, 1986.

Freudenthal, Gad, and Mauro Zonta. "Avicenna Among Medieval Jews: The Reception of Avicenna's Philosophical, Scientific and Medical Writings in Jewish Cultures, East and West." *Arabic Sciences and Philosophy* 22 (2012): 217–87.

Fricke, Hannes. *Das hört nicht auf: Trauma, Literatur und Empathie.* Göttingen: Wallstein, 2004.

Fujii, Lee Ann. *Killing Neighbors: Webs of Violence in Rwanda.* Ithaca, N.Y.: Cornell University Press, 2010.

Galinsky, Judah. "An Ashkenazic Rabbi Encounters Sephardic Culture: R. Asher b. Jehiel's Attitude Towards Philosophy and Science." *Simon Dubnow Institute Yearbook* 8 (2009): 191–211.

———. "Of Exile and Halakha: 14th Century Halakhic Literature and the Works of the French Exiles Aaron b. haKohen and Jeruham b. Meshulam." *Jewish History* 22 (2008): 81–96.

———. "On the Legacy of R. Judah ben haRosh, Rabbi of Toledo: A Chapter in the History of Responsa Literature from the Sages of Christian Spain" [Hebrew]. *Pe'amim* 128 (2011): 175–210.

Galipapa, Hayim ben Avraham. "*Sefer Emeq Refaim* and Several Responsa by R. Hayim Galipapa" [Hebrew]. In Saul Israeli, Norman Lamm and Isaac Rafael, eds., *Sefer yuval likhvod . . . Rabbi Yosef Dov haLevi Soloveitchik.* Jerusalem: Mossad haRav Kook, 1984, 1211–59.

García-Ballester, Luis. *La búsqueda de la salud: Sanadores y enfermos en la España medieval.* Barcelona: Peninsula, 2001.

———, Lola Ferre, and Eduard Feliu. "Jewish Appreciation of Fourteenth-Century Scholastic Medicine." *Osiris* 6 (1990): 85–117.

García-Ballester, Luis, Michael McVaugh, and Agustín Rubio-Vela. *Medical Licensing and Learning in Fourteenth-Century Valencia.* Philadelphia: Transactions of the American Philosophical Society, 1989.

García-Ballester, Luis, and C. Vázquez de Benito. "Los médicos judíos castellanos del siglo XIV y al galenismo arabe." *Asclepio* 42.1 (1990): 119–47.

Gautier-Dalché, J. "La Peste Negra dans les états de la Couronne d'Aragon." In *Mélanges offerts à Marcel Bataillon.* Bordeaux: Féret, 1962, 65–80.

Ginzburg, Carlo. *Threads and Traces: True False Fictive.* Berkeley: University of California Press, 2012.

Ginzburg, David. "*Be'er Lehi*: The Plague Tract of R. Isaac ben Todros" [Hebrew]. In Curatorium der Zunz-Stiftung, eds., *Tif'eret Seivah* (Jubelschrift zum Neunzigsten Geburtstag des Dr. L. Zunz). Berlin: Louis Gerschel, 1884, 91–126.

Gómez Menor, José Carlos. "Algunos datos sobre el cementerio judío de Toledo." *Sefarad* 31.2 (1971): 363–73.

Gorrini, Giovanni. *L'incendio della R. Biblioteca Nazionale di Torino.* Turin: Renzo Stregio, 1905.

Grau i Montserrat, Manuel. "Metges Jueus del Vell Comtat de Besalú." *Gimbernat: Revista Catalana d'història de la medicina i de la ciència* 8 (1987): 81–90.

Grayzel, Solomon. "Confession of a Medieval Jewish Convert." *Historia Judaica* 17 (1955): 89–120.

Green, Monica, ed. *Pandemic Disease in the Medieval World, The Medieval Globe* 1.1 Kalamazoo, Mich.: ARC Medieval Press, 2014.

Greenblatt, Rachel. "The Shapes of Memory: Evidence in Stone from the Old Jewish Cemetery in Prague." *Leo Baeck Institute Year Book* 47 (2002): 43–67.

Greenblatt, Stephen. "Murdering Peasants: Status, Genre and the Representation of Rebellion." *Representations* 1 (1983): 1–29.

Gross, Jan. *Neighbors: The Destruction of the Jewish Community in Jedwabne, Poland.* Princeton, N.J.: Princeton University Press, 2000.

Gruber, Mayer. "Floating Letters." In Steven L. Jacobs, ed., *Maven in Blue Jeans: A Festschrift in Honor of Zev Garber.* Lafayette, Ind.: Purdue University Press, 2009, 44–45.

Gruber, Samuel D. "Lessons from Medieval Jewish Center Discoveries." Jewish Heritage Report. *International Survey of Jewish Monuments* (ISJM) online newsletter, August 27, 2008, http://www.isjm.org/SitesMonuments/Europe/Spain/tabid/134/Default.aspx.

Guilleré, Christian. "La Peste Noire à Gérone (1348)." *Annals de l'Institut d'estudis Gironins* 27 (1984): 87–161.

Gutwirth, Eleazar. "Penso's Roots: The Politics and Poetics of Cultural Fusion." *Studia Rosenthalia* 35.2 (2001): 269–84.

Gyug, Richard F. *The Diocese of Barcelona During the Black Death: The Register Notule Communium 15 (1348–1349)*. Toronto: PIMS, 1994.

———. "The Effects and Extent of the Black Death of 1348: New Evidence for Clerical Mortality in Barcelona." *Mediaeval Studies* 45.1 (1983): 385–98.

Hacking, Ian. "Memory Sciences, Memory Politics." In Paul Antze and M. Lambek, eds., *Tense Past: Cultural Essays in Trauma and Memory*. New York: Routledge, 1996, 67–89.

Halkin, Hillel. *After One Hundred and Twenty: Reflecting on Death, Mourning and the Afterlife in the Jewish Tradition*. Princeton, N.J.: Princeton University Press, 2016.

Hamilton, Michele. *Beyond Faith: Belief, Morality and Memory in a Fifteenth-Century Judeo-Iberian Manuscript*. Leiden: Brill, 2014.

Havatselet, Abraham Joseph, A. I. Goldmintz, and Yoel Qatan, eds. *Zikhron Yehuda: Lerabbenu Yehuda ben haRosh*. Jerusalem: Makhon Shlomo Oman, Makhon Or haMizrah, Makhon Yerushalayim, 2005.

Hess, Cordelia. "Jews and the Black Death in Fourteenth-Century Prussia: A Search for Traces." In idem and Jonathan Adams, eds., *Fear and Loathing in the North: Jews and Muslims in Medieval Scandinavia and the Baltic Region*. Berlin: Walter de Gruyter, 2015, 109–26.

Hinton, Devon S., and Roberto Lewis-Fernandez. "Idioms of Distress Among Trauma Survivors: Subtypes and Clinical Utility." *Culture, Medicine and Psychiatry* 34.2 (June 2012): 209–18.

Hollan, Douglas. "Coping in Plain Sight: Work and Trauma." *Transcultural Psychiatry* 50.5 (October 2013): 726–43.

Hollender, Elisabeth. "Narrative Exegesis in Ashkenas and Zarfat: The Case of Piyyut Commentary." In Judit Targarona Borrás and Angel Saenz-Badillos, eds., *Jewish Studies at the Turn of the Twentieth Century*. Leiden: Brill, 1999, 429–35.

Hoogewood, F. J., and Falk Wresenmann. "Sephardic Cemeteries: A Selective Bibliography." In Henriques de Castro, ed., *Keur van Grafstenen: Selected Gravestones from the Dutch Portuguese Jewish Cemetery*. Ouderkerk aan de Amstel: 1999, 17–23.

Horowitz, Donald L. *The Deadly Ethnic Riot*. Berkeley: University of California Press, 2001.

Horowitz, Elliot. "Speaking to the Dead: Cemetery Prayer in Medieval and Early Modern Jewry." *Journal of Jewish Thought and Philosophy* 8 (1999): 303–17.

Israeli, Shaul, Norman Lamm, and Yizhak Rafaeli, eds. *Sefer Yuval likhvod . . . Rabbi Yosef Dov haLevi Soloveitchik*. Jerusalem: Mosad haRav Kook, 1984.

Jordan, William C. *The French Monarchy and the Jews*. Philadelphia: University of Pennsylvania Press, 1989.

———. *The Great Famine: Northern Europe in the Early Fourteenth Century*. Princeton, N.J.: Princeton University Press, 1996.

———. "Problems of the Meat Market of Béziers 1240–1247: A Question of Anti-Semitism." *Revue des Études Juives* 135 (1976): 31–49.

Kacki, Sacha, and D. Castex. "Reflexions sur la variété des modalités funéraires en temps d'épidémie: L'exemple de la Peste Noire en contexts urbain et rural." *Archéologie Médiévale* 42.1 (2012): 1–22.

Kahana-Smilansky, Hagar. "The Commentaries by Medieval Jews on Avicenna's Canon of Medicine: A Hypothesis." Unpublished lecture, IAS-Hebrew University, May 10, 2007.

Kalyvas, Stathis. *The Logic of Violence in Civil War.* Cambridge: Cambridge University Press, 2006.

———. "The Ontology of Political Violence: Action and Identity in Civil Wars." *Perspectives on Politics* 1.3 (2003): 475–94.

———. "The Paradox of Terrorism in Civil War." *Journal of Ethics* 8.1 (2004): 97–138.

Kanarfogel, Ephraim. *The Intellectual History and Rabbinic Culture of Medieval Ashkenaz.* Detroit: Wayne State University Press, 2012.

Kansteiner, Wulf. "Finding Meaning in Memory: A Methodological Critique of Collective Memory Studies." *History & Theory* 41.2 (2002): 79–97.

———. "Genealogy of a Category Mistake: A Critical Intellectual History of the Cultural Trauma Metaphor." *Rethinking History* 8.2 (2004): 193–221.

King, Charles. "The Micropolitics of Social Violence." *World Politics* 56.3 (April 2004): 431–55.

Klein, Kerwin L. "On the Emergence of Memory in Historical Discourse." *Representations* 69 (2000): 127–50.

Kleinman, Arthur, and Robert Desjarlais. "Ni patients ni victimes: Pour une ethnographie de la violence politique." *Actes de la recherche en sciences sociales* 104 (1994): 56–63.

Kleinman, Arthur, and Joan Kleinman. "The Appeal of Experience: The Dismay of Images: Cultural Appropriations of Suffering in Our Times." *Daedalus* 125.1 (Winter 1996): 1–23.

LaCapra, Dominick. *Writing History, Writing Trauma.* Baltimore: John Hopkins University Press, 2001.

Lacave, José Luis. "Antiguos cementerios judíos en España." *Raíces revista judía de cultura* 78 (2009): 76–78.

Laqueur, Thomas. "The Deep Time of the Dead." *Social Research* 78.3 (2011): 799–820.

———. *The Work of the Dead: A Cultural History of Mortal Remains.* Princeton, N.J.: Princeton University Press, 2015.

Laub, Dori, and N. Auerhahn. "Knowing and Not-Knowing Massive Psychic Trauma: Forms of Traumatic Memory." *International Journal of Psychoanalysis* 74.2 (1993): 287–302.

Lemos, Tracy M. "Dispossessing Nations: Population Growth, Scarcity and Genocide in Ancient Israel and Twentieth Century Rwanda." In Saul Olyan, ed., *Ritual Violence in the Hebrew Bible.* New York: Oxford University Press, 2016, 29–65.

León Tello, Pilar. "Judiós toledanos víctimas de la Peste Negra." *Sefarad* 37 (1977): 333–37.

Leys, Ruth. *Trauma: A Genealogy.* Chicago: University of Chicago Press, 2000.

López de Meneses, Amada. "Una consecuencia de la Peste Negra en Cataluña: El pogrom de 1348: Appendices (Documentos inéditos)." *Sefarad* 19 (1959): 321–64.

———. *Documentos acerca de la Peste Negra en los dominios de la Corona de Aragón*. Zaragoza: Imprenta Heraldo de Aragón, 1956.

Luckhurst, Roger. *The Trauma Question*. New York: Routledge, 2008.

Luzzatto, Samuel David. *Avnei zikkaron*. Prague: J. Landau, 1841.

Malkiel, David. "Christian Hebraism in a Contemporary Key." *Jewish Quarterly Review* 96.1 (Winter 2006): 123–46.

———. "Poems on Tombstone Inscriptions in Northern Italy in the Sixteenth and Seventeenth Centuries" [Hebrew]. *Pe'amim* 98–99 (2004): 120–54.

Mamdani, Mahmoud. *When Victims Become Killers*. Princeton, N.J.: Princeton University Press, 2001.

McVaugh, Michael. *Medicine Before the Plague: Practitioners and Their Patients in the Crown of Aragon, 1285–1345*. Cambridge: Cambridge University Press, 1993.

———, and Luis García-Ballester. "The Medical Faculty at Early Fourteenth-Century Lerida." *History of Universities* 8 (1989): 1–25.

———. "Jewish Appreciation of Fourteenth-Century Scholastic Medicine." *Viator* 23 (1990): 201–13.

Meister, Robert. "Human Rights and the Politics of Victimhood." *Ethics and International Affairs* 16.2 (2002): 91–108.

Melechen, Nina. "The Jews of Medieval Toledo: Their Economic and Social Contacts with Christians from 1150 to 1391." Ph.D. diss., Fordham University, 1999.

Mengel, David. "A Plague on Bohemia? Mapping the Black Death." *Past & Present* 211 (May 2011): 3–34.

Merback, Mitchell B. *Pilgrimage and Pogrom: Violence, Memory and Visual Culture at the Host-Miracle Shrines of Germany and Austria*. Chicago: University of Chicago Press, 2012.

———. *The Thief, the Cross and the Wheel*. Chicago: University of Chicago Press, 1999.

Miller, Christopher Patrick. "A Just Grammar: Unspeakable Speech in Robert Meister." *Qui Parle: Critical Humanities and Social Sciences* 22.1 (2013): 203–22.

Milton, Gregory B. *Market Power: Lordship, Society and Economy in Medieval Catalonia 1276–1313*. New York: Palgrave Macmillan, 2012.

Miret y Sans, Joachim. "Le Massacre des juifs de Montclus en 1320." *Revue des Études Juives* 53 (1907): 255–66.

Montanés, José Angel. "Staring Black Death in the Face in Barcelona." *El País* [English]. August 15, 2014, http://elpais.com/elpais/2014/08/15/inenglish/1408097721_483831 .html.

Morey, J. "Les juifs au Franche-Comté au XIVe siècle." *Revue des Études Juives* 7 (1883): 1–39.

Müller, Karlheinz, Simon Schwarzfuchs, and Avraham Reiner, eds. *Die Grabsteine vom jüdischen Friedhof in Würzburg aus der Zeit vor dem Schwarzen Tod*. Würzburg: Monumenta Germaniae Historica, 2011.

Muntané i Santiveri, Josep. "Aproximació a les causes de l'avalot de Tàrrega de 1348." *Tamid: Revista Catalana Annual d'Estudis Hebraics* 8 (2012): 103–29.

———. "Itinerari pels documents relatius a l'assalt del call de Tàrrega de l'any 1348." *Urtx* 23 (2009): 158–79.

———. "Metges jueus contractats pel govern municipal de Tàrrega durant els segles XIV i XV." *Urtx* 26.1 (2012): 135–47.

———, ed. *Moixé Natan: Qüestions de vida / Tots'ot hayim.* Barcelona: Institut Món Juic, Promociones y Publicaciones Universitarias, 2010.

———. "Proposta d'ubicació del fossar dels jueus de la vila de Tàrrega a partir dels testimonis documentals continguts en els libres d'estimes (1501–1510)." *Urtx* 20 (2007): 103–18.

Nijenhuis, Ellert. *The Trinity of Trauma: Ignorance, Fragility and Control.* Göttingen: Vandenhoeck & Ruprecht, 2015.

Nirenberg, David. *Anti-Judaism: The Western Tradition.* New York: Norton, 2013.

———. *Communities of Violence.* Princeton, N.J.: Princeton University Press, 1996.

O'Callaghan, Joseph F. *The Gibraltar Crusade: Castile and the Battle for the Strait.* Philadelphia: University of Pennsylvania Press, 2011.

Paladilhe, Dominique. "Les Pastoureaux contre les juifs." *Historia* 410 (January 1981): 116–24.

Passerat, Georges. *La croisade des Pastoureaux.* Cahors: La Louve, 2006.

———. "Les derniers juifs du pays toulousain victîmes des émeutes populaires." In Gilbert Dahan, ed., *L'expulsion des juifs de France, 1394.* Paris. Cerf, 2004, 69–77.

Petrucci, Armando. *Writing the Dead: Death and Writing Strategies in the Western Tradition.* Palo Alto, Calif.: Stanford University Press, 1998.

Phillips, William D., Jr. "*Peste Negra*: The Fourteenth-Century Plague Epidemics in Iberia." In Donald Kagay and Theresa Vann, eds., *On the Social Origins of Medieval Institutions: Essays in Honor of Joseph O'Callaghan.* Leiden: Brill, 1998, 47–62.

Pieters, Bert. *De Akkorden van Barcelona (1354): Historische en kritische analyse.* Barcelona: Promociones y Publicaciones Universitarias, 2006.

Pilocane, Chiara. "I manoscritti ebraici della Biblioteca Nazionale di Torino." *Materia Giudaica: Bollettino dell' Associazione italiana per lo studio del giudaismo* 9 (2004): 183–89.

Pinkhof, H. *Abraham Kashlari, over Pestachtige Koortsen.* Amsterdam, 1891, 51–35 (pagination backward to accommodate Hebrew order).

Polonsky, Antoni, and Joanna Michlic, eds. *The Neighbors Respond: The Controversy over the Jedwabne Massacre.* Princeton, N.J.: Princeton University Press, 2003.

Rabin, Haim. "A History of the Translation of the Canon into Hebrew" [Hebrew]. *Melilah* 3–4 (1950): 132–47.

Radstone, Susannah. "Trauma Theory: Contexts, Politics, Ethics." *Paragraph* 30.1 (2007): 9–29.

Raspe, Lucia. "Sacred Space, Local History and Diasporic Identity: The Graves of the Righteous in Medieval and Early Modern Ashkenaz." In Ra'anan Boustan, Oren Kosansky, and Marina Rustow, eds., *Jewish Studies at the Crossroads of Anthropology and History.* Philadelphia: University of Pennsylvania Press, 2011, 147–63.

Ray, Jonathan. "Beyond Tolerance and Persecution: Reassessing Our Approach to Medieval Convivencia." *Jewish Social Studies* 11.2 (2005): 1–18.

Rechtman, Richard. "L'enquête sur la condition de victime." *Études* 414 (2011): 175–86.

———. "Être victime: Généalogie d'une condition clinique." *Evolutionary Psychiatry* 67 (2002): 775–95.

Régné, Jean. *History of the Jews in Aragon: Regesta and Documents 1213–1327.* Ed. Yom Tov Assis. Jerusalem: Magnes Press, 1978.

Reif, Stefan, Andreas Lehnardt, and Avriel Bar-Levav, eds. *Death in Jewish Life: Burial and Mourning Customs Among Jews of Europe and Nearby Communities.* Berlin: De Gruyter, 2014.

Reiner, Rami (Avraham). "Epitaph Style of Tombstones from the Würzburg Cemetery, 1147–1346." In Karlheinz Müller et al., *Die Grabsteine vom judischen Friedhof in Würzburg aus der Zeit von dem Schwarzen Tod.* Würzburg: Monumenta Germaniae Historica, 2011, 263–95.

———. "Inscribed on a Stone: Descriptions of the Deceased on the Gravestones from the Würzburg Cemetery, 1147–1346" [Hebrew]. *Tarbiz* 78.1 (2008): 123–52.

———. "Shard Drawn to Shard: Discoveries from the Jewish Cemetery in Würzburg" [Hebrew]. *Zemanim* 95 (2006): 52–57.

Richler, Benjamin. *Guide to Hebrew Manuscript Collections.* 2nd rev. ed. Jerusalem: Israel Academy of Sciences and Humanities, 2014.

———. "Manuscripts of Avicenna's Kanon in Hebrew Translation: A Revised and Up-to-Date List." *Korot* 8.3–4 (1982): 145*–168* in English sec.; 137–43 in Hebrew.

Riera i Sans, Jaume. *Fam i fe: L'entrada dels pastorells (juliol de 1320).* Lleida: Pages Editors, 2004.

———. "Los tumultos contra las juderías de la corona de Aragón en 1391." *Cuadernos de Historia* 8 (1977): 213–25.

Roberts, Charlotte, and Keith Manchester. *The Archaeology of Disease.* 3rd ed. Ithaca, N.Y.: Cornell University Press, 2007.

Romano, David. "Restos judíos en Lérida." *Sefarad* 20.1 (1960): 50–65.

Roskies, David. "A Revolution Set in Stone: The Art of Burial." In idem, *The Jewish Search for a Usable Past.* Bloomington: Indiana University Press, 1999, 120–45.

Rothberg, Michael. "Beyond Tancred and Clorinda: Trauma Studies for Implicated Subjects." In Gert Buelens, Sam Durrant, and Robert Eaglestone, eds., *The Future of Trauma Theory.* London: Routledge, 2014, xi–xviii.

Ruiz, Teofilo. *Crisis and Continuity: Land and Town in Late Medieval Castile.* Philadelphia: University of Pennsylvania Press, 1994.

Ruíz Taboada, Arturo. "Comments on Muslim, Jewish and Christian Burial Practices in Medieval Toledo (Spain)." *Journal of Islamic Archaeology* 2.1 (2015): 51–73.

———. "La nécropole juive de Tolède: Type, construction et distribution des tombes." In Paul Salmona and L. Sigal, eds., *L'Archéologie du judaïsme en France et en Europe.* Paris: La Découverte, 2011, 287–300.

Ruiz Ventura, Jordi, and Eulàlia Subirà de Galdacàno. "Reconstrucció antropològica del pogrom de 1348 a Tàrrega." *Urtx* 23.1 (2009): 126–37.

Salmona, Paul, and L. Sigal, eds. *L'Archéologie du judaïsme en France et en Europe.* Paris: La Découverte, 2011.

Sárraga, Marian, and Ramón F. Sárraga. "Early Links Between Amsterdam, Hamburg and Italy: Epitaphs from Hamburg's Old Sephardic Cemetery." *Studia Rosenthaliana* 34 (2000): 23–55.

———. "Sephardic Epitaphs in Hamburg's Oldest Jewish Cemetery: Poetry, Riddles and Eccentric Texts." *AJSR* 26 (2002): 53–92.

Schirmann, Hayim, with Ezra Fleischer. *Toldot haShirah ha'Ivrit biSfarad haNotzrit uveDrom Tzarfat.* Jerusalem: Magnes, 1997.

Schwab, Moïse. *Rapport sur les inscriptions hebraïques de l'Espagne.* Paris: Imprimerie Nationale, 1907.

Seroussi, Edwin. "The Songs of Grief and Hope: Ancient Western Sepharadi Melodies of Qinot for the 9th of Av." *Yuval* 7 (2002): 201–32.

Shatzmiller, Joseph. *Jews, Medicine, and Medieval Society.* Berkeley: University of California Press, 1994.

———. "Les juifs de Provence pendant la Peste Noire." *Revue des Études Juives* 133 (1974): 457–80.

——— . "On Becoming a Jewish Doctor in the High Middle Ages." *Sefarad* 43 (1983): 239–50.

Shaw, Albert. "The Loss to Literature by the Turin Library Fire." *American Monthly Review of Reviews* 30 (1904): 234–35.

Shirk, Melanie. "The Black Death in Aragon 1348–1351." *Journal of Medieval History* 7 (1981): 357–67.

Shoham-Steiner, Ephraim. *On the Margins of a Minority: Leprosy, Madness, and Disability Among the Jews of Medieval Europe.* Detroit: Wayne State University Press, 2014.

———. "Pharaoh's Bloodbath: Medieval European Jewish Thoughts About Leprosy, Disease and Blood Therapy." In Mitchell Hart, ed., *Jewish Blood: Reality and Metaphor in History.* New York: Routledge, 2009, 99–115.

———. "An Ultimate Pariah: Jewish Social Attitudes Toward Jewish Lepers." *Social Research* 70.1 (2003): 237–68.

Silberman, Neil Asher. "Qui doit se soucier des morts? Droits religieux et responsabilité citoyenne." In Paul Salmona and L. Sigal, eds., *L'Archéologie du judaïsme en France et en Europe.* Paris: La Découverte, 2011, 225–34.

Siraissi, Nancy. *Taddeo Alderotti and His Pupils: Two Generations of Italian Medical Learning.* Princeton, N.J.: Princeton University Press, 1991.

Smelser, Neil. "Psychological and Cultural Trauma." In Jeffrey Alexander et al., eds., *Cultural Trauma and Collective Identity.* Berkeley: University of California Press, 2004, 31–59.

Smith, John Masson. "Mongol Campaign Rations: Milk, Marmots and Blood?." *Journal of Turkish Studies* 8 (1984): 223–28.

Smith, Robert S. "Fourteenth-Century Population Records of Catalonia." *Speculum* 19.4 (October 1944): 494–501.

Soifer Irish, Maya. "Beyond *Convivencia*: Critical Reflections on the Historiography of Interfaith Relations in Christian Spain." *Journal of Medieval Iberian Studies* 1.1 (2009): 19–35.

———. *Jews and Christians in Medieval Castile: Tradition, Coexistence, and Change*. Washington, D.C.: Catholic University Press, 2016.

Stearns, Justin. "New Directions in the Study of Religious Responses to the Black Death." *History Compass* 7.5 (September 2009): 1363–75.

Stocks, Claire. "Trauma Theory and the Singular Self: Rethinking Extreme Experiences in the Light of Cross-Cultural Identity." *Textual Practice* 21.1 (2007): 71–92.

Strauss, Scott. "How Many Perpetrators Were There in the Rwandan Genocide? An Estimate." *Journal of Genocide Research* 6.1 (2004): 85–98.

Summerfield, Derek. "A Critique of Seven Assumptions Behind Psychological Trauma Programmes in War-Affected Areas." *Social Science and Medicine* 48 (1999): 1449–62.

Surribas Camps, Maria Jose. *Destruction of the Jewish Community of Tàrrega in 1348 and Its Reconstitution*. Jerusalem: International Institute for Jewish Genealogy and Paul Jacobi Center, JNUL, 2015.

Tartakoff, Paola. *Between Christian and Jew: Conversion and Inquisition in the Crown of Aragon 1250–1391*. Philadelphia: University of Pennsylvania Press, 2012.

TeBrake, William. *A Plague of Insurrection: Popular Politics and Peasant Revolt in Flanders 1323–28*. Philadelphia: University of Pennsylvania Press, 1993.

Tolan, John, ed. *Expulsion and Diaspora Formation: Religious and Ethnic Identities in Flux from Antiquity to the Seventeenth Century*. Turnhout: Brepols/RELMIN, 2015 .

Triplett, K. N., et al. "Post-Traumatic Growth, Meaning in Life and Life Satisfaction in Response to Trauma." *Psychological Trauma: Theory Research Practice Policy* 4 (2012): 400–410.

Urbach, Ephraim. *Ba'alei haTosafot*. Jerusalem: Mosad Bialik, 1955.

van der Kolk, Bessel. *The Body Keeps the Score: Mind and Body in the Healing of Trauma*. New York: Viking, 2014.

Veltri, Giuseppe, and Gianfranco Miletto. *R. Judah Moscati and the Jewish Intellectual World of Mantua*. Leiden: Brill, 2012.

Veny i Clar, Joan. *"Regiment de Preservació de Pestilència" de Jacme d'Agramont*. Tarragona: Excelentisima Diputación Provincial, 1971.

Veny, Joan, and Francesc Cremades, eds. *Regiment de preservació de pestilència (1348): Jacme d'Agramont (nova edició)*. Barcelona: Universitat de Barcelona, 2015.

Vidal, J.-M. "L'émeute des Pastoureaux en 1320." In *Lettres du pape Jean xxii: Déposition du juif Baruc devant l'inquisition*. Rome: Ph. Cuggiana, 1898.

Winslow, C. E., and M. L. Duran-Reynals. "Jacme d'Agramont and the First of the Plague Tractates." *Bulletin of the History of Medicine* 22 (1948): 747–65.

———. "Regiment de Preservació a Epidèmia o Pestilència e Mortaldats." *Bulletin of the History of Medicine* 23 (1949): 57–89.

Young, Alan. "Suffering and the Origins of Traumatic Memory." *Daedalus* 125.1 (Winter 1996): 245–60.

Ziegler, Joseph. "Bodies, Diseases, and the Preservation of Health as Foci of Interreligious Encounters in the Middle Ages." In L. Berlivet et al., eds., *Médecine et religion: Compétition, collaboration, conflit: Cas de figures*. Rome: École française de Rome, 2013, 37–57.

Zunz, Leopold. *Literaturgeschichte der synagogalen poesie*. Berlin, 1865.

Index

"Abi'a miqreh" (Let me tell the story), 18–22
Abraham ben Solomon Hen, 83
Abulafia haMerari, Joseph, 107–12
Aguiló, Francesc, 120–21, 124, 128, 137,
    145–46
Akiva ben Eleazar, 49
"Alei ra'anan" (Fragrant Leaves) (Caslari), 61,
    85
Alexander, Jeffrey, 52
Alfonso de Córdoba, 62, 64, 76–77
Alfonso XI (King of Castile), 88
aljamas: attacks on, 9–10, 48, 58–59, 86,
    119–22, 198n.27; petitions submitted by,
    118–19, 121, 136–37; in Tàrrega, 118, 129
aljamiado (Jewish Romance vernacular
    narratives), 10–13
Almanzi, Joseph, 8, 91, 99, 189n.19
Amin, Shaid, 171n.47, 171n.55
'Amudei ha'avodah (Landshuth), 38
Anti-female violence, in Solomon's lament,
    21–22
anti-Jewish violence: Black Death and, 3–13,
    57–59; forensic evidence in Tàrrega of,
    130–36; migration following, 167n.2;
    Pastoureaux violence, 14–30, 165n.17; in
    plague tractates, 64–65
Arabic medical works, plague tractates and,
    68
Arab lands, Jewish migration to, 44–45
Aragon: anti-Jewish violence in, 3, 5, 7, 45, 60,
    82, 116–17; Black Death in, 2–3, 29, 88,
    116–17; Muslim threat in, 138; Pastoureaux
    violence in, 14–30; physician licensing
    system in, 67
Arba'Turim (Four Columns) (Jacob ben
    Yehiel), 101
Arrizabalaga, Jon, 64, 77, 79, 186n.2
Ashkenaz: liturgical laments by, 29, 32, 35,
    140; plague laments of, 48–49; suicide-
    martyrdom commemorations of, 42; in
    Toledo, 9, 100–102
ATID congregation, 124–25

Avicenna (Ibn Sinā), 58, 64, 66–73, 81, 83–84.
    See also Canon, Avicenna's

Balaguer, Jewish community in, 122
Bale, Anthony, 28
Baraz, Daniel, 28
Barcelona: anti-Jewish violence in, 59, 118,
    198n.17; Jewish community in, 122,
    200n.41
Barkai, Ron, 61
Bar-Tikva, Benjamin, 23
Baruch the Jew, 17, 28
Barzilay, Hillel, 80
Barzilay, Tzafrir, 118
Bedersi, Abraham, 61
Bedersi, Yedaiah, 68–69
begging letters, 194n.66
Bernfeld, Simon, 38, 44–45, 48
Besalú, Jewish community in, 7–8, 58–60, 82
biblical proof-texts: in epitaph poetry, 94–98,
    105–16; in liturgical laments, 20, 32, 46–48;
    in medical tractates, 78–81; in Nathan's
    "Mi gam bakhem," 143–45
Biblioteca Palatina, 37
Black Death: anti-Jewish violence during,
    29–30; brutality associated with, 178n.4;
    burial grounds, 93–94; epitaph poetry in
    Toledo linked to, 92–98; geography of,
    119–20; images in Emanuel's lament of, 35,
    42–43; impact and mortality studies of, 2,
    44, 58, 62, 88, 163n.5; interdisciplinary
    research on, 1–4; in Jewish studies, 3–13;
    pandemics, history of, 163n.1; physician's
    tractates on, 7–13, 57–87; in Tàrrega, 118;
    victims in Toledo cemetery of, 98–116,
    191n.33. See also plague tractates
Blois, victims of auto-da-fé in, 35, 42
Bonadona sa Sala, 60–61
Bos, Gerrit, 83–84
burial practices: grave excavations in Valencia
    and Tàrrega and, 130–36; in Toledo, 95–96,
    190n.27, 191n.40

Cabrilllana, Nicolás, 110
Calabria, anti-Jewish violence in, 6–7
Callico, J., 110
Calvo Gálvez, Matías, 131, 135
Campbell, Bruce, 2
Canon, Avicenna's, 58, 64, 68–73, 81, 83–84;
    Hebrew translations of, 68–69
Cantera, F., 91–93, 99, 189n.21, 190n.25
Caribbean, epitaph poetry in, 91
Carmichael, Ann, 73–74
Caruth, Cathy, 50, 136
Caslari, Abraham, 7–8, 165n.17; emotional and
    psychological factors ignored by, 83–85;
    Galipapa and, 80–81; literary aspects in
    tractate of, 74–87; marriages and family of,
    59–61, 86–87; plague tractate of, 57–74
Caslari, David, 57, 61
Castile: absence of violence in, 5, 89–91; Black
    Death in, 8, 88–91, 96–98; Jewish
    communities in, 11, 34, 187n.7
Catalonia: anti-Jewish violence in, 43, 116–17;
    Black Death in, 8, 62–63, 116–17, 119–20,
    122, 196n.1; Department of Cultural and
    Communications Media, 124–26; Muslim
    threat in, 138
cattle panzootic of Great Famine, 7, 20–21
Cervera: anti-Jewish violence in, 119–21, 129,
    198n.17; Jewish community in, 122
Chase, Melissa, 62
Christians: anxiety and fear of Jews by, 28;
    emotions in medical tractates of, 83–85;
    plague tractates by, 57–58, 61–62, 66;
    representation in Emanuel's lament of, 43,
    45–46; revenge in Ashkenaz laments
    against, 48–49; in Tàrrega, anti-Jewish
    violence and, 123–24, 128–47
Cohen, Mark, 194n.66
Cohen-Hanegbi, Naama, 83
Cohn, Samuel, 3
Colet, Anna, 130–32
collateral consolation, anti-Jewish violence
    and, 31
collective trauma: culture carriers and, 52,
    173n.6; martyrological proximity and,
    26–27, 171n.44, 171n.55; theories of, 11–13,
    165n.22, 166n.26
commemorative genre: absence of history in,
    41–42; suicide-martyrdoms of Ashkenaz
    in, 42–43
Commission for Jewish Heritage (Barcelona),
    124–26

communal narrative, in laments, 22–24,
    30–31, 47–49, 169n.32, 170n.42
Comtadin Jews, liturgical laments of, 24,
    34–35
Comtat Venaissin, 34, 52, 82
Corbera, Gilabert de, 120–21
Córdoba, Alfonso de, 8
Corteilles, Berenguer de, 120–21, 198n.21
Crémieux, Adolphe, 3
cultic meal offerings, in Solomon's lament,
    19–22
cultural carriers, collective trauma and, 52,
    173n.6, 175n.33

danza de la muerte (danse macabre), 10
Davidson, Israel, 51
Dayas Quinoni, 13, 36–37, 53–56
debts: in Emanuel's lament, 48; Tàrrega's
    anti-Jewish violence linked to, 121–22,
    198n.30
della Penna, Giovanni, 77
disease, plague tractates' theory of, 66–72,
    81–82
Duran-Reynals, M. L., 65–67

Eleazar, Judah, 144
Emanuel ben Joseph, 6–7, 18, 23–30, 32–56,
    144, 147
Emeq haBakha, 118
emotions, omission in medical tractates of,
    83–85
Ephraim of Bonn, 35, 42
epitaph poetry: in Amsterdam, 90–91;
    biblical texts in, 94–98, 105–16; children
    in, 95–96; dating convention, 94–95; early
    accounts of, 91–92; honorifics in, 96–98,
    103–4; in Prague, 90; selected readings
    from, 98–110; in Toledo Jewish cemetery,
    8–9, 89–116; translations from Hebrew of,
    148–62; women in, 98–100, 102–3; for
    Würzburg Jews, 97–98
equilibrum, in narratives of violence, 28–30,
    127–28
ethnic violence: analysis of instigators of,
    135–36; "micro" studies of, 127–28
"Ez'aq bemar" ("I shall cry out bitterly")
    (Emanuel), 23–30, 50

famine, 67, 76–79, 110, 119, 138, 145–46,
    184n.28, 197n.34, 209n.69. *See also* Great
    Famine

fast-day liturgies, 37, 173n.9
Federation of Jewish Communities in Spain, 126
feminist movement, collective trauma models and, 12
fever: Caslari's analysis of, 74–87; in plague tractates, 62, 72–74
flattened representation, in liturgical laments, 23–24, 27, 43
Folquet, Ramon, 120–21, 137, 198n.18
Fournier, Jacques, 17
French Revolution, Jewish emancipation following, 34
French Tosafists, 25–26
Friemann, Abraham Hayyim, 101

Fujii, Lee Ann, 135–36
Galen, 66, 83
Galipapa, Hayim, 29, 80, 86, 118, 120, 123, 131, 139, 173n.13, 197n.13
genetics, research on Black Death and, 1–4
Gentile da Foligno, 62, 83
Gerard of Cremona, 68
Germany, anti-Jewish violence in, 3–4, 35
Girona: Black Death in, 62; Jewish community in, 58–59, 82
Graus, František, 3
Great Expulsion of French Jews (1306), 34–35, 101
Great Famine (1315–21), cattle panzootic during, 7, 20–21
Greenblatt, Rachel, 90
Gross, Jan, 136
Gruber, Samuel D., 200n.42
Guilleré, Christian, 62

haCohen, Joseph, 18, 29, 80, 118, 188n.14
haLevi, Joseph, 112–16
haLevi, Meir, 98–100
haLorqi, Joshua, 68
Hamilton, Michele, 10–11
haRosh, Judah ben, 101–7, 109, 116, 195n.79
Havatselet, Abraham Joseph, 101
Haverkamp, Alfred, 3
Hebrew Canon, 68–69
Hebrew language: epitaph poetry translations from, 148–62; medical tractates in, 68, 83–87; in plague tractates, 57–58; survival of sources in, 10
history: penitential liturgy in context of, 33–34, 41–43; trauma and, 126–28, 174n.28

Holocaust, collective trauma models and, 11–13, 136, 170n.44
honorifics, in epitaph poetry, 96–98, 103–4
Horowitz, Elliot, 109
Hyères, anti-Jewish violence in, 3

Ibn Ezra, Abraham, 143
Ibn Shushan, Abuomar Yucef, 192n.45
individual vignettes: in liturgical laments, 21–22, 36; of trauma, 56
Institute for Microfilmed Hebrew Manuscripts, 51
Isaac bar Shalom, 35

Jacme d'Agramont, 8, 57–67, 69–79; Caslari compared with, 69–79, 82; tractate of, 8, 57–67, 82–83, 138
James (Count of Urgell), 122, 198n.26
Jaume II, 17
Jazzar, Ibn al-, 84
Jean Alamand (Johannen Alamanum), 28, 171n.50
Jean de Sant-Victor, 14
Jean XXII (Pope), 17
Jewish Encyclopedia, 3
Jewish prayer book, 33–34
Jewish property in Toulouse, auctioning of, 28
Jewish studies, Black Death in, 3–13
John XXII (Pope), 26
Jordan, William, 16
Justinian Plague, 163n.1

Kahana-Smilansky, Hagar, 68
kharja, in epitaph poetry, 100
Kleinman, Arthur, 22

La Baume, anti-Jewish violence in, 53–56
Lacave, José Luis, 200n.47
Landshuth, Lazar, 38
Languedoc, Jewish communities in, 60, 82
Laqueur, Thomas, 193n.59
Lemos, Tracy M., 135–36, 199n.32, 199n.34
Lepers' Plot, 26, 82
leprosy, in plague tractates, 81–82
Les Roquetes grave pits, 124–25, 130–36
"Let me lament in bitterness and fasting" ("Aqonen bemarah vetzom") (Emanuel ben Joseph), 37–51
libel narratives, 24
liturgical laments (qinot): antifemale violence in, 21–22; biblical prototypes for, 32; during

Black Death, 29–30; Black Death and, 6–13; calendar year in, 50; collective trauma in, 36; communal voice in, 22–24; evolution of, 50; individualized vignettes in, 21–22, 36; by Nathan, 139–45; Pastoureaux violence and, 14–30; as public genre, 22; survivors of violence and, 24–30

Lleida: anti-Jewish violence in, 7–8, 57–60, 120, 197n.17; Black Death in, 63–65; Jewish community in, 122, 196n.4; as rebel stronghold, 122

local agency, ethnic violence and, 128–36

Luzzatto, Samuel D. (Shadal), 8, 38, 91–98, 99, 110, 173n.15, 189n.19

Makhir, Joseph ben, 114–15

Malkiel, David, 90

martiha (lament incipit), appearance in litigurical laments of, 51

martyrological proximity, in social and sacred narratives, 26–27, 170n.44

martyrological vignettes: contemporary examples of, 170n.42; in liturgical laments, 19–22, 169n.32, 173n.9

Me'ati, Nathan ha, 68, 70, 81

medical practitioners: Caslari's relations with, 75–87; emotions in work of, 83; theology in works by, 78–81

Medieval Climate Anomaly, 2

medievalists: research on Black Death and, 1–4; trauma theory and, 30–31

Meir, R., 48, 100–101

Melechen, Nina, 187n.5

memory: in liturgical poetry, 33–34, 41–42, 44–46; trauma and, 126–28, 174n.28

Mengel, David, 5

Merback, Mitchell, 24

"micro" studies of ethnic violence, 127–28

"Mi gam bakhem" (Moses Nathan), 139–45

Millás, J. M., 91–93, 99, 189n.21, 190n.25

Montclus, Pastoureaux violence in, 17–18

Montpellier plague tractate, 57–58, 67, 76–77

moral pestilence, in Jacme's plague tractate, 63–65

MS Parma 1929/1935 (Calabrian codex), 37–38, 51–52

Mueller, Frederik, 189n.19

Muntané, Josep, 121–24, 129, 136–38, 145

Muslim plague tractates, 61–62

muwashshah lyrics, in epitaph poetry, 100

Nachmanides, 20–21

Nahmias, Judah ben, 111–12

Narboni, Moses b. Joshua, 69

Narbonne, expulsion of Jews from, 60

Nathan, Moses, 9–10, 35, 119, 121, 138–47, 178n.4, 205n.94

Nathan, Solomon, 121, 138, 204n.88

Nirenberg, David, 3, 28, 122

nonlinear narrative, Emanuel's lament as, 41–42

On Pestilential Fevers. See *Tractate on Pestilential and Other Types of Fevers*

Oral Law (rabbinic custom), 103

Passerat, Georges, 16, 28–30

Pastoureaux violence, 14–30; Black Death and, 6; in Hebrew liturgical laments, 18–30; pardons for perpetrators of, 28–30; perpetrators and victims in, 126–28; royal accounts of, 168n.26

penitential liturgical poetry *(piyyutim)*: communal voice in, 24–25, 35; generic content of, 34–35; genres of, 178n.2; linearity in, 41–42; liturgical laments and, 32; memory contained in, 33–34, 41–42, 44–46; in MS Parma 1929/1935 codex, 37; by Nathan, 139–45; from northern Africa, 52–53; Pastoureaux violence and, 18–24

Pentateuch, Dayas's invocation of, 53–56

Pere III of Catalonia (Pedro IV of Aragon), 43–44, 59, 118–19, 122–23, 173n.13

perpetrators of violence: classification of, 30, 119, 123–24, 191n.51; in trauma theory, 27–28, 126–28, 171n.47, 171n.55

Peyron, B., 92

Philip IV (King of Spain), 60

Philip V (King of France), 16

Philip the Tall, 17

Pierre de Saverdun, 28–29

Pinkhof, H., 66

plague. See Black Death

plague tractates, 7–13, 57–87

print liturgies, generic content of, 34–35

Provence: anti-Jewish violence in, 3, 59; Black Death in, 8; Jewish liturgies from, 34–35; Pastoureaux violence in, 14–30, 165n.17; plague-related violence in, 29

proximate martyrdom, in social and sacred narratives, 26–27

public fasts, liturgy for, 51–52

qilur (collyrium), 26–27
Qimhi, David. *See* Radaq (David Qimhi)
Qüestions de vida (Nathan), 138–39

Radaq (David Qimhi), 20, 100, 144
Rashi, 20, 81, 100, 144
Rechtman, Richard, 28, 191n.51
Regensburg, Germany, excavations in Jewish
    quarter of, 143
Regiment de Preservacio (Jacme d'Agramont),
    57–58, 63–65
Reiner, Rami, 97–98, 194n.72
resistance: by Christian clerics, 28–29; martyr
    figure in laments and, 22
revenge motif, in Ashkenaz laments, 48–49
Richler, Benjamin, 68, 92
Riera i Sans, Jaume, 16–17, 30, 126–27
Rimos, Moses, 192n.47
Rindfleisch massacres, 14
Rivera, Domingo, 93
Rosh. *See* Yehiel, Asher ben (Rosh)
Rwandan genocide, 135–36, 199n.32, 201n.55,
    204n.80

"sacred path" imagery, in epitaph poetry,
    98–107, 132
Sahwan dynasty, 99
Sasson (Ibn Shushan) family, 112, 115, 192n.45,
    196n.96
Seder qinot le-'arba' ta'aniyyot (Order of
    laments for the four fast days), 50
Sefer haDema'ot, 38
Sephardic liturgy: absence of revenge in, 48–50;
    Black Death in, 6–7; laments in, 33, 35
Seville, Jewish community in, 196n.97
Shadal. *See* Luzzatto, Samuel D. (Shadal)
Shatzmiller, Joseph, 3, 53–54
"She'erit Sheleimei" (Solomon b. Jacob), 22–23
Sheva'im (people of Sheba), Emanuel's
    references to, 44–45
sin, in Emanuel's lament, 47–48
"Sitbona," epitaph poem for, 98–100
Soifer Irish, Maya, 89, 187n.7
Solomon, Crescas, 144
Solomon b. Jacob, 22–23
Solomon b. Joseph of Avalon, 18–22, 24
Solomon ibn Verga, 18
Stock, Brian, 54
suffering, medieval and modern views of, 30
suicide-martyrdom in commemorative genre,
    41–42

Summerfield, Derek, 56
Surribas Camps, Maria Jose, 123, 199n.32,
    201n.49
survivors: of Pastoureaux, 24–30; of Tàrrega,
    137–47; trauma theory and role of, 204n.85

tajnis technique, in Emanuel's lament, 46
Tallarn, Atarn de, 121
Talmud: confiscation of, 25–26; women in, 103
Tarbut Sefarad de Lleida, 124–25
Tàrrega: anti-Jewish violence, 9–11, 29–30, 44,
    59, 117, 120–47, 198n.17; Christian
    community in, 123–24; forensic analysis of
    skeletal remains in, 128–36, 146–47, 193n.69,
    202nn.61–64; grave pits discovered in, 119,
    124–26, 130–36, 200n.42, 200n.46,
    201n.49; Jewish community in, 120–24,
    197n.6; penalties for violence in, 137–47
textual community, 54
Todros, Isaac ben, 25–26, 84
Toledo: burial practices in, 95–96, 190n.27,
    191n.40; epitaph poetry in, 8–9, 91–116;
    Jewish community in, 89–91, 187n.5
Torah, women in, 103
Toulon, anti-Jewish violence in, 3, 165n.17
Toulouse, Pastoureaux violence in, 18, 28–30
Tractate on Pestilential and Other Types of Fevers
    (Caslari), 7–8, 57, 62–63, 66–74, 78–87
Trastámara, Enrique, 187n.7, 187n.9
trauma theory: absence of singularity for, in
    lament genre, 42; "aesthetic" in, 174n.25;
    "anti-mimetic" strand of, 165n.22; Black
    Death in context of, 5–6; collective trauma,
    11–13, 165n.21, 166n.26; contemporary
    research on, 56; defined, 15–16; language
    and, 174n.28; martyrological proximity in,
    170n.44; medicalization of trauma and,
    191n.53; medieval studies and role of, 30–31;
    "mimetic" model of, 165n.22; perpetrators
    of violence and, 27–28, 171n.47, 171n.55; in
    social and sacred narratives, 26–27;
    Tàrrega anti-Jewish violence and, 136–47;
    triad of victims, perpetrators and witnesses
    in, 126–27; witness concept in, 170n.45
Tzedah laDerekh (Zerah), 190n.29
Tzemah, Simon b. (Rashbatz), 51

Usque, Samuel, 18

Valencia, Jewish grave excavations in, 128, 131,
    135–36, 193nn.76–77

Valperga-Calusio, Tommaso, 91
Victor Amadeus II (King of Sardinia), 91
Vietnam War, collective trauma models and,
    12, 171n.47

weapons, in Tàrrega anti-Jewish violence, 136
Winslow, C. E., 65–67
witnesses, in trauma theory, 126–28, 170n.45
women: anti-female violence in laments and,
    21–22, 44; Black Death impact on, 44; in
    Dayas's recollection, 55–56; in epitaph
    poetry, 98–100, 102–3; as martyr figures,
    22; omission in laments of, 43–44
Würzburg Jews, epitaph poetry for, 97–98,
    116, 194n.72

Yehiel, Asher ben (Rosh), 100–107, 188n.14,
    192n.53
Yehiel, Baruch bar, 48
Yehiel, Jacob ben, 101–7
Yehiel, Judah. *See* haRosh, Judah ben
Yehiel, Simon ben, 101–7
"Yom Sefarad" hyms, 37
"Yom Tzarfat" hymns, 37
Yuval, Israel, 49

Zakhor organization, 124–25, 200n.41
Zechariah ben haQadosh, 26–27
Zerah, Menahem ben, 93, 190n.29
Zerahiah ben Shealtiel Hen (Gracian), 68
Zusselin, Israel bar Joel, 48–49

Acknowledgments

LIKE MOST BOOKS, this one owes its making to the kindnesses of others. Wendy Turner graciously included a much earlier version of Chapter 1, on the Pastoureaux lament, in her edited volume on medieval trauma; my views have evolved considerably since that early iteration, as evidenced here. I am greatly indebted to the generosity of Monica Green, Lori Jones, Michael McVaugh, and Jon Arrizabalaga for their comments and suggestions on my treatment of Abraham Caslari's plague tractate in Chapter 3. Monica was also responsible for putting me in touch with Tàrrega archaeologists Anna Colet and Clara Jaurequi and their historian colleague Josep Muntané. The work of this team of historians and archaeologists inspired much of Chapter 5; their extraordinary dedication to uncovering the Jewish past is an inspiration. Benjamin Bar-Tikva of Bar-Ilan University provided a transcription of Emanuel bar Joseph's lament, discussed in Chapter 2, and Judah Galinsky, also of Bar-Ilan University, supplied bibliography and careful reading of the treatment of the Rosh family epitaphs in Chapter 4. Naoya Katsumata meticulously voweled and commented on my transcriptions of Emanuel ben Joseph's and Moses Nathan's laments. The University of Pennsylvania Press's two anonymous readers took up two very different lenses for reading the early draft of the chapters, and I owe both of them thanks for comments large and small; the result is, hopefully, better because of their efforts, and if it is not, it is no fault of theirs. I have had the privilege of Jerry Singerman's friendship and editorial guidance for two books, and I am grateful for his attention and unfaltering support.

I am always indebted to a long list of librarians and libraries, and this time is no exception. This work took shape over a period of several years and encompassed two geographical moves. The loss of easy access to my old library at the Hebrew Union College in Cincinnati is irreparable, but the librarians have continued to provide books, scans, manuscripts, and hospitality during my visits—my special thanks to Marilyn Krider, Noni Rudavsky, and Laurel Wolfson. Librarians Sandy Gallup and Michael Young of the University of Connecticut repeatedly found ways to overcome the limitations of UConn's library holdings and obtain sources. Without Yael Okun and the staff at the Institute for

Microfilmed Manuscripts at the Israel National Library in Jerusalem, a work like this could never be written in New England; the Countway Library for the History of Medicine at Harvard University provided me with an early edition of the Hebrew Canon, along with quiet and assistance in their reading room. A fellowship at UConn's Humanities Institute during 2015–16 gave me partial relief from teaching and the needed time to write; most of these chapters were drafted over that academic year. Cesar Abadia, Carolyn Betensky, Carlos Gardeazabal-Bravo, Caroline Bynum, Eva Haverkamp, Saul Olyan, Osvaldo Pardo, and Sallie (Sarah) Spence listened and offered thoughts and insights on various sections at various stages of the writing. Invitations to Brown, Harvard, and Rice Universities, along with Ludwig-Maximilians University in Munich and two talks at the International Medieval Congress at Western Michigan University, all gave me an opportunity to test my ideas with different but universally hospitable audiences. My thanks also to Diana Witt, who has now ably provided the index for all three of my books.

For many years, my mother has been my sharpest critic, and she put in her two cents' worth on the lecture version of Chapter 5. My father asked me frequently what this book was about. A man of equations and statistics, he marveled when I tried to explain—and as every scholar knows, that work of explaining usually benefits us more than the asker. It is a great sorrow to me that he did not live to see this book completed, and his encouragement in the course of our daily conversations was a great and precious gift. The same is true of my aunt, Evelyn Sommer, and my friend Regine Ransahoff, both of whom were unflagging in their encouragement over the years. To Bristol, Dutzi, Hayden, Jacqueline, and the yogis at Jala, I give thanks for the lessons in focus, determination, and the willingness to grow and reach without causing harm to others. To Shango, I am grateful for the wisdom that seems to come so naturally to cats. My friend Bill in Cincinnati has loyally and uncomplainingly given his presence, insight, and support over many years and moves. I dedicate this book to him.